Praise for Walter R. Borneman's

AMERICAN SPRING

"Likely to be one of the enduring accounts of the opening of the American Revolution. . . . Loaded with intriguing details, sort of historical nonpareil candies sprinkled throughout the account. . . . A pleasing marriage of scholarly research and approachable language."
—David Shribman, *Boston Globe*

"Walter Borneman has written an engaging and illuminating account of some of the most critical weeks in American history. Here is how it all began."　　　—Jon Meacham, author of
Thomas Jefferson: The Art of Power

"Borneman delivers a gripping, almost moment-by-moment account of the nasty exchanges and bloody retreat of British troops followed by hundreds and then thousands of militia who camped around Boston and laid siege. . . . A first-rate contribution."
—*Kirkus Reviews* (starred review)

"An exceptionally detailed account of the first six months of 1775. . . . A balanced and thorough narrative."
—Douglas King, *Library Journal*

"Borneman's approach gives the reader not just a comprehensive understanding of the rebels' motives, obstacles, and overall tensions, but also makes the setting of the colonies during the spring of 1775 vivid and real to a twenty-first-century audience. . . . An enjoyable and accessible read."　　　　　—*Publishers Weekly*

"An excellent history of the origins of the American Revolution."
—*Army* magazine

"Walter R. Borneman's superb *American Spring: Lexington, Concord, and the Road to Revolution* tells the story of that period in significant detail with descriptions of military engagements and legislative actions, but never loses sight of the personalities at all levels. To a great extent, Borneman relies on the original affidavits, correspondence, and memories of the participants and views events from their perspective—before they knew what the outcome would be—giving us a remarkably fresh look at this transformative period. . . . Borneman's authoritative, carefully structured, and very well-written account often seems to place readers in the moment with events that changed the course of history."
—Roger Bishop, *BookPage*

AMERICAN SPRING

AMERICAN SPRING

LEXINGTON, CONCORD, AND THE
ROAD TO REVOLUTION

WALTER R. BORNEMAN

BACK BAY BOOKS
LITTLE, BROWN AND COMPANY
New York Boston London

Back Bay Books / Little, Brown and Company
Hachette Book Group
1290 Avenue of the America, New York, NY 10104
littlebrown.com

Originally published in hardcover by Little, Brown and Company, May 2014
First Back Bay paperback edition, April 2015

Back Bay Books is an imprint of Little, Brown and Company. The Back Bay Books name and logo are trademarks of Hachette Book Group, Inc.

The publisher is not responsible for websites (or their content) that are not owned by the publisher.

The Hachette Speakers Bureau provides a wide range of authors for speaking events. To find out more, go to hachettespeakersbureau.com or call (866) 376-6591.

Maps by David Lambert

ISBN 978-0-316-22102-3 (hc) / 978-0-316-22099-6 (pb)
LCCN 2014932742

10 9 8 7 6 5 4 3 2 1

RRD-C

Printed in the United States of America

Once again for Marlene

CONTENTS

~

LIST OF MAPS

~

AMERICAN SPRING

Patriots' Day

~

*P*resent!*" Red-coated British regulars in precise formation level their muskets across the expanse of green grass. Fifty yards to their front, colonials
in dark homespun wait with a mixture of trepidation and resolve. How has it
come to this? Several late arrivals, muskets in hand, run, panting, to join the
ragged line of locals. As they do so, a shrill command fills the morning air
from behind the Redcoat ranks. "Fire!" A thundering retort rings out. The
line of leveled muskets disappears in a cloud of white smoke, and the smell of
gunpowder quickly wafts across the field.*

*Among the local militia, several men are down, blood oozing from their
garments. Others are moving toward the shelter of adjacent buildings and a
nearby stand of trees. But most of the militiamen stand their ground and
dare to return fire — a cacophony of sporadic shots that crisscross the field in
front of them. Into this void, the British regulars move forward at the quick-
step with glistening bayonets fixed. In seconds, they will sweep the militiamen before them.*

*Then, from the crowd of spectators gathered around, come the sounds of
cameras clicking and a chorus of oohs and aahs. And it is over. The regulars
halt their advance, and a cheer goes up from both sides. The "wounded"
effortlessly rise to their feet. Hats and caps are doffed on both sides, and
handshakes all around are the order of the day.*

*   *   *

ON THE THIRD MONDAY OF every April, the people of the Commonwealth of Massachusetts celebrate. Around the towns of Lexington and Concord and in between, along what is called Battle Road, the sounds of fifes and drums and the rattle of reenactors' muskets fill the spring air. Individuals in period costumes tell stories, march in military formations, and pose for photographs. Tour buses line the routes to Lexington Green and Concord's North Bridge, and parking spots of any size are highly prized for miles in every direction. Down the road in Boston, the annual marathon is under way. The Patriots are a football team, Samuel Adams is a beer, and John Hancock is an insurance company.

The celebration is Patriots' Day, and who now would not be a patriot? The outcome of what began in earnest that long-ago morning on Lexington Green seems preordained and inevitable. But in the spring of 1775, the central issue—blind obedience to Great Britain, no matter how oppressive its rule, versus independence and the freedom to form a more representative government—was very much in doubt and the opposing sides not yet irrevocably defined. Who were the rebels? Who were the loyalists? Who were those caught in the middle? Liberty and independence were noble concepts, but how far across the populace would their bounty be spread?

Boston and the surrounding villages and towns of Massachusetts had long been flash points in relations between Great Britain and its North American colonies. New England's hardy lifestyle, both on sea and on land, had put a stubborn streak of independent thought into its inhabitants. Given the abundance of trade flowing in and out of Boston Harbor, taxes, duties, and royal decrees tended to fall more onerously here and be met with stiff opposition. But while events in the spring of 1775 focused on Boston and its environs, the fundamental questions vexing its inhabitants—loyalty or rebellion, servitude or freedom—were no less trying to residents in front of the statehouse in Philadelphia, on the streets of Williamsburg, Virginia, or on the wharves at Charleston, South Carolina.

In history's shorthand, and from an American viewpoint, the Redcoats were the bad guys and the "embattled farmers" of Ralph Waldo Emerson's epic poem the good guys. But it was hardly that simple. There were neighbors on opposite sides, and, surprising to some, there was significant support in Great Britain for colonists' rights. Some who had liberal political leanings supported the colonists, feeling that the rights they cherished should apply to *all* Englishmen—at least those who were white and male. Others in England supported the colonists because they wanted to preserve the lucrative trade between the ports of the British Isles and North America.

Whether one had loyalist or rebel leanings or was intractably resolved toward one side or the other, the first six months of 1775 were a critical transition period—a spring of uncertainty, a spring of change, a spring of hope. Only in retrospect—after a long seven years that would come to be filled with names such as Saratoga, Valley Forge, and Yorktown—could it be said that this six-month period was truly an *American* spring. But after the spring of 1775, there was no question that both sides would fight fiercely to achieve or defeat the goal of independence from Great Britain.

The spring of 1775 was filled with a rush of decisive events that ultimately brought a war no one had planned to fight. Yet men and women on both sides determined to do so before compromising their beliefs in either the prerogative of king and Parliament or representative government. None knew how the conflict would play out. After Lexington and Concord, it brought horror to both sides. After Bunker Hill, the only certainty was that this battle had turned the struggle into a deadly confrontation between confirmed adversaries.

It is particularly powerful and insightful to return to the original affidavits, correspondence, and remembrances of the

participants in these events and see history from their perspective —
before two centuries of interpretation clouded their words. It is
equally interesting to explore the roles of women, American loyalists, and African Americans, who were given little notice in many
earlier histories. As sweeping as the cries for liberty and equality
sounded to some, not all were to be the beneficiaries. This narrative strives to provide an immediacy to these events through the
words of the participants, show that there were far more kinds of
people involved than white males in three-cornered hats, and mark
the spring of 1775 as one of the most decisive periods in American
history. The conflict could have gone either way, and that we would
be celebrating Patriots' Day generations hence was not a certainty.

Today, amid the cacophony of Patriots' Day sights and sounds,
there is — if one listens closely — a background quiet that filters
down to the present. Some of the buildings that stood more than
240 years ago still stand about Lexington Green, throughout Concord, and along Battle Road. The steeple of the Old North Church
looks out across the Charles River to the granite spire honoring
those who fought on the slopes around Bunker Hill. One can walk
past Parker's Revenge, Merriam's Corner, and the spot where a
messenger named Paul Revere was captured. But look deeper. Who
were those who once walked these same streets, endured great
anxiety and hardship, and ultimately made a choice? Who were
those at risk in the spring of 1775?

~

Tuesday, December 13, 1774

L ashed by a bitterly cold northeast wind, a lone horseman galloped along the Post Road north of Boston. He moved in broad
daylight, though the heavy gray clouds of a New England winter
dimmed the low-angled sun. *Galloped* is perhaps too ambitious a
word. A deep snowfall a few weeks before had first turned mushy
and then solidified as the temperature dropped to sixteen degrees
Fahrenheit at sunrise, leaving the road a jagged obstacle course of
icy ruts and rock-hard ridges.

But onward the rider pressed. From his start early that morning
in Boston, it had been twenty-four miles to Topsfield, then fourteen
miles more to cross the Merrimack River at Newburyport. As the
day waned, and with twenty-two miles still to go, the rider grew
weary, but he was no stranger to such hardship. The horseman's
name was Paul Revere, and he was determined to reach Portsmouth, New Hampshire, and spread the alarm: "The regulars are
coming!"

In the fleeting light of this short December afternoon, Revere
rode into Portsmouth and went straight to the home of Samuel
Cutts, a prosperous merchant whose substantial residence stood
opposite his wharf and warehouse on the Piscataqua River. Cutts
was a member of Portsmouth's committee of correspondence, one

of many such associations throughout Great Britain's thirteen colonies that were increasingly trading information and voicing grievances against the British Crown. Put more bluntly, Cutts and the half-frozen messenger who knocked at his door were rebels.

The reason for Paul Revere's urgency was that George III's government had recently banned the importation of arms and gunpowder into North America in an effort to restrain this rebel faction in its deeds if not its words. Existing stores of arms and ammunition had immediately become highly prized. The principal New Hampshire cache was housed in aging Fort William and Mary on New Castle Island, several miles off Portsmouth Harbor.

Technically, these munitions were the king's, kept in storage for use by both British regulars and colonial militia for their mutual self-defense. But as rebels exerted increasing influence over provincial legislatures, the distinction between Crown property and that of the individual provinces deepened. In response, General Thomas Gage, the British commander in chief in North America, had begun to exercise strict control over these stores for the Crown. The gist of Revere's warning was that New Hampshire rebels should seize these weapons before British regulars en route from Boston could do so.

As Revere warmed himself by the hearth, members of Portsmouth's committee of correspondence answered the summons to the Cutts residence. Some voiced concern that Revere had acted precipitously in delivering a warning from "only two or three of the Committee of Correspondence at Boston" when no fewer than seven were empowered to act. Lacking a quorum, the Portsmouth committee deferred action until a full meeting could be held the next day. But several committee members shared Revere's sense of urgency. Rather than another meeting, daylight on Wednesday, December 14, was greeted by the beating of drums to summon volunteers to march on the fort.

By the time these Portsmouth men rowed to New Castle Island and joined inhabitants of New Castle, the resulting force numbered some four hundred. To oppose these local insurgents, Captain John Cochran commanded a total garrison of five men. But more than the soldiers under his command, Cochran was relying on the Union Jack flying from the fort's flagpole to dissuade an attack. What better symbol of the power of his post? What colonial would dare assail it? To do so would be treason.

But that charge seemed of little concern to the local men who ignored Cochran's refusal to open the gates, swarming over the walls despite the defenders' discharge of several small cannons. The attackers quickly overpowered Cochran and his meager garrison. They "struck the King's colours, with three cheers, broke open the Powder House, and carried off one hundred and three barrels of Powder, leaving only one behind." [1]

By nightfall, it was New Hampshire royal governor John Wentworth's turn to send a hasty message in the opposite direction of Revere's ride. Briefly recounting the "most unhappy affair perpetrated here this day," Wentworth warned General Gage that with the gunpowder seized, another rebel force was forming "to carry away all the Cannon and Arms belonging to the Castle...unless some assistance should arrive from Boston in time to prevent it." Far from taking responsibility for this occurrence, Wentworth went on to complain: "This event too plainly proves the imbecility of this Government to carry into execution his Majesty's Order in Council, for seizing and detaining Arms and Ammunition imported into this Province, without some strong Ships-of-War in this Harbour." [2]

The British regulars were indeed coming, but they were taking their time about it. On this particular ride, Paul Revere's warning — based on rebel intelligence in Boston — proved a bit premature. In fact, while General Gage had contemplated the possibility of a raid, he did not start troops northward from Boston to Portsmouth on board the sloop HMS *Canceaux* until December 17, the day *after* receiving Governor Wentworth's anguished plea for assistance. By then it was too late. On the morning after the first raid, Wentworth issued an order to assemble thirty local men from the First Regiment of Militia — supposedly loyal to the king — to assist Cochran's garrison in withstanding another round of pilfering. As his officers later reported to the governor, they "caused the Drums to be Beat, & Proclamation to be made at all the Publick corners, & on the Place of Parade," but no person appeared "to Enlist."[3]

That same afternoon of December 15, another band of rebels rowed out to Fort William and Mary and made off with small arms, "fifteen 4-pounders, and one 9-pounder, and a quantity of twelve and four and twenty pound shot." Waiting for the tide to come in, they then spirited their prizes away by boat up the estuary of the Piscataqua River to Durham. According to one loyalist, "a few flaming demagogues" had persuaded the good people of New Hampshire "to commit a most outrageous overt act of treason and rebellion."[4]

British regulars finally arrived in Portsmouth on board the *Canceaux* late on December 17, and another contingent disembarked from the frigate HMS *Scarborough* two days later. By then, the rebel cause in New Hampshire was safe and well supplied, but the Redcoats would march again.

PART I

~

AN IRREPRESSIBLE TIDE

January–March 1775

It seams we have troublesome times a Coming for there is a great Disturbance a Broad in the earth & they say it is tea that caused it.

—Diary of Jemima Condict, October 1774

Chapter 1

~

New Year's Day 1775

Throughout Great Britain's thirteen American colonies, New Year's Day 1775 dawned with grave feelings of anxiety and uncertainty. Relations with the colonies' mother country had grown increasingly strained over the last decade — too many taxes; Crown troops quartered in colonists' homes; intransigence at every turn when some measure of compromise might have better served both sides. And no matter which side one was on, there was an uncomfortable feeling of sitting on a powder keg and watching a fiery fuse burn ever shorter.

The thirteen colonies stretched more than one thousand miles along the Atlantic Seaboard from Georgia northward to Massachusetts, which still claimed Maine as its own. The many ranges of the Appalachian Mountains generally marked the colonies' western boundaries, although a few frontier outposts had long been established beyond the mountains. The first complete census of these provinces would not be taken until 1790, but in 1775, the population was an estimated 2.5 million. About a fifth of them were enslaved.

The white population was descended largely from ancestors in the British Isles — England, Scotland, Ireland, and Wales — though a Dutch population remained from the days when New York was New Amsterdam, Germans were concentrated in Pennsylvania,

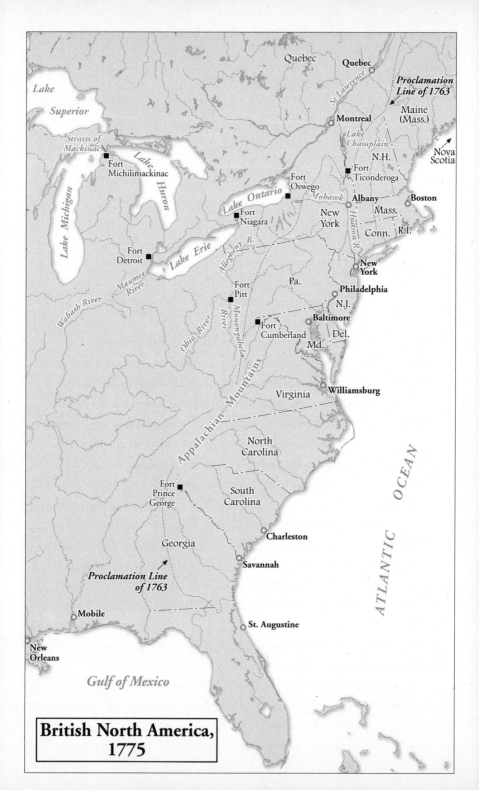

British North America,
1775

and French Huguenots resided in parts of Virginia and the Carolinas. Most slaves traced their roots to Africa or the West Indies, but particularly in New England, some came from subjugated Native American tribes. The bulk of the slave population worked in agriculture in the middle and southern colonies, but it was common to find both field and domestic slaves owned by upper-income families throughout New England and in metropolitan areas such as New York City and Philadelphia.

These urban areas were definitely the exception, as the colonies were largely agrarian and the countryside was filled with small villages, hamlets, and farms. The principal towns were Philadelphia, Pennsylvania, with a booming population of thirty-five thousand inhabitants; New York City, New York (at the time including only Manhattan Island), with twenty-five thousand; and Charleston, South Carolina, supporting about twelve thousand. New Haven (Connecticut), Newport (Rhode Island), and Baltimore (Maryland) were smaller but growing in both size and influence. Boston's population in 1775 has been estimated at sixteen thousand, but increasing friction between British regulars stationed in the city and its inhabitants had contributed to a steady exodus of its citizenry as many fled the town for the countryside.[1]

While there was a great measure of self-sufficiency among local farmers, artisans, and shopkeepers, the colonies were also a vital part of the trading network of the greater British Empire. New England shipwrights built oceangoing sailing ships from fine stands of hardwood forests. Southern planters shipped rice and tobacco to Europe. A ready supply of sugar, often in liquid form as molasses, went from the West Indies to New England or Europe, where it was distilled into rum. Textiles and manufactured goods were transported back across the Atlantic to North America or Africa. The shipment of slaves from the latter formed another leg of these trading triangles.

London merchants who sold finished goods to the North American colonies were among those profiting the most from this trading network. Despite a certain degree of self-sufficiency, many colonists—particularly in urban areas—were grateful for their ability to purchase these finished goods from colonial importers who were only too glad to make their own profits on the transactions.

On the surface, these trading relationships were mutually beneficial, but they also raised issues of import duties and consumer taxation. While the causes of the revolution were many and could trace their roots back at least a decade, it was the importation and taxation of tea—and the stiff reaction of some colonials to it—that had escalated emotions throughout 1774—until this New Year's Day, when Boston was effectively an armed camp garrisoned by British regulars.

Boston in 1775—long before massive landfills in the surrounding waters expanded its girth—lay like a craggy lobster. Its two "claws," Barton's Point and Hudson's Point, reached north into the Charles River toward Charlestown. The "body" of the lobster itself was crowned by Beacon Hill, below which the broad Common occupied the westward edge along the Charles River, while the Long Wharf and numerous shorter wharves encircled Boston Harbor on the seaward, or eastern, side. Only the thin causeway at Boston Neck connected the "tail" of the lobster to the mainland. The causeway led south past the town gate to higher ground at Roxbury and Dorchester Heights. This irregular landform didn't lend itself to a rigid grid of wide avenues but rather a helter-skelter of narrow dirt streets and alleys that jogged every which way off a main thoroughfare of cobblestones running northward from Boston Neck.

The week between Christmas and New Year's in Boston saw the landing of the latest contingent of British troops, about six hundred Royal Marines commanded by Major John Pitcairn. They arrived aboard several men-of-war that dropped anchor in Boston Harbor and showed no sign of leaving. The marines were billeted in barracks in the north part of town within easy sight of the steeple of the Old North Church and the heights of Bunker Hill across the river to the north.

Boston definitely felt like an occupied town, but not all was

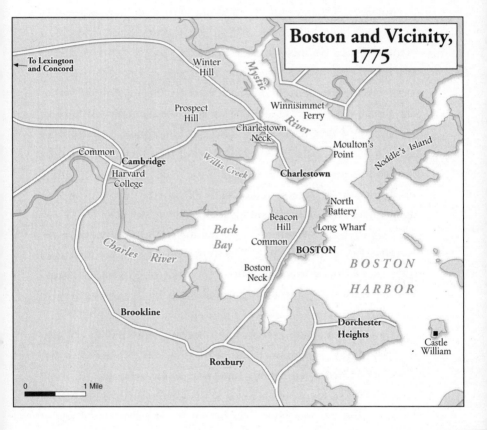

Boston and Vicinity, 1775

To Lexington and Concord

Winter Hill

Mystic

Winnisimmet Ferry

Prospect Hill

River

Charlestown Neck

Moulton's Point

Noddle's Island

Common

Cambridge

Harvard College

Willis Creek

Charlestown

North Battery

Back Bay

Beacon Hill

Long Wharf

Common

BOSTON

Charles River

Boston Neck

BOSTON

HARBOR

Brookline

Dorchester Heights

Castle William

Roxbury

0   1 Mile

tense between Bostonians and this garrison of British troops. Four days before New Year's, on a wild and stormy afternoon, "a seafaring Lad" fell from a wharf in Boston Harbor and appeared to be drowning. A British regular from the Tenth Regiment of Foot jumped in to rescue him. "The Lad," according to press reports, "was saved," but the soldier himself drowned in the attempt.[2]

But even British regulars could not ensure holiday tranquillity in Boston. Shortly before midnight on the day after Christmas, "some *well-bred Gentlemen* took the *Liberty* of breaking my Windows in a *most spirited Manner*," one John Troutbeck reported sarcastically in an advertisement in the *Boston Gazette and Country Journal*'s January 2 issue. "If any Person will be pleased to inform me of the Place of their Residence, (if they have any,) that I may make them a proper Acknowledgement for this *publick Mark of their Civility*, he shall be intitled to a Reward of Ten Dollars."[3]

The same newspaper contained an announcement of a one-dollar reward for information regarding a separate incident:

"Any Person that will give information to the Printers of an old Negro Fellow named Caesar, who went away some Time since, and is suppos'd to be strolling about in some of the neighbouring Towns, walks lame and talks much about being free, shall receive the above Reward. Had on when he went away a blue Jacket."[4]

The *Boston News-Letter* reported other tragedies of daily colonial life. An obituary mentioned the death of a Mrs. Silence Thwing, who succumbed at a sprightly ninety-three but who was recorded only as the "Relict of the late Mr. Wm. Thwing." A person named Jeremiah Ballard was much less fortunate. He died at the age of eighteen, the victim of an accidentally self-inflicted gunshot wound. His weapon discharged while he was climbing over a fence.[5]

In Milton, south of Boston, "the Wife of Mr. Ebenezer Houghton"—her given name, in the manner of the time, was considered of secondary importance—was drawing a pail of water from a well when "she accidentally slipt into the Well, Head first, and was drowned." No mention was made of her husband's whereabouts at the time. Farther south, in Rochester, Asa Richer also met his end. He "was fixing a Ramrod into the Pipes of a loaded Gun, when it accidentally went off, and the Contents entered his Bowels; of which Wound he expired in about Half an Hour." [6]

Among these grim clippings there was evidence — despite the then-current political turmoil — of just how close many in the colonies still felt to their mother country. In addition to regular reports on London politics, economics, and entertainment, a number of colonial newspapers, including the January 2 issue of the Boston Evening-Post, published a complete list of newly elected members to the House of Commons. Of the 558 members, about one hundred were freshmen. Time would tell whether these new members would carry enough weight — or inclination — to reverse the punitive legislative measures invoked by the last session against the American colonies. [7]

Parliament's edicts weighed heavily on the man who was charged with enforcing them in the colonies: General Thomas Gage, long-time commander in chief of British forces in North America and, since May 1774, governor of the errant province of Massachusetts. In that capacity, Gage had moved his headquarters from New York to the increasingly tense confines of Boston. The question on many minds was what Gage thought personally about Parliament's heavy hand and whether he might have some sympathy for the frustrations of his constituency. Among those believed to have a persuasive influence on his thinking was his American-born wife, the former Margaret Kemble of New Jersey.

One Bostonian who cared not a whit for what General Gage or Parliament thought was John Hancock, who entered the New Year his usual cocky self. Hancock had taken over his uncle's shipping business as a young man and grown to become one of Boston's wealthiest and most influential merchants. There were more than a few whispers that he routinely found ways to circumvent onerous customs duties, but if nothing else, the practice made for loyal and appreciative customers. His partner in intrigue against the British Crown, Samuel Adams, had chaired a town meeting at Faneuil Hall on December 30 to craft a reply to a stern missive from General Gage. Politics and business aside, Hancock was looking forward to a year that would see his wedding to the spirited Dorothy Quincy.

John Andrews, a Boston merchant of only slightly less standing than Hancock, was also looking ahead. To his brother-in-law, William Barrell, a merchant in Philadelphia, Andrews extended his New Year's wishes "that we may have a less troublesome year than the last." Andrews had many economic reasons to preserve relations with Great Britain, but he nonetheless hoped "Great Britain may see her error in distressing the Colonies, and restore to them their *just* rights and liberties; that we may *once* more see that harmony prevail which formerly us'd to subsist between them."[8]

In Plymouth, thirty-five miles south of Boston, Mercy Otis Warren, a housewife, mother, and clandestine author, was putting the finishing touches on her latest political satire. Her anonymous writings had already attracted a following, and this effort, *The Group*, was a harsh condemnation of the role of mandamus councilors — those appointed by the king to carry out royal laws. Men who held such offices, Warren editorialized, had succumbed to royal bribes at the price of liberty. But Warren's writings also had a strong secondary theme. In a culture and time that accorded women and family life a decidedly subservient role to men and their public lives, Warren compared the oppressed marital status of women with Parliament's suppression of the assumed rights of male colonists.[9]

At the other extreme from Mercy Warren's feminist viewpoints were those of a twenty-year-old New Jersey woman named Jemima Condict. Her diary musings were mostly concerned with biblical texts from church services and a hope chest that her father was in the process of procuring, despite Jemima's pensiveness about the eventual marriage such an acquisition foreshadowed. But even in rural New Jersey, the prospect of war was not far from her daily thoughts. If people would quarrel about such a trifling thing as tea, Jemima asked in her diary, "What must we expect But war & I think or at least fear it will be so."[10]

War was certainly a possibility. In Dedham, just south of Boston, the martial spirit was judged so high that a militia company of more than fifty, "several of whom [were] above 70 Years of Age," organized and elected a slate of officers. Most other small towns either had already formed or were in the process of forming similar local units. The British regulars who would oppose them were judged by some to be well-trained troops, but few had as yet been tested in battle. On this New Year's Day, one British officer complained that there was "Nothing remarkable but the drunkenness among the Soldiers, which is now got to a very great pitch; owing to the cheapness of the liquor, a Man may get drunk for a Copper or two." [11]

Attorney John Adams was at home in Braintree, a dozen miles south of Boston, with his wife, Abigail, and their brood of four children, which included seven-year-old John Quincy. Adams's frequently extensive diary was silent on the occasion of New Year's for just that reason: he was home — not traveling, as he had done that fall to Philadelphia for the First Continental Congress, or making his rounds for various legal matters. His time with fellow delegates in Philadelphia had hardened his resolve to speak out strongly — not that he had been quiet to date — against what he judged to be increasingly heavy-handed British oppression. Indeed, it is likely that Adams was already making notes for a series of letters he would soon publish in the *Boston Gazette* in opposition to letters from a Tory supporter who signed himself "Massachusettensis." [12]

On the outskirts of the village of Lexington, some dozen miles west of Boston, Prince Estabrook, a black slave of about forty years of age, went about his chores as usual. He was owned by Benjamin Estabrook, who farmed substantial acreage and operated a gristmill on Vine Brook Road just east of the village green. Prince was a Lexington native who had been born as Estabrook family property and inherited by Benjamin from his father. Prince and Benjamin were at opposite ends of the social spectrum, but there is at least circumstantial evidence that, being about the same age, they shared bonds of friendship that went beyond their master-servant relationship. Perhaps because

Benjamin was occupied with his businesses, a family of eight children, and service in a variety of town government roles, he encouraged Prince to join the local militia. Prince had been routinely drilling with the Lexington company for almost two years.[13]

BOSTON AND MASSACHUSETTS, WHILE THE focal point of British punishment and colonial resolve, were certainly not alone in their unease. Bostonians read in their New Year's newspapers that the colony of Maryland had taken similar steps to train and arm local militiamen because "a well regulated militia . . . is the natural strength and only stable security of a free government." The Maryland legislature went on to say, perhaps with tongue in cheek, that creating such a force on its own would "release our mother country from any expence in our protection and defence [and] will obviate the pretence of a necessity for taxing us on that account." Consequently, it was recommended that all Maryland inhabitants between sixteen and fifty years of age "form themselves into companies of 68 men . . . and use their utmost endeavours to make themselves masters of the military exercise."[14]

There was plenty of intrigue in New York, too. On January 2, the publishers of the *New-York Gazette and Weekly Mercury* teased readers by announcing, "In our next Paper, the Public may possibly be entertained with some little Account of a certain Spy that has lately made his Appearance in this City, and of whom all Gentlemen are requested to be on their Guard."[15]

Tempers were particularly high in New York because the customs collector, Andrew Elliot, had come under verbal attack from locals for confiscating certain firearms that had been legally imported into the province from Great Britain. Elliot nonetheless seized them and secured them aboard a British man-of-war in the harbor. On December 27, Elliot received an unsigned letter that characterized his actions as an arbitrary step by which "you have declared yourself an inveterate enemy to the liberties of North-America" and advised him that the weapons' rightful owners would soon demand their return. "Do not slight this admonition or treat it as a vain menace," the unsigned threat continued. Elliot would find no protection against "our just revenge, which will be soon done." [16]

In Virginia, a planter and member of the Virginia House of Burgesses named George Washington spent New Year's at Mount Vernon with his wife, Martha, and an assortment of relatives. His mind was occupied by the political turmoil, but in part this was because such events had had a major impact on his business operations. A week later, Washington wrote a testy letter to a trade representative, complaining about a delay that "was never done before!" in unloading a cargo of herring from the brigantine *Farmer* in Jamaica. The ship sat dockside for six weeks before it could be loaded with Washington's rum for the return journey, an expense in port that Washington was being asked to assume. He was also miffed that "the Sugar and other Articles" he had ordered had not yet arrived and that under the nonimportation measures recently enacted by the First Continental Congress he would be "obliged to return them if they arrive in Virginia after the first day of next Month." [17]

But Washington was also busy giving instructions for work to be done farther west, on lands he had acquired that the British Crown now said belonged to others. "I am resolved," he wrote an overseer, "if no unforeseen accident happens to prevent it, to have my people at work upon my lands on the Ohio, by the last day of March." [18]

There was also news that faraway Georgia, which had not sent delegates to the recent Continental Congress, was falling into line with the other colonies. "By Account just received from Georgia," the *Boston News-Letter* reported, "we are informed, that all Opposition to their Concurrence with the other Colonies has ceased . . . [and] that they have fully resolved to retrieve their late Neglect; and do heartily join in the Association of the General Congress." [19]

ON THE OTHER SIDE OF the Atlantic this New Year's Day, there was no less a general feeling of unease and apprehension. The exceptions were those staunch royalists whose intractable regard for the authority of their monarch was exceeded only by their disdain for *anything* having to do with the colonies. Great Britain's right to do as George III and Parliament decreed was absolute, they said. Others in England weren't so sure.

Save for a two-year sabbatical back in Philadelphia, Benjamin Franklin had spent the better part of the preceding seventeen years in London, initially as an agent for Pennsylvania business interests but increasingly as a de facto ambassador at large for greater colonial concerns. Franklin's son, William, was the royal governor of New Jersey, and it made for a strained family relationship. In the spring of 1774, Franklin had encouraged William to resign his governorship, forewarning that if he did not do so, he would find himself "in no comfortable Situation."[20]

Although Franklin did not yet know it this New Year's Day, his son had written him on Christmas Eve to notify him of the death of Franklin's long-suffering common-law wife, Deborah Read. Despite Franklin's absences of many years and rumors of his extramarital liaisons, Deborah had kept the home fires burning in Philadelphia while Franklin reveled in the gaiety of London society. William gently chided his father that Franklin's failure to return the previous year as Deborah lay dying had "preyed a good deal on her Spirits," but the bulk of William's letter concerned Franklin's own political fate.

If there were any prospect of swaying those in power in Parliament to Franklin's way of thinking, or any prospect of those of Franklin's political persuasion coming into power, it would have happened by now, William wrote. "But as you have had by this Time pretty strong Proofs that neither can be reasonably expected and that you are look'd upon with an evil Eye in that Country, [you] are in no small Danger of being brought into Trouble for your political Conduct. . . ." Return to America while you are physically able, William told his soon-to-be-sixty-nine-year-old father, "where the People revere you, and are inclined to pay a Deference to your Opinions."[21]

Benjamin Franklin was in fact planning to sail back to America soon, but the holidays brought one last round of political intrigue in London. It started innocently enough before Christmas, when Caroline Howe, a widow of considerable standing in London society, invited him to play chess, "fancying," in Franklin's words, "she could beat me." Whether she did is unknown, but both players found the company so engaging that they quickly met a second time. Only after a few games did the social gossip turn political, and Mrs. Howe asked pointedly, "And what is to be done with this Dispute between Britain and the Colonies? I hope we are not to have a Civil War." Franklin laughed and said they should kiss and be friends because "Quarrelling can be of Service to neither but is Ruin to both." This appears to have been the opening Mrs. Howe was seeking, and she offered the opinion that she had long thought Franklin himself should be employed to mediate the dispute.

On Christmas Day, Franklin again called on Caroline Howe for a chess game, but she immediately asked if he would like to meet her brother Richard Howe, an admiral in the Royal Navy and a member of Parliament. Here was more than merely London social elite. Admiral Howe, his brother William, a general in the army, and sister, Caroline, who had retained her Howe surname by marrying a distant cousin, were among a faction of powerful British strongly in favor of some form of reconciliation with the colonies. Their oldest sibling, Lord George Howe, had caught the attention and admiration of colonials during the French and Indian War, when as a young brigadier he led an assault on French-held Fort Carillon in northern New York. A stray bullet cut Lord Howe down in his prime, but the surviving Howes were among those who found it difficult to contend that the liberties they took for granted in England should be denied to other Englishmen in the colonies. Perhaps Franklin was their conduit to some form of accommodation.

Franklin readily agreed to meet Richard Howe, but after hearing a flow of silken compliments from him, Franklin grew leery. They talked generally of the merits of reconciliation, and Howe asked

Franklin to draft propositions upon which "a good Understanding might be obtained." The two men agreed to meet several days later at Caroline's home under the pretext of another game of chess.

Franklin was already the author of a lengthy defense of the key points that the First Continental Congress demanded as conditions of reconciliation, including the repeal of recent duties and taxes imposed without the consent of the provincial legislatures. Howe knew this, but hoped that Franklin might now reconsider, moderate his stance, and form some compromise plan that might be acceptable to both sides. Franklin's holiday partying kept him from completing a draft by their next meeting, but Howe again stressed the need for reconciliation and went on at great length about "the infinite Service it would be to the Nation" and "the great Merit" to Franklin himself "of being instrumental in so good a Work."

But then Howe stuck the fork in. He said "he should not think of influencing me by any selfish Motive," Franklin recalled, "but certainly I might with reason expect any Reward in the Power of Government to bestow." Franklin, the wily chess player, recognized an out-and-out bribe when he saw it. "This to me," he later wrote, "was what the French call *Spitting in the Soup*." [22]

But Franklin played out the game. He drafted a plan for resolving the crisis that carefully reiterated his prior arguments and the steps necessary "to cement a *cordial Union*, and remove, not only every real Grievance, but every Cause of Jealousy and Suspicion." Franklin continued to play chess with Mrs. Howe and engage in discussions with Lord Howe after New Year's Day, but subsequent to receiving Franklin's steadfast missive, Howe admitted to his sister that any hope of working with Franklin "threatens to be attended with much greater difficulty than I had flattered myself." [23] Whatever else 1775 was to be, it would not be a good year for moderates.

~

Chapter 2

Drumbeats of Dissension

A s 1775 began, a great many British subjects on both sides of the Atlantic asked themselves, how had it come to this? What had led to such polarization? In truth, drumbeats of dissension had been increasing in intensity for more than a decade.

It was not lost on observers on both sides of the Atlantic that a principal impetus for the original British settlement of North America had been the flight of citizens from religious persecution by the British government. But in the century and a half since the Pilgrims landed at Plymouth, enlightened reforms by Britain's monarchy and Parliament had mitigated much of that suffering, and swelling immigration and trade had made for strong ties between Great Britain and its colonies. There was no better evidence of this than the enthusiastic colonial participation in the war for empire so recently waged by Great Britain against France.

Called the Seven Years' War in Europe, the struggle at times also involved Prussia, Austria, Russia, and Spain, but it was the Anglo-French phase in North America — there called the French and Indian War — that decided the fate of that continent. Thanks in no small measure to the sacrifices of British colonials — including a young George Washington — who ably fought for their mother country as well as for their own commercial interests, Great Britain expelled France from most of North America.

But it had been a costly affair in terms of finances as well as blood. With a scratch of a pen on the 1763 Treaty of Paris, Great Britain won an empire that stretched from Canada to the Caribbean and on to Africa, India, and the Philippines. The royal treasury was suddenly saddled with the expense of administering these acquisitions as well as retiring a staggering war debt. Great Britain chose to pay these costs in part by imposing a series of increasingly onerous financial burdens on its American colonies, because they were far and away the most economically developed of its new overseas empire.

Taxes to support Great Britain's colonial administration and provincial infrastructure had long been a part of colonial life, but they had been levied by the legislative assemblies in each colony, which enjoyed some measure of representative government. Although a Crown-appointed royal governor presided over each province, voters—generally limited to white male property owners over the age of twenty-one—elected delegates to colonial legislatures to approve such business. As citizens of the British Empire and as royal subjects, these colonists considered themselves endowed with certain rights well established by Parliament—among them the right to representative government.

THE FIRST MAJOR DISRUPTION TO this harmony came when Parliament passed the American Duties Act of 1764. Known as the Sugar Act, it placed tariffs not only on sugar but also on coffee, wine, and other imports to the American colonies. Ominously to some, including Boston importer John Hancock, the act also called for aggressive new enforcement measures to end smuggling and collect all taxes due. Minor tariffs were previously not unknown—a sixpence-per-gallon tax had been imposed on foreign molasses as early as 1733—but this new resolve to enforce them was a different matter. "The publication of orders for the strict execution of the

Molasses Act," the royal governor of Massachusetts noted, "has caused a greater alarm in this country than the [French] taking of *Fort William Henry* did in 1757."[1]

Egregious as these new tariffs were to colonial importers and consumers alike, they arguably flowed from Parliament's power to regulate commerce. When Parliament passed the Stamp Act the following year, it went a step further and levied a direct tax on the use of paper. Any paper in the American colonies, including newspapers, advertisements *in* newspapers, licenses, legal documents such as wills and powers of attorney, and a host of other printed matter—even playing cards—was required to have a revenue stamp affixed certifying that the appropriate tax had been paid. Colonial reaction was predictable.

In Virginia, Patrick Henry, a twenty-nine-year-old attorney just elected to the House of Burgesses, went so far as to suggest that only the Virginia legislature held the "sole exclusive Right and Power to lay taxes" within the province, and he refuted any measure of compliance with the act. In but a preview of the divisive debates to come, conservative members from Virginia's Tidewater region were aghast at Henry's insolence, while liberal delegates from the western reaches of the colony heartily applauded it. Years later, when Henry's defiant words on another occasion stirred patriot souls, he would be misquoted with historical hindsight and hyperbole as having said, "If this be treason, make the most of it."[2]

In Massachusetts, the legislature immediately called for representatives from the disgruntled colonies to coordinate a response to the Stamp Act. Twenty-seven delegates from nine colonies (New Hampshire, Virginia, North Carolina, and Georgia did not participate) met in New York City in mid-October of 1765. But what really got the attention of the British government was the outpouring of protests from a broad spectrum of the colonial population. Many not only signaled their refusal to buy stamps when the act became effective on November 1, they also boycotted British imports.

"What used to be the pride of the Americans?" Benjamin

Franklin was asked when called before the House of Commons to testify on the Stamp Act and the resulting boycott. "To indulge in the fashions and manufactures of Great Britain," the best-known colonial in London replied evenly. "What is now their pride?" he was asked. "To wear their old clothes over again," Franklin answered, "till they can make new ones."[3]

Dr. Franklin was already well versed in such gamesmanship, but his reading of the underlying determination of certain colonials was sound. Before the year was out, lawyer John Adams confided to his diary that the powers in London "are determined to inforce the Act . . . [but] will find it a more obstinate War, than the Conquest of Canada and Louisiana."[4]

William Smith Jr., another young lawyer and assemblyman in New York who helped draft petitions asking Parliament to reconsider the Stamp Act, was more blunt. He noted that by refusing even to consider the arguments of the New York petitions, Parliament could expect nothing "but discontent for a while, and in the end open opposition." This single stroke, Smith maintained, "has lost Great Britain the affection of all her Colonies."[5]

By the following spring, thanks in no small measure to a damning denouncement of the measure in the House of Commons by former prime minister William Pitt, Parliament grudgingly repealed the Stamp Act. But this did little to erase a lingering bitterness, especially in light of other tax burdens placed on the colonies. By 1768, in an effort to quell antitax demonstrations, British regulars began to be concentrated in key cities, including Boston. While there were many flare-ups over the next five years — physical as well as verbal — events reached an exclamation point on the dark, moonless night of December 16, 1773. The issue was tea, but not entirely the taxation of it.

To get around almost a decade of tariffs on tea, colonial merchants' lucrative smuggling operations with the Dutch West Indies flourished. There were also many in the colonies who simply paid the tariff and quietly drank British tea. Then, in May of 1773, Parliament passed the Tea Act, a statute that at its core was designed as a government bailout of the floundering British East India Company. The company had a surplus of tea, commodity prices were falling, and to prop up the entire operation, Parliament gave the company a monopoly on the tea trade in the colonies and also retained its threepence-per-pound tariff.

Truth be told, not much of substance changed. One could still buy smuggled Dutch tea on the black market or continue to buy English tea and pay the duty. But then the propagandists took over. The very fact that the East India Company now had a monopoly *and* was collecting a tariff for the government was evidence to some that Parliament was once again doing whatever it chose with no consideration of, let alone input from, the colonies.

What made the politically charged situation ironic was that, given the glut of tea in East India Company warehouses, prices actually came down. According to the late historian John C. Miller, "There seemed excellent prospect, therefore, that this cheap tea would 'overcome all the Patriotism of an American' and that the colonists would hail [Prime Minister] Lord North as one of the great benefactors of thirsty humanity."[6]

Many colonists didn't embrace that view, however, and for once, Boston lagged behind New York, Philadelphia, and Charleston in its outrage. Citizens leading the anti-tea charge in those cities included a strong faction of smugglers who stood to lose the most in profits should cheap tea glut the market. In New York and Philadelphia, East India Company ships laden with tea were eventually turned away amid threats of violence, and in Charleston, unloaded tea was left to rot in a warehouse for nonpayment of duties.[7]

In Boston by late October, the local consignees of the East India Company, who happened to include two sons of Massachusetts royal governor Thomas Hutchinson, took the offensive by pointing out the inconsistency of suddenly protesting the tea tax after years of paying it, particularly when colonists were still paying duties on sugar, molasses, and wine, "from which more than three quarter parts of the American Revenue has and always will arise."[8]

As in Philadelphia and New York, those who shouted the loudest in opposition had distinct financial interests at stake. Boston importer John Hancock declared that if the Tea Act were not opposed, "We soon should have found our trade in the hands of foreigners [i.e., Englishmen] . . . nor would it have been strange, if, in a few years, a company in London should have purchased an exclusive right of trading to America."[9]

For the better part of three weeks, Boston merchants wrestled with the question of whether East India Company tea on board three ships would be unloaded or returned to England. When Governor Hutchinson refused permission for the ships to sail out of port and ordered the tea unloaded, Samuel Adams announced to a public meeting on the evening of December 16 that "there was nothing else they could do to save their country." There was, of course, more that could be done, and these were in fact code words for action. By midnight, thinly disguised "Indians," encouraged if not actually led in person by Adams and Hancock — this has always been a matter of debate — were dumping tea into Boston Harbor. "This destruction of the Tea," confided Samuel's second cousin John Adams to his diary, "is so bold, so daring, so firm, intrepid and inflexible, and it must have so important consequences."[10] It did.

NEWS OF THE BOSTON TEA PARTY reached England on January 19, 1774. Lord North's government and most in Parliament coalesced more strongly than ever around their long-sung theme: if the supremacy of the Crown and Parliament over affairs in America was not asserted, the government's absolute control would be lost, and Great Britain might just as well abandon its colonies. This, of course, Lord North had no intention of doing.

Instead, Parliament passed a quartet of laws meant to punish the province of Massachusetts and enforce its proper subordination. Great Britain would call them by the shorthand term Coercive Acts, while to most colonials they were the Intolerable Acts—a difference far greater than semantic that showed the depth of the underlying divide.

The first of these acts, the Boston Port Act, closed the port of Boston to all meaningful commercial traffic, effectively shutting down most of the business of the seaport. Two administrative measures severely limited any semblance of local government in the province, even requiring royal approval to hold town meetings and designating royally appointed sheriffs to empanel juries. Finally, the Quartering Act of 1765, which required local authorities to provide provisions and housing for troops in public accommodations and empty buildings, was expanded to permit the quartering of troops in private dwellings. Now the Redcoats would not just march by, they would sit down to dinner with you.

Boston, whose direct act of the destruction of tea was being punished, recoiled, but so, too, did the other colonies. In Farmington, Connecticut, almost one thousand people gathered to resolve that "blocking up the port of *Boston*, is unjust, illegal, and oppressive; and that we, and every *American*, are sharers in the insults offered to the town of *Boston*." Similar resolutions in Philadelphia decried the port closure as "unconstitutional; oppressive to the inhabitants of that town; [and] dangerous to the liberties of the British colonies." [11]

Virginia was not yet ready to shed blood in the defense of Massachusetts, but the House of Burgesses expressed "Apprehension of the great Dangers to be derived to *British America*, from the hostile Invasion of the City of *Boston*" and ordered a day of fasting and prayer. One of those delegates wrote to a neighbor later that summer from Mount Vernon. "For my own part," said George Washington, "I shall not undertake to say where the line between Great Britain and the colonies should be drawn; but I am clearly of opinion, that one ought to be drawn, and our rights clearly ascertained." [12]

*   *   *

THE FIRST CONCERTED STEP IN drawing that line came when delegates from all the colonies except distant Georgia convened in Philadelphia on Monday, September 5, 1774, for what came to be called
the First Continental Congress. The date is not much celebrated by
history, but it is nonetheless a landmark in the evolving cooperation
between the individual colonies. "It is," wrote delegate John Adams
to Mercy Otis Warren's husband, James, in anticipation, "to be a
school of political prophets, I suppose, a nursery of American
Statesmen."[13] Besides the Adams cousins and Robert Treat Paine
from Massachusetts, the assembly included John Jay and Philip Livingston from New York, Joseph Galloway and John Dickinson from
Pennsylvania, and George Washington, Richard Henry Lee, and
Patrick Henry from Virginia.

Henry lost no time in making his voice heard, but, as with the
Stamp Act debate almost a decade before, his sentiment was again a
little premature — declaring a spirit of unification that most of the
delegates did not yet share. "The distinctions between Virginians,
Pennsylvanians, New Yorkers and New Englanders are no more,"
Henry thundered. "I am not a Virginian, but an American."[14]

Joseph Galloway of Pennsylvania, for one, thought Samuel Adams
and his cohorts were far too radical for their own good. If the assembly followed Adams's star, the only acceptable destination would be
independence. Galloway favored colonial representation in Parliament, but, recognizing that was a pipe dream, he promoted what
would essentially be a second-tier Parliament in America. The colonial assemblies would elect its members, and while the individual
colonies would oversee their internal affairs, this "Grand Council"
would work with Parliament on matters affecting them all, including
the contentious issue of taxation. In such a way, Galloway hoped to
convince all but the most radical that "British sovereignty was com-
patible with colonial freedom" without the recourse of revolution.[15]

While the Congress debated these diverse ideas, there came to

Philadelphia some rather startling news from Suffolk County, Massachusetts, which contained Boston. Though the Massachusetts legislature had been dissolved under the Intolerable Acts and no town meetings were allowed without royal assent, delegates had nevertheless met secretly and quite illegally in county conventions. The Suffolk assembly overwhelmingly approved a series of resolutions drafted by Joseph Warren, a doctor and member of Boston's committee of correspondence. Collectively, the resolutions arrived in Philadelphia as "the Suffolk Resolves," hand-delivered to the congress by messenger Paul Revere.

Invoking the reasons their forebears had left England for the New World in the first place, the men of Suffolk County minced no words from their first sentence on: "Whereas the power but not the justice, the vengeance but not the wisdom of Great Britain, which of old persecuted, scourged, and exiled our fugitive parents from their native shores, now pursues us, their guiltless children, with unrelenting severity." [16]

Damning the Crown's past heavy-handedness and the recent tyranny of the Intolerable Acts, the Suffolk Resolves also took Parliament to task for the just-passed Quebec Act, which many judged to be the final straw. On its face, the Quebec Act had very little to do with punishing an insolent Boston; only its timing and the reaction to it meant it would be lumped together with the Intolerable Acts in colonial minds. Designed by Parliament as an attempt to limit the spread of radicalism in the colonies, the Quebec Act tightened the noose around Boston and all the colonies.

In the aftermath of the French and Indian War, Parliament had passed the Proclamation of 1763, a document that drew a line roughly along the crest of the Appalachians and forbade permanent settlement west of it. The western boundaries of the existing colonies—many of which had been thought to extend westward to . . . well, no one was quite sure—were now given a finite demarcation, and British lands west of that line, just won from France, were designated a vast Indian reserve. Even hard-won Fort Duquesne, rechristened Fort Pitt and quickly morphing into Pittsburgh, was west of the line. The truth of the matter was that this settlement prohibition was rarely enforced, and for a decade it did little to deter men like George Washington and others who had land interests there.

But now the Quebec Act gave much of this vast reserve— all British land north of the Ohio River and westward to the Mississippi—to the province of Quebec. It and Nova Scotia were in fact Great Britain's fourteenth and fifteenth colonies in North America. This destroyed the westward expansion schemes of the other thirteen colonies—but there was more. The Quebec Act restored French civil law in the province of Quebec and gave full tolerance to the dominance of the Roman Catholic Church. To British colonials the intent was clear: the recently vanquished French in Quebec were being treated better than they were.

Put in its most crude terms, a young Alexander Hamilton noted, "a superstitious, bigoted Canadian Papist, though ever so profligate, is now esteemed a better subject to our Gracious Sovereign George the Third, than a liberal, enlightened New England Dissenter, though ever so virtuous." [17]

Some American propagandists conjured up ridiculous plots that had the pope dividing up the colonies, but the real threat was not in Rome. Rather, it lay along the borders with Quebec, where Frenchmen now appeared to be aligned with the British in London. In a debate in Parliament, Lord North readily acknowledged that if the king's unruly colonies could not be brought to obedience by present forces, it was "a necessary measure to arm the Roman Catholics of Canada, and to employ them in that service." [18]

The Intolerable Acts had been directed against Massachusetts, but now, by seeming to threaten the rights and religion of all colonies, the Quebec Act inadvertently went a long way toward unifying them. The protests of moderates like Joseph Galloway were swept aside and the full text of the Suffolk Resolves placed before the Continental Congress on September 17. The delegates voiced their support for the "firm and temperate conduct" of Massachusetts to date and approved the Suffolk Resolves as submitted. They trusted that the united efforts of the colonies would convey their convictions "of the unwise, unjust, and ruinous policy of the present administration" and encourage the introduction of "better men and wiser measures." [19]

When John Adams heard the outcome of the vote, he was elated. "This Day convinces me," he wrote in his diary, "that America will support Massachusetts or perish with her." [20]

MORE THAN MERELY VOICING MORAL support for Boston and Massachusetts, the First Continental Congress debated significant — some said drastic — action. As the colonies had learned from the Stamp Act crisis, there was power in unity of purpose and action, particularly if it struck a financial nerve. The question was whether or not the colonies would once again endorse the nonimportation of British goods and, if so, whether they would be able to enforce it.

The earlier boycott in response to the Stamp Act and other tariffs had largely run its course by 1770. Not only had the Stamp Act been repealed in 1766, merchants who honored the embargo had increasingly seen that it benefited the pockets of importers who ignored the ban without much regard for the cause of American freedom.

Now, however, the Continental Congress was determined to curry wide popular favor for a trio of agreements forbidding the importation of British goods, the exportation of colonial crops to the British Isles, and the consumption of British goods that might arrive in North America via whatever circuitous route an importer might devise. Measures supporting all three issues were passed in October of 1774 and came to be called the Continental Association. The ease with which the nonimportation and nonconsumption measures passed showed how quickly moderates such as Joseph Galloway had been overshadowed by the radical members of the assembly.

Indeed, one of the few controversies that arose during the drafting of the nonimportation agreement, which was to take effect December 1, 1774, was whether to include French wine imported via Great Britain. Madeira, higher in alcoholic content than French wine and available from Portugal's Madeira Islands, saved the day. "I drank Madeira at a great Rate [instead of wine]," boasted John Adams, "and found no Inconvenience in it." [21]

The exportation ban was more problematic because it affected the middle and southern colonies disproportionately. Major rice exports to Great Britain from South Carolina, for example, were far more important to that colony's economy than lumber exports were to New England. Virginia had similar concerns when it came to the 1774 tobacco crop now curing for next year's delivery. The delegates resolved this matter by postponing the implementation date of the nonexportation provision until September of 1775, after which most of that summer's crops would have been shipped. When this still wasn't good enough for South Carolina, rice was excluded from the exportation ban altogether.

As for enforcement, the delegates bypassed the suspect merchants and importers and asked the general populace to pledge itself to the nonconsumption agreement. If the citizenry united in not consuming British products, there would be little incentive for importers to break the nonimportation measures. Nonconsumption compliance would be "encouraged" by local committees of compliance. The irony to some was that these local committees, invariably spearheaded by the more radical among the populace, inspected importers' bills of lading and merchants' ledger books with a fervor that surpassed the most stringent methods of royal customs officers. Some rebel sympathizers and most of those loyal to Great Britain asked themselves what the difference was between being told what to do by Parliament and the Crown and being governed by the sweeping edicts of the First Continental Congress. [22]

Loyalist Samuel Seabury, the Episcopal rector of a church in Westchester County, just north of New York, put it bluntly. Writing as A. W. Farmer, a pseudonym for "a Westchester farmer," Seabury taunted his rural neighbors, exhorting them to "do as you please" in supporting local committees "chosen by half a dozen fools in your neighborhood," but warned that if they opened their doors to such a mob, it would next be inspecting "your tea canisters, and molasses-jugs, and your wives' and daughters' petty-coats."[23]

But women could play an important role in determining whether the nonconsumption mandates succeeded or failed. While only a very few upper-class men wrote pamphlets and engaged in legislative debates, everyone—men *and* women—could join the political campaign against Great Britain by adjusting their eating, drinking, and sartorial habits. Since the choice of whether to boycott the marketplace and make or mend at home was largely domestic in nature, women were essential—perhaps even more than equal—partners in the rank and file's support for the nonimportation and nonconsumption provisions. Christopher Gadsden, a leading merchant in Charleston, South Carolina, readily conceded that "without the assistance of our wives" it would be impossible for the boycott to succeed.[24] More than one woman may have thought that ironic as she listened to pleas for equality and freedom that did not extend to her.

Having passed a boycott of trade with Great Britain, the First Continental Congress used its final days to delineate the rights of "the English Colonies in North America." Voicing words and sentiments that would foreshadow future declarations, the delegates proclaimed they were "entitled to life, liberty, and property." And they reminded their brethren across the Atlantic that "at the time of their emigration from the mother country, [our ancestors had been] entitled to all the rights, liberties, and immunities of free and natural-born subjects within the realm of England."[25] How could Englishmen enjoy those rights while denying them to others of the common tree?

As to the anticipated reaction of Great Britain to these words, as well as to the boycott, there was little optimism. "I expect no redress, but, on the contrary, increased resentment and double vengeance," John Adams remarked to Patrick Henry, showing him a letter to the Massachusetts delegation from a rebel leader in western Massachusetts. "We must fight. It is *now* or never, that we must assert our liberty," Joseph Hawley had admonished Adams. "By God," replied Henry, "I am of that man's mind."[26]

Word that the Continental Congress had passed the Suffolk Resolves reached England in early November. Lord Dartmouth, Lord North's stepbrother and Secretary of State for the Colonies, was beside himself. "If these Resolves of your people are to be depended on," Dartmouth told exiled former Massachusetts governor Thomas Hutchinson, "they have declared War against us." Dartmouth later wrote to General Gage, characterizing the situation in Massachusetts as one of "actual Revolt, and shew a Determination in the People to commit themselves at all Events to open Rebellion."[27]

George III seemed almost relieved. On November 18, 1774, the king wrote Lord North, "I am not sorry that the line of conduct seems now chalked out, which the enclosed dispatches thoroughly justify; the New England governments are in a state of rebellion, blows must decide whether they are to be subject to this country or independent."[28] It was a rather bold statement, as in the colonies there were many who had yet to wish themselves independent.

Chapter 3

~

Who Would Be True Patriots?

In the spring of 1775, the inhabitants of the thirteen colonies were forced to make a choice between loyalty to the existing government of King George III or the hope of a less oppressive political structure. Perhaps most troubling, the lines between colonists loyal to the king and those advocating rebellion were not clearly drawn, and this uncertainty made for uneasy relationships, particularly among families, neighbors, and friends. In the absence of a united groundswell of popular uprising, the political situation was complicated, and it carried with it an ugly overtone of civil war.

Who were the true patriots—rebels who fought for a change of government or loyalists who stood by their sovereign? In hindsight, American propagandists would glory in the term *patriot* for those who had risen up against British oppression and apply *Tory* in a derogative fashion to those who fled the country, fought against them, or merely tried to avoid the fray. The political labels of Whigs and Tories were also applied. But at the beginning of 1775, *rebels* or *loyalists* were the terms usually employed.

Either way, mere labels could not adequately convey the emotional cost to personal relationships. Jonathan Sewall and John Adams were lawyers, close friends, and intellectual confidants. As early as 1759, it was Sewall who, sensing the financial burdens that

Great Britain would impose on the colonies after the French and Indian War, encouraged Adams to write his first political letters for publication. "Mr. Sewall was then a patriot," Adams later recalled. "His sentiments were purely American."

But as the divide between the colonies and the Crown deepened, highly placed loyalists aggressively courted Sewall. Over time, they promoted his law practice and saw to his appointment first as solicitor general for the province and later as attorney general. Adams eschewed such offers, but he and Sewall "continued our friendship and confidential intercourse, though professedly in boxes of politics as opposite as east and west," until just after Adams was chosen as a delegate to the First Continental Congress.

In that summer of 1774, finding themselves in court together in what is now Portland, Maine, the two old friends went for an early morning walk. Sewall was vehement in opposing Adams's participation in the congress. "Great Britain was determined on her system," Sewall lectured his friend; "her power was irresistible, and would certainly be destructive to [Adams], and to all those who should persevere in opposition to her designs." But Adams was equally determined. "The die was now cast," Adams replied. "I had passed the Rubicon; swim or sink, live or die, survive or perish with my country, was my unalterable determination." The two men parted, and each took his own path, not to meet again as friends.[1]

Families suffered similar rifts. Colonel Josiah Quincy, a Boston merchant of some standing, had three sons. The eldest, Edmund, followed his father into business and adopted his political leanings, becoming "a zealous whig" and political writer during the Stamp Act crisis. There is little doubt Edmund's persuasions and activities would have continued had he not died in 1768 at the age of thirty-five. The second son, Samuel, went to Harvard and became a lawyer. As with Jonathan Sewall, Samuel Quincy was courted by loyalists and later appointed solicitor general of Massachusetts. As a family biographer later delicately noted, "Influenced by his official duties and connexions, his political course was opposed to that of the other members of his family." The third son, Josiah Quincy Jr. (sometimes referred to as Josiah Quincy II), also went into law but picked up where his brother Edmund had left off. Josiah became a blazing though short-lived meteor of rebel rhetoric, which culminated in a strident pamphlet published in May of 1774 in which he argued against the bill closing the port of Boston. Josiah sent a copy to Samuel, who, while opposing his brother's views, rather mournfully acknowledged, "The convulsions of the times are in nothing more to be lamented, than in the interruptions of domestic harmony." [2]

Later that fall, while John Adams was in Philadelphia for the Continental Congress, his wife, Abigail, who was a distant Quincy relation, dined at Colonel Quincy's home in Braintree and found Samuel's wife, Hannah, and the junior Josiah and his wife, another Abigail, present. Hannah remarked that "she thought it high time for her husband to turn about; he had not done half so cleverly since he left her advice" and stood by the loyalists. It is not entirely clear whether Samuel himself was there for this family gathering, but Abigail Adams reported to John, "A little clashing of parties, you may be sure." [3] Josiah junior was likely rather discreet on the occasion, as he was even then planning to leave in several weeks on a secret trip to London in an attempt to rally friendly merchants and members of Parliament to the rebel cause.

JUST HOW DEEPLY DIVIDED A region might be was evidenced in and around Marshfield, a community of about twelve hundred inhabitants roughly halfway between Boston and Plymouth. The town had a long history of outspoken loyalty to Great Britain and in the aftermath of the Boston Tea Party had passed a town resolution decrying the action as "illegal and unjust and of a dangerous Tendency." [4]

In mid-January of 1775, one hundred and fifty Marshfield residents voted against supporting the trade edicts of the Continental Congress. Instead, they voiced support for an association promoted by Timothy Ruggles, a Massachusetts lawyer who had been president of the 1765 Stamp Act Congress but who was now a staunch loyalist. The Ruggles Covenant, as some called it, promised that its signers would do everything in their power to enforce "obedience to the rightful authority of our most gracious Sovereign; King George the third, and of his laws."[5]

To that end, Marshfield residents formed a local militia to counter those of the rebels and called themselves "the Associated Loyalists of Marshfield." But when this became known down the road in Plymouth, "the faction there," as one loyalist termed the rebel movement, threatened to march en masse and either force the Marshfield loyalists to recant or drive them off their farms. Marshfield appealed to General Gage for assistance, and Gage dispatched four officers and about one hundred men via two small ships to Marshfield along with three hundred stands of arms "for the use of the gentlemen of Marshfield."[6]

This response had the desired effect, and when the local rebel militia attempted to muster in opposition, "no more than twelve persons presented themselves to bear Arms" against the king. As another loyalist gloated, "It was necessary that some apology should be made for the scanty appearance of their volunteers, and they coloured it over with a declaration that 'had the party sent to Marshfield consisted of half a dozen Battalions, it might have been worth their attention to meet and engage them.'"[7]

Meanwhile, the British troops were quartered outside Marshfield on the fifteen-hundred-acre estate of Nathaniel Ray Thomas, one of the mandamus councilors scorned by the rebels. "The King's troops are very comfortably accommodated, and preserve the most exact discipline," boasted the same observer. And to the rebels' chagrin, they showed no inclination to leave anytime soon. To the loyalists, the troops provided an extra measure of security in town so that "now every faithful subject to his King dare freely utter his thoughts, drink his tea, and kill his sheep as profusely as he pleases."[8] (One of the Continental Association's many mandates in

preparing for a full-scale boycott against Great Britain was to pro-
hibit the slaughter of sheep under the age of four, a measure
intended to build domestic flocks.)

General Gage was quite pleased by this request for assistance
from Marshfield. While he was forced to acknowledge that despite
his efforts, "the Towns in this Province become more divided,"
Marshfield was a glowing example of local opposition to the rebels.
"It is the first Instance of an Application to Government for assistance," Gage reported to Lord Dartmouth, "which the [rebel] Faction has ever tried to perswade the People they would never obtain."[9]

Even though they had not put up a military resistance to Gage's
rescue of Marshfield, rebels in nearby towns did not take this intrusion of British regulars lightly. Selectmen in six towns in the county
of Plymouth petitioned General Gage to remove the public disgrace
they felt the military deployment reflected upon their county.
Swearing a regard for the truth that they claimed their adversaries
had overlooked, these representatives asserted that the fears and
intimidation of Marshfield residents "were entirely groundless" and
that "no design or plan of molestation was formed against them."
This petition came from the neighboring towns of Plymouth,
Kingston, Duxbury, Pembroke, Hanover, and Scituate, and one
look at the map showed that, at least geographically, the rebels had
Marshfield surrounded.[10]

And even in Marshfield there was not unanimity. At a subsequent Marshfield town meeting — with British regulars still
encamped near town — a motion was put forth to determine
whether the town would support the resolves and proclamations of
both the Continental Congress and the Massachusetts Provincial
Congress. It failed to pass, and instead the town voted letters of
thanks to General Gage and Admiral Samuel Graves of the Royal
Navy for their prompt support. But sixty-four Marshfield residents,
being "sensible of the high colouring which the Tories never fail to
bestow on every thing that turns in their favor," boldly protested
not only the results of the vote but also the procedures of the town

meeting. The Marshfield selectmen—three assumed loyalists—"gave but a day's warning for the said Meeting" and ordered it held without notice of the agenda in a location where a town meeting had never been held before.[11]

It was little wonder that when the Provincial Congress met in Concord in February, there was no representative present from Marshfield, and the congress thanked the six rebel towns of Plymouth County for "detecting the falsehoods and malicious artifices of certain persons belonging to Marshfield."[12]

But the loyalists of Marshfield and elsewhere had good reason to be concerned. The rebel movement possessed a very ugly side. Boycotts, protests, and propaganda were one thing, but intimidation, abuse, and physical violence were quite another. Even as Plymouth rebels were joining neighboring towns in assuring General Gage that Marshfield loyalists had nothing to fear, Plymouth loyalists were under assault. When loyalist women gathered at a meeting hall for a social event, a mob surrounded the building and threw stones, breaking shutters and windows. When the ladies attempted to flee to the supposed safety of their homes, they were "pelted and abused with the most indecent Billingsgate language."[13] (Billingsgate, a section of London that was home to a fish market of the same name, was known for its foul talk and seamy ways.)

Even if one tried to keep a low profile, any association with the royal government posed a risk. Israel Williams, "who was appointed of his Majesty's new Council, but had declined the office through infirmity of body"—or quite possibly out of fear of reprisal—was nonetheless "taken from his house by a mob in the night, carried several miles, put into a room with a fire, the chimney at the top, and doors of the room being closed, and kept there for many hours" until he was literally smoked. He barely made it out alive.[14]

"To recount the suffering of all from mobs, rioters, and trespassers, would take more time and paper than can be spared for that purpose," one loyalist said in an appeal to the Provincial Congress after a lengthy listing of intimidations and destruction of property. "It is hoped the foregoing will be sufficient to put you upon the use of proper means and measures for giving relief to all that have been injured by such unlawful and wicked practices."[15]

Since the Provincial Congress then assembled in Concord was decidedly pro-rebel, such loyalist pleas fell on deaf ears. The congress had recently elected John Hancock its president, and its pro-rebel sentiments were fueled in large part by the machinations of Samuel Adams. What an interesting pair they were.

JOHN HANCOCK WAS SUPPOSED TO have become a Congregationalist minister; he would have been the third generation of John Hancocks to be so ordained. His grandfather, the first John, was so widely known and respected among Congregationalists in Massachusetts that he unofficially came to be called the Bishop of Lexington. The "bishop" saw to it that his eldest son, the second John, went to Harvard, as he had, and after serving three years as a librarian there because he could not find a ministry, the second John was finally ordained and established in a church in Braintree. The new minister took his time, but seven years later, in December of 1733, he married a local farmer's daughter. When their second child and first son was born on January 12, 1737, there was little doubt that his name, too, would be John Hancock.[16]

Among their neighbors was the family of Deacon John Adams, which included a son, also named John, who was two years older than the youngest John Hancock. The two boys would sometimes play together, but years later John Adams would remember his playmate with some exasperation. Young Hancock "inherited from his father," John Adams wrote, "a certain sensibility, a keenness of feeling, or—in more familiar language—a peevishness that sometimes disgusted and afflicted his friends." But, allowed Adams, "if his vanity and caprice made me sometimes sputter ... mine, I well know, had often a similar effect upon him."[17]

Young Hancock's inclination to outbursts of temper and

self-importance probably came more from his grandfather, the bishop, than from his father. Grandfather John put so much emphasis on his eldest son's education and well-being that his second son, Thomas, was sent to Boston at the age of fourteen to become an apprentice in a bookbinding business. The ministerial path was clearly the prestigious one, and grandson John was groomed for it from an early age. But then the bishop's long-range plans fell apart.

The second John died suddenly just short of his forty-second birthday, leaving a widow and three small children. Grandfather John invited them to live with him in the manse at Lexington. It was tight financially, but the combined family attempted to make the best of it. A few months later, a handsome carriage, drawn by four matched horses and attended by four liverymen, pulled up. Who should alight but Thomas, the bishop's second son, who twenty-seven years previously had left home in poverty. Not only had the bookbinding business proven profitable but a partnership with one of Boston's leading merchants and subsequent shrewd investments had also turned Thomas Hancock, apprentice, into Thomas Hancock, respected merchant. In addition to his trading empire, the House of Hancock, Thomas had a wife, his partner's daughter, Lydia, and a mansion on Beacon Hill. About the only thing Thomas didn't have was an heir after thirteen years of trying.

Thomas Hancock's offer was too good to pass up. He would provide his father and his brother's widow and children with additional income if young John, then age seven, would come to Boston to be raised as his and Lydia's own. Thus John Hancock went from a Congregational manse in Lexington to a mansion on Beacon Hill and detoured forever from the path his grandfather had laid out for him. Instead, he would follow his uncle Thomas into business.

In only twenty years, Thomas Hancock had built the House of Hancock into a lucrative conglomerate. Starting with the bookbinding business, it had quickly grown to include publishing, paper manufacturing, and Boston's most complete general store. There was nothing that his shelves did not contain or that he could not get — for a price. His ships plied the Atlantic with cargoes of rum, cotton, fish, whale oil, and more. He came to own warehouses and wharves along Boston's harbor. And, as did many successful businessmen, he negotiated profitable government contracts, providing food, munitions, and supplies to various military expeditions, including William Pepperell's 1745 expedition against the French at Louisbourg.

What didn't change in John Hancock's young life after moving in with Uncle Thomas and Aunt Lydia was that he was still bound for Harvard. After graduating in 1754, he entered his postgraduate training at the House of Hancock. The French and Indian War was brewing, and once again Thomas was a key military supplier. Grooming John for an eventual partnership, his uncle sat him down in the ledger room and began to reveal the complex transactions that had turned the House of Hancock into such a powerhouse. Only Thomas and John had access to all the accounts and records. His shrewd uncle "had set up the books so that no one clerk could put the entire puzzle together and become a competitor." [18]

As the war wound down, Thomas and Lydia sent John to London not only to collect on some of his uncle's overseas accounts but also to give him a certain cultural polish. This graduate course in monetary negotiations stood John in good stead, but he almost failed his uncle's expectations of personal economy. "I find Money some way or other goes very fast," John wrote Thomas somewhat apologetically. "But I think I can Reflect it has been spent with Satisfaction and to my own honour." [19]

John enjoyed London's refinements and was inclined to linger there, but Thomas was beginning to feel his age, particularly after Lydia's father, who had been Thomas's mentor and patron, fell ill and died. Thomas and Lydia wanted their nephew safely back in America, and John arrived in Boston on October 3, 1761, having been away sixteen months.

That winter Thomas, too, fell ill, and it scared him. He put more and more control of the business into John's hands and a year later, on New Year's Day of 1763, announced to his associates that he was taking "my Nephew Mr. John Hancock, into Partnership with me having had long Experience of his Uprightness [and] great abilities for Business."[20]

With his uncle's blessing, over the next months John readily took ever greater control of the affairs of the House of Hancock, no doubt exhibiting some of that ego and intransigence that John Adams recalled as "peevishness." Nineteen months after making John a partner, in August of 1764, his uncle died suddenly of a stroke as he made his way into a meeting of the Governor's Council. He left generous bequests to Lydia, relatives, and community causes, but the prize of his estate, the House of Hancock and its many properties, he left solely to his nephew John, whom "he had loved as a son" and who was now at age twenty-seven suddenly one of the wealthiest men in America and Boston's undisputed merchant king.[21]

But there was more. Hancock buried his uncle on the Monday after his death; five days later, his Aunt Lydia handed him a deed to the family mansion, its furnishings, and the Beacon Hill land on which it sat, requesting only that she be allowed to live out her life there. Having always adored his aunt, John was happy to honor her proposal. Lydia became Hancock's hostess, his social conscience, and — when he seemed to drag his feet in choosing a suitable wife — his matchmaker.

All this set up John Hancock as an example of profound paradox when it came to the mounting tension between Great Britain and its colonies. Hancock had everything he could possibly want under the British colonial system. True, a tightening of the customs laws and ever-higher taxes threatened to take some of his wealth away. But thanks both to his uncle's legacy and his own innate knack for business, John Hancock was the epitome of success in colonial America. Yet, in perhaps even more of a paradox, a decade later the rank and file of rebels in Massachusetts — be they the farmers of Lexington and Concord or the blue-collar tradesmen of Boston, who would readily burn the mansions and businesses of entrenched loyalists—would come to revere the likes of John Hancock, who was as elite and patrician as anyone.

So how was it that John Hancock, merchant king, came to be John Hancock, rebel leader? The answer lies in part with a ne'er-do-well former tax collector, failed businessman, and part-time brewer named Samuel Adams. Few men were further apart in business practices, but each had a personality that thrived on risk. In addition—and this was perhaps easier to read on Adams's coarse veneer than on Hancock's polished sophistication—each man could be calculatingly cold and purposeful.

SAMUEL ADAMS WAS BORN ON September 16, 1722, and was fifteen years Hancock's senior. There has been a tendency among historians to call him, familiarly, Sam—especially given the popularity of a certain twentieth-century brewing company—but the contemporary evidence points strongly to the fact that he was "Samuel." Indeed, the modern incarnation of the brand of beer that bears his name, made by the Boston Beer Company, is officially "Samuel Adams."[22]

As young Samuel entered Harvard, at fourteen, his father, the elder Samuel Adams, was well on his way to joining Thomas Hancock on the top rung of Boston's power-broker ladder. Samuel senior used his brewery operations to cement ties to local taverns and, in turn, the political types who gathered there, eventually founding a political machine called the Boston Caucus. His next venture was a rural bank outside Boston that circulated its own paper money to farmers based on the value of their lands and crops. It was a rather creative approach at a time when hard currency, in the form of British sterling, or barter—either one of which was available through the House of Hancock—held sway. But it ran counter to the established norm, backed by certain merchants under the leadership of Thomas Hutchinson. At their urging, Parliament outlawed the land bank, indicted its organizers—including

Samuel senior—and ordered all money bought back with Massa-chusetts currency. Samuel senior lost a good share of his life's sav-ings, and his son, who was then in his third year at Harvard, swore eternal revenge on Thomas Hutchinson.[23]

But young Samuel's problem was that he did not seem to have the golden touch that Thomas and John Hancock did. After Har-vard, Samuel went to work for a merchant friend of his father's, but he was fired for spending more time writing political rants than keeping the company's books. Despite his own financial straits, Samuel senior bankrolled his son so that he could start his own ven-ture, but Samuel junior loaned half the stake to a friend, who promptly lost it; young Samuel then lost the other half on his own. The son tried his hand in the family brewery, but once again reveled in the political discussions of the taverns more than he attended to business.

His father died soon afterward. Adams squandered much of his inheritance, leaving both the brewery and his father's mansion in marginal condition. Political cronies of his father at the Boston Caucus tried to bail him out in 1756 by arranging his appointment as Boston tax collector. But that didn't work, either. Within a year, Adams owed the town for taxes that he had either failed to collect or had collected and carelessly allowed to drop into his own pocket.

His second cousin John Adams recalled that Samuel once acknowl-edged to him that he had "never looked forward in his life; never planned, laid a scheme, or formed a design for laying up any thing for himself or others after him."[24] That was likely true when it came to his shabby personal finances—which in any event Samuel blamed not on his own shortcomings but on a festering hatred for Thomas Hutchinson and the merchants of his class. It was certainly not true, however, that Samuel was a laggard when it came to lay-ing the foundation for a political scheme.

And when it came to politics, Samuel Adams did not pull any punches. At the time, the only man in Massachusetts more vocifer-ously against British rule than Samuel Adams was James Otis, a firebrand attorney whose revolutionary role was cut short by mental illness. (Otis's married sister, Mercy Warren, was as yet too busy raising children to think about adding her own pen to the fray.) Adams and Otis were both fiercely independent, champions of individual liberties, and ardently antiestablishment.

What pushed the seeming opposites of Samuel Adams and John Hancock together was money—or, more precisely, the lack of it in the post–French and Indian War period. With the French driven from Canada and Indian affairs west of the Appalachians relatively calm after the defeat of Pontiac's Rebellion, there was no one left to fight. This meant that there were no more lucrative government contracts for the House of Hancock or anyone else. In good times, the additional taxes levied by the Stamp Act might have been swallowed, but in this postwar depression, they loomed large and were the catalyst for Samuel Adams to rally opposition to all things British.

In addition to his pen, Adams's arsenal included his personal influence over an increasing number of fellow rebels. Taken at their best, they formed an idealistic corps devoted to self-government; at their worst, they roamed the streets as an unruly mob. When it was announced that the Stamp Act collector for Boston was to be Andrew Oliver, a well-to-do merchant who happened to be Thomas Hutchinson's brother-in-law, the mob took over. Oliver was hung in effigy from an elm tree on High Street that would soon be called the Liberty Tree. Then these rowdies marched on Oliver's house. Oliver had long fled with his family, but the marchers broke down the doors and ransacked its contents.[25]

Among those who abhorred this violence was John Hancock. Oliver was a fellow merchant and Harvard graduate. If such a mob could vent anger on Oliver's mansion, what was to stop them from marching up Beacon Hill to Hancock's own stately residence? While Samuel Adams thought that the night's events "ought to be forever remembered... [as] the happy Day, on which Liberty rose from a long Slumber," Hancock beseeched his agent in London to do all he could to encourage repeal of the Stamp Act, which he called "a Cruel hardship upon us," in the interest of avoiding further violence.[26]

His torn interests put Hancock decidedly on the fence. He began to spend more and more time in Boston taverns, including the Green Dragon, headquarters of his Masonic lodge. He wasn't being driven to drink; rather, he sought firsthand intelligence on how the political winds were blowing. Samuel Adams routinely stopped by the Green Dragon on his tavern rounds, and before long he began to spin his dreams of political rebellion in the younger man's ear. From 1758 to 1775, Adams "made it his constant rule," according to his cousin John, "to watch the rise of every brilliant genius, to seek his acquaintance, to court his friendship, to cultivate his natural feelings in favor of his native country, to warn him against the hostile designs of Great Britain, and to fix his affections and reflections on the side of his native country."[27]

This Samuel Adams did in spades with John Hancock. Never mind that Adams was still under scrutiny for his deficiencies as tax collector. Hancock soon decided that the best way to protect his property and business interests — not only on Beacon Hill but also throughout Boston and its waterfront — was to guarantee their safety by funding part of Adams's growing political movement — rowdy though it might be at times.[28]

In October of 1765, Hancock joined 250 British merchants, among whom he was clearly a kingpin, in supporting a boycott of British goods until the Stamp Act was repealed. For Hancock it was definitely a win-win. With the depressed economy, his business was at low ebb. His remaining credit in London was nil, and he could not have ordered a shipload of British goods if he had wanted to. Joining the boycott gave him an excuse to unload existing inventories at bargain prices. The boycott was actually good for his business, and it made him look like a hero to the Adams crowd. As for his own debts, he craftily pointed out to his London agent that without stamps, "he was legally unable to issue any remittances."[29]

It helped John Hancock immensely that he was well liked by his hundreds of employees and related operators who depended on his many businesses. By one later estimate, perhaps a little high, "a thousand families were, every day in the year, dependent on Mr. Hancock for their daily bread."[30] So when Hancock showed up at the Green Dragon, or any other establishment in Boston, the rank and file sang his praises as someone who treated them kindly and honestly.

In the end, the people hurt the most by this boycott were British merchants whose flow of orders from America and accounts receivable from past business took a substantial dip. By one account, British exports to the colonies dropped 14 percent, and London merchants pleaded with Parliament as readily as did their American cousins to consider "every Ease and Advantage the North Americans can with Propriety desire."[31]

A wealthy planter in Virginia who was watching events throughout the colonies held a similar view. "I fancy the merchants of Great Britain, trading to the colonies, will not be among the last to wish for a repeal of the act," George Washington wrote to the uncle of his wife, Martha, in London. As for Hancock, he declared to his London agent "that not a man in England, in proportion to estate, pays the tax that I do." He would not be a slave, Hancock declared. "I have a right to the Libertys & Privileges of the English Constitution, & I as an Englishman will enjoy them."[32]

With Adams's blessing and the support of the Boston Caucus, Hancock won a seat in the Massachusetts legislature, polling five votes more than Adams himself received in his own race. Hancock thought that he was championing commercial freedom, but what his election really did was bring him to the full attention of the government in London, which now identified him as "one of the Leaders of the disaffected." This impression was particularly solidified when, in one of Hancock's tavern campaign talks, he had boasted that he "would not suffer any of our [English customs] Officers to go even on board any of his London ships."[33]

Out for a walk that election day, John Adams happened to run into cousin Samuel and they took "a few turns together." Coming in view of Hancock's mansion on Beacon Hill, Samuel pointed to the impressive structure and remarked to John, "This town has done a wise thing to-day. They have made that young man's fortune their own." [34]

Ten days later, lightning struck. One of Hancock's ships docked in Boston with news that Parliament had repealed the Stamp Act. Samuel Adams's mob — dignified in some circles by the name Sons of Liberty — set off a huge fireworks display on Boston Common. Then they marched on John Hancock's Beacon Hill property, just as Hancock had once feared. But now they came to crown Hancock the hero of the hour for championing the boycott. He responded with fireworks of his own "in answer to those of the Sons of Liberty" and set out a pipe of Madeira wine — a cask of about 125 gallons — to treat the crowd. The only casualty of the night occurred when a giant wooden pyramid bedecked with lanterns, which had been erected on the Common, caught fire by accident and burned to the ground. [35]

The end result was that John Hancock and Samuel Adams emerged from the Stamp Act crisis as somewhat unlikely political partners. As the years went by, there would never be any question which side they were on. Others would vacillate, even up until the final hour, but together Hancock and Adams would stay the course toward rebellion and, ultimately, independence. As for those who wavered in their views, "Their opinions," noted Samuel's cousin John with disgust as he sat down to the First Continental Congress, "have undergone as many changes as the moon." [36]

Chapter 4

~

Volleys of Words

In the decade before 1775, rebels and loyalists aggressively used political propaganda to promote their individual agendas — just as political leaders have done throughout history. When events such as the Boston Tea Party and the Intolerable Acts occurred, both sides were quick to put their respective spins on the issues and to circulate their ideas as widely as they could. What gave colonial media wider distribution and greater weight than merely a local readership would have conferred was the postal system, which sped newspapers and letters from committees of correspondence to every corner of the colonies.

By 1775, thanks to Benjamin Franklin's efforts years before, the thirteen colonies enjoyed a state-of-the-art postal system. Franklin was appointed postmaster of Philadelphia in 1737. At the time, there was little communication between the colonies — at least not on an urgent basis — and mail delivery even between principal cities was a matter of "maybe it gets there, maybe it doesn't." Most often, mail was entrusted to a private traveler known to be going that way.

By 1753, Franklin was deputy royal postmaster for North America, essentially a postmaster general for the colonies. By the time Franklin left Philadelphia for his extended stay in England, he had eliminated this haphazard approach and unified and streamlined mail delivery into a truly reliable postal system. His post riders pioneered twenty-four-hour travel, using lanterns when necessary, horse relays, and centralized offices in major towns. Not only did his system reduce delivery times and increase reliability, it also proved profitable. The canny Franklin may or may not have realized at the time that he was nurturing what would one day become an essential component of revolutionary communication.

Riders carrying letters and newspapers made the trip from Boston to Philadelphia in five days and reached as far south as Charleston, South Carolina, in a month. This gave newspapers wide and relatively timely circulation, and it was common for papers in Boston and New York to reprint news of interest from Georgia and the Carolinas and vice versa. As political events heated up, rebels and loyalists — there were newspapers aligned with both sides — could read what their brethren were doing throughout the colonies.

Perhaps even more important, rebel committees of correspondence had direct and speedy — for the times — access to committees in other colonies. Initially, these committees were formed for a limited duration in response to a specific event — such as the committees in Massachusetts and New York, which promoted the Stamp Act Congress — but by 1775, some committees of correspondence had become shadow governments. This was particularly true after Parliament disbanded colonial legislatures with the passage of the Intolerable Acts. The postal system allowed rebel committees of correspondence to exchange news, formulate cooperative plans, and direct concerted action.

For much of the heyday of American newspapers during the twentieth century, major cities boasted at least two papers of competing political persuasions. It was no different in Boston in 1775. Among the newspapers in Boston that year, Isaiah Thomas's *Massachusetts Spy* and the *Boston Gazette*, published by Benjamin Edes and John Gill, trumpeted the rebel cause. Brothers Thomas Fleet Jr. and

John Fleet's *Boston Evening-Post* and Richard Draper's *Massachusetts Gazette* — variously known as or published in tandem with the *Boston News-Letter* and *Boston Post-Boy* — were bastions of loyalist thought.

In just one example of the heated exchanges that occurred early in 1775, a writer signing himself only as "a Friend to Peace and Good Order" — who was in truth loyalist Harrison Gray — published a pamphlet containing inflammatory criticism of the recent Continental and Massachusetts Provincial Congresses. Calling the adoption of the Suffolk Resolves nothing "short of high *treason* and *rebellion*," Gray charged that "the only apology that could be made for their conduct was, that they came into this vote immediately after drinking thirty two bumpers of the *best madeira*," and that by the following morning "they were ashamed of what they had done; but it was then too late for a reconsideration of the vote." Gray claimed that to avoid such mistakes in the future, the delegates "prudently determined to do no business after dinner." [1]

Edes and Gill, writing in the *Boston Gazette* in rebuttal, termed Gray's pamphlet "despicable" and noted it was "commonly called the *Gray Maggot*." As for Gray's "most impudent and false Assertion," the *Gazette* replied that as the minutes of the congress showed, "they never did any Business after Dinner." The Suffolk Resolves, the *Gazette* concluded, "were acted upon on a Saturday in the Forenoon." [2]

Perhaps the longest-running war of words occurred between two writers signing themselves "Massachusettensis" and "Novanglus." As John Adams recalled many years later, upon his return from the First Continental Congress in November of 1774, he "found the *Massachusetts Gazette* teeming with political speculations, and Massachusettensis shining like the moon among the lesser stars" in defense of the loyalist cause. Adams immediately surmised that Massachusettensis was none other than his estranged friend, Jonathan Sewall. Told that Massachusettensis "excited great exultation among the tories and many gloomy apprehensions among the whigs," Adams "immediately resolved to enter the lists with him." [3]

If his suspicion of Sewall's involvement was indeed his belief at the time, it brings a particular poignancy to the exchange. Not only were the two men advocates of their respective causes, they also were estranged friends turned determined adversaries. But in fact, as Adams acknowledged later, he was in error. Massachusettensis was not Jonathan Sewall but yet another Massachusetts lawyer named Daniel Leonard.

Born in Norton, Massachusetts, in 1740, Daniel Leonard was the son of the owner of an iron foundry in nearby Taunton. Entering Harvard in 1760, Leonard finished second in his class and felt compelled to prove his merits by delivering his commencement speech in Latin. He returned to Taunton and practiced law with Samuel White, who was also the speaker of the Massachusetts Assembly. Leonard married White's daughter, Anna, in 1767, but she died in childbirth the following year. Later, he married Sarah Hammock and had three children with her. In 1769, he became king's attorney for Bristol County.

Smart, wealthy, well connected, and recognized as one of the finest legal minds in Massachusetts, Leonard was a prime example of just how difficult it sometimes was to determine which side one was on — or even that a crisis requiring a choice of sides was at hand. Not only did Leonard have all the trappings of royally connected power and esteem, he was also a lieutenant colonel of the Bristol County militia. In this capacity, he reportedly spoke coolly of King George, king's attorney though he was.

Then in 1774, royal governor Thomas Hutchinson appointed Leonard a mandamus councilor. Now his allegiance was really being tested. Leonard denied that he had changed his position, but he chose to don the robe of loyalist rather than be further swayed by rebel arguments. When rebels in Taunton challenged his decision, Leonard's home was attacked by a mob firing shots and breaking windows. Like many rural mandamus councilors, Leonard sought refuge in occupied Boston.[4]

Whether or not this thirty-four-year-old lawyer and businessman—

run out of his own town by rebels — took it upon himself to speak out for the loyalist status quo or was possibly encouraged to do so by General Gage is not known. But in December of 1774, Leonard began his series of articles — in the form of letters to the editor — that were published in the *Massachusetts Gazette and the Boston Post-Boy and Advertiser*. Leonard chose to sign himself Massachusettensis, a concocted name with a Latin flair.

The use of pseudonyms or pen names by contributors was not at all unusual in those days, but just why writers adopted them is an interesting question. There usually was little mystery — among the well informed, at least — as to the true identity of an author. Newspapers were leaky sieves of gossip and innuendo. Libel laws may have been of some concern, but prosecution was usually reserved for blatant assaults on individual character rather than advocacy of general political views. Such presumed anonymity tended, however, to allow authors to express views more pointed and accusations more personal than if they had signed their own names. Some authors no doubt also felt that such pseudonyms — particularly when they referenced noted Roman statesmen or were otherwise Latin flavored — added a mark of distinction and gravity to their words.

Samuel Adams appears to have used at least twenty-five pseudonyms, including Candidus, Populus, and A Son of Liberty, and Alexander Hamilton (Publius, Americanus), Benjamin Franklin (Silence Dogood, Richard Saunders), Robert Livingston (Cato), and James Madison (Helvidius) all employed pen names. Another advantage, according to journalism historian Eric Burns, was that the more pseudonyms an author used, "the more likely it was that readers would think of him as several authors [and] his views, therefore, would seem to be held by many rather than simply one man with a prolific pen."[5]

Daniel Leonard was somewhat of an exception to the hate-mongering that frequently sprang from such pseudonymous columns; the impassioned pleas he made as Massachusettensis for loyalty to the king began in a balanced and moderate tone. "When a people, by what means soever, are reduced to such a situation, that every thing they hold dear, as men and citizens, is at stake," Leonard wrote in his first letter, dated December 5, 1774, "it is not only excusable, but even praiseworthy for an individual to offer to the public any thing that he may think has a tendency to ward off the impending danger."[6]

A main theme of the loyalist argument that Leonard underscored was the impossibility of the colonies surviving on their own or prevailing in a direct struggle against the assembled might of Great Britain. "With the British navy in the front, Canadians and savages in the rear, [and] a regular army in the midst," Massachusettensis noted, "desolation will pass through our land like a whirlwind, our houses be burnt to ashes, [and] our fair possessions laid waste."[7]

As January of 1775 passed, Leonard's weekly missives became more strident. "You are loyal at heart, friends to good order," Massachusettensis told his readers. "But you have been most insidiously induced to believe that Great-Britain is rapacious, cruel and vindictive."[8] Two weeks later, he warned: "To deny the supreme authority of the state is a high misdemeanor . . . to oppose it by force is an overt act of treason, punishable by confiscation of estate and most ignominious death."[9]

John Adams chose to answer Massachusettensis as Novanglus, meaning "New Englander," but he took his time doing so. His first Novanglus letter appeared in the *Boston Gazette* on January 23, 1775, seven weeks after Massachusettensis's opening salvo. Adams's tone was uncompromising from the start, particularly about the inevitability of Great Britain's power. Massachusettensis was mistaken, Adams wrote, when he said "the people are sure to be loosers in the end. They can hardly be loosers, if unsuccessful," Adams maintained, "because if they live, they can but be slaves, after an unfortunate effort, and slaves they would have been, if they had not resisted." Death, Adams went on to assert, "is better than slavery."[10]

That same week, not yet knowing that he had a direct adversary in the field, Massachusettensis continued to develop the theme of the dangers of the colonies surviving on their own. "Destitute of British protection," he asked, "what other Britain could we look to when in distress?" Would not the trade, navigation, and fisheries, which no nation dared to violate while protected by British colors, "become the sport and prey of the maritime powers of Europe?" [11]

Adams chose to address himself to Leonard's arguments in the order of their publication, pursuing him "in his own serpentine path." His adversary, Adams wrote, "conscious that the people of this continent have the utmost abhorrence of treason and rebellion, labours to avail himself of the magic in these words." As to the charge that rebels had subverted the long-cherished freedom of the press, Adams termed it but one example of his opponent's wily art "intended to excite a resentment against the friends of liberty." Both sides had their respective newspapers at their service, even if Adams was slightly disingenuous in concluding, "the Massachusetts Spy, if not the Boston Gazette, has been open to them as well as to others." As for the pro-loyalist papers, Adams maintained "the Evening-Post, Massachusetts Gazette & Boston Chronicle, have certainly been always as free for their use as the air." [12]

WHILE MASSACHUSETTENSIS AND NOVANGLUS ENGAGED in this war of words, Samuel Adams was also getting his writings, if not always his real name, in newspapers in Massachusetts and throughout the colonies. As Boston suffered under the deprivations of the closure of its port, support in the form of cash, goods, livestock, and crops poured in not just from surrounding Massachusetts counties but also from other colonies, including far-off Georgia. As chairman of the Boston committee of correspondence, Adams frequently either wrote or directed the writing of acknowledgment letters for those expressions of support and then made sure to give them wide circulation.

Of course, Samuel Adams never shied away from a political

controversy. When loyalists cast aspersions upon those administering these donations, the Boston committee of correspondence was quick with a response over Adams's signature as chairman. "The Printers in this and the other American Colonies," Samuel Adams wrote, "are requested to insert the following in their several News Papers." (Here again an effort was being made to gain a much wider circulation than just Boston.) "The Committee appointed by the Town of Boston . . . think themselves obliged, in this publick Manner, to contradict a slanderous Report raised by evil minded Persons, and spread in divers Parts of this Province, and perhaps more extensively thro' the Continent." There was absolutely no truth, Adams asserted, to reports that each member of the Boston committee was compensated six shillings, or, as some claimed, as much as half a guinea (ten shillings) a day for their attendance, in addition to receiving a commission on donations received. Any such reports were "in every part . . . groundless and false."[13]

But there were also other writers—besides the small group that might be called "the usual suspects": white, male, and upper-class—dipping their pens for the rebel cause and their own individual agendas. History's shorthand has long spoken of April 1775 in decidedly masculine terms: minutemen, alarm riders, armed men and boys. But in an era when women could neither vote nor own property without restrictions, women shared the heady dangers of revolution as rebels or bemoaned the upheaval of their lifestyle as loyalists.

The writer Mercy Otis Warren was a strong-willed woman whom one would not want on an opposing side. Warren's diminutive frame and gentle features belied the determination that burned behind her dark eyes when they focused on a mission. She was born in West Barnstable, on Cape Cod, on September 25, 1728, the third child and first daughter of James and Mary Otis. Her father was a merchant, attorney, and local judge who had prospered enough to own a substantial house with three dormers crowning the second story and employ laborers and indentured servants to look after the surrounding fields. Among the help were at least one African American and several Native American slaves.

Mercy's mother was dour, reserved, and frequently depressed. There seems little doubt that having thirteen children over twenty years, only seven of whom survived, may have had something to do with her outlook. James Otis, on the other hand, was outgoing, gregarious, and an affable host. He had a keen wit and a penchant for ideas that he passed on to his children. His only regret was that he lacked a formal education. This he determined to remedy in his eldest sons, and in due course James Jr. — known as Jemmy — and Joseph were sent off to Harvard. Such a path was unthinkable in that day for Mercy, but she learned to read and write and sharpened her intellect in father-daughter discussions that went well beyond domestic conversations. She also joined her brother Jemmy's tutoring sessions with the local minister as he prepared for college.

At Harvard, Jemmy Otis met James Warren, two years his junior. Warren's father was the high sheriff of Plymouth County and well acquainted with Jemmy's father, but exactly when James Warren first met Mercy Otis is uncertain. What is certain is that their marriage in a civil ceremony on November 14, 1754, found Mercy at twenty-six almost an old maid by the standards of the day and James at twenty-eight an aspiring merchant and farmer with political ambitions.[14]

James Otis dispatched one of his domestic servants to help Mercy and James in the Warrens' saltbox-style home in Plymouth. And Mercy soon needed that help, as beginning in 1757 she bore five healthy sons over the next nine years. Her focus was what was expected of colonial women: home, hearth, and husband, but by their own accounts, Mercy and James adored one another. "I again tell you that on your happiness depends mine," he wrote her during an absence nine years into their marriage. "I am uneasy without you . . . [and] . . . wish for the time that I am to return . . . everything appears so different without you." Years later, her own ardor had not cooled. He was "the center of my early wishes," Mercy told

James, and he continued to be "the star which attracts my attention."[15]

The Warrens' circle of friends came to include John Adams and his wife, Abigail. Mercy Warren was sixteen years Abigail Adams's senior, and Abigail found an intellectual mentor in her. "You, Madam," Abigail wrote Mercy just before the Boston Tea Party, "are so sincere a Lover of your Country, and so Hearty a Mourner in all her Misfortunes that it will greatly aggravate your anxiety to hear how much she is now oppressed and insulted." Abigail called tea "this weed of Slavery."[16]

By now, Mercy Warren's youngest was seven, and she was increasingly turning her pen to political issues. Mercy herself had found a mentor in Catharine Sawbridge Macaulay, a British historian who flouted strictures against feminine intellectual engagement. Beginning in 1763, Macaulay published a liberal Whig history of England in eight volumes, essentially arguing the importance of personal liberty. Mercy's brother had maintained a correspondence with Macaulay, but after Jemmy Otis deteriorated mentally, Mercy assumed his role. When asked by Mercy "whether the genius of Liberty has entirely forsaken our devoted isle [England]," Macaulay replied that Parliament's regrettable Intolerable Acts were "a complete answer," but encouraged Mercy not to lose hope. There were still liberal Whigs in Great Britain "who strenuously and zealously defended the injured rights of your countrymen."[17]

Mercy Warren hoped so but was dubious about their ability to carry the American cause in Parliament. "America stands armed with resolution and virtue," Warren told Macaulay as 1774 came to an end, "but she still recoils at the idea of drawing the sword against the nation from whence she derived her origin. Yet Britain, like an unnatural parent, is ready to plunge her dagger into the bosom of her affectionate offspring."[18]

But Mercy Warren desired a broader audience for her political thoughts. To publish openly as a woman in Puritan Massachusetts would have been regarded as scandalous at best. Her first anonymously published work, a play entitled *The Adulateur*, which satirized the administration of Massachusetts governor Thomas Hutchinson, had been published in Isaiah Thomas's rebel-friendly *Massachusetts Spy* in the spring of 1772. Political commentary thinly disguised as a fictitious play was a generally safe vehicle, particularly as plays in Puritan society were read by individuals at home rather than acted out.[19]

The Adulateur was well received and particularly championed by Mercy's husband, James, who, like Samuel Adams and many others, thought Governor Hutchinson a two-faced scoundrel, serving Great Britain while giving lip service to Massachusetts interests. When Benjamin Franklin leaked Hutchinson's personal letters favoring a stronger role for the governor to the press in 1773, Adams seized on them to prove the point. The disclosures were perfectly timed to coincide with the publication of Warren's second play, *The Defeat*, which portrayed Hutchinson as the diabolical Rapatio and ended with his gubernatorial downfall.[20]

A rather convoluted poem about the Boston Tea Party, entitled "The Squabble of the Sea Nymphs; or the Sacrifice of the Tuscararoes," followed. It was written with the encouragement of John Adams, but Mercy nonetheless told Abigail that she would not be upset if John told her to stop writing and "lay aside the pen of the poet (which ought perhaps to have been done sooner)." Instead, Adams arranged the poem's publication in the *Boston Gazette*.[21]

A few months later, after James Warren was elected to the Massachusetts Provincial Congress, Mercy wrote Abigail Adams of her increasing apprehensions about the looming rebellion. "No one has at stake a larger share of Domestic Felicity than myself," she told her younger admirer. "I see no Less than five sons who must Buckle on the Harness And perhaps fall a sacrifice to the Manes of Liberty."[22]

It was during this period of heightened anxiety that Warren committed her fears to parchment and anonymously published *The*

Group. Characters reappeared from her earlier plays, and she gave voice to the difficulty of choosing a side and sticking with it. One character named Beau Trumps, who loudly espoused loyalty to the king, was assumed by alert readers to be modeled after Daniel Leonard, the king's attorney for Bristol County who was then safely ensconced in Boston writing as Massachusettensis. A character named Simple Sapling—before accepting a royal bribe—took note that the opposing rebels were "Resolv'd to die, or see their country free."[23]

But there was more to *The Group* than the bashing of mandamus councilors. A strong secondary theme, according to Warren biographer Nancy Rubin Stuart, carried "a pro-female message that lamented the personal hardships of war forced upon women married to greedy husbands."[24]

Here Warren was publicly espousing political views about the status of women that went back to early conversations with her father and brothers about basic liberties. Before his mental breakdown kept him from writing, Mercy's brother Jemmy Otis had asked the bombshell question quite pointedly in a 1764 pamphlet: "Are not women born as free as men?" If that was indeed so, he continued, should not they also have "a natural and equitable right to be consulted . . . in the formation of new original compact or government?"[25] Mercy Otis Warren and her confidante Abigail Adams thought so, but both their husbands, adoring of their wives though they were, were not so sure.

While striking this chord of equal rights and liberty, Mercy Warren still sought reassurance from men about the worth of her writing. Husband James was perhaps too biased in his effusive praise, but Mercy coyly expressed her doubts to others that "it has sufficient merit for the public eye." John Adams, for one, demurred and once more arranged publication in the *Boston Gazette* of the first two acts of *The Group*, which appeared in the same issue as Adams's first missive as Novanglus.[26] By February of 1775, *The Group* and its anonymous author were the talk of rebel Boston.

*   *   *

THERE WAS ANOTHER WRITER WHO published his views on liberty and freedom but who brought a vastly different perspective to the issues and framed the debate in even more inclusive terms than did Mercy Otis Warren. His name was Caesar Sarter, and he was a black former slave of about fifty years of age. Sarter had been captured in Africa and brought to Massachusetts as a youth. His exact ownership is a mystery, but by 1774, after twenty years in bondage, he was living as a freeman in Newburyport, just north of Boston.

There was a strong Quaker influence among freed blacks at the time because of the Religious Society of Friends' pioneering stance in favor of abolition, and much of what Sarter had to say carried strong biblical overtones. Whether or not Sarter had help drafting his letter is open to question, but there can be no question that the agony of Sarter's personal experience flowed through his words. It must have taken courage to put his thoughts on paper and perhaps even more courage for the printers of the *Essex Journal and Merimack Packet* of Newburyport to publish them.

Sarter began by reminding readers that the political climate in which they lived was "a time of great anxiety and distress among you, on account of the infringement . . . of the natural rights and privileges of freeborn men. [Permit me] to tell you, and that from experience," Sarter went on, "that as Slavery is the greatest, and consequently most to be dreaded of all temporal calamities; so its opposite, Liberty, is the greatest temporal good, with which you can be blest!" Surely, he wrote, the freemen of Massachusetts recognized this because they were engaged in "struggles to preserve it."

Like others in the fight, Sarter harked back to the quest for freedom that had prompted so many Europeans to come to America in the first place. Unlike his own experience of being brought to America against his will, those white forefathers had fled England because of strong feelings about the "worth of Liberty" as well as "their utmost abhorrence of that curse of curses, slavery." As for those who piously thought Africans happier in America, "every man," wrote Sarter, "is the best judge of his own happiness, and every heart best knows its own bitterness."

The first step in any quest for freedom from Great Britain, Sarter maintained, was for Americans to "let the oppressed Africans be liberated." Not until then could rebels look "with consistency of conduct" for a blessing on their own endeavors to cast off the shackles of British rule. "I need not point out," Sarter concluded, "the absurdity of your exertions for liberty, when you have slaves in your houses." [27]

One of those who heartily agreed with Caesar Sarter was Abigail Adams. While John was attending the First Continental Congress in the fall of 1774, there had been what Abigail termed "a conspiracy of negroes," the first major indication that slaves in Boston were asking to fight for General Gage on the loyalist side in exchange for their freedom. The entire episode was "kept pretty private," according to Abigail, but she did not refrain from telling John her wish that "there was not a slave in the province."

Then Abigail, who had had her own conversations with Mercy Warren about women's rights, echoed Caesar Sarter's incredulity. "It always appeared a most iniquitous scheme to me," Abigail wrote John, "to fight ourselves for what we are daily robbing and plundering from those who have as good a right to freedom as we have." [28]

Truth be told, however, most of the rebels firing off volleys of words about liberty and freedom reserved them for a limited group of white males from the middle and upper classes. *Equality* was a cherished word, but one not widely or freely shared. To apply it universally to include females and black and Indian slaves was as yet unthinkable.

Chapter 5

~

"Fire, If You Have the Courage"

General Thomas Gage was certainly no stranger to North America. In fact, he had spent the better part of twenty years there. In the spring of 1775, Gage was fifty-five or fifty-six years old, the exact date of his birth being of some question. His father was the first Viscount Gage and for a time a member of Parliament. As the second son in the family, Thomas went into the military while his older brother, William, inherited the peerage. William used his contacts with Thomas Pelham-Holles, the first Duke of Newcastle, to further his younger brother's military career. By 1751, Thomas had fought without apparent distinction at Fontenoy in Flanders (1745) and Culloden in Scotland (1746) and was a lieutenant colonel with the Forty-Fourth Regiment of Foot.[1]

When the Duke of Newcastle, as de facto prime minister, decided to counter French expansion in the Ohio River valley, the Forty-Fourth Foot was ordered to North America late in 1754 to serve under Major General Edward Braddock. The following spring, with an expedition that included George Washington as the general's aide-de-camp, Braddock attempted to drive the French from Fort Duquesne (modern-day Pittsburgh).

Gage's military acumen now came under harsh criticism. On the morning of July 9, 1755, Braddock's column forded the low waters of the Monongahela River just below Turtle Creek. Gage was in the lead, commanding an advance guard of some three hundred regulars. When French troops and their Indian allies appeared across his line of march and began to encircle his force, Gage ordered a retreat back toward Braddock's main column of about one thousand men.

Hearing the sounds of this initial action, Braddock, instead of standing firm with his main force until the full extent of Gage's contact with the enemy could be determined, elected to advance in column along the narrow path. The result was that Gage's retreating troops and Braddock's advancing forces telescoped inward upon one another in a tangle of confusion. The French and Indians quickly seized a hilltop to the right of the British advance that Gage had failed to secure and poured deadly fire into the massed British troops. Gage abandoned two six-pound cannons in his hasty retreat, and the French turned them against the head of the British column. More than five hundred men from Braddock's command, including the general himself, were killed. Gage was slightly wounded.

Three years later, Gage was to have an even worse combat experience on the shores of Lake Champlain. In the wake of the Monongahela disaster, he received permission to organize a regiment of light infantry. Critics said the new regiment was an easy way for Gage to obtain a full colonelcy, but Braddock's defeat clearly argued for more agile tactics. Light infantry was designed to be more mobile and more rapidly deployed than regular British units and was an answer to the tactics being employed successfully by colonial frontiersman Robert Rogers. Indeed, it was Rogers' Rangers and the colonials' favorite general, Lord George Howe, who led an advance guard that included Gage's regiment during Lord Abercromby's attack against Fort Carillon, later renamed Ticonderoga.

When Abercromby inexplicably ordered Rogers' Rangers, who knew the ground better than anyone, to detour some distance away from the main force, Howe and Gage continued the advance and met with initial French resistance. This time, the British advance guard prevailed, but not before the likable Lord Howe lay dead with a bullet through his chest. Suddenly Colonel Gage was Abercromby's second in command.

Two days later, Abercromby ordered Gage to lead a massive frontal assault against a maze of fortifications spread across the slopes below Fort Carillon. The result was as predictable as it was catastrophic and proved to be the French and Indian War version of the Charge of the Light Brigade. By nightfall, the British had suffered almost two thousand casualties in front of a French force they outnumbered four to one, though Gage himself survived.[2]

Gage's star remained undimmed — both personally and professionally. On December 8, 1758, he married the quite eligible Margaret Kemble in an Anglican ceremony in New Brunswick, New Jersey. She was twenty-four and, if a later portrait is any indication, quite a beauty, with thick dark hair and pensive, some might even say moody, brown eyes. Margaret's father, Peter Kemble, was well settled in New Jersey and had been appointed to the governor's council of the province by George II in 1745. Her brother Stephen was a young infantry officer who first served under Gage at Ticonderoga and may have arranged Gage's introduction to his sister. About fifteen years older than Margaret, Thomas Gage was a good catch. Along with his high forehead, long, angular nose, and rounded chin, his drooping brown eyes conveyed stability if not daring, comfort if not dash. Together they would have nine children.[3]

At the beginning of 1759, the commander in chief in North America, Jeffery Amherst, gave Gage command of the western outposts on the Great Lakes, and a year later Gage led a force down the Saint Lawrence River to complement Amherst's attack on Montreal. His reward was a promotion to major general and the military governorship of Montreal. Amherst, worn out from five years of war, finally returned to England in 1763, when peace was signed with France, and Thomas Gage succeeded him as commander in chief of British forces in North America with headquarters in New York City.

In the wake of the French and Indian War, Gage was initially concerned with maintaining security along the western frontier. Despite the prohibitions of the Proclamation of 1763, which drew colonial borders along the crest of the Appalachians, continuing cross-Appalachian trade and limited settlement demanded his attention. But in 1768, ministers in London ordered Gage to withdraw British troops from most western forts and post them instead along the Eastern Seaboard, in part to garrison key cities where opposition was growing to Parliament's various taxing schemes.

When Massachusetts royal governor Francis Bernard — quite unpopular in the aftermath of the Stamp Act crisis — asked Gage to post troops in Boston, Gage declined to do so on his own authority. He was quite willing to follow orders from London, but if Gage took such a step on his own, he wisely foresaw that he would become a lightning rod for criticism, both in America and among Whigs in England.[4]

There are also indications that Gage found himself torn — or at the very least disturbed — by the notion that he should be using troops to suppress rights that he took for granted as an Englishman. Gage was a loyal soldier of the king, but he was not a royalist. His concept of English government and what it meant to Englishmen was more in keeping with the Whig tradition of a government of Parliament and men.

Still, in letters to his superior, secretary of war Lord Barrington, Gage held to the party line. When Boston protested the garrisoning of two regiments at Castle William in Boston Harbor, Gage called it "very disagreeable News" and told Barrington, "The People there grow worse and worse, and if any thing is Rebellion in America, they seem to me in an actual State of Rebellion." Gage was also quite derogatory in his statement that the colonials would never take decisive action — an attitude he would carry with him until the end. "I am very much of the Opinion," Gage told Barrington in the midst of the Stamp Act crisis, "they will shrink on the Day of Trial . . . They are a People, who have ever been very bold in Council, but never remarkable for their Feats in Action."[5]

Despite minor outbursts of colonial frustration, tensions in Massachusetts eased for a time, and in the spring of 1773, for the first time in eighteen years, Gage was granted leave to return to England. Margaret, who had never been out of North America, went with him. One of those who attended General Gage's farewell dinner in New York was an old comrade from the days of the French and Indian War, a Virginian named George Washington, who happened to be in town enrolling his stepson at King's College.[6]

From what is known, Thomas and Margaret Gage enjoyed the better part of a year in and around London, although one of Margaret's first acts upon arriving that summer was to give birth to their seventh child, a daughter named Charlotte Margaret. Three of their children had accompanied them on the Atlantic crossing, while the three oldest offspring were already in England attending school. With all the family together and no sign that Thomas's brother, Viscount Gage, would produce a viable heir (his seven children all died in infancy), there were strong familial and economic reasons to remain in England. Indeed, their stay might well have become permanent.

But in Gage's absence, tea was dumped into Boston Harbor, and royal governor Thomas Hutchinson was finally driven out of office by the relentless campaign of Samuel Adams and his followers. Soon after news of the Tea Party reached London, Gage had a command audience with George III. The precise timing is uncertain, but given that Gage had been in England seven months without such a summons, it was likely made in response to the tea news. The king was livid over the action, and Gage may have overplayed his hand in asserting his readiness "to return at a day's notice" should the conduct of the colonies warrant it. George III was impressed with Gage and soon decreed not only that Gage return to North America but also that he assume the dual role of military chieftain *and* royal governor of the errant province of Massachusetts.

By the time he was informed of this decision by Lord Dartmouth, Gage was likely having second thoughts. Parliament passed the punitive Boston Port Act, which he would have to enforce, shortly before his appointment as governor was formally signed on April 7, 1774. Given what Gage knew from almost twenty years of experience in North America, he found no reason to rejoice in either the bill or his appointment. In his mid-fifties, he may well have reveled in the idea of remaining in England. After a successful career, there was little in the way of fame or honor that he could hope to achieve, even if he should be successful in taming the rebel faction, and there was a high probability that if things went badly he would be seen in London as the principal scapegoat. As both the political and military leader in Massachusetts, there would be no one else to blame.

But loyal soldier that he was, Thomas Gage sailed for Boston without open complaint and, after a particularly speedy crossing on HMS *Lively*, arrived in Boston Harbor on Friday, May 13, 1774. Margaret Gage left England three weeks after the general's departure and, with her brother Stephen and all but two of her children, landed first in New York to visit friends and relatives then joined her husband in Boston in mid-September. Little did she know how tumultuous her stay would be.[7]

BECAUSE THE BOSTON PORT ACT made Salem the new Massachusetts capital as part of Boston's punishment, General Gage spent some of the summer of 1774 there before returning to Boston just prior to Margaret's arrival. In late September, he sent two dispatches to Lord Dartmouth that gave a gloomy outlook for the province, highlighting the illegal convening of both the Continental Congress and the county convention that passed the Suffolk Resolves. Gage offered Dartmouth "no Prospect" of enforcing the Intolerable Acts unless "by first making a Conquest of the New-England Provinces." The movement that the general characterized as a "Disease" was not confined to Boston, "but now it's so universal there is no knowing where to apply a Remedy."[8]

Before he heard back from Dartmouth, there was more bad news for Gage to report. "The Proceedings of the Continental Congress astonish and terrify all considerate Men," Gage acknowledged. As for the Massachusetts Provincial Congress, Gage assured Dartmouth that he had published a proclamation condemning its latest proceedings at Cambridge. Then, in what might be described as wishful thinking, Gage suggested to Dartmouth, "People are cooler than they were, and grow Apprehensive of Consequences. The Congresses have gone greater Lengths than was expected."[9] Greater lengths than perhaps Gage expected, but Samuel Adams, John Hancock, and others had little regard for such conservative thought.

Then came the seizure by rebels of the king's stores at Portsmouth. Ironically, Gage had almost forecast the outcome by telling Dartmouth a few days before: "Your Lordship's Idea of disarming certain Provinces would doubtless be consistent with Prudence and Safety, but it neither is nor has been practicable without having Recourse to Force, and being Masters of the Country."[10]

Given the pace of events in North America, the delay in cross-Atlantic communications between Gage and his superiors must have been maddening. Even in the fastest of circumstances, it took at least two months, and sometimes three, from the time Gage wrote a letter to London until he received a reply. A lot could happen during that interval, and Gage knew well that at a local level he was on his own. But in the broadest sense, he was also well aware that only Parliament and the king could resolve the status between mother country and colonies and either announce a reconciliation or tighten the screws of control.

"The Eyes of all are turned upon Great Britain, waiting for her Determination," Gage told Dartmouth three weeks into the new year. He might well have stopped there, but, characteristically, he went on to say what so many from the king on down wanted to hear: "It's the opinion of most People, if a respectable Force is seen in the Field, the most obnoxious of the Leaders seized, and a Pardon proclaimed for all other's, that Government will come off Victorious, and with less Opposition than was expected a few Months ago." [11]

It would take some months for Dartmouth's response and his instructions in the matter to reach Gage in Boston. In the meantime, all Thomas Gage could do was suffer through an uncomfortable winter. Not until February 6, 1775, did he receive a reply to his admonitions of late September. "The state of the Province as represented in those Dispatches," Dartmouth told Gage, "is now under consideration." Dartmouth hoped that it would "not be many days" before he could direct a course of action in response. Waiting "with Impatience" for further letters from Gage, Dartmouth "ardently" wished for "a better prospect of the restoration of public tranquility than is held forth in those which I have already received." [12]

WHILE HE WAITED FOR FURTHER instructions from London, General Gage pressed to undertake two important missions, both cloaked in secrecy. On February 22, the general gave instructions to two officers, Captain John Brown of the Fifty-Second Regiment of Foot and Ensign Henry De Berniere of the Tenth Regiment of Foot, to make a clandestine reconnaissance of rural towns west of Boston. These officers were instructed to make a sketch of the country they passed and note in particular the heights, passes, rivers, and fords as well as "advantageous spots to take post in, and capable of being made defencible." As evidence that Gage was anticipating more than a day or two in the field, they were also instructed to record what provisions might be had off the land and from local farms, including "Forage, Straw, &c., the number of Cattle, Horses, &c., in the several Townships." [13]

To travel as inconspicuously as possible through the Massachusetts countryside, these two proper British officers attempted to disguise themselves as farmers, donning "brown Clothes and reddish handkerchiefs" around their necks. Such attire was questionable, but what made the pair really stand out was that Captain Brown chose to take his servant along. When a sentry from the Fifty-Second Regiment recognized Brown as the trio was leaving Boston, the servant "bid him not to take any notice," and they "passed unknown to Charlestown," thinking their disguise secure.

Commenting favorably on the brick buildings of Harvard College, the "farmers" passed through Cambridge and reached Watertown, about six miles to the west. De Berniere thought their real identities "were not suspected," but a lunch stop at Brewer's Tavern proved otherwise. Brewer was a Whig, and while the black woman who brought their food was at first very civil, she soon excused herself to report her suspicions to her employer. When she returned, Brown tried to engage her in conversation about what "very fine country" this was, which she acknowledged, but then she warned, "And we have got brave fellows to defend it, and if you go up any higher [into the hills] you will find it is so."

With some trepidation, the two officers and their "man" walked west toward Worcester, seeking out loyalists who could provide them with food and shelter and doing their best to avoid rebels who frequently shadowed or fell in with them. Even if they did not know the political persuasions of their hosts with certainty, the proffered choice of drink usually told them what they needed to know. If they were presented with only coffee, it raised an alarm that the house was observing the tea boycott, but if they were freely given a choice of coffee or tea, they were among loyalist friends.

Having reconnoitered Worcester — where a substantial cache of rebel arms and ammunition was stored — and the roads leading to it, they arrived on the fifth night of their journey at Buckminster's Tavern in Framingham. To their surprise, the local militia was drilling on the village green. About an hour after Brown, De Berniere, and their servant retired to their room, the militia drew near the tavern and drilled right under their window. Whether this was meant as bluster, so that the officers might report back on the readiness of the militia, or whether it was merely a convenient spot to practice before all were dismissed to enter the tavern for rounds of drinks is debatable. In any event, the thinly disguised British officers slept there all night, and De Berniere's report that "nobody in the house suspected us" is almost certainly not true.

From Framingham, they doubled back on a different road to sketch the lay of the land toward Sudbury and Marlborough, a long day's walk of thirty-two miles through snow and muddy roads. Once again, their identities and purpose seemed well known as rebels made one excuse or another to follow them or bump into them. By the time they returned to Boston after seven nights on the road, about the only person who failed to recognize them for what they were was General Gage, who happened to be walking on Boston Neck as they came into town.[14]

Before Brown and De Berniere returned, and before receiving any additional instructions from London, General Gage nonetheless dispatched a second mission of even greater importance, continuing his attempts to seize powder and arms from the rebels. To date, he had not been very successful. Though his troops had reclaimed two field pieces in nearby Cambridge the previous September, his attempts to secure the king's stores at Newport, Rhode Island, and Portsmouth, New Hampshire, had failed. Now, in the last week of February 1775, Gage focused on nearby Salem, Massachusetts, and a cache of cannon barrels that rebels were in the process of mounting on gun carriages for use on land as field guns.

The cannons were twelve-pounders thought to have originally belonged to the French in Nova Scotia during the French and Indian War. David Mason, a colonel in the local militia, reportedly purchased at least twelve and perhaps as many as seventeen of the pieces from Salem merchant and seafarer Richard Derby. Mason's wife and daughters were busy sewing flannel cartridges to hold gunpowder.

Gage ordered Lieutenant Colonel Alexander Leslie and about 240 men of the Sixty-Fourth Regiment of Foot to sail the fifteen miles from Boston to Marblehead and then march on nearby Salem. Well aware that the rebels' intelligence network in Boston might detect such a movement and again send Paul Revere galloping to spread an alarm, Gage used troops that were quartered at Castle William in Boston Harbor and not in the town proper. They could be embarked more stealthily, and two hours after sunset on Saturday, February 25, they were.

About noon the following day — a Sunday, when the pious of New England could be expected to be focused on church — a transport, "apparently manned as usual," according to the *Essex Gazette*, arrived at Marblehead, about four miles south of Salem. Somewhere between two and three o'clock that afternoon, as soon as most people had gone back to afternoon church services, the decks of the transport were suddenly covered with soldiers, "who having loaded and fixed their Bayonets, landed with great Dispatch; and instantly marched off." [15]

Certain men with sharp eyes who were not in church suspected Leslie's destination and sped word to Salem in advance of his column. A youngster named William Gavett later remembered, "My father came home from church rather sooner than usual, which attracted my notice, and said to my mother, 'The reg'lars are come and are marching as fast as they can towards the Northfields bridge.'" Telling his wife to keep the children indoors, Jonathan Gavett then stepped into his front yard in time to see Leslie's troops march past. His minister from the nearby First Meeting House, Thomas Barnard, soon joined Gavett, and together they followed the force through town. Meanwhile, David Mason, the colonel of the militia, had also received word of Leslie's approach and burst into the North Meeting House to interrupt the service with a similar shout: "The reg'lars are coming after the guns and are now near Malloon's Mills!"[16]

There is some evidence, however, that Colonel Leslie was not yet sure of the location of the cache of cannon barrels. Coming into Salem from the south, his line of march crossed the inlet of the South River at Malloon's Mills via a drawbridge and reached the courthouse square. His advance guard turned eastward, toward the town's long wharf—perhaps as a diversion, perhaps to seek information—while Leslie paused in front of the courthouse and sought a local informant.

John Sargent, a well-known Tory and half brother of the local mandamus councilor, appeared and "was very soon whispering in the Colonel's Ear." When they parted, Leslie led his troops onward

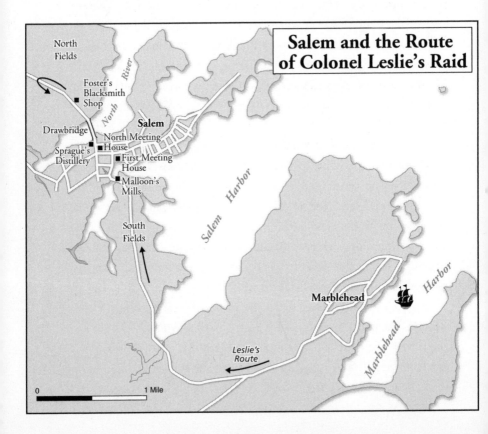

through town and past the North Meeting House to another bridge, this one spanning the inlet of the North River that led to the North Fields section of town. The column boldly started across the long bridge only to discover that the drawbridge portion was in the raised position, exposing a deep, watery chasm of some forty feet. The bridge was clearly under the control of a group of townspeople on the opposite (northern) shore who had raised the span to stop the troops in their march. Some people on that side even climbed to the top of the raised span with the help of the chains that held it. As many as could fit defiantly perched there like hens at roost.

The *Essex Gazette* initially reported that Leslie "ordered an Officer to face his Company to the Body of Men standing on a Wharf on the other Side of the Draw-Bridge, and fire." A Salem man, by some accounts the Reverend Barnard and by other accounts a militia captain named John Felt, immediately intervened and told Leslie he had no right to fire without further orders, "and if you do fire (said he) you will be all dead Men." [17]

A week later, the *Gazette* noted there was some question as to whether or not Leslie had given a specific order to face and fire or been prevented from doing so by locals. "There was no Intention to detract from Col. Leslie's Courage, Honour or Prudence," the newspaper's proprietors wrote in response, but the end result was still the same: "The Company neither fired or faced." [18]

Meanwhile, locals scuttled three large gondolas on the riverbank that might have been used to ferry troops across. While Joseph Whicher, the foreman of the nearby Sprague's Distillery, was directing the sinking of the distillery's own gondola, a party of some twenty soldiers swarmed aboard it and ordered Whicher to cease and desist at the points of their bayonets. Whicher reportedly opened his shirt in defiance and "dared them to strike," which one did, with a gentle jab that nonetheless drew some blood. Whicher bragged about it the rest of his life. [19]

Seeing the squabble in the sinking gondola, Leslie withdrew to the center of his command and held a brief council with his officers.

Whether he cautioned them against an unauthorized errant shot is unknown but likely. Most of the townspeople for the moment appeared unarmed, and Leslie did not want another Boston Massacre incident on his hands. Instead, the colonel advanced again to the open span and made one more appeal to the crowd. "I am determined to pass over this bridge before I return to Boston," Leslie declared — "[even] if I remain here until next autumn." That was an empty enough threat, but then Leslie announced that he would seize barracks for his troops in two nearby stores until the bridge was lowered. Most in Salem did not want such permanent company.

Captain Felt of the local militia, to whom this remark was particularly addressed, answered that "nobody would care for that," upon which Colonel Leslie, "nettled no doubt by this expression of contempt," replied, "By God I will not be defeated." To which Felt coolly responded, "You must acknowledge that you have been already baffled."[20]

By another recollection, in the midst of this standoff, Colonel Leslie pompously exclaimed that he was upon the King's Highway and would not be deterred from crossing over the drawbridge. That wasn't so, replied a gutsy old man named James Barr. "It is *not* the King's highway, it is a road built by the owners of the lots on the other side, and no king, country or town has anything to do with it."

"There may be two words to that," Leslie replied.

"Egad," Mr. Barr responded. "I think that will be the best way for you to conclude the King has nothing to do with it."[21]

What seems to have become clear, however, is that most of the British column stood shivering in the cold in the fading afternoon light of a wintry day. They might have been better served if they had brought their overcoats instead of fife and drums. Numbed by the cold, they endured the taunts of a growing group of townspeople: "Soldiers, red-jackets, lobster-coats, cowards, *damnation to your government!*" In addition, members of militia from neighboring towns were beginning to appear and could be seen taking up positions behind nearby buildings. Many more militiamen were on the way, and to Leslie's rear, the hardened Marblehead fishermen were preparing to block his line of retreat.

Leslie was in a box, and he knew it. Had he pushed the issue, leveled arms, and fired, he might well have put Salem—instead of the green at Lexington—on the map as the tinderbox of the American Revolution. In desperation, he proposed a win-win. If the Salem folk would lower the bridge, Leslie promised to march his troops across it no more than about five hundred feet and not disturb anything or anyone. He would then turn them about and march them back again, à la the Duke of York in a certain nursery rhyme.

The objects of Leslie's quest had likely been stored in Robert Foster's blacksmith shop on the northern shore, but the delay at the drawbridge of "about an Hour and an Half" had given locals time to have "every Thing . . . secured." By one account, a Quaker named David Boyce lent his team of horses to the effort, and the cannons were moved farther out of town. With the cannons thus secure, David Mason, sitting atop the open drawbridge, gave the decisive order. His men on the northern shore lowered the drawbridge, and Leslie ordered his freezing troops to march across.[22]

But there was to be one more moment of tension—at least it was remembered as tense in hindsight. As Leslie's regulars reached their promised turnabout point, Sarah Tarrant, a woman of about thirty, stuck her head out of an open window and shouted at them, "Go home and tell your master he has sent you on a fool's errand and broken the peace of our Sabbath." By one account, one of the soldiers aimed his firearm at her, but that only made her more defiant. "Fire, if you have the courage," Tarrant shouted. "But I doubt it."[23]

The tale of Sarah Tarrant aside, Leslie led his men back over the drawbridge to the waiting ship at Marblehead and returned to Boston. There he was able to report to General Gage that he had indeed marched the length of Salem but found no arms. Gage may have taken the entire Salem incident as proof that he could send troops into the countryside with impunity. But had Leslie's troops opened fire at the drawbridge, there is little doubt that their retreat would have been met with considerable return fire—if not immediately then upon their homeward trek.

The lesson of the Salem raid to the rebels was that their local militias could quickly be warned, assembled, and dispatched to the point of a contest. One company of armed men arrived in Salem from Danvers, about five miles away, just as Colonel Leslie's force was departing. Had a stand-down message not been circulated on the heels of the initial warnings, the *Essex Gazette* estimated that "not less than 12 or 15,000 men would have been assembled in this town within 24 hours after the alarm." As it was, Salem "immediately dispatched Messengers to the neighbouring Towns to save them the Trouble of coming in; but the Alarm flew like Lightening so that great Numbers were in Arms, and some on the March, before our [recall] Messengers arrived."[24]

Just how General Gage and the British learned about the cache of Salem cannons in the first place was a matter of great debate. In Salem, as in every town in America, all were not on the same side. But when fingers were pointed, at least one suspect just as quickly took it upon himself to deny any involvement. "As it is reported about this Town, much to my Injury," Andrew Dalgleish professed in an advertisement two days after Leslie's raid, "that I gave Information of certain Pieces of Artillery, which was the Occasion of a Regiment's marching to this Place Yesterday;—I take this public Method of acquainting the good People, that the Character of an *Informer*, is of all Characters the most odious to me; that I was in no Way instrumental in bringing Troops hither, and shall be ready to satisfy any one, who will call upon me, of my intire Innocence."[25]

"Col. Leslie's ridiculous expedition," as the *Essex Gazette* termed it, was given mention in John Trumbull's epic poem of the Revolution, *M'Fingal*.

Thro' Salem straight without delay,
The bold battalion took its way,
March'd o'er a bridge, in open sight
Of sev'ral Yankees arm'd for fight,
Then, without loss of time, or men,
Veer'd round for Boston back again;
And found so well their projects thrive,
That ev'ry soul got home alive.[26]

By yet another anecdotal account, fifers in Leslie's column supposedly played "The World Turned Upside Down" as they returned to their ship off Marblehead.[27] The irony, of course, is that if the story is true, this is the same tune that the British would play after the surrender of Lord Cornwallis at Yorktown at the end of the American Revolution. But as it was, the British raid on Salem was not even the beginning, much less the end.

Chapter 6

Boston in the Bull's-Eye

Boston was long accustomed to being the focal point of both American rebellion and British resolve. News of the Salem raid made headlines there just as the town prepared to commemorate the five-year anniversary of one of its most infamous events. The catalyst for that event had been jobs — more precisely, the lack of them. At the time, Boston was still feeling the economic pinch of the nonimportation boycott promoted in the wake of the Stamp Act crisis. Compounding the unemployment problem, British soldiers stationed in town were permitted to moonlight with part-time jobs. The result was competition for much-sought-after openings in the workforce, and it also increased friction with locals as soldiers came into daily interactions with Bostonians — and, inevitably, flirted with local women.

Monday evening, March 5, 1770, was a bitterly cold night. It had not been a peaceful weekend. On the previous Friday, there had been a bloody brawl between local workers and about forty off-duty soldiers looking for work at John Gray's ropewalk. Higher-ups on both sides quickly got control of the situation, but groups of workers and soldiers, fueled by ample amounts of brew from various taverns, roamed the streets over the weekend, looking to restart the trouble.

No confrontations occurred on Saturday or Sunday, but that Monday evening a wig maker's apprentice attempting to collect an overdue bill from a British officer got into a squabble with a lone sentry at the door of the Custom House on King Street near Boston's Long Wharf. The sentry struck the apprentice with the butt of his musket. A small group of locals quickly appeared to support the apprentice, and the sentry called for assistance from Captain Thomas Preston, the officer of the watch. Someone sounded a downtown Boston alarm bell, usually reserved for fires or other great calamities, and men on both sides poured into the streets. With more bells ringing, about three hundred locals converged on the Custom House. They took up positions in front of Preston's small detachment of eight British regulars who had been hastily dispatched to reinforce the building.

The crowd taunted the soldiers with angry words, including ill-advised shouts of "Fire, Fire!" Next they started throwing snowballs, rocks, and chunks of ice. When one soldier — greatly outnumbered as he and his fellow soldiers were — was knocked down by such a missile, he got to his feet and, undoubtedly partly in fear for what might happen next and perhaps partly in rage, fired one shot into the crowd. At the sound of his musket discharging, other soldiers fired as well. As the crowd surged forward, more shots — perhaps as many as a dozen or more — rang out before Captain Preston got control of his troops. But it was too late. Four Bostonians lay dead, and several others were badly wounded, one of whom died early the next morning. For Boston, what locals would call the Boston Massacre immediately became that generation's Kent State shooting.[1]

Blame was laid on both sides. General Gage placed it squarely on Samuel Adams and his cohorts. Gage claimed that the entire provocation had been "contrived by one Party," meaning Adams's radical leadership of Boston's rebels.[2] On the other side, the *Boston Gazette* was quick to call the incident "a recent and melancholy

Demonstration of the destructive Consequences of quartering Troops among Citizens in a Time of Peace." [3]

But in a demonstration that civil law was still supreme in Boston, General Gage agreed to permit the soldiers who had fired to stand trial in a Massachusetts court. Given local sentiments, they would need one of the best lawyers in Boston to defend them. Despite his growing rebel beliefs, John Adams agreed to do so. Captain Preston, who had never given an order to fire, was acquitted, as were six of his soldiers. Two others were convicted only of manslaughter, not murder.

Certainly John Adams took a risk by representing such unpopular clients, but on the third anniversary of the shootings, while Adams acknowledged such representation had caused him great "anxiety," he nonetheless called it "one of the best pieces of service I ever rendered my country." Condemning those soldiers to death for murder would, Adams believed, have been "as foul a stain upon this country as the executions of the quakers or witches anciently." [4] What, after all, was his cousin Samuel Adams agitating for if not an unalienable system of justice?

Samuel Adams used the Boston Massacre as a rallying cry to denounce every act of British occupation and oppression. Illustrations and editorials in the *Boston Gazette* and the *Massachusetts Spy* and a number of privately published pamphlets spread the Adams version of events throughout the colonies: despicable British regulars had fired on unarmed Americans without provocation. For his part, General Gage appears not even to have attempted to counter this stream of rebel propaganda, though his chances of success had he tried are open to question.

After the trial of the soldiers, tempers on both sides eased for a time. In the broadest sense, this period of relatively calm occupation lasted for almost three and one-half years, until the next flash point — the Boston Tea Party. But these were hardly quiet years for Samuel Adams, who was instrumental during this interlude in keeping up a torrent of political opposition in correspondence and

editorials. In particular, Adams went to great pains to commemorate the tragedy of the Boston Massacre with annual memorials and
speeches. Given the events of the previous six months, the fifth
anniversary commemoration, on March 5, 1775, was to be one of
his finest efforts.

THE KEYNOTE SPEAKER FOR THE gathering in the Old South Church
was Dr. Joseph Warren, frequently confused with Mercy Warren's
husband, James, but in fact there was no connection between them
other than their shared passion for the rebel cause. Joseph Warren
was a medical doctor who had been the principal author of the Suffolk Resolves and was a member of Samuel Adams's inner circle on
Boston's committee of safety, essentially an executive committee
charged with military preparedness.

Joseph Warren was definitely one to command attention. Even
among a relatively young generation of rebel leaders, Warren was
younger than most, still only thirty-three years old that March. He
was five years younger than John Hancock and nineteen years
younger than Samuel Adams. He was an articulate writer and polished public speaker, and he had also been invited to give the 1772
commemoration address. Men on both sides of the issue listened to
his words with attention, and it was generally acknowledged that
his handsome good looks gave women cause to fixate on him as
well.

Born in nearby Roxbury, where his father had been a farmer,
Joseph Warren graduated from Harvard in 1759 and began his
medical apprenticeship after a year of teaching school. In 1764, at
age twenty-three, he married eighteen-year-old Elizabeth "Betsy"
Hooton, who even by the standards of the day was something of a
child bride. Betsy's merchant father had just died, and their wedding announcement in the *Boston Gazette* described her as "an
accomplished young Lady with a handsome Fortune." [5]

The couple's first child, also named Elizabeth, was born at some vague date in the spring of 1765, quite probably less than nine months after their wedding. Over the next eight years, Joseph and Betsy Warren had three more children, but Betsy died suddenly in May of 1773, leaving Joseph a widower with four small children between the ages of ten and three. Neither his medical practice nor his family responsibilities, however, kept Warren from a consuming participation in the rebel cause. Commenting two days before on Warren's scheduled speech, Samuel Adams noted, "It was thought best to have an experiencd officer in the political field on this occasion, as we may possibly be attackd in our Trenches."[6]

Because the March 5 anniversary fell on a Sunday in 1775, the memorial service was held on the following Monday. The church was packed to the limit. Samuel Adams, John Hancock, Joseph Warren, and other members of Boston's revolutionary council occupied seats near the pulpit, but there was also a good showing of British officers in attendance near the front of the church. After preliminaries, Warren was introduced. Graciously saying that his audience should not expect "the enrapturing strains of eloquence which charmed you" from prior years' speakers, including John Hancock, Warren nonetheless assured his audience that "with a sincerity, equal to theirs, I mourn over my bleeding country."[7]

As always, Adams and Warren had scripted both a strong political message of the wrongs of British rule and an equally strong emotional reminder of images of their fellow citizens bleeding red on the white snow. "The baleful images of terror crowd around me," Warren intoned, "and discontented ghosts with hollow groans, appear to solemnize the anniversary of the fifth of March."[8]

By one Tory account, soon sent to the loyalist *Rivington's New-York Gazetteer*, the British officers present "frequently interrupted Warren, by laughing loudly at the most ludicrous parts . . . to the great discontent of the devoted citizens."[9] Undeterred, Warren forged ahead. Independence from Great Britain was not their aim, Warren maintained, but he acknowledged to his listeners, "However difficult the combat, you never will decline it when freedom is the prize."[10]

After Warren was finished, Samuel Adams rose to move the appointment of an orator for the following year's commemoration. As usual, he did not mince words in describing the event to be honored as a "Bloody Massacre," words that even Warren had avoided. This was too much for the assembled British officers, and they took up cries of "Fie! Fie!" and "To Shame!"[11]

To the assembled audience, especially to those in the balconies some distance from the pulpit, this came across and was repeated as "Fire! Fire!" and thinking the building ablaze, by one Tory report, they "bounced out of the windows, and swarmed down the gutters, like rats into the street." By apparent coincidence, the Forty-Third Regiment of Foot, "returning accidentally from exercise," was marching by with drums beating, and its appearance "threw the whole body into the utmost consternation."[12]

At least one officer exchanged heated words with Adams at the pulpit, but by then the audience had largely made for the exits. Had a confrontation taken place, one British officer later speculated, it "wou'd in all probability have proved fatal to Hancock, Adams, Warren, and the rest of those Villains, as they were all up in the Pulpit together." But the officer claimed he was glad that such had not occurred, because "it wou'd indeed have been pity for them to have made their exit in that way, as I hope we shall have the pleasure before long of seeing them do it by the hands of the Hangman."[13] Clearly, neither side took these annual rites as an opportunity for reconciliation.

MEANWHILE, BOSTON REMAINED IN THE bull's-eye. General Gage had some four thousand soldiers under his command in Boston, roughly one for every four Bostonians. But he was surrounded by dozens of rural towns inhabited by tens of thousands of musket-toting rebels who seemed quite willing and able to rally great numbers of militia at a moment's notice. No doubt Gage was inclined to agree with a London traveler who a few months before opined of

British forces in North America: "They are too numerous indeed for ambassadors, and too few for soldiers."[14]

Two of Gage's regiments were quartered at Castle William, in the harbor, but ten other regiments and Major Pitcairn's marines were quartered in encampments, makeshift barracks, and private dwellings throughout the town. The population of Boston had been steadily declining as rebels opted to evacuate to the countryside, but the loyalist population had been increasing to balance this exodus as mandamus councilors and other loyalists took shelter there. Samuel Adams boasted two days before the Boston Massacre anniversary, "We have almost every Tory of Note in the province, in this Town, to which they have fled for the Generals protection."[15]

And four thousand troops did not necessarily mean four thousand effectives ready to take the field. It had been a hard winter on everyone. Many of Gage's troops had been sick, and some had died. Samuel Adams believed that others had deserted; in addition, he wrote, "many I believe intend to desert" come spring. Adams estimated in early March that there were not more than 2,200 effective men under Gage's command. Adams told a correspondent, "I have seen a true List of the 65th & the Detachment of Royal Irish, in both of which there are only 167 of whom 102 are effective."[16]

This situation did not, however, keep most British officers from looking with disdain upon their colonial opponents. In fact, from General Gage on down, the greatest weakness of the British army might have been their underestimation of the rebels at every turn. "It is a curious Masquerade Scene," one British officer wrote after observing Boston militia at drill, "to see grave sober Citizens, Barbers and Tailors, who never looked fierce before in their Lives, but at their wives, Children, or Apprentices, strutting about in their Sunday wigs in stiff Buckles with their Muskets on their Shoulders, struggling to put on a Martial Countenance."[17]

When a member of the House of Lords dared to suggest "the impracticability of conquering America," the Earl of Sandwich, First Lord of the Admiralty, responded that he did not "think the noble Lord can be serious on this matter." So what if the colonies abound in men? Sandwich asked. "They are raw, undisciplined, cowardly men . . . [and] believe me my lords, the very sound of a cannon would carry them off." [18]

Major John Pitcairn of the Royal Marines held similar opinions and was not afraid to put them in writing to Sandwich. He had arrived in Boston the previous November as part of a six-hundred-man force of marines. "I often wish to have orders to march to Cambridge," Pitcairn wrote Sandwich in February of 1775, "and seize those impudent rascals that have the assurance to make such resolves." Pitcairn acknowledged that he had "no orders to do what I wish to do, and what I think may easily be done," which was to seize all the troublemakers and "send them to England." [19]

Two days before the Boston Massacre commemoration, Pitcairn wrote again to the Earl of Sandwich and noted that General Gage had met with "some of the Great Wigs, as they are called here," and swore to them that "if there was a single man of the King's troops killed in any of their towns [General Gage] would burn it to the ground." Whether Gage meant it, or whether the words made any impression on the local leaders, is debatable, but they did make for impressive rhetoric when repeated among Gage's junior officers. Indeed, Pitcairn remained "satisfied that one active campaign, a smart action, and burning of two or three of their towns, will set everything to rights." Nothing less, Pitcairn firmly believed, "will ever convince those foolish bad people that England is in earnest." [20]

As the British occupiers of Boston looked down their noses at their rebel adversaries, Samuel Adams, under the auspices of the Boston committee charged with receiving and distributing donations, continued to crank out letters of thanks for the material support that other colonies were sending to Boston. He was always sure to include with his thanks exhortations to the greater collective cause. From the county and borough of Norfolk and the town of Portsmouth, both in Virginia, came "seven hundred and fifteen bushels corn, thirty-three barrels pork, fifty-eight barrels bread, and ten barrels flour." Unfortunately, the ship carrying these provisions floundered, but not before the Boston men had "the good fortune of saving the most part of the cargo." [21]

From Henrico County, surrounding Richmond, Virginia, came "three hundred twenty-nine and a half bushels wheat, one hundred thirty-five bushels corn, and twenty-three barrels flour." In hindsight, Adams's thank you carried some irony with it. "Having been born to be free," Adams assured the Virginians of his fellow Bostonians, "they will never disgrace themselves by a submission to the injurious terms of slavery." [22] The skin color and legal status of the laboring hands that had grown that Virginia produce in the first place was not acknowledged as part of the communication.

Such generosity from other colonies was not lost on loyalists who despised the show of support and hoped that Boston might suffer more. "In God's name," asked loyalist writer and Anglican clergyman Samuel Seabury, "are not the people of Boston able to relieve their *own* poor? Must they go begging . . . from Nova-Scotia to Georgia, to support a few poor people, whom their perverseness and ill conduct have thrown into distress?" [23]

But such donations were not always without controversy. When the schooner *Dunmore* brought a cargo of "valuable donations from our friends in Virginia," Adams responded with the usual thanks, but added a warning that a recently built vessel had lately sailed from Boston to Virginia under a master named Crowel Hatch. Rebel tradesmen in Boston, feeling the economic downturn resulting from the closure of the port, had proposed to Hatch that they do the construction at a 5 percent discount. Refusing to work with rebels, Hatch demurred, got his ship built by "more ordinary workmen from the country," and then, according to Adams, "proposed that the Committee should employ our smith, in making anchors for his vessel, at a price by which they could get nothing but their labor for their pains."

When the rebel blacksmiths declined to work without a profit, Hatch, in Adams's words, grew very angry and threatened repeatedly "that he would stop all the donations he could, and that no more should come from the place where he was going to, meaning Virginia." Adams closed this letter by asking the Virginians "to use your influence that Capt. Hatch may not have it in his power, (if he should be disposed,) to traduce the Committee and injure the sufferers in this Town, for whose relief our friends in Virginia have so generously contributed."[24]

These donations to beleaguered Boston from throughout the colonies were the surest signs yet that Massachusetts was not standing alone. Other letters in the Boston press went to great lengths to emphasize this. "We have the Pleasure to inform you," a correspondent identified only as "a Gentleman in South Carolina" wrote, "that in this Colony the [Continental] Association takes Place as effectually as Law itself." Vessels from England had been obliged to return with their merchandise unloaded, he claimed, and Bostonians were assured of the "fixed Determination" of their southern cousins to adhere to the trade restrictions.[25]

The number of similar anonymous letters appearing in colonial newspapers raises at least some question as to their veracity. It is not unthinkable that rebels, particularly the politically savvy and media-conscious Samuel Adams, desperately trying to rally the spirits of occupied Boston, might have occasionally fabricated some good news of solidarity and support with letters from "a Gentleman" somewhere.

On a more personal note, Samuel Adams also wrote to Arthur Lee, who was a trade representative in London and a brother in the famous clan of Richard Henry and Francis Lightfoot Lee, both of whom would later sign the Declaration of Independence. Adams told Lee that he understood the reluctance of many in England to risk support for the colonies "lest we should desert our selves" and give up the fight. "But assure them," Adams continued, that "the people hold the Invasion of their Rights & Liberties the most horrid

rebellion and a Neglect to defend them against any Power whatso-
ever the highest Treason." [26]

ONE OF GENERAL GAGE'S CHIEF lieutenants in this "Invasion of
their Rights & Liberties" was Hugh Percy. In many respects, Percy
epitomized all that most colonials with rebel leanings despised
about the English ruling class, which largely resolved as a matter of
right to be lord and master over them. Percy was the oldest son of
Sir Hugh Smithson, who in 1766 became the first Duke of Northumberland. Thereafter, his son Hugh was known as Lord Percy or
Earl Percy. Educated at Eton and St. John's College, Cambridge,
before he turned eighteen, Lord Percy then received a commission
in the army. With his father's influence, he rose rapidly to become a
lieutenant colonel in a newly raised regiment of foot by the time he
was twenty, in 1762. The following year, and again in 1768, Percy
was elected unopposed as a member of Parliament, where he voted
against the repeal of the Stamp Act. By December of 1768, he was
appointed colonel of the Fifth Regiment of Foot, distinguished by
its natty gosling-green facings, and in May of 1774 he departed with
his regiment for service in occupied Boston.

Percy had a large, hooked nose that looked like the beak of a
hawk, and he immediately came to view the rebel faction as appropriate prey. While praising Gage for his "great coolness & firmness," Percy found the populace in general to be rash and timid. "To
hear them talk," he wrote his father soon after his arrival in Boston,
"you would imagine that they would attack us & demolish us every
night; & yet, whenever we appear, they are frightened out of their
wits." [27]

On his infrequent trips outside Boston, Percy found the surrounding countryside to be "the most beautiful country I ever saw
in my life," but bemoaned the people as just the opposite. "The people here," he told his second cousin, "are a set of sly, artful, hypo-

critical rascalls, cruel, & cowards. I must own I cannot but despise them compleately." [28]

As his time in Boston wore on, Percy was careful not to criticize Gage directly, but he did tell his father, "The general's great lenity and moderation serve only to make them more daring & insolent. . . . He has given them every proof that his utmost wish is to restore peace & tranquillity without coming to violent measures." His father's response was to obtain an order permitting General Gage to send his son home to England, but the thirty-two-year-old colonel felt it his duty to remain with his regiment. [29]

As the winter of 1774–75 wore on, Percy shared the anxiety of the "strange unsettled state" in Boston. By February, six months after his landing, disease had caused the deaths of two officers and 123 men, women, and children of the various regiments. [30] Percy put the best possible spin on it when he wrote a mentor and member of Parliament that the rebel leaders "undoubtedly grow more desperate as they see less hopes of escaping, and do all they can to drive the others to extremities."

Meanwhile, Percy said, the British troops were "waiting with impatience the determinations and orders from yr side of the water." That was undoubtedly true from General Gage down to the lowliest private. But Percy couldn't refrain from letting his mounting frustrations show. Rather pointedly, he told the MP that whatever actions Parliament took, "I hope they will be pointed and effectual ones; for you left so many loopholes in the last acts you passed, that it was found not possible to enforce them." [31]

Percy told his father much the same thing and foreshadowed the conclusions that Lord North's government was reaching in London. Gage might well wish to be lenient and hope for some accommodation that would stem the irrepressible tide toward open warfare, but the choices were becoming increasingly black and white. "If Gt Britain relaxes in the least," wrote Percy, "adieu to the colonies. They will be lost forever." [32]

Chapter 7

~

Independence or Reconciliation?

Even as Bostonians sat on the hot seat, no one but the most ardent of rebels was yet talking openly about inevitable independence from Great Britain. Loyalist Daniel Leonard, writing as Massachusettensis, found such a thought deplorable. "It is our highest interest to continue a part of the British empire," Massachusettensis lectured, "and equally our duty to remain subject to the authority of parliament."

John Adams quoted this line in his rejoinder—addressing Massachusettensis as "our rhetorical magician"—and was quick to mention the prospect of the roles being reversed. "We are a part of the British dominions . . . and it is our interest and duty to continue so," Novanglus acknowledged, but the time might not be far off "when the colonies may have the balance of numbers and wealth in [their] favour." If that happened and the colonies should then in turn attempt to rule Great Britain "by an American parliament, without an adequate representation in it," Novanglus predicted Great Britain would "infallibly resist us by her arms." [1]

But it was American arms that were on the minds of some two hundred delegates to the Massachusetts Provincial Congress when it convened in Concord on March 22 for another session. Two days later, under the hand of John Hancock, its newly elected president, the congress voted to continue "most vigorously" the defensive measures recommended by the prior session because "any Relaxation would be attended with the utmost Danger to the Liberties of this Colony and all of America."[2]

Similar preparations were being undertaken throughout the colonies. In Richmond, Virginia, the House of Burgesses reconvened in a church after the royal governor dissolved its official proceedings in the capital at Williamsburg. Delegate George Washington wrote to his brother John Augustine Washington, thanking him "for the holly berries and cotton-seed" and expressing pleasure over John's "laudable pursuit" in training an independent company of militia. George had already promised to review the Richmond militia company, of which he had been offered command, sometime during the coming summer. He told his brother that he could at the same time "review yours, and shall very cheerfully accept the honor of commanding it, if occasion require it to be drawn out, as it is my full intention to devote my life and fortune in the cause we are engaged in."[3] Surely George Washington must have sensed that the coming summer would bring much more action than military reviews.

As the Virginia legislature convened, one of its first acts was to ratify the nonimportation and nonconsumption measures of the First Continental Congress—the "*American* Continental Congress," as its proceedings reported with emphasis—and thank Virginia's loyal delegates to the same. Then it was Patrick Henry's turn to speak to the military needs of the colony. Henry introduced a resolution on the tactical concerns of military preparation that was closely modeled on a resolution that had been passed by a Fairfax County convention chaired by George Washington. Henry's strategy was clear. If the Virginia assembly, illegally convened though it was in the eyes of the king, chose to act on a plan of military preparedness, it would be following the same path as the Massachusetts Provincial Congress and establishing a de facto provincial government independent of Great Britain.

Debate on the resolution was heated and certainly not one-sided. Finally, Henry rose to defend his motion with words that held the attention of all assembled. To those who claimed that the resolution went too far, Henry asserted that events had already taken them that far down that road and more. "Gentlemen may cry peace, peace," Henry proclaimed, "but there is no peace," and any day might bring word of "the clash of resounding arms" from Boston. War was inevitable, Henry maintained. "Let it come," he intoned, "let it come." Then he dramatically flung his arms apart and pronounced the words for which he would best be remembered. "I know not what course others may take," he told the assembly, "but as for me — give me liberty or give me death."

Dead silence followed for a moment or two, as the gravity of Henry's words took hold. Then, after another round of spirited debate, the moderates were voted down by five votes, and Patrick Henry was named chairman of a committee authorized to produce a colony-wide militia plan. Among those on his committee were George Washington, Richard Henry Lee, and Thomas Jefferson.[4]

THE DAY BEFORE PATRICK HENRY's speech, Edmund Burke, one of the most distinguished orators, authors, and political theorists in England, rose to speak in the House of Commons. Ingrained though he was in the British system, Burke was a native of Ireland, and that island's experience with British rule may well have colored his thinking on the crisis in America. Burke was decidedly opposed to Lord North's unrelenting policies of coercion rather than conciliation toward the American colonies.

This was hardly Burke's first time speaking out against such policies. Almost a year before, in the heat of the debate over the restrictions placed on Massachusetts by the Intolerable Acts, Burke argued against the effectiveness of such punitive measures, particularly that of bringing accused insurgents to trial in England. "If you govern America at all, Sir," Burke told the House of Commons, "it must be by an army . . . they never will consent without force being used." [5]

On that occasion, Lord North rose in rebuttal to say that while he did not profess to know the proper time "to lay a fresh tax on America," he did know "this is not the proper time to repeal one." But then North underscored the secondary status that many in his government accorded the Americans. "I will answer," North went on with the haughty tone of an overly strict and superior parent, "that when they are quiet, and have a respect for their mother country, the mother country will be good-natured to them." [6]

Whatever his strengths in other matters, Lord North had two personal drawbacks when it came to finding a peaceful resolution of the looming crisis in America. First, North was intensely, perhaps blindly, loyal to George III, and second, he was haughtily contemptuous of colonials in America, particularly those who opposed his policies. One should never allow contempt to color an appraisal of one's enemies, and Lord North made this error repeatedly in his dealings with North America.

While Edmund Burke, former prime minister William Pitt, and others championed the cause of English liberty and sought to apply it evenly across the empire, a solid majority in Parliament supported Lord North's views. Samuel Adams and others in the colonies had long hoped that the House of Commons would "be purgd at the next Election," but that election, late in 1774, had only swelled the ranks of North's Tories. Adams previously thought it "best that the Tories in their house have acted without Disguise," but their actions did not as yet find disfavor among the majority of the British electorate. [7] By the time the results of America's renewed nonimportation and nonconsumption measures were felt on British merchants and manufacturers, North's majority was safely ensconced for another seven-year term.

But that did not mean that Lord North and his government were without critics in Parliament. On January 20, 1775, William Pitt, the great commoner who as prime minister had won Great Britain a global empire during the Seven Years' War and who now sat in the House of Lords as the Earl of Chatham, introduced a resolution calling for the immediate removal of all British troops from Boston. It was a gutsy move, but Pitt followed it with an even gutsier speech.

Listening in the gallery as Pitt's specially invited guest was Benjamin Franklin. "The spirit which now resists your taxation in America," Pitt told the assembled lords, "is the same ... spirit which established the great fundamental, essential maxim of your liberties, *that no subject of England shall be taxed but by his own consent.*" That was the crux of the matter: rebels in the colonies wanted equal standing in the British Empire. Then Pitt urged Lord North and his administration to take the step that it was increasingly clear they would never take: "With a dignity becoming your exalted situation, make the first advances to concord, to peace, and happiness. . . . That *you* should first concede is obvious, from sound and rational policy." [8]

The House of Lords overwhelmingly voted down Pitt's troop-removal resolution by a margin of sixty-eight to eighteen. George III's response to the man who had won him an empire when he was but a boy king was to hope for the man's early earthly demise.

Two months later, it was Edmund Burke's moment to sound the same concerns in the House of Commons. He spoke passionately for hours and argued from numerous angles that the advantages of cooperation between Great Britain and its colonies far outweighed any advantages that might be derived from an intractable insistence on a right to tax them without due representation. "To prove that the Americans ought not to be free," Burke bluntly noted, "we are obliged to depreciate the value of freedom itself; and we never seem to gain a paltry advantage over them in debate, without attacking some of those principles, or deriding some of those feelings, for which our ancestors have shed their blood." [9]

Lord North's government, Burke charged, had led them down the path of the Intolerable Acts, dispatched General Gage and more and more troops, and sought to punish at every turn, but all these things had only made matters worse. "When I see things in this situation," said Burke, shaking his head in despair, "after such confident hopes, bold promises, and active exertions, I cannot, for my life, avoid a suspicion, that the plan itself is not correctly right." [10]

There was a growing spirit and greatness in America, Burke maintained, and "English privileges have made it all that it is; English privileges alone will make it all it can be." Nearing his conclusion, he again urged Great Britain to take the first step, even as he leveled a dig at Lord North. "Magnanimity in politics is not seldom the truest wisdom," concluded Burke, "and a great empire and little minds go ill together." [11]

But Burke's words in the House of Commons fell on ears as unresponsive as Pitt's pleas had in the House of Lords two months before. To implement his plan, Burke introduced six resolutions that he hoped would bring about reconciliation with the colonies. The first was supposed to be a plain statement of fact: essentially that the colonies of Great Britain in North America — including, by Burke's count, Quebec — did not have "the liberty and privilege of electing and sending" representatives to Parliament. But even this was too much for Lord North and his hardliners. Who knew where such acknowledgment might lead? Burke's speech was highly praised by Whigs of similar mind, but after this first attempt toward reconciliation was voted down 270–78, Burke held no hope for the passage of his remaining resolutions. [12]

On the American side of the Atlantic, not yet knowing of Burke's speech or resolutions, John Adams, writing as Novanglus, nonetheless offered thoughts that coincided with Burke's views. Noting that Scotland and Wales sent representatives to the British Parliament even though they were originally conquered countries, Adams asserted "the extreme difficulty, the utter impracticability, of governing a people who have any sense, spirit, or love of liberty, without incorporating them into the state, or allowing them in some other way equal privileges." [13]

*　　*　　*

As UNCERTAINTY OVER THE FUTURE continued to weigh on the leaders on both sides of the issue, it also affected men and women across all points of the social and economic spectrum. From Kensington, near Philadelphia, Eliza Farmar wrote her nephew, Jack Halroyd, who was a clerk for the East India Company in London. "Your wine is all unsold for there was no demand for it when it came," she told him. Because of the nonimportation measures, "that sort is not so much drank here as Madeira." As for herself, Mrs. Farmar admitted, "I never drank so little wine since I knew what it was."

As if to underscore that the economic situation for wine was unlikely to change, Farmar noted, "the Non Importation is Strictly adheard to and after this month No Tea is to be bought sold or drank and there are Committees chosen for every Town to see that the Resolves of Congress are strictly observed and those that dont are lookd on as Enimies to America." [14]

In the hills of Essex County, New Jersey (near present-day West Orange), twenty-year-old Jemima Condict was fighting a different battle. Having procrastinated for days over a troublesome toothache, she finally resolved one Monday morning "if Possible to have my toth out." So down she went "to Dr. C. and he got his Cold iron ready." But when he put his pliers in Jemima's mouth, she quickly pulled them out, to the laughter of assembled onlookers. According to Jemima, they teased her and "Said if I dast not have A tooth Drawd I Never would be fit to marry. I told them I never Recond to be if twas as Bad as to have a toth Drawd." Amid the ensuing laughter, the doctor gave a good yank, and Jemima "could put my Toth in my pocket & laugh with the Best of them." [15]

A week or two later, on a Monday that she called Training Day, Jemima went with her father to see several companies of militia drill together. Jemima wrote in her diary that it would have been "a mournful Sight to see if they had been fighting in earnest." That was indeed an obvious possibility, although "how soon they will Be

Calld forth to the feild of war we Cannot tell, for by What we Can hear the Quarrels are not like to be made up Without bloodshed." Jemima had "jest Now heard Say that All hopes of Conciliation Between Briten & her colonies are at an end for Both the king & his Parliment have announced our Destruction." [16]

Across the ocean in London, Lord Dartmouth received a letter from William Franklin, the royal governor of New Jersey. Given the recent actions of the Continental Congress, William Franklin — inadvertently, perhaps — put his finger squarely on the heart of the matter when he implied that royal ego rather than the calls of Pitt and Burke for reconciliation seemed to be guiding British policy. "It seems apprehended by many sensible and moderate Men here," Franklin, speaking for his loyalist friends, told Dartmouth, "that it will be the Opinion of the Mother Country that the Congress has left her no other alternative then either to consent to what must appear humiliating in the Eyes of all Europe, or to compel Obedience to her Laws by a Military Force." [17]

Benjamin Franklin, the royal governor's father, was about to depart London and sail back into the American cauldron. His chess moves with Lord Howe and Howe's sister had come to naught, in part because Franklin would not be drawn into a more moderate position than he knew many of his brethren held in North America. Given the delays in cross-Atlantic communications, Franklin was only now writing Joseph Galloway of Pennsylvania a response to Galloway's stillborn compromise plan for a "mini-American Parliament." It had been voted down at the Continental Congress six months before. "I cannot but apprehend," Franklin told Galloway, "more Mischief than Benefit from a closer Union." [18]

Joseph Galloway was a moderate who had strived for compromise but by now had irrevocably hung his hat with the loyalists. In the Pennsylvania Assembly, he spoke out strongly against the measures of the Continental Congress. His pro-loyalist resolution condemning its actions failed to pass, although more than one-third of the delegates — fourteen out of thirty-eight members — voted with him, a clear sign how divided that province was on the issue of open rebellion.

Galloway tried to put a positive spin on the outcome by telling William Franklin, "The People of this Province are altering their sentiments and conduct with amazing rapidity. We have been successful in baffling all the attempts of the violent Party to prevail on the People to prepare for war against the Mother Country." That, of course, was unwarranted optimism. Galloway was an example of how difficult it was to know at what point, in the words of historian Henry Steele Commager, "the conflict between colonies and mother country became a war between America and Britain, and at what point, therefore, lack of enthusiasm for separation, or for war, became treason." [19]

DURING THE LATTER PART OF March 1775, the front pages of the competing rebel *Boston Gazette* and loyalist *Massachusetts Gazette and the Boston Post-Boy and Advertiser* were filled in their entirety with the writings of Novanglus and Massachusettensis, respectively. Novanglus continued his essays into April, but Massachusettensis published his last column on March 27—perhaps because he thought his arguments had run their course or been overtaken by mounting tensions as all awaited some definitive word from England. "There is an awful disparity," Massachusettensis concluded, "between troops that fight the battles of their Sovereign and those what follow the standard of rebellion." [20]

But as Massachusettensis's pen fell silent, others spoke for the loyalist cause while casting themselves as compromising moderates. One letter, dated April 7, from "A Friend to Both Countries" appeared in the *Boston Evening-Post*. Inadvertently, perhaps, the author's choice for framing the debate—"Both Countries" as opposed to "both sides" or even "both factions"—suggested how deep the split had already become. "At a time when the hostile parade of these colonies portend the most disagreeable effects," wrote the author, signing himself only as "A Customer," "it is evidently the duty of the moderate of all parties to unite . . . as the only probable means of rescuing this country from all the tragical concomitants of a civil war." [21]

The truth of the matter was, as Joseph Galloway had learned, that it was too late for moderates. "A Customer's" belief that "the first appearance of moderate measures adopted on our part, will be eagerly seiz'd by the ministry for accommodating this unnatural contest" was a belated hope. Parliament's sweeping rejections of William Pitt's and Edmund Burke's reconciliation efforts were not yet known in America, but it would be only a matter of days before they were. And on the heels of this news, General Gage would receive instructions from Lord Dartmouth, dated January 27, 1775, as to how the general should proceed to deal with Massachusetts.

Meanwhile, the Massachusetts Provincial Congress continued to meet in Concord into the first week of April. On Thursday, April 6, James Warren wrote from there to "My Dear Mercy." He had hoped to be home with her in Plymouth that day, but the congress had narrowly voted to sit another week in the hope of news, "and News we have," he told her. Unofficial reports from England indicated that Parliament had not extended even a hint of reconciliation despite the efforts of Pitt and Burke. "I dare say," James Warren went on, "you would not desire to see me till I could tell you that I had done all in my power to secure and defend us and our Country. We are no longer at a loss [about] what is Intended us by our dear Mother. We have Ask'd for Bread and she gives us a Stone, and a serpent for a Fish." [22]

What orders were coming to General Gage could only be surmised, but there was strong evidence afoot, and, for the rebels, there were ominous warnings. The April 10 issue of the *Massachusetts Gazette and the Boston Post-Boy and Advertiser* carried a report from London dated "*War Office, Feb. 24.*" It went on to say: "It is his Majesty's pleasure that all officers, absent from regiments in North-America, do join their respective corps without delay." [23] Likely the same ship that brought the report of Parliament's recalcitrance also brought news that the sloop HMS *Falcon*, mistakenly reported as "the Faulkland," had sailed from Spithead four days before the recently arrived ship "with dispatches for the General and Commander in chief." Ninety-five feet in length, with a crew of 125, *Falcon* was nimble and quick. It could be expected any day. Among the rumors was the report that Lord Howe "was to come with two regiments of horse." Regardless of such speculation, the rebel *Massachusetts Spy* reported, "The army in this town seem to be preparing for a matter & a considerable number of waggons are made and now ready for their use." [24]

If General Gage appeared to be showing great patience and restraint during this uncertain time, the same could not be said for most of his officers, particularly after informal word reached Boston that Parliament appeared resolved not to offer the colonies even a single leaf of an olive branch. "This has convinced the Rebels (for we may now legally call them so)," Lord Percy wrote a friend, "that there is no hopes for them but by submitting to Parliament." The rebels remaining in Boston were evacuating, Percy claimed, and "have proposed in Congress, either to set it on Fire & attack the troops before a reinforcement comes, or to endeavour to starve us." Which course they meant to adopt, only time would tell. "The Gen. however has received no Acc. whatever from Europe," Percy concluded, "so that [on] our side no steps of any kind can be taken as yet." [25]

So, anticipating what increasingly seemed an inevitable clash of arms, partisans on both sides waited. Finally, the sloop HMS *Falcon* came into view off Boston Harbor. Many an eye fixed on the vessel with a sense of foreboding. Perhaps no one watching its arrival did so with more mixed emotions than General Thomas Gage. He was about to receive the orders a part of him had been dreading for almost fifteen years. [26]

PART II

~

"LET IT BEGIN HERE"

April 1775

The violences committed by those who have taken up arms in Massachusetts Bay, have appeared to me as the acts of a rude Rabble without plan, without concert, & without conduct, and therefore I think that a smaller Force now, if put to the Test, would be able to encounter them with greater probability of Success.

—Lord Dartmouth to General Thomas Gage,
received around April 16, 1775

Chapter 8

~

The General's Dilemma

Springtime in New England is usually something of a tease. One smells the coming season long before it arrives, then discovers bursting buds and blades of green only to turn about once and find them covered with a foot of wet snow or lashed by an icy wind. "The Weather here for the last three weeks has been cold & disagreeable, a kind of second Winter," Lord Percy wrote home to England in early April. "However as this day is remarkably warm & fine I flatter myself our good Weather is now beginning." Roughly one hundred and fifty years later, an American expatriate who became a British subject characterized April as "the cruellest month," but in 1775, April was destined to be among the most decisive months of the year.[1]

Despite a warm fire and ample board, General Thomas Gage and his American-born wife, the former Margaret Kemble, had endured an uncomfortable winter. While no one questioned his loyalties as a British officer, Gage was having difficulty squaring the intransigence of Lord North's government with his twenty years of experience in North America and his own personal beliefs about English liberty.

On the one hand, Gage had issued the strictest orders to his soldiers to treat the inhabitants "with Lenity, Moderation and Justice" so they might "be permitted to enjoy unmolested, the common Rights of Mankind."[2] But on the other hand, Gage found that such "lenient Measures, and the cautious and legal Exertion of the coercive Powers of Government," served only to make some colonists "more daring and licentious."[3]

The particular irony was that these instructions and Gage's observations were not given in the spring of 1775 but seven long years before, during the Stamp Act crisis. The general had been wrestling with this dilemma for a long time. He well understood Edmund Burke's statement in the House of Commons during his fruitless reconciliation plea. "An Englishman," Burke noted, "is the unfittest person on earth, to argue another Englishman into slavery."[4]

Margaret Gage was vexed as well. Her father remained a wealthy New Jersey land baron, for the moment seemingly above the fray. Her brother Stephen was the general's deputy adjutant general and perhaps his closest aide. Stephen had accompanied the Gages on their recent visit to England. Another of Margaret's brothers, Samuel, served as Gage's confidential secretary, and her distant cousin Captain Oliver De Lancey had lately arrived on the *Nautilus* with a backup copy of Lord Dartmouth's most recent orders for her husband. Through these relationships, and indeed through her marriage to Gage, Margaret was well aware of the perks of belonging to the upper echelons of British society. But she had also enjoyed similar status as the daughter of one of New Jersey's landed gentry. It was difficult for her to reconcile the differences between them.

There is evidence in his letters and military directives that by the spring of 1775, Thomas Gage was tired of walking the tightrope between respecting the colonials' English liberties and resisting the extremist acts of avowed rebels. For both the Gages, Boston in all its turmoil was a drudgery compared to their previous pleasant post in New York and particularly compared to what by all accounts were happy times during their recent respite in England. It seemed increasingly certain that either Gage or his children would inherit the Gage peerage and estates from his childless older brother. After twenty years in America fighting the French, Indians, and an increasingly angry horde of American rebels, the prospect of a quiet retirement to an English estate undoubtedly looked appealing. In his midfifties, Thomas Gage was simply worn out.

THE ORIGINALS OF LORD DARTMOUTH's orders of January 27, 1775, reached General Gage via HMS *Falcon* on April 16. They left little doubt that Dartmouth expected Gage to undertake prompt and decisive action. While Gage's reports from the fall of 1774 presented the state of affairs in Massachusetts "in a very unfavourable light," Dartmouth had not found any facts in them "tending to shew that the Outrages which had been committed were other than merely the Acts of a tumultuous Rabble." But by the time Dartmouth received Gage's letters of December 1774 and replied, he had changed his mind. The long-awaited answer to what Great Britain intended was now clear. "The King's Dignity, & the Honor and Safety of the Empire, require," Dartmouth asserted, "that, in such a Situation, Force should be repelled by Force."

More troops were on the way, and still others were to be dispatched. Gage was to encourage the recruitment of loyalists "from among the friends of Government" and "take a more active & determined part" not only "to keep possession of Boston" but also to extend the protection of His Majesty's government. The "first & essential step to be taken towards re-establishing Government," Dartmouth instructed, "would be to arrest and imprison the principal actors & abettors in the Provincial Congress" should they again assemble despite Gage's proclamation forbidding it. Dartmouth termed the proceedings "in every light to be acts of treason and rebellion." Dartmouth did not mention them by name, but Samuel Adams and John Hancock would have been understood to be at the top of the list of "principal actors & abettors."

While Dartmouth left the timing and details to Gage's "own Discretion," his letter was also filled with specific suggestions about troop dispositions and fortifications. The implication was clear and well known to a soldier of Gage's long standing. If Gage succeeded in quashing the uprising, Lord Dartmouth and George III's government would take the credit. If Gage failed, Dartmouth had given him just enough room that the failure would be the general's fault in execution.

As if to bring home this point, Dartmouth closed his instructions with a less-than-subtle admonishment. "Be more than ever on your guard," he told Gage, and warned him not to permit the inhabitants "of at least the Town of Boston, to assemble themselves in arms on any pretense." If those instructions seemed unnecessary to someone who was supposed to be the firm hand of the king, Dartmouth rather snidely added, "I rather mention this, as a Report prevails that you have not only indulged [the rebels] in having such a Guard, but have also allowed their Militia to train and discipline in Faneuil Hall." If Gage needed any more of a prodding than that, Dartmouth concluded with a by-the-way observation that there was a clause in the Massachusetts charter that empowered the governor to declare martial law "in time of actual War, Invasion, or *Rebellion*."[5]

WHILE AWAITING THESE SPECIFIC INSTRUCTIONS from London, General Gage had certainly not been idle. In late February, he had dispatched Colonel Leslie to Salem, looking for cannons, and sent officers Brown and De Berniere snooping around the countryside as far west as Worcester. In mid-March, Gage had sent Brown and De Berniere on another clandestine outing, this time northwestward to Concord. They left Boston once again in their country-folk disguises and walked through Roxbury and Brookline along the direct road to Concord. Despite its straightforward approach, they found the route "woody in most places, and very close and commanded by hills," making it susceptible to surprise and ambush.

In Concord, their appearance was greeted with more open hostility than they encountered on their visit to Worcester several weeks before. They were directed to the home of Daniel Bliss, one of the few loyalist lawyers not hunkering down in Boston. But the woman who gave them directions soon pounded on Bliss's door seeking refuge from rebels who, she claimed, "swore if she did not leave town, they would tar and feather her for directing Tories in their road." Scarcely had she left when Bliss received an ominous warning that "they would not let him go out of town alive that morning."

Brown and De Berniere offered their protection, and Bliss left for Boston with them via a slightly circuitous but "very open and good" road that took them first to Lexington and then through Menotomy (present-day Arlington) en route back to Cambridge and Boston. When the two British officers reported this reconnaissance to General Gage, they may well have recommended their return route as the safest approach to Concord.[6]

During these weeks, General Gage was also receiving intelligence from other loyalist sources throughout the countryside. What would become clear only in hindsight is that Gage also had the benefit of a well-placed informant among the rebels' innermost circle. Whoever this spy was, he had an intimate knowledge of the disposition of rebel arms and supplies at Concord. Indeed, beginning on March 8, Gage received no less than eight letters from this source, two in poorly written French, which was probably meant to disguise the sender. These communications described the exact locations of the hiding places of munitions and provisions and disclosed in detail the secret deliberations of the Massachusetts Provincial Congress — the illegally convened body whose leaders Dartmouth had ordered him to arrest.

Given this inside information, it is probable that Gage's informant was himself not only a member of the Provincial Congress but also one of the handful of operatives to whom Samuel Adams and John Hancock entrusted their very lives. "The stricktest secrecy is enjoined to every member of the Congress," this mole wrote Gage on March 30, "& it is therefore necessary that none of this intelligence should be mentioned to any person whatever."[7]

Perhaps most disconcerting to Gage was the informer's report that the numbers of militia available on call throughout the province might far exceed previous estimates. There was still great uncertainty about how these numbers would be integrated into anything approaching a formal army, but the fact that earnest discussions were taking place about doing so and that instructions had been given for the remittance of funds into a common treasury to pay for its support were definite signs of an organized opposition government.

There were also reports of disagreements within the Provincial Congress. Some members opposed the organization of a formal New England army, which would be seen as an offensive posture in contrast to the defensive character of the local militias. Others wanted to solicit opinions from their constituents, and many delegates were concerned that the other colonies, particularly their neighbors in New Hampshire, Connecticut, and Rhode Island, would not follow their lead and assemble troops in the field to assist Massachusetts.

All this meant that time was of the essence if the British were to make a preemptive strike against the rebel cause. Gage knew that the rebels were proceeding to raise an army; he had specific information about the locations of key munitions and stores invaluable to that effort, and he also knew that there was still some division of opinion among the provincial delegates. On April 11, a few days before Gage received his firm orders from Dartmouth, the general's informer noted the obvious: "A sudden blow struck now or immediately on the arrival of the reinforcements from England should they come within a fortnight would oversett all their plans."[8]

BASED ON THIS STREAM OF intelligence, General Gage began to draft operational orders. With great specificity, the first draft repeated almost verbatim the information Gage had learned in his informant's letter of March 9. For example: "Four Brass Cannon and two Mortars or Cohorns with a Number of small arms in the Cellar or out Houses of Mr. Barrett a little on the other side the Bridge where is also lodged a Quantity of Powder & Lead." But by the time Gage received a missive from his Concord spy dated April 18, most of the cannons—"four excepted which are now in Concord Town House"—and all but "a few Barrels" of powder had been removed to nearby towns in anticipation of just the sort of strike Gage was planning. The principal remaining prize appeared to be great quantities of beef and flour, as well as "a Quantity of [musket] Balls."[9]

As will be seen, April 18 was a rather hectic day for the British in Boston. In moving quickly to provide a final set of orders to his field commander, Gage chose to condense the intelligence information about specific cache locations onto a map of Concord—which, unfortunately, has been lost to history—rather than include them in his written orders. Sometime during the afternoon of the eighteenth, Gage handed these instructions and the map to Lieutenant Colonel Francis Smith of the Tenth Regiment of Foot to carry them out. Given the events of the next thirty-six hours, they are of interest in their entirety:

> Having received Intelligence, that a Quantity of Ammunition, Provision, Artillery, Tents and small Arms, have been collected at Concord, for the Avowed Purpose of raising and supporting a Rebellion against His Majesty, you will March with the Corps of Grenadiers and Light Infantry, put under your command, with the utmost expedition and Secrecy to Concord, where you will seize and destroy all the Artillery, Ammunition, Provisions, Tents, Small Arms, and all Military Stores whatever. But you will take care that the Soldiers do not plunder the Inhabitants, or hurt private property.
>
> You have a Draught [map] of Concord, on which is marked, the Houses, Barns, &c., which contain the above Military Stores. You will order a Trunion to be knocked off each Gun, but if its found impracticable

on any, they must be spiked, and the Carriages destroyed. The Powder and flower, must be shook out of the Barrells into the River, the Tents burnt, Pork or Beef destroyed in the best way you can devise, And the Men may put Balls or lead in their pockets, throwing them by degrees into Ponds, Ditches &c., but no Quantity together, so that they may be recovered afterwards.

If you meet with any Brass Artillery, you will order their Muzzles to be beat in so as to render them useless.

You will observe by the Draught that it will be necessary to secure the two Bridges as soon as possible, you will therefore Order a party of the best Marchers, to go on with the expedition for that purpose.

A small party on Horseback is ordered out to stop all advice of your March getting to Concord before you, and a small number of Artillery go out in Chaises to wait for you on the Road, with Sledge Hammers, Spikes &c.

You will open your business, and return with the Troops, as soon as possible, which I must leave to your own Judgment and Discretion.[10]

What additional verbal instructions Gage gave Smith, if any, will never be known. The one glaring omission that differentiated these orders from Lord Dartmouth's instructions to Gage was that Gage made no mention of arresting provincial leaders—Adams, Hancock, or anyone else. Whether Gage made this omission on purpose, perhaps fearing that such arrests would only make martyrs out of a few who would likely be quickly replaced in the evolving rebel hierarchy, or whether, given his leanings on individual liberties, he simply focused on the military purpose of the expedition is open to speculation. The pressing question at that moment, however, was whether or not the rebel leaders in Concord knew that British regulars were about to march.

Gage wasn't the only one with spies. The strength of the rebel intelligence network came from the eyes and ears of Adams's and Hancock's band of tradesmen and skilled workers who frequented the Green Dragon and other Boston taverns. These Sons of Liberty took note of troop movements, ship arrivals and departures, and anything out of the ordinary and reported the same along a clandestine network that ultimately led to the committee of safety of the Provincial Congress. And in the first two weeks of April, there was plenty going on in Boston to report. On Friday, April 7 — even before Gage had received his action orders from Dartmouth — rebels observed longboats being moored under the sterns of British men-of-war in the harbor for ready access and concluded that an attack somewhere was imminent. Perhaps it would even come on a quiet Sunday morning, as had Colonel Leslie's Salem raid.

Paul Revere once again saddled up and the next day carried a message of alarm to Concord — the likely target, given its stockpiles of munitions and supplies and the Provincial Congress then meeting there. It proved a little premature, considering Gage's timetable, but this warning was the impetus for removing much of the rebel cannons and gunpowder from Concord, as was subsequently reported to General Gage by his informer. Certainly Revere's message heightened the state of alert in Concord. "We daily expect a Tumult," wrote a local resident to a friend. "There came up a post [Revere's warning] to Concord Saturday night [April 8] which informs them that the regulars are coming up to Concord the next day, and if they come I believe there will be bloody work." [11]

This alarm to Concord and the subsequent report from Gage's informer about the disposition of the rebels' heavy ordnance and gunpowder should have made Gage question the secrecy and effectiveness of his operation. Certainly it raises the question of why Gage continued with his plans if indeed he had strong intelligence that the most important pieces of the rebels' armaments had been moved from Concord to other locations. The last thing the general wanted was to come up empty-handed again, as Colonel Leslie had done at Salem. But instead of altering his target, Gage — no doubt feeling pressure from Dartmouth's recently received orders — chose to strike as planned to secure the rebel munitions remaining in Concord. To ensure the expedition's success, Gage attempted to impede the rebel warning system between Boston and Concord.

Accordingly, early on Tuesday, April 18, a patrol of about twenty men, commanded by Major Edward Mitchell of the Fifth Regiment and heavy with junior officers from other regiments, departed Boston via Boston Neck. They soon fanned out toward the key intersections on the roads leading to Concord. This was the "small party on Horseback" that was "ordered out to stop all advice of your March getting to Concord before you," of which Gage so confidently assured Colonel Smith in his orders. But it didn't work out that way.

Mitchell's men rode with no apparent haste, but this in itself caused a stir among locals. Their actions were in sharp contrast to the hurry-scurry of previous British maneuvers into the countryside. They appeared in no rush to return to Boston by nightfall. Then, too, these were not casually dressed men out for exercise but fully uniformed troops with regimental cockades in their hats and sidearms and swords plainly visible beneath their riding coats.

The greatest number of these soldiers, about eight or nine, drifted toward Lexington. In Menotomy, about halfway between Lexington and Cambridge, the Massachusetts committees of safety and supply had just adjourned after an all-day meeting at Weatherby's Black Horse Tavern. As committee members Richard Devens and Abraham Watson rode eastward in a chaise toward Charlestown, they encountered "a great number of British officers and their servants on horseback." With jaunty waves, Devens and Watson passed by and then casually turned their buggy around and rode back westward, passing the officers again.

Once out of sight of the officers, the two hurried back to Menotomy to warn several committee members who had intended to spend the night at the Black Horse Tavern. Among them was Elbridge Gerry. He immediately scribbled a hasty note of warning to Samuel Adams and John Hancock, who were staying at the home of Jonas Clarke in Lexington, and dispatched it via a messenger who was instructed to keep to the back roads and avoid encountering the British patrol.[12]

Later that evening, Elijah Sanderson, a cabinetmaker from Lexington, "saw a party of officers pass up from Boston, all dressed in blue wrappers." Given the late hour, "their passing, excited the attention of the citizens," and Sanderson took his gun and cartridge box and, "thinking something must be going on more than common, walked up to John Buckman's tavern, near the meeting-house."[13]

Ironically, the warning that General Gage tried to stem was thus spread through the Massachusetts countryside by his own men even before Paul Revere yet again saddled his horse. And if news of British regulars riding about was not enough to raise the alarm that something was afoot, the daylight hours of April 18 in Boston offered plenty of other evidence. The shrill whistles of boatswains' pipes and the creaking of block and tackle told all who cared to look across Boston Harbor that the longboats moored to the sterns of the men-of-war were about to get under way. "The town was a good deal agitated and alarmed at this Movement," noted Frederick Mackenzie, the adjutant of the Royal Welch Fusiliers, officially the Twenty-Third Regiment of Foot, "as it was pretty generally known, by means of Seamen who came on shore from the Ships, about 2 o'clock, that the boats were ordered to be in readiness."[14]

There were other signs as well. The grenadier and light infantry companies were conspicuously absent from their regular duties around town with their regiments. "I dare say," Lieutenant John Barker of the Fourth Regiment of Foot noted in his diary, "they have something for them to do." By evening, British longboats were moving about like so many water bugs and congregating around HMS *Boyne*.[15]

With Adams and Hancock first in Concord for the Provincial

Congress and later at Lexington, command of the rebel intelligence network in Boston devolved upon Dr. Joseph Warren, to whom Adams had entrusted the Boston Massacre commemorative oration six weeks before. Dr. Warren was also a member of the Provincial Congress, but at some point during the previous days he had chosen to return to Boston. Perhaps because of his valuable medical expertise, Warren was one of the few rebel leaders who still felt secure from British harassment there. Warren may also have stayed in Boston because of his concern for his motherless children, although by now they were under the care of a housekeeper, Mercy Scollay, who aspired to become the second Mrs. Warren.[16]

All afternoon and into the evening of April 18, reports flowed into Warren's medical office about British activity. Paul Revere received similar intelligence throughout the day, but before Warren would dispatch Revere to ride once again to Concord, the doctor had to be certain that this time an attack was not only imminent but in fact under way. And so into the story intrudes speculation about a minor episode that nonetheless has mushroomed into one of the purported great historical mysteries of those April days.

The speculation—magnified in some quarters into a bald assertion—is that Dr. Warren had a secret informant close to General Gage upon whom he relied to confirm the general's plan of attack. In the words of one eminent historian, "circumstantial evidence strongly suggests that it was none other than Margaret Kemble Gage," the general's American-born wife.[17]

The first question that must be asked is, did Dr. Warren really have a secret informant close to General Gage? The Sons of Liberty intelligence network was full of rebels who routinely gleaned information from sources that ran the gamut from British officers who haughtily ignored locals as they conversed in taverns to enlisted men who spilled their guts in Boston whorehouses. Paid informants who provided information for a fee likely augmented these sources. But if Warren also had a highly placed source in Gage's headquarters—paid or otherwise—would he have risked exposing this spy in the rush of a few hours on the night of April 18 only to confirm what was increasingly obvious from other indications?

Six months after the fact, Jeremy Belknap, a Congregationalist minister from New Hampshire who became an early American historian, wrote in his diary of his visit to New Hampshire troops stationed at Cambridge with what was becoming the Continental Army. Either upon Belknap's return to Dover or while he was in Cambridge, a Mr. Waters gave him a detailed account of the British preparations on the evening of April 18. (The diary entry was dated October 25, the day after Belknap's return to Dover, but whether the conversation with Waters happened in Dover or in Cambridge is not clear.)

Belknap recorded Waters as saying, "The design of the regular troops, when they marched out of Boston the night of April 18, was discovered to Dr. Warren by a person kept in pay for that purpose." After a lengthy description of the British attempts to keep the expedition a secret and the circumstances that contributed to its discovery — including the movements of the longboats and the advance patrol — Waters concluded that after these reports were communicated to Dr. Warren, "he applied to the person who had been retained, and got intelligence of their whole design." Upon this bit of hearsay — and who knows where Mr. Waters got the information? — rests the existence of Dr. Warren's secret informant, a paid one at that.[18]

But suppose one did exist. Would this person have had knowledge of what Gage considered a top-secret operation? Here is the oft-repeated second piece of the puzzle. By one account, as the longboats were gathering beneath the *Boyne* on the evening of April 18, General Gage summoned Lord Percy, the commander of his First Brigade, who was not yet directly involved with Colonel Smith's expedition. Gage told Percy of the orders he had given Smith to seize the stores in Concord. Despite the flurry of activity about them, Gage supposedly admonished Percy that the mission was "a profound secret" and that he should tell no one.

As Percy left their meeting and returned to his quarters, he passed a group of local men talking in whispers on the Common. When he asked the gist of their conversation, one man replied, "The British troops have marched, but will miss their aim."

"What aim?" Percy demanded incredulously.

"Why, the cannon at Concord," came back the reply.

Percy did an about-face and hurried back to Gage to tell him that the mission had been compromised. Upon hearing this, Gage reportedly confessed great anguish that "his confidence had been betrayed, for he had communicated his design to one person only besides his lordship." [19] The truth is, of course, Gage was likely aware from his own secret informant that the cannons at Concord had been dispersed.

This story of Percy eavesdropping, and Gage's response, has appeared in one form or another in almost every account of the march on Concord. All references can be traced, directly or via subsequent secondary sources, to Charles Stedman's history of the American Revolution, written from the British point of view and first published in London in 1794. Where Stedman got the story is not documented, but it is not unheard of for military commanders to blame subsequent operational shortcomings on some form of betrayal. In any event, from this one account and its many progeny springs the assertion that Gage told only "one person" of his plans and that person must have betrayed him. The truth of the matter was that while General Gage may have told only "one person" of his plans, as he supposedly claimed, he had telegraphed them to all of Boston. No informant was necessary to observe that British troops were about to leave Boston and to guess that Concord was their likely aim.

Richard Frothingham's 1865 biography of Joseph Warren, which is the first major account of Warren's life, is one early source that repeats this story of Percy and Gage, but it makes no mention of Warren obtaining information from a secret informer or of Warren seeking to obtain confirmation of the intelligence reports flowing into his office. Quoting an earlier history, Frothingham says that Warren reportedly learned of the British troops embarking from the Common only "by a mere accident." [20]

This brings us to Margaret Kemble Gage. On the basis of sketchy information that Joseph Warren had a highly placed informant in Gage's headquarters, and the even more dubious claim that General Gage believed the Concord operation had airtight secrecy and that he confided in only one person about it, historians have long pointed fingers at possible suspects. No one has appeared a more intriguing possibility than Mrs. Gage.

There is strong evidence that Margaret Gage was deeply conflicted by the events around her. Born in America, daughter of colonial aristocracy, married to arguably the most powerful Englishman in America, mother of a brood of children who were being educated in England, Margaret Gage was seeing her placid lifestyle turned upside down. But then so, too, were a great many others. Some, such as Abigail Adams and Mercy Warren, were unequivocally on the rebel side. Others, such as former governor Thomas Hutchinson, had already sailed for refuge in England. There were still many others deeply troubled by the question of where their ultimate loyalties lay. And sometimes making that determination disrupted marital bonds.

One of the early American histories of the Revolution is William Gordon's *The History of the Rise, Progress, and Establishment, of the Independence of the United States of America*, published in 1788. Without initially mentioning Dr. Warren, Gordon wrote of the warning of the British march: "A daughter of liberty, unequally yoked in point of politics, sent word, by a trusty hand, to Mr. Samuel Adams, residing in company with Mr. Hancock at Lexington, about thirteen miles from Charlestown, that the troops were coming out in a few days." Only a page later does Warren make an appearance and learn "by mere accident" of the threat. [21]

Once again, this one reference has spawned a plethora of blind repetition. It is easy enough to translate. "A daughter of liberty, unequally yoked in point of politics" refers to a woman of rebel sympathies married to a man who did not share her politics and who was probably a loyalist. The rift that Abigail Adams had noted between Samuel and Hannah Quincy was but one example of this. But does it apply to Thomas and Margaret Gage? We know relatively little about Margaret's political beliefs, but even if such a rift existed, would Margaret choose to betray her husband so aggressively? Even more incredibly, if Thomas had had the slightest hint of Margaret's rebel leanings—if indeed she had them—would he have confided his secret plans to her, of all people?

Assuming that Gage told only "one person" of his plans and was obtuse enough not to recognize that Boston was full of rumor, gossip, and misinformation, whom else might he have told? Margaret's brother Major Stephen Kemble was the general's good friend, faithful adjutant, and trusted specialist in intelligence matters. Another Kemble sibling, Samuel, served as the general's private secretary. Samuel may even have transcribed Gage's final orders to Colonel Smith.

While no one will ever know what pillow talk may or may not have taken place between the general and his American-born wife, if the strict, by-the-book—some might even say stodgy—Gage should have trusted anyone with a highly confidential matter of a military nature, it seems far more likely that Gage, in the manner of the time, would have confided in one of his closest aides, not his wife.

No less a hated symbol of the loyalists than exiled Massachusetts governor Thomas Hutchinson spoke in Margaret's defense when her loyalty to her husband was questioned. A Mr. Keen visited Hutchinson in London in the summer of 1775 and complained of Gage's previously lenient conduct toward the rebels. As for Mrs. Gage, Keen reported, "She hoped her husband would never be the instrument of sacrificing the lives of her countrymen." Hutchinson replied that he doubted Margaret had made such a statement, and Keen retorted that he did not doubt it, "but did not chuse to be quoted for it."[22]

Margaret Gage's subsequent accusers have pointed to this statement—once again in the form of hearsay—to suggest her willingness to betray her husband. But even if Margaret did utter such a comment, is it really anything more than evidence of her inner turmoil? After all, what wife would not abhor the thought of her husband at war, let alone a war against her neighbors?

There is little doubt that Margaret Gage was anguished by the prospect of her husband's country—indeed, it was her mother country as well—drawing the blood of those in the land of her birth. But perhaps the person even more troubled by such a prospect was General Gage himself. If Gage had been a strict royalist, he might well have attempted to crush the rebels' streaks of independence with overwhelming force long before their movement could gain any traction. But Gage was politically a Whig, one from a long line of political thought that recognized not only certain limits to the power of the monarchy but also the basic rights of all men. How could he deny to some subjects of George III—who had fought alongside him as brothers in arms during the French and Indian War—those privileges he believed were foundational to all Englishmen? Edmund Burke was right. Englishman Gage was ill suited to argue another Englishman into slavery.

So as the sun set over Boston's Back Bay on the evening of April 18, 1775, General Thomas Gage faced not one, not two, but perhaps as many as three dilemmas. First, despite his orders to Colonel Smith to take care not to plunder or disturb individuals or private property, what might happen to Gage's cherished views of English liberties if Smith were opposed by armed force? Second, with his plans for marching on Concord apparently exposed to the point that rebels had moved major stockpiles of munitions, could the mission still meet with success? And third, despite his attempts at secrecy, if Gage did have the reported conversation with Lord Percy and it was in fact true that the general had "told" but one other person, who was his betrayer? Meanwhile, his troops were on the march.

Chapter 9

~

Two Lanterns

Despite the day's activities in Boston Harbor and the obvious signs of unusual troop movements around town, some British soldiers would later remember making stealthy preparations for their departure from Boston late on the evening of April 18. By most accounts, it had been a rather rainy day. Evening brought clearing skies and shifting easterly winds. In some quarters, sergeants moved among their sleeping troops and, "putting their hands on them, and whispering gently to them," urged them to rise quietly and don their gear. They were ordered to "equip themselves immediately with their arms and 36 rounds of powder and ball." They had not been asleep for very long. Other troops likely had only the benefit of late-afternoon naps before pulling on their field uniforms and forming ranks with full cartridges boxes, heavy muskets, and haversacks filled with one day's provisions. There would not be any sleep that night.[1]

The companies of the Royal Welch Fusiliers were "conducted by a back-way out of their barracks, without the knowledge of their comrades, and without the observation of the sentries." They made their way through deserted streets and were the first to arrive at the embarkation point, on a remote beach below the Common at the edge of the Back Bay. This location was across the Charles River from Cambridge and was chosen on the Boston side because it was "in the most unfrequented part of town."[2]

Next at the rendezvous were companies from the Fourth Regiment of Foot, the storied King's Own, which was bivouacked near the Common. Other companies soon arrived from all over Boston, including from Fort Hill, near Roxbury, encampments around Boston Neck, and warehouse barracks near the Long Wharf. Several companies formed below the spire of the North Church in the North End and slipped quietly southward to below the Common. Altogether about seventy-five officers and eight hundred enlisted men from twenty-one companies assembled that evening for the expedition to Concord.[3]

That they deployed as individual companies rather than as part of their full regiment would contribute to a serious lack of command and control as the evening and following day progressed. Each of the twelve British regiments then in Boston was composed of approximately thirty-five officers, twenty noncommissioned officers (sergeants), a dozen or so fifes and drums, and about four hundred rank and file organized into about ten companies. The total effective strength of any particular regiment varied widely from time to time because of deaths, desertions, sick call, underenlistments, or, occasionally, postings of some companies of a regiment in other locations.[4]

Within each regiment there were two special-purpose units accorded elite status. These were the grenadier and light infantry companies. They were, as one contemporary put it, "the flower of the army."[5] The grenadiers were tall, husky lads whose original task in the European wars of the eighteenth century had been to hurl rudimentary hand grenades at their opponents. Over time, the grenadier companies evolved into a tough band of shock troops designed to lead ferocious assaults and punch a hole in an enemy's line or storm a fortified position. The light infantry company had just the opposite composition and role. These soldiers were smaller, leaner, and more agile men chosen for stealth and speed. To the light infantry fell the roles of advance and flank guards, skirmishers, sharpshooters, and special operations troops. The light infantry companies owed their existence to the British experiences in the French and Indian War, when General Gage himself had recommended the establishment of units in the British regular army modeled after colonial forces like Robert Rogers's backwoods rangers. Initially organized into their own regiment, the light infantry companies were subsequently scattered among regiments.

Gage might well have chosen two or three full regiments for the Concord mission. Instead, he cherry-picked the companies of grenadiers and light infantry from each regiment and placed them under the command of Lieutenant Colonel Francis Smith, with Royal Marine Major John Pitcairn as Smith's second in command. This had the disadvantage of placing many company-level officers under the command of superior officers they did not know and likewise gave Smith and Pitcairn command of junior officers with whose strengths and weaknesses they were not closely acquainted.

This arrangement also placed company commanders from different regiments, who had not regularly trained or maneuvered together, side by side. All were trained officers following orders, but in no force was regimental esprit de corps and routine more fiercely revered than in the British army. Individual companies, no matter how well trained, simply did not respond as effectively in nonregimental conglomerations without their practiced lines of communication.

This lack of regimental structure carried a potential for confusion that manifested itself when the first independent companies began to arrive on the Back Bay beach. Frederick Mackenzie of the Royal Welch Fusiliers was admittedly somewhat of a perfectionist, but he was appalled at the disorganization he found as companies from other regiments joined the grenadier and light infantry companies of his own. Company commanders milled around with their troops, but without any regimental structure there was no general direction, in part because Smith and Pitcairn were slow in arriving.

Lieutenant John Barker of the Fourth Regiment found that "few but the Commandg. Officers knew what expedition we were going upon."[6]

The longboats from the Royal Navy were indeed on the beach, but they numbered only about twenty—half the number required to transport the eight-hundred-plus troops in one trip. Thus the boats were required to make two trips across the Charles River estuary. This left half the command standing around on the Boston side for nearly an hour as the first wave was rowed across by British seamen, and then the other half, similarly, stood idling around on the western shore while the second wave crossed. At some point early in the course of the first wave's crossing, a waning moon, three days past full, began to climb above Boston Neck.

The water crossing itself was a little over a mile and ran diagonally downstream from the Back Bay beach toward Lechmere Point, near Cambridge. It didn't help matters that an incoming tide on the Charles River slowed progress on the outbound leg and pushed the boats farther upstream from Lechmere Point than intended. This meant that the landing point on the Cambridge shore, while indeed isolated and unpopulated, was squarely in the middle of the wetlands of the Cambridge marshes. With the incoming tide just beginning, the boats grounded in knee-deep water and four hundred pairs of boots were quickly soaked. Once the men were ashore, the swampy ground offered no respite for those wishing for a quick hour's nap while the boats made a second trip.[7]

Not until after midnight, more than two hours after assembling on the Back Bay, were all Smith's troops disembarked on the Cambridge shore. But there was more confusion there. Without regimental structure, the companies once again looked about for direction. Colonel Smith prided himself on strict, by-the-book formations, but open-field, parade-ground maneuvers were ill suited for the soggy banks of the Charles River in the middle of the night—moonlit or not.

In arranging his order of march, Smith chose to follow the

established practice of the British army. The light infantry company from his own Tenth Regiment of Foot would go first, as Smith was the overall formation commander. This company was followed by the light infantry companies in order of seniority as determined by their regiment's number. Hence the light infantry of the King's Own (formally the Fourth Regiment of Foot) came next, followed by those of the regiments of the Fifth, Eighteenth, Twenty-Third (Mackenzie's Royal Welch Fusiliers), and so on. These were followed by the companies of grenadiers in the same order of regimental seniority. Pitcairn's marine detachment of one company each of light infantry and grenadiers trailed this formation, as marines were clearly part of the navy—to their pride, but to the disdain of the army.

The most distinctive difference between the grenadier and light infantry companies, even in the early moonlight, was the headgear of the troops. The light infantry wore "tight helmets of black leather, adorned with feathers or horsehair crests, and constructed with whimsical peaks in front or behind, according to the fancy of the regimental commander." To make them appear even taller than they were, the grenadiers wore "towering caps of bearskin, adorned with heavy metal faceplates and colorful cords and tassels, and emblazoned at the back with their regimental number in large Roman numerals."[8]

What distinguished these regiments' specialist companies were the colors on their red uniform coats. These colors were worn as well by the regular companies, or "hat companies," of the regiment, so called because of their standard-issue cocked hats. Lapels and cuffs revealed the facings of the regiment's colors. In the case of royal regiments, such as the King's Own of the Fourth Regiment and the Royal Welch Fusiliers of the Twenty-Third, these facings were what is still called royal blue. The light infantry and grenadier companies of Lord Percy's Fifth Regiment were there in their gosling-green facings. Other regimental colors slogging around the Cambridge marshes that evening were the pale yellow facings of the Thirty-Eighth, the buff facings of the Fifty-Second, and the bright purple of the Fifty-Ninth. Colonel Smith's own Tenth Regiment wore a rather vivid yellow.[9]

This was all very pretty but not terribly practical, particularly as the column was soon again in disarray as its soldiers slogged through marshes and oozy mud on the tidal flats. Some of the troops "were obliged to wade, halfway up their thighs, through two Inlets, the tide being by that time up." Ensign Jeremy Lister, who had volunteered for the mission at the last moment, when another officer feigned sickness, was in the van with the light infantry company of the Tenth Regiment. This company led the column "at first through some swamps and slips of the Sea till we got into the Road leading to Lexington."[10]

By now, as much as four hours had passed since the initial departure from the Back Bay, and it was approaching two o'clock on the morning of April 19. Given the delays in crossing the Charles and the folly in the marshes, Colonel Smith may have been wondering if he would have been better advised to have simply marched his entire command with dispatch across Boston Neck, over the Charles River by bridge at Cambridge, and on through Cambridge to the same point on the Lexington road. This route would have been about seven miles — double the distance across the river and through the marshes — but might well have been covered in much less than four hours. Time and secrecy had been of the essence, but it was not long after taking up the march on the road toward Lexington that Ensign Lister noted that "the Country people [have] begun to fire their alarm guns [and] light their Beacons, to raise the Country."[11]

MEANWHILE, THE COUNTRYSIDE FARTHER WEST was also full of alarms. Gage's initial patrol the day before had already had the effect of arousing the countryside around Lexington. Word was spreading well beyond the town when the most famous signal of the evening of April 18 briefly appeared on the Boston skyline.

Whether Dr. Joseph Warren indeed had a secret informer highly placed in General Gage's headquarters, or whether he assessed the reports coming into his medical office and concluded the obvious, by the time British companies were gathering to embark from below the Common there was little doubt that this was indeed a major British movement in force designed to strike at the heart of the rebel resistance.

Dr. Warren, however, seems to have identified the capture of Samuel Adams and John Hancock — and not the munitions and supplies at Concord — as the chief objective of the British march. Despite the absence in General Gage's written orders to Colonel Smith of any mention of capturing Adams and Hancock, it is certainly possible that Gage gave verbal orders to that effect — if not to Smith, then to Major Mitchell of the advance patrol. It is also possible that Warren was less concerned about the munitions because he knew that a goodly number had been spirited away from Concord.

On each of the three occasions that Paul Revere recorded his account of that night — twice shortly thereafter and a third time, in 1798 — he was very specific that his mission was to reach Lexington, where Dr. Warren knew Adams and Hancock to be staying, apprise them of the British movements, and alert them "that it was thought they were the objects." [12] Warren's decision to report to Adams and Hancock in their roles as the key leaders in the Provincial Congress was logical enough — particularly as Warren and, possibly, Dr. Benjamin Church Jr. were the last of the rebels' inner circle then in Boston. But Warren also perceived a grave personal danger to Adams and Hancock, or at least Revere remembered it that way.

Warren was so anxious to get word to Adams and Hancock in Lexington that he dispatched not one but two messengers, Paul Revere and William Dawes, the latter a Boston tanner whose business routinely took him in and out of town. Dawes carried the message on horseback through the guard post on Boston Neck and started for Lexington via the land route that Colonel Smith may have wished he had taken. Various accounts have Dawes passing the

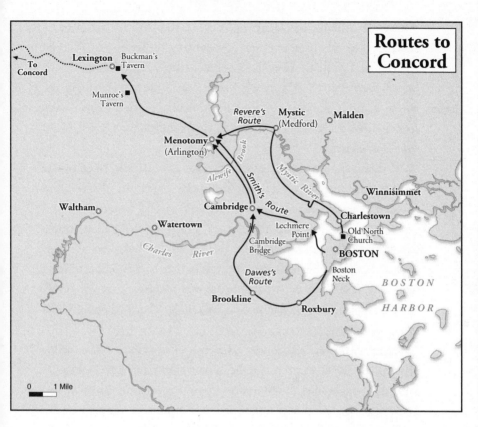

guard post on the neck by bluffing his way through, cajoling guards he knew from prior trips, or mingling with a larger party. But regardless of the circumstances, the question must be asked, why was *anyone* permitted to leave Boston that evening by any route? At least one account suggests that all traffic out of Boston was stopped shortly after Dawes passed the sentries, but why weren't these precautions taken before the regulars began to assemble on the Back Bay?

Indeed, only a few days before, Paul Revere had anticipated the prospect of rebel messengers getting bottled up in Boston — effectively cutting off communications with the countryside — and he devised a simple set of signals. Returning to Boston from Lexington on Sunday, April 16, after carrying a previous message from

Warren to Adams and Hancock, Revere stopped in Charlestown and met two rebel leaders there. According to Revere, he "agreed with a Col. [William] Conant, & some other Gentlemen, that if the British went out by Water, we would shew two Lanthorns in the North Church Steeple; & if by Land, one as a signal; for we were apprehensive it would be difficult to Cross the Charles River, or git over Boston neck." [13]

William Dawes was already on his way over Boston Neck by the time Revere answered his own summons from Dr. Warren and reached Warren's house. Upon hearing Warren's instructions and urgency, Revere left immediately and, in his words, "called upon a friend and desired him to make the Signals." [14] But who was this friend? Long-established tradition holds that it was Robert Newman, the sexton of what became known to history as the "Old" North Church. Revere had been a bell ringer there when he was a fifteen-year-old.

In 1775, this structure was a Church of England enclave properly called Christ Church. Anglican churches tended to be heavily loyalist, and Thomas and Margaret Gage, Major John Pitcairn, and many other British officers stationed in Boston were among its worshippers. The rector, Mather Byles Jr., became so outspoken in his defense of the king and about the foolishness of the rebel cause in his weekly harangues that he fell out with his moderate parishioners over both his politics and his salary. The very day before signal lanterns would be hung in the church's steeple, a committee of vestrymen "waited on Dr. Byles to know if he intended to leave the church" and evidently encouraged him to do so. Byles responded the next day, April 18: "For my part I am willing to give up the keys and quit the church," but he hoped the church would pay the balance due on his salary. [15]

Among those who may or may not have been involved with these negotiations was John Pulling, a member of the vestry whose rebel leanings went back to the early days of Samuel Adams Sr.'s Boston Caucus and who was enough of a known rebel to have made a London enemies list.[16] Given Revere's long relationship with the older Pulling, it may well have been Pulling whom Revere "called upon as a friend and desired him to make the signals." Pulling himself was well acquainted with Robert Newman in Newman's role as church sexton — essentially the building's caretaker. The twenty-three-year-old Newman was not openly supporting the rebel cause; some discretion was required on his part, as British officers were boarding at the home he shared with his mother and stepfather, his young wife, Rebecca, and their own two small sons. But Newman was known as an ally, and it did no harm that he was the first cousin of Isaiah Thomas, the fiery editor of the rebel *Massachusetts Spy*.

There is an intriguing story in a Newman family history that says that Revere — or perhaps it was Pulling, at Revere's request — arrived at the Newman house, across the street from the church, late on the evening of April 18 to summon Newman's assistance and/or get the sexton's keys. The boarding British officers were playing a rowdy game of cards at the parlor table and enjoying an after-dinner libation, so Revere slipped into the darkened garden behind the house and was pondering his next move when Newman stepped from the shadows. He had said good night to the boarders and pretended to go to bed before crawling out a bedroom window and dropping to a hiding place in the garden, much to the dismay of his wife, Rebecca, who was expecting their third child.

One way or the other, Revere, if he was present — or, more likely, John Pulling in his stead — told Newman what needed to be done. Crossing the darkened street — the moonlight was only a halo spreading above the southeastern horizon — the two men made their way to the church door, where Newman produced his key. Quite possibly, a third man, Thomas Bernard, was also present and likely stood guard as Newman and Pulling entered the building and in its darkened interior retrieved two lanterns from a closet. Using leather thongs, the two men draped the lanterns around their necks and climbed 154 creaking wooden steps up the church tower. It was the tallest building in Boston. At some point, perhaps on the platform beneath the great bells, Newman and Pulling took out flint and steel and showered sparks onto tinder with which to light the small candles in the lanterns. All that remained was the delicate climb up the narrow ladder leading past the bells to the uppermost perch at the base of the steeple.

Who made this climb and did the actual hanging remains a matter of some debate, but, as with other aspects of Paul Revere's storied ride — and, indeed, the entire rebel warning system — it was definitely a matter of teamwork. Assuming he could manage two lighted lanterns and still climb the ladder, it was probably the younger, more agile Robert Newman who did the deed. From the highest window, the glow of first one and then two lights flickered out to the northwest, in the direction of Charlestown.[17]

Revere, meanwhile, went to his house, got his riding boots and frock coat, and hurried to the northern part of town, where he kept a small rowboat. Two other friends — another example of a team effort — rowed him from Boston across the Charles River to Charlestown, a little to the east of where the man-of-war HMS *Somerset* lay at anchor. This was about the time that the first wave of Colonel Smith's force was in its boats a mile or so upriver. But unlike Smith, who crossed against the tide, Revere crossed the Charles where it curved eastward around the tip of Boston. Angling toward Charlestown from there, Revere's boat had the advantage of the incoming tide to help it along.[18]

If Revere or his two oarsmen caught a glimpse of the signal from the steeple of the North Church, he made no mention of it in his recollections. Historic images notwithstanding, these were not two searchlight beacons shining brightly above the north end of Boston. Newman's signal was dimly and briefly displayed. The lanterns emitted only a subtle glow, and to leave them visible for much more than a minute would have attracted the attention of patrolling British sentries. But it was enough. On the Charlestown shore, the rebel leader Colonel Conant and several others saw two lights briefly appear.

Revere may well have been busy enough nervously anticipating some shout of alarm from the decks of the *Somerset*. The warship's anchorage astride the Boston-to-Charlestown ferry route was no fluke: it was intended to thwart just the sort of clandestine, after-hours transit that Revere was attempting. Whatever the exact timing and location of the moonrise that evening, it seems clear that it occurred late enough and far enough to the southeast that the hills of Boston still shadowed the Charles River, cloaking Revere's crossing, and that the moon had not yet backlighted the steeple of the North Church.

One of Revere's biggest fears was that one or more of his brethren among the rebels' inner council had been routinely betraying them to General Gage. The extent of the secret correspondence the general had been receiving from Concord was as yet unknown, but Revere had firsthand knowledge that a traitor to the cause was abroad. Several months before, "a Gentleman who had Connections with the Tory party, but was a Whig at heart," had warned Revere that secret rebel meetings were compromised and as proof repeated "the identical words that were spoken among us the Night before."

This was particularly disconcerting, because every time this group met, they swore upon the Bible—no idle gesture—that no one would reveal "any of our transactions, But to Messrs. Hancock, Adams, Doctors Warren, Church, & one or two more."[19] Someone among this band of brothers thought more of British sterling than their cause. The traitor was not yet known in the final hour of April 18, as the rowboat carrying Revere touched on the Charlestown shore.

Meanwhile, Robert Newman's journey had been shorter but put him in potentially greater peril. Extinguishing the two lanterns, Newman, likely again with John Pulling's assistance, descended the ladder from the steeple and hurried back down the tower steps. British guards were already banging on the front door of the church, demanding to know the reason for the lights in the steeple. Thomas

Bernard, if indeed he had been left on guard, had faded into the darkness.

The oft-told tale is that to escape arrest, Newman and Pulling hurried down the center aisle of the sanctuary and climbed out the window to the right of the altar. The two men parted, and Newman circled into the backyard of his house, across the street, and retraced his route back through his bedroom window. When British troops, or possibly his family's boarders, banged on his chamber to determine his whereabouts, they found the sexton snugly in his bed, feigning sleep.[20]

Revere would get no sleep that night, feigned or otherwise. Colonel Conant and several others met him in Charlestown, and Revere "told them what was acting" while he hurried to secure a horse. As the horse was being saddled, Richard Devens appeared and told Revere about his encounter with the patrol of British officers as he had left Menotomy earlier that evening and that they were all "well mounted and armed." With this information in hand, Paul Revere thanked his comrades and "set off on a very good Horse."[21]

Chapter 10

~

Lexington Green

The thick grass on Lexington Green still smelled like the day's rain as John Hancock read the hasty note of warning that Elbridge Gerry had dispatched from the Black Horse Tavern after Gerry learned that Major Mitchell's patrol was at large. Hancock and Samuel Adams were staying at the home of Jonas Clarke, the minister at Lexington's Congregational meetinghouse. Hancock knew the home well, because Clarke had succeeded Hancock's grandfather in the pulpit, and it was from this house that Hancock's uncle Thomas had fetched him as a boy and taken him to the world of Boston business.

The Clarke home stood on the western side of Bedford Road, about four hundred yards north of Lexington Green's northernmost point. The white two-story house was oriented so that the front door looked almost directly down the road toward the green. Lexington Green itself was a long, triangular field of about three acres. Coming into Lexington from the east, the road from Menotomy and Cambridge split at the easternmost point of the green, with the northern leg running toward Bedford and the southern leg continuing westward toward Concord. The meetinghouse stood on the green behind this three-way intersection and across Bedford Road from Buckman's Tavern.

Gerry's warning reached the Clarke house about 8:00 p.m. on the evening of April 18, after Mitchell's patrol had passed through town en route to Concord. At this point, the principal fear seems to have been that Hancock and Adams themselves were the targets of capture or worse. Reverend Clarke later recalled that because "Mr. Hancock in particular had been, more than once, personally insulted, by some officers of the troops, in Boston; it was not without some just grounds supposed, that under cover of the darkness, sudden arrest, if not assassination might be attempted." [1]

Thinking Major Mitchell's patrol of eight or nine officers the main threat, a squad of eight armed men of Lexington militia under the command of Sergeant William Munroe stationed themselves around Clarke's parsonage to guard Hancock and Adams, while another thirty Lexington men, including Elijah Sanderson, the cabinetmaker who had passed Mitchell's group on the road, assembled at Buckman's Tavern. Sanderson and two others, Solomon Brown and Jonathan Loring, were soon detailed on horseback to shadow Mitchell's men westward and return with a warning should the British officers double back and make for the Clarke house. [2]

Meanwhile, Hancock took the time to reply to Gerry's warning. Writing that he was "much obliged for your notice," Hancock told Gerry, "It is said the officers are gone to Concord, and I will send word thither." Showing that he and Adams were not yet aware of the main British force about to come marching down the road, Hancock assured Gerry that he shared his concern about the seriousness of recent events and hoped that the decisions of the committee of safety would be effective. And then, thinking of another meeting of the committee in Menotomy, Hancock added, "I intend doing myself the pleasure of being with you to-morrow." [3]

With that, the Clarke household settled down for the night, confident in the guard posted outside. In addition to Reverend Clarke, his wife, Lucy, John Hancock, and Samuel Adams, Hancock's "female connections"—as James Warren termed them in a letter to Mercy—were present. Things had deteriorated to the point that neither Hancock nor Adams dared venture into Boston, and on April 7, Hancock's beloved aunt Lydia and his fiancée, Dorothy Quincy, had left Boston and found refuge in Lexington. Also present were other members of the Clarke family. Lucy Clarke was a granddaughter of the Reverend John Hancock, making her John III's second cousin.[4]

Sometime between midnight and one o'clock on the morning of April 19, the quiet outside the Clarke residence was broken by the sound of a horse hurrying up the road from the direction of Lexington Green. Sergeant Munroe and his men were at their posts, and Munroe blocked the rider's path as he dismounted and strode purposefully toward the front door. The sergeant did not recognize the man and admonished him to be quiet lest he wake the inhabitants with his noise. "Noise!" shouted the lone rider. "You'll have noise enough before long. The regulars are coming out." At this, he stepped around Munroe and pounded on the front door.

Reverend Clarke immediately opened an upstairs window and inquired who was there. Without answering that direct question, the rider instead announced that he wished to see Mr. Hancock. Clarke, in the usual deliberative way of ministers, sought to question him more about his business, but Hancock's head appeared at another window, and he said rather matter-of-factly, "Come in, Revere; we are not afraid of you."[5]

EVEN THOUGH PAUL REVERE REMEMBERED the early hours of April 19 as "very pleasant" weatherwise, the British column marching west from Cambridge toward Lexington on what is now Massachusetts Avenue was already showing signs of stress. Most if not all of Smith's command were wet and chilled from hours of waiting and stumbling around soggy marshes. They nonetheless set a brisk pace along the road, still muddy from the prior day's rain. For a time, they managed better than four miles an hour despite complaints that the pace was "hasty and fatiguing."[6]

Colonel Smith, however, was not one to consider the welfare of his men, and after the delays in crossing the Charles and wandering through marshy bogs, he focused on the part of Gage's orders that directed him to secure the two bridges at Concord "as soon as possible" with "a party of the best Marchers." Halting the main column for a brief rest at Menotomy, where the committee of safety of the Provincial Congress had just adjourned, Smith ordered Major John Pitcairn to take the six light infantry companies at the head of the column—about eighteen officers and 220 men, roughly 30 percent of his force—and march them at the quick to seize the Concord bridges and hold them until his main force arrived. Nothing was said about what might happen at the little crossroads of Lexington en route.[7]

John Pitcairn was by all accounts an able officer of long service. He was born in Scotland about 1722, the son of a Presbyterian minister. Commissioned a lieutenant in Cornwall's Seventh Marines in 1746, Pitcairn filled a variety of assignments and was finally promoted to major in 1771, a long twenty-five years later. Along the way, the rigors and postings of military life did not keep him from marrying Elizabeth Dalrymple and fathering nine children with her. By the time Pitcairn landed in Boston with a contingent of six hundred marines in December of 1774, he was in his midfifties, and the subsequent long winter no doubt brought thoughts of Elizabeth and retirement. One of their children, Robert, had become a midshipman in the Royal Navy and was on watch during a 1767 voyage when what would be named Pitcairn Island was discovered in the South Pacific. Another of their children, Catherine, was married to Captain Charles Cochrane of the Fourth Regiment, who was now somewhere on the road up ahead as part of Major Mitchell's advance patrol. Pitcairn's son William was with him on the march as a lieutenant in the light infantry company of the Royal Marines.[8]

John Pitcairn was the type of experienced commander a superior would want for a mission in which the lines between military and political considerations were blurred. Colonel Leslie had faced this sort of quandary six weeks before at Salem and had at least come away without bloodshed if not rebel cannons. But Colonel Smith was another matter. Like Pitcairn, Smith was an aging relic of the ponderous hierarchy of the British army. Somewhat overweight, meticulous to a fault, and deliberative in his rank and position, Smith might well have been called General Gage's ideal of what a military leader should be — which in itself was not necessarily a compliment to either man. Whether Smith's unhurried pace was due to studied calmness under fire or merely occasional befuddlement only time would tell.

But for now, the immediate concern as Major Pitcairn led his advance force forward at a brisk march along the road to Lexington may have been General Gage's tactical decision to assemble a force of independent companies without a regimental command structure. Smith acquiesced in this decision by sticking to traditional regimental seniority in the order of march. Pitcairn had behind him six company commanders, generally able and willing but largely unknown to him, and one wonders whether Smith might have been better advised to have moved Pitcairn's light infantry company of marines into the van of his advance force.

As it was, the company at the head of Pitcairn's column soon found plenty to keep it occupied. There was more activity in farmhouses and barns than there should have been at that hour — although it was by then approaching 4:00 a.m. Riders were encountered along the road, and all were detained and presumed to be rebel messengers out in the predawn dark to spread the alarm. Some, such as Simon Winship, may have had other business, or at least have been good actors. About halfway between Menotomy and Lexington, Pitcairn's advance guard met Winship "on horseback, unarmed, and passing along in a peaceable manner." When ordered to halt and dismount, Winship indignantly questioned the soldiers' right to detain him. He had not been out warning minute-men, he claimed, but merely returning to his father's house. Despite his protests, Winship was forced to march on foot in the midst of the British troops back toward Lexington, in the direction he had come.[9]

To Pitcairn, it soon became obvious from these encounters that surprise was not to be among his advantages. From the sounds of alarm bells and signal guns that were now resonating ahead of and behind his position, Colonel Smith was coming to the same conclusion. Major Mitchell and his patrol had set the alarm system in motion even as General Gage was giving Smith his orders. Smith made his first prudent decision of the long night and sent a messenger riding back toward Boston to advise the general that Smith might require reinforcements.

HAVING DELIVERED DR. WARREN'S MESSAGE and warned Hancock and Adams of the approaching troops, Paul Revere remounted and rode west toward Concord to spread the alarm. William Dawes, who had slipped across Boston Neck before it was sealed and arrived at the Clarke residence shortly after Revere, joined him. A third rider, Dr. Samuel Prescott of Concord, soon overtook them. Prescott had been out on an errand of love and was returning to Concord from a late evening courting Lydia Mulliken of Lexington. Revere and Dawes ascertained that Prescott was a rebel at heart, and the three took turns knocking on farmhouse doors as they rode toward Concord.

By now the moon was near its apex, and the road was bathed in moonlight. The brightness made it more difficult to see what dangers lurked in the shadows of tall trees. Near the tiny hamlet of Lincoln, about midway between Lexington and Concord, Revere scouted the road in the lead while Dawes and Prescott stopped to arouse the inhabitants of a farmhouse.

Suddenly two British officers rode out from the shadows. Revere shouted a warning to his companions, and for a fleeting moment the rebel trio considered bulling its way through, although they were unarmed. But then another two heavily armed regulars emerged from the shadows. Flight quickly seemed the better strategy. Prescott urged his horse over a stone wall and escaped into the darkness of the adjacent woods. Dawes, who was mounted on the slowest horse of the three, rode in the opposite direction and managed to find shelter in an abandoned farmhouse. Revere was about to outrun his pursuers when six more soldiers appeared across his path.

Revere found himself a prisoner, but he was not alone. Major Mitchell's patrol had also captured messenger Solomon Brown, who had been dispatched earlier from Lexington to Concord, and Elijah Sanderson and Jonathan Loring, who had been sent to follow the officers after they passed through Lexington. An officer who appeared to be in command ordered Revere to dismount and asked him where he had come from and when. Revere told him but thought the officer "seemed surprised" at his answers, either at the ground he had covered so quickly or the fact that he had slipped out of Boston at all. Asked his name, Revere told the truth on this point, too, which met with recognition. But rather than cower, Revere used his acknowledged notoriety to launch a verbal offensive against his captors.

They wouldn't find what they were after, Revere told them. He had warned the countryside all the way from Charlestown and would soon have five hundred men in the field. The British officer retorted that his side had fifteen hundred men coming but again seemed surprised at the extent of Revere's knowledge. The officer rode back to a group of officers still on the road. After a whispered conversation, they all came back to Revere at a gallop. This time it was Major Mitchell himself who "Clap'd his Pistol to [Revere's] head" and threatened to "blow [his] brains out" if Revere did not answer his questions.

Mitchell then grilled Revere with the same questions the first officer had asked, but he demanded more particulars. Revere gave him the same answers without further detail but with a like amount of swagger. No doubt annoyed by Revere's confidence and uncertain of the number of rebels who might be closing in around his small troop, Mitchell ordered Revere to mount his horse. As Revere did so, Mitchell snatched the reins out of his hands and exclaimed, "By G-d Sir you are not to ride with reins I assure you" and handed them to an officer to lead him.[10]

Mitchell's men put each of their four prisoners — Revere, Brown, Sanderson, and Loring — between two guards, and they all started east toward Lexington at a brisk pace. Elijah Sanderson's horse, "not being swift," had difficulty keeping up, and one of the officers pressed his own horse close and prodded Sanderson's mount with a blow from his scabbard.

As they neared Lexington, the boom of a signal gun reverberated through the crisp dawn air. What did it mean? Mitchell testily asked Revere. The express rider shrugged and repeated what he had already said twice before: the countryside knew that the regulars were about and was in a state of alarm. According to Sanderson's recollection, the bell at the meetinghouse on Lexington Green began to ring soon thereafter, and Jonathan Loring snapped to his captors, "The bell's a ringing, the town's alarmed, and you're all dead men."[11]

Even Major Mitchell seems to have considered that a strong possibility. Keeping his prize — Paul Revere — Mitchell ordered the other three rebels to dismount. "I must do you an injury," one soldier told Sanderson, drawing his sword. Expecting the worst, Sanderson, Brown, and Loring were relieved when their captors merely cut the bridles and saddles off their horses and drove them away. The three men, on foot but very near Lexington Green, were told they "might go about their business."

Revere asked Mitchell to dismiss him as well, but the major "said he would carry me, lett the consequences be what it will." But a few more minutes of riding brought them within sight of the meetinghouse and the sound of another alarm volley — likely fired by those gathered at Buckman's Tavern. Major Mitchell quickly quizzed Revere about the distance to Cambridge and ordered him to trade his horse for a burly sergeant's wearying mount. The exchange made, the bridle and saddle girth on the sergeant's original horse were also slashed. Then Major Mitchell's patrol and Paul Revere's horse hurried past the meetinghouse and disappeared down the road toward Cambridge at full gallop. Revere was left standing in the road near the edge of Lexington Green.[12]

WHILE PAUL REVERE HAD TAKEN his ride toward Concord and been returned to Lexington a prisoner, Lexington's militia had not been idle. Even before Revere had arrived, an initial guard had formed around the Clarke house, and another group gathered at Buckman's Tavern. The call to turn out Lexington's full complement was not given until after the receipt of Dr. Warren's warning, sent via Revere. According to Reverend Clarke, "the militia of this town were alarmed, and ordered to meet on the usual place of parade," that being Lexington Green. Clarke's account was decidedly one-sided as to the peaceful intent of the militia and the militant purpose of the approaching regulars. The call out was made "not with any design of commencing hostilities upon the king's troops," Clarke maintained, "but to consult what might be done for our own and the people's safety." They would be ready, however, "in case overt acts of violence, or open hostility should be committed by this mercenary band of armed and blood-thirsty oppressors."[13]

The commander of Lexington's militia company was Captain John Parker. In the tradition of the militia, his position was an elected one, as were those of his officers. The practical nature of hardened countrymen usually assured that they voted for military experience over popularity. Parker had plenty of both. He was forty-six that spring, dying of tuberculosis but not one to let such personal inconvenience stand in the way of duty. His family recalled him as "a great tall man, with a large head and a high, wide brow."

His military experience had been honed through some of the toughest fighting of the French and Indian War. Parker had been with Brigadier James Wolfe at the siege of Louisbourg and on the Plains of Abraham before the fall of Quebec. There were rumors that along the way he had spent some time with Rogers' Rangers.[14]

Despite Parker's position as captain, the seventy-some men who answered this middle-of-the-night summons had truly come—in Reverend Clarke's words—"to consult what might be done." While a far-reaching alarm system was already spreading word of the regulars' advance to similar militia units across much of eastern Massachusetts, at this particular moment Captain Parker's men were very much on their own. They looked to Parker for leadership, but as a volunteer force of independent-minded individuals they expected to have some say in whatever action they took. And whatever action that might be, they would first and foremost be concerned with the immediate safety of their persons, their families, and their homes.

So by ones, twos, and threes the men of Lexington assembled on their village green. Many were related by blood or marriage, and all were neighbors and friends. While their ages ranged from sixteen to sixty-six, most were middle-aged men of some substance—men who worked hard on their farms, ran businesses, and took active part in the affairs of the town and the Congregational church. Its meetinghouse was so central to the activities of the town that it served as a makeshift armory for guns and munitions. Many times its congregation had heard Reverend Clarke espouse the blessings of liberty and the rights of man. Benjamin Estabrook's slave, Prince, didn't share in those blessings, but having taken an oath as a militiaman, he was among those who assembled in the darkness.

Robert Munroe was an example of how connected the men were on Lexington Green that morning. He was two weeks shy of his sixty-third birthday, definitely of the older generation in that era. He had already given his service in the Louisbourg campaign of the French and Indian War. His daughter Anna was married to Daniel Harrington. His daughter Ruth was the wife of William

Tidd. These sons-in-law and Munroe's own two sons, Ebenezer and John, stood beside him on the green that morning. Tidd was a lieutenant in the company; Daniel Harrington owned the blacksmith shop that fronted on the northern edge of the green.[15]

As his company formed on the green, Captain Parker sent two scouts down the road toward Cambridge to attempt to locate the approaching column of regulars. It is unclear how far they traveled, but one of them returned between 3:00 and 4:00 a.m. and reported "no appearance of the troops, on the roads, either from Cambridge or Charlestown; and . . . that the movements in the army the evening before, were only a feint to alarm the people."[16]

Given the inactivity and the coolness of the early morning air, Parker decided to dismiss his company, provided the men stay within earshot of a drumroll so they might be readily reassembled. Some retired to nearby homes, but most sought refuge in the warm confines of Buckman's Tavern while Parker calmly awaited the return of his second scout. Little did he suspect — though perhaps he should have — that the scout was returning to Lexington as a prisoner of Major Pitcairn's advance guard.

HAVING BEEN LEFT STANDING IN the road by Major Mitchell and his patrol, Paul Revere avoided crossing Lexington Green and instead circled north across the town cemetery toward the Clarke house. Most likely he did so to avoid other soldiers, should they be lurking around the green. Like Major Mitchell, Revere may have been unsure of the meaning of the commotion coming from the direction of Buckman's Tavern — originating, unbeknownst to him, from Parker's men. Perhaps the regulars were already in town in force.

Just whom Revere expected to find at the Clarke residence is uncertain, but he certainly did not expect to find the objects of his midnight ride. But yes — some three hours after receiving Revere's urgent warning from Dr. Warren, John Hancock and Samuel

Adams were still ensconced in Reverend Clarke's parlor debating a course of action. When Hancock had written Elbridge Gerry a few hours before that "I intend doing myself the pleasure of being with you to-morrow," he had meant in a committee meeting and not on a field of battle, but now Hancock seemed quite determined to be present at the latter. Never mind that his only weapons at hand were a pistol and a ceremonial sword meant more for fashionable dress than rugged combat.

John Hancock had become who he was in Boston society and commerce through no lack of ego. Samuel Adams understood this completely and had long used Hancock's self-esteem to the advantage of the rebel cause. But Hancock, who had become an acknowledged political leader under Adams's tutelage, rather grandly considered himself a military leader as well. Until removed from the post some months before by General Gage, Hancock had held the title of captain of the First Corps of Cadets. It sounded very official, but the cadets more closely resembled a local fraternal order that turned out occasionally for ceremonial roles than a military force. Other than drilling with the cadet company, Hancock had never had the slightest military training, never commanded troops in battle, and never been in the line of fire.

Hancock was nonetheless quoted as saying, "If I had my musket, I would never turn my back upon these troops," and other words to that effect as he busily cleaned his pistol and polished his sword.[17] Adams was more at ease. The signal event that might spark the open and irrevocable break with Great Britain that he had been planning for more than a decade was likely at hand, but he had no desire to stand on Lexington Green. Their task, Adams assured his friend, was to focus on the bigger picture and avoid being struck down to little benefit. "That is not our business," Adams told Hancock of the coming confrontation on the green. "We belong to the cabinet."

As Hancock and Adams went around and around about this, the rest of the Clarke household was in an uproar. When Dorothy

Quincy fretted over the thought of her aging father stranded in Boston and vowed she would return to him in the morning, Hancock spoke to his fiancée as if she were a newly hired clerk in one of his warehouses. "No, madam," Hancock decreed. "You shall not return as long as there is a British bayonet left in Boston." Dorothy Quincy was cut from some of the same determined cloth as Hancock's aunt Lydia, and, according to Dorothy's reminiscence many years later, she replied, "Recollect, Mr. Hancock, I am not under your control yet."[18]

Finally, with Revere's added weight brought to bear on Hancock, he agreed with Adams to seek safety away from Lexington and up the road toward the north. Leaving Lydia Hancock and Dorothy Quincy with the Clarkes — arguably they were safer in the parsonage than on the open road with the rebels' two best-known leaders — Hancock, Adams, Revere, and John Lowell, who was one of Hancock's most trusted clerks, departed Lexington. When they arrived at what was judged to be a safe house several miles away, Revere and Lowell left Hancock and Adams and returned to the Clarke house in Lexington. For Revere, it was his third arrival there in the span of four hours in the early morning of April 19.

Perhaps it had been Hancock's design all along, but some way or another, young Lowell persuaded Revere to continue with him to Buckman's Tavern and rescue a heavy trunk of Hancock's that was located in one of the upper rooms. It was a treasure trove of papers from the Provincial Congress and also held Hancock's correspondence with committees of safety throughout the colony. Revere must have sighed just a little as he started off on yet another errand. But when the two men entered the tavern, they found a surprise.

The bulk of Parker's militia were still inside warming themselves. On the basis of the return of Parker's first scout and no other alarms from the east, the rumor that Revere's earlier shouts of alarm were false had gained strength. Revere doubted the false alarm rumors, but before he could sit down and savor a refreshment he was interrupted. A rider burst into the tavern with news that the regulars were not coming. They were here — marching into town at the quick less than half a mile from the tavern.

Whether a scout dispatched by Parker or a nearby farmer along the Cambridge Road raised this cry is not entirely clear from contemporary accounts. But Captain Parker immediately ordered nineteen-year-old William Diamond, a newcomer from Boston who had been taught "the art of military drumming by a kindly British soldier," to beat a loud roll on his drum and summon all men within earshot to assemble once more on the green.[19]

As the militiamen scrambled out of the tavern, Revere and Lowell exchanged looks and knew what they must do. Up the narrow stairs they climbed to the chamber containing Hancock's trunk. Loaded with papers, it was far more than one man could manage alone — four feet long, two feet wide, and some two and one-half feet high. As they bent to lift it and carry it downstairs, Revere chanced a glance out the window. The eastern sky was lightening, and he could make out the long column of British regulars approaching the three-way intersection adjacent to Lexington Green and the meetinghouse.

On the road, Major Pitcairn heard William Diamond's long roll on his rebel drum, halted his troops, and ordered them to load their muskets. Bells and signal guns were one thing, but to someone who had been a marine for almost thirty years, the ruffle of drums could only mean a call to battle.

Revere and Lowell lugged Hancock's trunk down the stairs and out the door of Buckman's Tavern. The Lexington men had assembled in front of the tavern and then followed Parker to form a line on the northern end of the green, adjacent to Bedford Road, which led to the Clarke parsonage. It is possible that Parker chose this position with a thought to protecting what until a short while before had been the safe haven of Hancock and Adams. More likely, he chose it to have a sweeping view of the green and the road to Concord in the early morning light. Revere and Lowell "made haste" and passed through the line of militia with the trunk. As they did so, Revere heard Parker tell his men, "Lett the troops pass by, and don't molest them, without They being first."[20]

These instructions appear to have been standing orders well known to all Massachusetts militia captains, and they dated back to the previous September, when the First Continental Congress, after approving the Suffolk Resolves, made it clear that the continued support of its sister colonies depended on Massachusetts showing restraint and being "on the defensive."[21]

This restraint may well have been the most likely reason for Parker's position on the far northern corner of the green. Outnumbered at least three to one by Pitcairn's advance guard — Colonel Smith and his main force were still well down the road toward Menotomy — the Lexington men sought no confrontation but were nonetheless out to show the regulars that they could not march freely through the town without notice. Later, Parker would be quoted as saying, "Stand your ground. Don't fire unless fired upon. But if they mean to have a war let it begin here."[22]

If Pitcairn's force had continued along the road to Concord at a brisk march, it is possible that no confrontation would have occurred on the green. But what triggered a halt by Pitcairn's men and gave rise to the confusion that so often breeds errant action in such situations was that one or more of Pitcairn's light infantry companies — likely the company from the Fourth Regiment, as well as those of the Fifth and Tenth, at the head of the column — turned the wrong way at the intersection and marched up Bedford Road between Buckman's Tavern and the meetinghouse instead of bearing left toward Concord and paralleling the southwestern edge of the green.

This took them directly toward Parker's force rather than past it at an angle. To add to the confusion, Major Mitchell and his mounted officers were scurrying around the advancing infantry. After a sleepless night — what with the anxieties of capturing messengers and listening to Paul Revere assure them of both the size

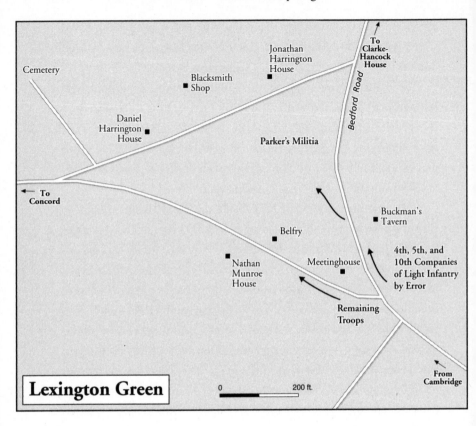

Lexington Green

Cemetery

Blacksmith Shop

Jonathan Harrington House

To Clarke-Hancock House

Bedford Road

Daniel Harrington House

Parker's Militia

To Concord

Buckman's Tavern

Belfry

Nathan Munroe House

Meetinghouse

4th, 5th, and 10th Companies of Light Infantry by Error

Remaining Troops

From Cambridge

0   200 ft.

and ready response of the rebel force — Mitchell was not displaying steady British calm. Again the issue of divided command dogged the British force. Lieutenant Jesse Adair of the Royal Marines was leading the van, but was he following Pitcairn's orders or did Mitchell issue different orders to Adair in the field?

By the time Pitcairn saw what was happening at the intersection, approximately half his force — some one hundred men — had followed Adair along the northern edge of the green. Pitcairn frantically tried to recall them as his remaining companies turned left and followed the Concord road. To Parker and his men, the result was that the lightening sky silhouetted British troops appearing on both sides of the meetinghouse and advancing on their position.

Given the morning light, it was difficult to see just how many soldiers were on the Bedford road coming straight toward them.

If the Lexington men were suddenly seized by the fear of being surrounded, Pitcairn was also gripped by similar thoughts. This was because, in addition to the line of militia on the green, there were two knots of would-be spectators—perhaps twenty or so each—lurking in the wings. One group gathered near Buckman's Tavern and the adjacent stable on Pitcairn's right flank, and the other stood partially hidden behind the home of Nathan Munroe along the Concord road, on his left flank. Their purpose was uncertain, but to Pitcairn, they appeared to be mostly male, armed, and threatening. Suddenly, he thought, it might be his command that was surrounded.

It is certainly possible, as many reports have claimed, that it was Major Pitcairn who galloped across the line of British infantry that had turned off the Bedford road and spread across the green behind the meetinghouse, facing across the green toward the assembled militia. It is also possible that this rider was Major Mitchell, still highly charged with the events of the previous night. Whoever it was, this officer yelled some version of, "Lay down your arms, you damned rebels, and disperse." [23]

Elijah Sanderson recalled that there were perhaps as many as five mounted British officers in front of the British line, which seems to suggest that Mitchell and at least some of the officers from his patrol were at the forefront. Sanderson stepped into line, but he had sent his musket home the prior evening before his nighttime ride toward Concord. He later wrote, "Reflecting I was of no use, I stepped out again from the company" and fell back about thirty feet as the regulars were "coming on in full career." [24] John Robbins, who stood in the militia's front line, later swore that "there suddenly appeared a number of the King's Troops"—about one thousand, he mistakenly believed—"about sixty or seventy yards from us, huzzaing and on a quick pace towards us, with three officers in their front on horseback, and on full gallop towards us; the foremost of which cried, 'Throw down your arms, ye villains, ye rebels.'"[25]

In the account of Captain Parker, given six days later, he reiterated that having "concluded not to be discovered, nor meddle or make with said Regular Troops (if they should approach) unless they should insult us; and upon their sudden approach, I immediately ordered our Militia to disperse and not to fire."[26] Indeed, for whatever confusion was about to ensue, "sixty-two depositions collected from American eyewitnesses all testified that Parker's militia was dispersing before it was fired upon."[27]

As bystander William Draper remembered the sequence of events, the Lexington men had "turned from said Troops" and were "making their escape," but in the meantime "the Regular Troops made a huzza and ran towards Captain Parker's Company, who were dispersing."[28] Thomas Fessenden, who was not in the militia ranks but rather standing "in a pasture near the meeting-house," also recalled three officers on horseback in front of the advancing infantry, one of whom "cried out, 'Disperse, you rebels immediately;' on which he brandished his sword over his head three times." A second officer was riding just behind him with a pistol in his hand.[29]

For a fraction of a second, the scene froze. Then a shot rang out.

Chapter 11

~

On to Concord

Who fired the first shot on Lexington Green early on the morning of April 19, 1775, has been debated ever since and likely will be forevermore. About the only thing both sides agree upon is the uncertainty of the moment.

Paul Revere, still struggling with John Lowell to carry Hancock's trunk away from Buckman's Tavern, heard the first shot. Many years later, perhaps influenced by other reports, Revere would say that he both "saw, & heard, a Gun fired, which appeared to be a Pistol." But in a deposition only a few days after the event, Revere specifically recalled that he had to turn his head to view the action. "When one gun was fired," Revere then testified, "I heard the report, turned my head, and saw the smoake in front of the Troops, they imeditly gave a great shout, ran a few paces, and then the whole fired." [1] When Revere turned around at the shot, he could not see the Lexington militia. A building, probably Jonathan Harrington's house, blocked Revere's view of that part of the green closest to him.

Captain Parker, having already "ordered our Militia to disperse and not to fire," testified only that the regulars "rushed furiously" and fired "without receiving any provocation therefor from us." [2] John Robbins, who was in the militia's front rank, agreed that the company was dispersing when three British officers yelled, "'Fire, by *God*, fire;' at which moment we received a very heavy and close fire from them." Robbins believed that Parker's men "had not then fired a gun."[3]

Local spectators reported much the same thing. Timothy Smith of Lexington was near the green when he "saw the Regular Troops fire on the *Lexington* Company, before the latter fired a gun." Smith, who was likely standing behind and to the right of the front militia line, had started to run away when another volley was unleashed in his general direction. By the time Smith cautiously returned to the common, he saw "eight of the *Lexington* men who were killed, and lay bleeding, at a considerable distance from each other," suggesting they had in fact been dispersing.[4]

As VEHEMENT AS THE REBELS were in their insistence that they had not fired first, the British were equally so. Major Pitcairn, who in advance of Colonel Smith was the senior British commander on the field, rode onto the green after at least two and perhaps three of the light infantry companies that had mistakenly taken Bedford Road were advancing across it. The rebels to their front were apparently moving, but whether they were dispersing, as they later claimed, was questionable. Pitcairn saw rebels sprinting toward the cover of stone walls to the north of the green and took the movement to be a threat on the British right flank.

According to Pitcairn's report to General Gage, the light infantry, "observing this, ran after them. I instantly called to the soldiers not to fire, but surround and disarm them, and after several repetitions of those positive orders to the men, not to fire, etc. some of the rebels who had jumped over the wall fired four or five shots at the soldiers."[5]

But Pitcairn refrained in this report from discussing a "first" shot and hurried on to describe the next exchange. Lieutenant John Barker, who was in the Fourth Regiment's light infantry company in Pitcairn's van, was almost as terse in his account, particularly given the detail elsewhere in his diary. Barker estimated the rebels at three or four times the number actually assembled and said his company "continued advancing, keeping prepared against an attack tho' without intending to attack them." When the distance had closed, Barker claimed the rebels "fired one or two shots, upon which our Men without orders rushed in upon them, fired and put 'em to flight."[6]

One of the most detailed of the British reports is that of Lieutenant William Sutherland of the Thirty-Eighth Regiment. If Sutherland is to be believed as a reliable source—and time will tell in that regard—he knew nothing of the expedition to Concord until troops were preparing to embark from below Boston Common late on the evening of April 18. Without apparent orders and unassigned to any particular unit—the light infantry and grenadier companies of his own Thirty-Eighth were on the expedition, but they were under their regular commanders—Sutherland nonetheless seems to have been readily received by Smith and Pitcairn.

One wonders if this was truly a last-minute lark by Sutherland or whether he was possibly some sort of special observer dispatched on the sly by General Gage. Either way, on the face of things, Sutherland's prior service did not necessarily boast of competence. He was commissioned a lieutenant in 1761 and had been with his regiment since 1766. Even in the slow-ordered system of the British army, this fourteen-year tenure in grade was hardly evidence of blooming talent. Whether Pitcairn ordered him directly or Sutherland once again merely seized the initiative, Sutherland ended up with Lieutenant Jesse Adair in Pitcairn's van after Colonel Smith dispatched Pitcairn's command ahead of his main force.

Sutherland was rather definite in his recollection, written a week later, that a line of British officers on horseback—be they four, five, or six, as various reports describe—"rode in amongst" the rebels and called out both commands to throw down their arms and assurances that they would "come by no harm." Sutherland heard Pitcairn's entreaties to his own troops to hold fire and main-tain their ranks. But then "some of the Villains," as Sutherland termed them, got over a stone wall and opened fire on the regulars. It was only "then & not before," Sutherland maintained, that the regulars returned fire.[7]

Sutherland was very specific — almost as though he were trying to provide exculpatory evidence, if one is a skeptic — that it was "very unlikely our men should have fired on them immediately as they must certainly have hurt" the officers on horseback to their front, which by Sutherland's account included Major Edward Mitch-ell, Captains Charles Lumm and Charles Cochrane, and Lieutenant F. P. Thorne of Mitchell's advance patrol as well as Sutherland himself.

Sutherland also mentioned a Lieutenant "Baker," but this only serves to confuse the matter and show how muddled any account of those brief moments can be. There was, in fact, a Lieutenant Thomas Baker of the Fifth Regiment, but he was posted with that regiment's grenadier company, which was back down the road a piece with Smith's main body. Quite probably Sutherland was recalling Lieutenant John Barker of the Fourth, who was on the green but failed to mention in his own brief account any ride among the rebels on horseback or even if he himself was mounted.

However and by whomever the first shot was fired, the first con-certed fire from the British ranks caused Sutherland's horse to bolt, and it took off at a full gallop and carried him "600 yards or more" along Bedford Road, which ran toward the Clarke parsonage. If Sutherland — who was prone to overestimate numbers, at least those of opposing forces — was correct in the distance he traveled, he must have ridden by the Clarke house. What a sight that must have been — a lone British officer riding madly through militia and spectators and then dashing off down the road alone on a runaway horse. Somewhere along the route, Sutherland may have passed close to where Revere and Lowell were lugging Hancock's trunk, but if they in fact saw one another, neither made mention of it.

Finally, Sutherland got his horse under control and galloped back to the green through what he described as a fusillade of fire from which he could hear "the Whissing of the Balls." [8]

Sutherland was not, however, the only rider to have trouble with his mount. Benjamin Tidd of Lexington and Joseph Abbott of nearby Lincoln were on Lexington Green that morning and "mounted on horses" when they "saw a body of Regular Troops marching up to the *Lexington* Company which was then dispersing." The British officers riding to the front of their troops paid these two horsemen, who evidently were unarmed observers, no mind, so Tidd and Abbott for a moment had front-row seats. They testified that "the Regulars fired first a few guns, which we took to be pistols from some of the Regulars who were mounted on horses, and then the said Regulars fired a volley or two before any guns were fired by the *Lexington* Company." But at the sound of the first volley, Tidd's and Abbott's horses also bolted, and they raced off down the road toward Concord. [9]

Two other spectators testified that they not only heard what they took to be a pistol shot but also saw a British officer fire it. Thomas Fessenden, having observed the officer in the lead brandishing his sword, claimed, "Meanwhile the second officer, who was about two rods behind him, fired a pistol pointed at said Militia." In his reminiscences, Reverend Clarke — who may or may not have witnessed the scene in person — agreed with these details and wrote, "The second of these officers, about this time, fired a pistol towards the militia, as they were dispersing." [10]

While these partisan witnesses were likely showing strong bias, it seems quite possible, perhaps even probable, that the first shot came from a pistol held by one of the British officers riding into the rebel lines. Given that Major Pitcairn appears to have been momentarily preoccupied with his advance companies having taken the wrong road and rushing toward the assembled militia, the likely suspects are Major Edward Mitchell, exhausted and clearly keyed up after a tense night without sleep, and Lieutenant William

Sutherland, who had been scurrying to the forefront all night long. Whether this officer fired intentionally or whether the pistol discharged accidentally as he rode is another matter.

The evidence suggests that Sutherland was mounted on a horse he took from a rebel courier who was stopped on the road earlier that morning. So in Sutherland's defense, it was quite likely not his regular mount. Nonetheless, as one historian shrewdly noted — while admitting it was only his personal hypothesis — "riders who have the most trouble controlling their horses are those least able to control themselves."[11] Sutherland's horse, by its rider's own admission, had gone for quite an uncontrolled gallop, and it is certainly possible that Sutherland's pistol discharged by accident as he rode his frisky mount into the rebel lines.

The other possibility is that the pistol shot came from among the spectators or even from someone hidden from view who had a not-so-hidden desire to provoke an incident. Sergeant William Munroe swore that he saw someone, possibly Solomon Brown, fire from the back door of Buckman's Tavern, but this appears to have been after the initial volley from the regulars.[12] Given that there were groups of spectators clustered around the green and no absence of firearms, almost anything is plausible.

In the end, a preponderance of evidence suggests that the first shot did not come from the rebel militia or from the rank and file of the advancing British infantry. Whether it was a pistol shot discharged on purpose or by accident by a British officer or a rebel onlooker remains a point of debate.

Lieutenant Edward Gould from the light infantry company of the Fourth Regiment may have been among the most objective of observers — or at least he may have summarized the majority opinion. Among the first to move forward across the green, Gould acknowledged that the rebels were dispersing as his command approached, and "soon after firing began; but which party fired first, I cannot exactly say." But even Gould's testimony must be considered in light of its circumstances: having been wounded in the action at the North Bridge later that day, Gould was being treated by rebels at Medford when he gave his deposition. [13]

Regardless how that first shot was fired, it quickly spread into sporadic and then volley fire from the British regulars. After the first volley apparently caused no casualties among the rebels, John Munroe remarked to his brother Ebenezer, who was standing beside him, that the regulars were only firing powder—a scare but no harm. But on the second volley, a ball ripped into Ebenezer's arm, and he exclaimed otherwise. "I'll give them the guts of my gun," he cried in surprise, and, leveling his piece, he returned the fire. [14]

According to one well-worn anecdote of questionable veracity, John Hancock and Samuel Adams were walking through the woods, continuing their escape from Lexington, when they heard this fusillade of musketry. "It is a fine day," Adams remarked with no little satisfaction. Hancock glanced about, thinking that Adams was talking about the weather. "Very pleasant," he agreed. Adams suppressed a small smile. "I mean," he said—for one brief moment, Hancock's tutor once again—"this day is a glorious day for America." [15] It makes a great story, and, then again, it may have happened, but it certainly conveys the true feelings of Samuel Adams in the matter.

IN THE MAZE OF LEADEN musket balls flying in all directions it was remarkable that there were not more casualties. The black powder of the day was so dense, and so much of it had been discharged, that a thick veil of smoke settled on the green, and John Munroe recalled, "The smoke prevented our seeing any thing but the heads of some of their horses." But he fired back nonetheless. After his first shot, he retreated some yards and "then loaded my gun a second time, with two balls, and, on firing at the British, the strength of the charge took off about a foot of my gun barrel." Ebenezer Munroe also fired again, recalling that as he did so, "the balls flew so thick I thought there was no chance for escape, and that I might as well fire my gun as stand still and do nothing." [16]

Then came the bayonets. Jonas Parker, Captain John Parker's aging cousin, had been "standing in the ranks, with his balls and flints in his hat, on the ground, between his feet" when he declared he would "never run." He didn't, but he was shot down on the second volley. William Munroe "saw him struggling on the ground, attempting to load his gun . . . [when] as he lay on the ground they run him through with the bayonet." [17]

Jonas Parker, Jonathan Harrington, Isaac Muzzy, and John and Ebenezer Munroe's father, Robert, were found dead near the place where the militia line had formed. Harrington died almost on his own doorstep, which was just behind the militia line on the edge of the green. No one could say that he hadn't been defending his home. Samuel Hadley and John Brown died after they had limped off the green. Asahel Porter and Caleb Harrington were shot down on the other end of the common, near the meetinghouse. Porter had been taken prisoner earlier and was trying to escape; Harrington had been minding the powder cache in the meetinghouse with an eye toward blowing it up should the regulars attempt to seize it. [18] Among the nine wounded was Prince Estabrook.

The only casualties on the British side were one infantryman wounded in the leg and Major Pitcairn's horse, which was nicked in two places. Some, including Reverend Clarke, would cite this as evidence that "far from firing first upon the king's troops; upon the most careful enquiry, it appears that but very few of our people fired at all." [19]

Onto this scene of bloodshed, pungent with the smell of black powder, marched Colonel Smith and his remaining companies of light infantry and grenadiers. Smith, though he never admitted it, must have been aghast as his horse bore his ample girth to within sight of the meetinghouse and Buckman's Tavern. Pitcairn's six companies of the advance guard were in disarray, and dead and wounded rebels littered the green. This was not Salem, and Smith was not going to get off as easily as Colonel Leslie did. What words Smith spoke to Pitcairn were never recorded, but they can certainly be imagined. And what of the hyper Major Mitchell? What angst did he add to Smith's grim view? And then there was Lieutenant Sutherland.

Once again, Sutherland — by his own account, at least — found himself at the center of the action. Colonel Smith turned to him in this chaos and asked him where a drummer was. Sutherland found one, and Colonel Smith immediately ordered him to beat to arms and bring some order to his troops. It was not easy. The first exchange of deadly fire had had as profound a psychological effect on the regulars as it had on the militia. Adrenaline was at a fever pitch. "We then formed on the Common but with some difficulty," Lieutenant Barker of the Fourth Regiment recalled. "The Men were so wild they cou'd hear no orders."[20]

Within Sutherland's hearing, Smith and Pitcairn expressed dismay at the behavior of their troops in not obeying the junior officers more readily and in not keeping to their ranks. In Sutherland's words, they recommended "a more steady Conduct to them for the future." When some troops lingered and attempted to break into some neighboring houses from which they surmised rebel fire had come, Smith, fearing more bloodshed, stopped them.[21]

As the sergeants goaded their men back into ranks, Colonel Smith held officers' call and for the first time told his subordinates the objective of their march — the stores at Concord. Some officers expressed surprise and then skepticism. Others objected almost to the point of insubordination. Contrary to Gage's and Smith's delusion, they had never had any hope of surprise, and now the countryside was alarmed all around them with the scent of fresh blood on the ground. Mackenzie's account suggests that Smith was more patient in hearing these concerns than circumstance or his position required. They would press on, the colonel decreed, if for no other reason than that he was "determined to obey the orders" he had received.[22]

With his officers' call finished, Smith directed his command to fire their weapons in a victory salute and raise three cheers. Likely he did so to clear muskets and avoid any accidental firing while on the march. How much of a morale boost his excited troops needed—despite the uncertainty of advancing even farther from home after a sleepless night—is questionable. Certainly the roar of some eight hundred muskets and the subsequent hurrahs echoing across their green had just the opposite effect on the inhabitants of Lexington.[23]

Colonel Smith gave the order to march toward Concord, but as his column of regulars disappeared to the west, Captain Parker reassembled his company of militia on the green. More men had arrived in the meantime from outlying farms. They joined the morning's survivors in stunned disbelief at the sight of dead and wounded friends and relatives. Quite suddenly, without Parker or anyone saying anything of particular note, the entire atmosphere changed. This assemblage was no longer a military version of a town meeting called to discuss a course of action or make a demonstration of readiness. Their blood had been spilled, and now they would march with but one aim—that of revenge.

AHEAD OF SMITH'S COLUMN, CONCORD had been on the alert since Dr. Samuel Prescott galloped into town after eluding Major Mitchell's patrol as it captured Paul Revere. Prescott had ridden through woods and fields that he knew well and avoided further detection. The town's elders gathered at the parsonage of the Reverend William Emerson, the future grandfather of Ralph Waldo Emerson. While the Concord militia was assembled, a saddle maker named Reuben Brown was dispatched eastward to Lexington to gather intelligence. He witnessed the initial firing from the far western edge of the green, but then hurried back to give the alarm without waiting to determine the outcome. Upon Brown's arrival back in Concord, Major John Buttrick of the Concord militia company asked him if he thought that the regulars were firing ball. Brown wasn't sure, but thought it highly probable.[24]

As the Concord militia formed, there was much more debate among the volunteers than had occupied the hours of waiting by the Lexington men in Buckman's Tavern. In Lexington, there had then as yet been no irrevocable sense of doom. In Concord, especially after Reuben Brown's report, it was pretty clear that doom was on its way to them. The younger men wanted to march eastward and meet the advancing regulars as far from town as possible. The middle-aged men wanted to stay closer to their families and businesses and defend the town proper. The town elders, most of whom had seen some measure of bloodshed in the French and Indian War or in combat against Indians, were more cautious. However many regulars were on the march, the Concord men were likely outnumbered. It might be wise to melt into the surrounding hills and await reinforcements from neighboring towns. Already members of the militia from neighboring Lincoln, just to the east, were joining them.[25]

Most of these men were not "minutemen," as history has so often characterized them. All were militiamen, but per long-standing custom and later suggestions from the Provincial Congress — *directives* was still too strong a word to these independently minded locals — only about one-quarter of the militia were designated as being able to assemble and march in the shortest time possible. They were the first responders of the day. The remaining militia formed and responded in a much more deliberative manner. Lexington — the minuteman statue that stands on its green to this day notwithstanding — had no company of true minutemen, but larger Concord did, and Amos Barrett was one of them.

As Barrett remembered it fifty years later, "The bell rung at 3 o'clock for alarm. As I was a minute man, I was soon in town and found my captain and the rest of my Company at the post." When the Concord men decided to send a scouting party in force to reconnoiter the regulars' advance, Barrett's minuteman company was among the 150 or so men who took up positions on the crest of a hill east of town. "We thought we would go and meet the British," Barrett recalled. "We marched down towards Lexington about a mile or mile and a half and we see them coming. We halted and staid till they got within about 100 rods, then we were ordered to the about face and marched before them with our drums and fifes going, and also the British (drums and fifes). We had grand music."[26]

As these minutemen fell back into Concord, there was still debate about whether the militia would form and defend the town or withdraw to surrounding high ground—both to ascertain the regulars' intentions and to await the arrival of more militia. To the consternation of some of the younger men, the counsel of sixty-four-year-old Colonel James Barrett prevailed. As the colonel of the combined Middlesex County regiment of militia, Barrett led them north out of Concord, across the North Bridge over the Concord River, and up to the high ground of Punkatasset Hill, about a mile north of Concord Common. A short pause of prudence seemed in order, and, as Reverend Emerson noted, "We were the more careful to prevent a Rupture with the King's Troops, as we were uncertain what had happened at Lexington, & Knew not they had begun the Quarrell there by 1st firing upon our People."[27]

So Colonel Smith's men, with fifes and drums playing in an attempt at intimidation—because there was certainly by then no secret of their advance—marched into Concord unopposed and came to a halt opposite the common. At that point it was about 8:00 a.m. The Concord Common, unlike the triangle patch of Lexington Green, was long and rectangular, extending along the southern edge of the main road as it curved north through town toward the North Bridge. In about the middle of the common, a road led west to the South Bridge across the Sudbury River, which joined the Assabet River to form the Concord River just upstream from the North Bridge.

Now it was time for Colonel Smith once again to remember General Gage's orders. Having caught up with Major Pitcairn's

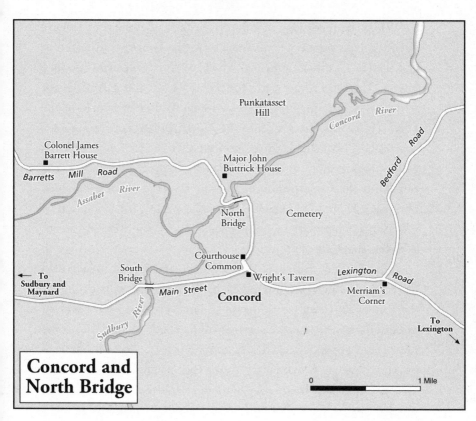

Concord and North Bridge

advance force after its delay at Lexington and marched with it as one force the six miles into Concord, Smith again ordered that the two Concord bridges just beyond the town be seized. But instead of dispatching Major Pitcairn to command the North Bridge force, Smith chose Captain Lawrence Parsons, the commander of the light infantry company of Smith's own Tenth Regiment of Foot.

No firm reason has survived for why Smith chose Parsons over Pitcairn for this assignment, but it is interesting to speculate that Smith was no doubt disturbed over the bloodshed at Lexington. Whether or not the turn of events had been Pitcairn's fault, he was the commander of the advance troops and responsible, short of an overt first volley by the rebels, for their firing. Parsons marched off for the North Bridge with six companies of light infantry.

While the record is not completely clear, these appear to have been the light infantry companies from the Fourth, Fifth, Tenth, and Thirty-Eighth Regiments, which were in Pitcairn's advance into Lexington, along with the Forty-Third and Fifty-Second, which were not. In short order, Captain Walter S. Laurie of the Forty-Third was left guarding the North Bridge and its western approaches, while the companies of the Fourth and Tenth deployed to low hills a short distance westward. Captain Parsons and the remaining three companies, numbering about 120 men and guided by Ensign Henry De Berniere, marched on toward Colonel Barrett's farm, where Gage's intelligence had told him there was a considerable stockpile of munitions.[28]

Indeed, there had been until mere days earlier, when Paul Revere had ridden into town with his first message of warning for the Provincial Congress. Much of the matériel had been removed to outlying towns, and what remained had been hidden with some measure of creativity. Only several days before, Colonel Barrett's sons had plowed a field on his farm and then planted muskets instead of corn, covering them over with dirt. De Berniere, who had scouted this area surreptitiously with Captain Brown only a month earlier, was forced to report, "We did not find so much as we expected, but what there was we destroyed."[29]

Meanwhile, Colonel Smith also detailed a smaller force to the South Bridge, about a mile west of the common, both to look for munitions in that area and to form a defense against any rebel militia coming into town from that direction. Captain Mundy Pole of the grenadier company of Smith's Tenth Regiment — again the colonel seemed to be going with men he knew well — led this detachment to the South Bridge. But for the steady calm of a rebel minuteman officer, the first shots of the Concord battle might have been fired here.

Captain John Nixon was in command of a minute company of West Sudbury men attached to Colonel Abijah Pierce's regiment. Nixon and his company reached Dugan's Corner, on the Sudbury side of the South Bridge, about 9:00 a.m. and awaited orders either to advance into Concord over the South Bridge or march to the west and rendezvous at Colonel Barrett's farm. Nixon had what seems to have been standing orders—witness Parker's actions a few hours earlier at Lexington—not to fire unless fired upon. But then came word that Captain Mundy Pole's contingent had occupied the South Bridge in a manner calculated to prevent rebel forces from converging in Concord, exactly as General Gage's orders had intended.

Nixon was content to obey his orders and stand his ground, but a member of the town's exempt company—those advanced in years and excused from active service—had nonetheless tagged along and now exhorted Captain Nixon, "If you don't go and drive them British from that bridge, I shall call you a coward!" There were murmurs of assent from among his men, but Nixon stood his ground. "I should rather be called a coward by you," Nixon replied evenly, "than called to account by my superior officer, for disobedience of orders." Soon afterward, the West Sudbury company received orders to march westward to Barrett's farm, and Captain Pole continued his occupation of the South Bridge without incident.[30]

The remaining companies of light infantry and the bulk of the grenadiers stayed in the center of Concord under Colonel Smith's direct control. All in all, his force was getting spread rather thin—about one hundred men at the South Bridge, a mile to the west of the town common; another 120 at or near the North Bridge, a mile to the north; 120 with Captain Parsons a good two miles beyond that, digging around Barrett's farm; and the remaining number of about five hundred searching the buildings in Concord proper. (Whether the light infantry company of the Twenty-Third with its complement of thirty-eight officers and men had belatedly joined Parsons or was somewhere in between Barrett's farm and Concord has never been entirely clear.) Meanwhile, up on Punkatasset Hill, Colonel Barrett's militia companies were growing increasingly restless. Many were itching for a fight.

Chapter 12

~

By the Rude Bridge

At the North Bridge, Captain Walter Laurie of the Forty-Third Regiment was growing increasingly nervous. He had only forty-some men to defend this key point, and the numbers of rebel militia looking down from Punkatasset Hill appeared to be growing with each passing minute. Captain Parsons and three companies were up the road about two miles to the west at Barrett's farm, while two other companies, those of the Tenth and Fourth Regiments, had been left tenuously positioned atop two knolls about four hundred yards beyond the bridge in advance of Laurie's position. Laurie had had no communication with them or with Colonel Smith in his rear. He was feeling alone and surrounded when once again Lieutenant William Sutherland put himself at the center of things.

Without a command of his own and no direct orders from Colonel Smith, Sutherland had been free to tag along with Captain Parsons's force as it initially marched out of Concord. When Parsons momentarily posted the light infantry company of Sutherland's own Thirty-Eighth Regiment on yet another knoll along the road to Barrett's farm, as he had done with those of the Tenth and Fourth, Sutherland appears to have lingered near the bridge. Now Sutherland told the nervous Captain Laurie that he would saunter up the road and make contact with the companies of the Tenth and Fourth as well as his own.

Meanwhile, the commanders of the companies of the Tenth and Fourth also got nervous atop their little knolls. Seeing these clumps of redcoats pop up on the two hilltops, the assembled rebel militia had cautiously moved toward them for a closer look. Lieutenant Waldron Kelly, momentarily in command of the company from the Tenth because Captain Parsons was off commanding the combined force at Barrett's farm, reacted first. As Ensign Jeremy Lister of Kelly's company recalled, "We saw a large Body of Men drawn up with the greatest regularity and approach'd us seemingly with an intent to attack, when Lt Kelly who then Commanded our Compy with myself thought it most proper to retire from our situation and join the 4th Compy which we did." [1]

As this was happening, Lieutenant Sutherland arrived and became "exceedingly vexed" that Captain Parsons had gone on farther — although that appears always to have been the plan. Sutherland begged Lieutenant Kelly of the Tenth "to give me 2 men to go after them," which Kelly did. But as this trio started up the road toward Barrett's, the rebels "still approached," and the officers of the Tenth and Fourth Companies made the decision to retire together and join Captain Laurie at the bridge. "Luckily for us," Ensign Lister remembered, "we joined the 43ᴿᴰ Compy [Laurie's] and not a shot [was] Fired." [2]

Sutherland and his two enlisted men might well have continued ahead in search of Parsons and wound up being captured by the advancing rebels, but one of the soldiers called out to him, "Sir, the Company of the 4th are retiring." Upon hearing this Sutherland expressed surprise but then looked to his right and "saw a large body of men marching almost within Pistol shot of me, [and] it struck me it would be disgracefull to be taken by such Rascals & I made the best of my way for the Bridge never out of reach of Musquet shot of this party." [3]

Thus Captain Laurie ended up with three companies, as well as the always eager Sutherland, at the bridge instead of his own single company. But the increasing numbers arrayed against Laurie made him no less nervous. Rebels continued to move down Punkatasset Hill and occupy the knolls west of the bridge that the regulars had just vacated. They appeared content to continue their waiting game, albeit at much closer range.

Captain Laurie consulted with Lieutenant Sutherland—"was kind enough to ask me," in Sutherland's words—if they had not better alert Colonel Smith about the rebel forces now not only arrayed near them but also seemingly threatening Captain Parsons's line of withdrawal from Barrett's farm. Sutherland agreed "by all means as their Disposition appeared to be very regular & determined." Laurie sent Lieutenant Alexander Robertson of his own Forty-Third Regiment riding hard back down the road to Concord.[4]

By now, the rebel militia closest to the North Bridge numbered about five hundred men. These were divided into two regiments of five companies each. One was a regiment of minuteman companies commanded by Major John Buttrick of Concord. His home stood about a quarter of a mile to the north of the bridge on the far side. Under his command were companies from Acton, Bedford, Lincoln, and two from Concord. The regiment of regular militia was composed of five older, slower companies from the same towns under the command of Colonel James Barrett. As the senior officer present, Barrett assumed overall command of both regiments. If Barrett and Buttrick represented older, more cautious warriors who had seen the face of war, their adjutant was a young hot-spur lieutenant named Joseph Hosmer.[5]

As Barrett and Buttrick held a council with their officers, not everyone in their ranks was ready to fight. One of the men from nearby Lincoln, James Nichols, was remembered as an amusing sort of fellow and a fine singer. "If any of you will hold my gun," Nichols remarked to his neighbors that morning, "I will go down and talk to them," meaning the British. Someone took his gun, and Nichols strolled down to the bridge by himself and had quite a conversation with the regulars. No one knows what was said, and Lieutenant Sutherland in his detailed account made no mention of this lone rebel dropping by for a chat. But afterward Nichols returned to his militia unit, retrieved his gun, and said simply that he was going home, and he did.[6]

Meanwhile, the grenadier companies in Concord proper were going about their search for weapons and supplies. By some accounts, they did so in the most genteel manner. The readily apparent matériel had long since been spirited away, and what was left had been hidden in ingenious ways. When a British officer pounded on Timothy Wheeler's door and demanded entrance to his barn, where a large quantity of provincial flour was stored, Wheeler got his key and graciously granted him admission. But when the officer expressed pleasure in his find, Wheeler launched into quite an act. "This is my flour," he told the officer indignantly. "I am a miller, Sir. Yonder stands my mill. I get my living by it. In the winter I grind a great deal of grain, and get it ready for market in the spring." Pointing to other barrels with exaggerated bluster, Wheeler proceeded to identify numerous barrels of "his" flour, "his" wheat, and "his" rye.

"Well," replied the officer rather glumly, "we do not injure private property," and with that he and his men withdrew, leaving the cache untouched.

Ephraim Jones doubled as a tavern keeper and the town jailer, but he had also been given custody of important papers from the provincial treasurer. Jones was initially taken prisoner and detained by a guard of five men with fixed bayonets, but after a short while they decided that he could be of better service if he opened his tavern and set up a round of drinks, which he did. But before they partook, the soldiers entered his house to search for rebel supplies. As the regulars approached the bedroom where the records were hidden, Hannah Barns, who boarded with the Jones family, defiantly stood in the doorway and insisted that it was her bedroom and contained only her property. Perhaps hearing the call that drinks were being served, the regulars left Miss Barns and the room unmolested.[7]

Similar incidents were taking placing near the South Bridge, where Captain Mundy Pole and his detachment had been dispatched. Entering several homes just beyond the bridge, Pole's troops ordered milk, potatoes, meat, and other refreshments for a late but much-needed breakfast. In the house of Ephraim Wood, one of those instrumental in hiding most of the stores a few days before, the regulars sought to arrest the owner, but he was not home. At the nearby home of Amos Wood, Ephraim's brother and a sergeant in a minuteman company, Pole's men graciously paid the female members of the household a guinea apiece for their breakfast. Searching the house, an officer found one room tightly locked and asked Dorothy Wood, Amos's wife, whether there were other females hiding there. Mrs. Wood, too, played her role well and by her answer, the officer took that to be the case. Gallantly, he told his troops, "I forbid any one entering this room!" and once again another cache of military stores was saved.[8]

All in all, it was estimated that the grenadiers broke open just sixty barrels of flour — out of a total of three or four hundred hidden around town — and "knocked off the trunnions of three iron twenty-four pound cannon, burnt sixteen new carriage wheels, and a few barrels of wooden trenchers and spoons."[9] It was a rather poor haul, but the fire that was started to destroy these pieces was to have severe consequences. A pile was set ablaze near the courthouse on the northernmost corner of the village common. This was on the road to the North Bridge and easily visible from the knolls to the west of the bridge that were now occupied by Barrett's and Buttrick's regiments. The fire got out of control and quickly spread to the nearby walls of the courthouse.

Martha Moulton, a seventy-one-year-old widow living next door, had found herself the unwilling hostess of some fifty or sixty officers and men who had been "in and out the house, calling for water and what they wanted" for some time. Initially, they ignored her cries to extinguish the blaze even as she stood in her doorway with a single pail of water in hand. Moulton recalled that only after she "ventured to put as much strength to her arguments as an unfortunate widow would think of" did the troops form a bucket brigade and put "one pail of water after another" on the fire. Whether they did so out of genuine concern or in response to Mrs. Moulton's fevered assertion that the upper floor of the building was filled with powder that was likely to explode and kill them all is open to speculation. So the courthouse and town buildings were saved, but the billowing smoke from the fire had already set events in motion at the North Bridge.[10]

On the rise to the west of the North Bridge, Colonel Barrett and Major Buttrick were still conferring with their officers. Their companies were formed in a line with those of Buttrick's regiment of minutemen on the right and Barrett's regular militia on the left as they faced the bridge. Lieutenant Joseph Hosmer interrupted this conference and pointed to a cloud of black smoke rising from near the town common. Unaware that Mrs. Moulton was goading her unwelcome guests into a bucket brigade, the observers surmised that the British had set fire to one or more buildings in town.

It is interesting that most contemporary and secondary accounts of the battle at Concord's North Bridge focus almost exclusively on the rebel militia facing the bridge and the town beyond it. Little is said of the British force at their rear—the 120-some men then deployed with Captain Parsons at Barrett's farm. To be sure, Barrett's and Buttrick's two regiments were being reinforced by companies and full regiments arriving from surrounding towns, and Parsons's numbers soon paled in comparison. But the fact that the militiamen ignored or at least downplayed this potential threat in their rear simply underscores their overriding concern for what the British were doing in the town. Protection of their families, homes, and property was their primary concern, not an armed confrontation with British forces.

For a moment or two, all stood transfixed by the smoke curling up from near the courthouse. Then Lieutenant Hosmer, not so much as a call to arms but as a "what-in-the-world-are-we-waiting-for" question, asked of his commanders the obvious: "Will you stand here and let them burn the town down?" The answer came in Colonel Barrett's command to march, with the minuteman companies on the right leading the column. And so down off the hill they came.[11]

There is an oft-told tale that the two regiments of rebel militia marched the final yards toward the North Bridge to the spirited sounds of fifes and drums playing "The White Cockade." The background to the story makes it almost too good to be true—but it may well be true. The tune was a traditional Scottish air that had been an unofficial standard of Charles Stuart, known to history as Bonnie Prince Charlie, during his attempt to restore the House of Stuart to the British monarchy. Stuart wore a white rose in his bonnet as a symbol of rebellion before his cause was defeated at Culloden in 1746. While Robert Burns's lyrics, including the famous line "He takes the field wi' his White Cockade," would not be written until 1790, the tune itself was a country dancing set piece much earlier.

To suggest, as some participants and historians did afterward, that this march was played to gall the British regulars with memories of Stuart's earlier rebellion is probably overreaching. Truth be told, the British rank and file were far too young to have seen service at Culloden or to have been much influenced by it. The only British officer near Concord to have been on the field at Culloden was General Gage, and he was miles away in Boston, for the moment blissfully ignorant of the extent of the calamity about to befall Colonel Smith's troops.

More likely, if "The White Cockade" was played at all that morning, it was chosen because it was a well-known and catchy tune. What does seem certain is that with the Acton company leading the regiment in column toward the North Bridge, Luther Blanchard, its

Rebel Triumvirate

Samuel Adams Politically savvy, media-conscious, and single-minded almost to a fault in his long-range goal, Adams enticed men from all walks of life with his talk of liberty. *Library of Congress*

John Hancock Fortuitously given a silver spoon by his uncle, Hancock used the greatest fortune in Boston as well as his ego to promote and defend the rebel cause. *Library of Congress*

Joseph Warren Young, charismatic, and able, Dr. Warren may have outshone both Adams and Hancock had he not sacrificed his life on Bunker Hill. *Library of Congress*

Thomas Gage Long Great Britain's military chieftain in North America, Thomas Gage walked a turbulent course between respect for his colonial neighbors and loyalty to his king. *Emmett Collection, Miriam and Ira D. Wallach Division of Art, Prints and Photographs, The New York Public Library, Astor, Lenox and Tilden Foundations*

Margaret Kemble Gage This John Singleton Copley painting showing a pensive and somewhat mysterious Mrs. Gage may have helped give rise to subsequent questions about her loyalties. *Putnam Foundation, Timken Museum of Art, San Diego, California*

James Warren and Mrs. James Warren (Mercy Otis), oils on canvas, John Singleton Copley
Only the younger John and Abigail Adams rivaled their mentors, James and Mercy Warren, as the power couple of pre-revolutionary Massachusetts. These paintings were likely commissioned about 1763 as Copley was achieving his reputation. James was a well-to-do merchant and farmer. Mercy was still largely occupied with raising five sons. When the time came, both had talked the talk of liberty for so long that there could be no turning back.
Bequests of Winslow Warren, Photographs © 2014, Museum of Fine Arts, Boston

Clarke-Hancock House "Come in, Revere; we are not afraid of you," John Hancock shouted down from an upper window in the wee hours of April 19. *Author's Collection, 2012 photo*

James Barrett House Colonel James Barrett was not home when British regulars came a-knocking, but his wife, Rebeckah, stood her ground in his stead. Their home has recently been restored. *Author's Collection, 2012 photo*

The Battle of Lexington Ralph Earl, an itinerant painter, and Amos Doolittle, an engraver, made a trip to Lexington and Concord to chronicle the recent action from first-person accounts. Regardless which side fired first, Earl's painting of Lexington Green clearly shows British regulars advancing on both sides of the meetinghouse after their confusion over choice of roads to Concord. *Print Collection, Miriam and Ira D. Wallach Division of Art, Prints and Photographs, The New York Public Library, Astor, Lenox and Tilden Foundations*

The Engagement at the North Bridge in Concord With the Buttrick House prominent on the bluff above, Earl depicted narrow ranks of British infantry firing in volleys and then retreating down the road toward Concord as rebel militia advanced to the bridge. Doolittle's caption on the subsequent engraving claimed it was "the Regulars who fired first on the Provincials at the Bridge." *Print Collection, Miriam and Ira D. Wallach Division of Art, Prints and Photographs, The New York Public Library, Astor, Lenox and Tilden Foundations*

Hugh, Earl Percy Lord Percy epitomized the British officer corps in his general disdain for all things colonial, but that opinion changed after he saw the rebels in action during the retreat from Lexington. *Library of Congress*

William Howe Brothers George, Richard, and William Howe had strong ties to North America. Campaigning for Parliament, William assured his constituents he would refuse to serve if ordered to fight against the colonies, but in the end, he could not refuse his king. *Library of Congress*

Ethan Allen and surrender Allen and his troops were not nearly as polished in uniform or manner as this painting suggests when he reportedly demanded the surrender of Fort Ticonderoga "in the name of the great Jehovah, and the Continental Congress." *Library of Congress*

William Prescott on the March Prescott led the way by lantern light to the heights of Bunker Hill and dug the entrenchments that would goad British regulars into a frenzied battle the next day. *Print Collection, Miriam and Ira D. Wallach Division of Art, Prints and Photographs, The New York Public Library, Astor, Lenox and Tilden Foundations*

Artemas Ward Forgotten by most, vilified by others, Ward was the first commander of what could be called a Continental Army. He understood that his key assignment was to protect the rebel encirclement of Boston.

Israel Putnam An experienced fighter from the French and Indian War, Putnam was eager to engage British regulars anywhere, any time. *Library of Congress*

John Stark Stark may have been the one indispensable man on Bunker Hill. Without his shrewd positioning and stalwart defense, Howe's plan to turn the rebel left may well have succeeded. *Emmett Collection, Miriam and Ira D. Wallach Division of Art, Prints and Photographs, The New York Public Library, Astor, Lenox and Tilden Foundations*

Burning of Charlestown Rebels would call it an outrageous act, but General Howe gladly accepted the Royal Navy's offer to burn Charlestown after snipers hidden in its buildings harried his left flank. *Emmett Collection, Miriam and Ira D. Wallach Division of Art, Prints and Photographs, The New York Public Library, Astor, Lenox and Tilden Foundations*

fifer, and Francis Barker, its young drummer, were giving the performance of their lives no matter which tune they called.[12]

But was the Acton company of minutemen supposed to be in front? Its commander was thirty-year-old Isaac Davis, a gunsmith by trade. The captain had left his wife, Hannah, and their four small children, the youngest of whom was but fifteen months old, and hurried eastward from Acton about five miles to the heights above the North Bridge. Davis was "serious and thoughtful" after the alarm that morning, Hannah later recalled, but he "never seemed to hesitate in the course of his duty." As he led his company away from his home, Davis turned toward his wife and appeared on the verge of uttering some parting endearment, but all he could manage was, "Take good care of the children."[13]

A half century later, what might be called the second battle of the North Bridge was fought in an exchange of letters and depositions from aging veterans of the engagement. The debate centered over whether a company of Concord men began leading the minuteman regiment down the slope from Major Buttrick's residence only to have Davis's company from Acton cut in front and take the lead. Some reports have the two companies arriving in tandem and drawing up alongside one another in front of the bridge. Whatever the exact order of march, there is little question what happened next.[14]

OBSERVING THE REBEL COLUMN COMING toward them, Captain Laurie and his troops at the bridge were genuinely surprised. This was not Captain Parker's small band hastily gathered on Lexington Green and then just as hastily dispersed. Here was a military column of apparently well-drilled and disciplined troops advancing toward their position. Ensign Jeremy Lister, who was with the company from the Tenth, recalled that the rebel advance was made "with as much order as the best disciplind Troops."[15]

With these men advancing toward him, Captain Laurie suddenly recognized what he should have known upon first crossing the bridge. The best defensive position was on the opposite (Concord) side of the bridge, with the bridge and river to his front and not to his rear. According to Laurie, his fellow company commanders and Lieutenant Sutherland, who among these higher-ranking captains was still being accorded a surprising degree of deference, heartily, if belatedly, concurred.

Laurie accordingly ordered the three companies to fall back across the bridge — and indeed they might have retreated all the way to Concord but for one of those little acts that suddenly and irrevocably changes the mood of a given moment. Ensign Lister claimed that it was his idea, but it may have come almost simultaneously from Laurie and the other officers. Thus Laurie's troops paused to rip up planks on the North Bridge to impede, if not outright prevent, the advancing rebel militia from pursuing them. (What Captain Parsons and his companies of regulars out on the road toward Barrett's farm may have thought about this maneuver is another matter.) Typical of his account, Lieutenant Sutherland asserted that he was the last to cross the bridge and in doing so "raised the first plank." [16]

Ripping up these planks was a destruction of property that galled the oncoming militia and, if anything, was just the sort of overt act that seemed to confirm that the smoke rising from the town was no accident. Major Buttrick announced, "If we were all his mind, he would drive them away from the bridge — they should not tear that up." Buttrick took no formal vote, but there were murmurs of approval among his men, and Amos Barrett remembered, "We all said we would go." Significantly, this rebel force, alarming though it appeared to Captain Laurie and his troops, had not yet loaded its weapons. That changed as Buttrick gave the order to load and gave further "strict orders not to fire till they fired first, then to fire as fast as we could." [17]

Colonel Barrett later testified that his orders had been largely the same: "to march to said bridge and pass the same, but not to fire on the King's Troops unless they were first fired upon." Accordingly, seeing the regulars continuing to rip up planks on the bridge, Captain Davis and the Acton company of minutemen "quickened our pace, and ran toward them." The companies behind them followed suit, and the approach of this determined column had the effect of hurrying the wrecking-party members off the bridge and back into their ranks.[18] Then, as on the green at Lexington that morning, an errant shot rang out.

Who fired this first shot is still a matter of conjecture. Thomas Thorp, who was a member of Captain Davis's Acton company, saw "a ball strike the water" of the Concord River on his right and then thought that "some other guns were fired over our heads." Thaddeus Blood, a private in Captain Nathan Barrett's company of Concord militia, also "saw where the Ball threw up the water about the middle of the river, then a second and third shot." Significantly, Blood also remembered that just before "a gun was fired," a British officer "rode up."[19]

Who was this man on horseback? By all accounts Captain Laurie was not mounted, nor, it seems, were his brother officers — except, quite possibly, for Lieutenant William Sutherland. It is impossible to know with certainty where and when Sutherland was mounted. If he indeed stopped, as he reported, and "raised the first plank" in destroying the bridge, he had to have been on foot at that point. He might easily have remounted and ridden to the left of the British line forming behind the bridge. This was the position that afforded the best view of the oncoming rebels. Did Sutherland fire the first shot — either as an excited accidental discharge or with more deliberate aim, as he may or may not have done that morning at Lexington? It is an intriguing question and an inviting proposition to blame one man — whatever his motives or inadequacies — for starting the firing at both confrontations.[20]

What is almost certain, however, is that the first shot came from the British side. Captain Laurie himself reported as much to General Gage in an after-action report: "I imagine myself that a man of my company (afterwards killed) did first fire his piece."[21] For his part, Sutherland was as adamant about the initial shot at Concord as he was about the first shot at Lexington. He claimed that the rebels had fired first at a cluster of men he was trying to form near the bridge and implied that he himself was dismounted at the time.[22]

These first shots—perhaps as many as three in total—were followed by a full volley from the British side. At least the front rank of one company of regulars that Laurie had positioned immediately at the eastern end of the bridge fired a ragged volley that wounded Luther Blanchard, the fifer, and put a stop to whatever music he was playing. Captain Davis gave the order to return fire, which the Acton men did, but another volley from the ranks of the regulars struck Davis and Abner Hosmer, a distant cousin of Joseph's, dead. Ezekiel Davis, a brother of the captain, came within a fraction of an inch of a similar fate when a ball passed through his hat and grazed his head.[23]

Solomon Smith wasn't sure whether it was Captain Davis or Major Buttrick as the regimental commander who had given the order to fire, but Smith quoted Buttrick as exclaiming, "Fire, for God's sake, fire!" Two British soldiers were killed, one of whom was left on the ground wounded and subsequently killed by a rebel with a hatchet blow to the head. This was a particularly grisly moment, and the British repeated accounts of it as an example of American savagery. For their part, the Americans were equally appalled, and it was excused "only by the excitement and inexperience of the perpetrator." The perpetrator later confessed that the deed "had worried him very much," but that he thought he was doing right at the time.[24]

Meanwhile, in Concord proper, Colonel Smith and Major Pitcairn had been supervising the search of the town and watching the bucket brigade save the courthouse at Mrs. Moulton's insistence. Into this scene rode Lieutenant Alexander Robertson with Captain Laurie's desperate plea for assistance at the North Bridge. If Smith in his usual deliberative way chose to consider the gravity of Laurie's situation and ponder his response, the sound of the first few scattered shots and then full-blown volleys sped his decision and told him that for the second time that day things had gotten decidedly out of hand. The colonel quickly assembled two companies of grenadiers—about sixty men—and personally set off for the bridge half a mile away.

But Colonel Smith was not the only British officer to be alarmed by the sounds of this firing. A mile and a half to the west of the North Bridge, at Colonel Barrett's farm, its mistress, Rebeckah Barrett, had been standing her ground in the face of Captain Parsons and his men. Parsons and his officers offered to pay Mrs. Barrett for refreshments—evidently water and perhaps some food, as a request by one of the sergeants for something stouter was refused both by Mrs. Barrett and his commanding officer. But Rebeckah Barrett also refused the proffered payments, saying, "We are commanded to feed our enemies."

In searching the Barrett house, the regulars took fifty dollars from a drawer but overlooked casks of musket balls, cartridges, and flints that were hidden in the attic and shrewdly covered by a layer of feathers. But then Parsons accosted Barrett's twenty-five-year-old son, Stephen, and on learning his identity ordered him ready to march for Boston in order to be sent to England to stand trial for treason.

Once again, Rebeckah Barrett showed some Yankee brass. She pointedly intervened and asserted that while Stephen was indeed her son, he was not the master of the house in his father's place and should not be detained. Parsons seems to have acquiesced and turned his attention to some gun carriages. He ordered them burned, but before his troops could get a blaze going they all heard the sound of musket fire coming from the direction of the North Bridge. Uncertain as to what was occurring, Captain Parsons formed his troops and started on the road back to Concord.[25]

With perhaps as many as one thousand rebels either assaulting the North Bridge or descending toward it from the nearby hills, there might have been quite a battle as Captain Parsons and Colonel Smith converged on Captain Laurie's tenuous position. But Laurie's men were not waiting around to find out. After firing several volleys and becoming entangled in some confusion as front ranks tried to drop to the rear and the others tried to step up, the three companies of the Fourth, Tenth, and Forty-Third regiments beat a hasty retreat back along the road toward Concord. "The weight of their fire," Ensign Lister wrote of the rebel onslaught, "was such that we was obliged to give way, then run with the greatest precipitance." [26]

Laurie's companies retreated until they met the reinforcements of grenadiers that Colonel Smith was hurrying from Concord. Once again, it would be fascinating to know the exact words that passed between Smith and one of his junior officers. Major Pitcairn had been in charge at the confrontation on Lexington Green, and now Captain Laurie had been responsible for another bloody encounter. What's more, Laurie had failed to secure the line of retreat for Captain Parsons's companies returning from Colonel Barrett's farm.

The remaining companies of rebel minutemen under Major Buttrick scrambled over the missing planks of the North Bridge behind the Acton and Concord men and found two regulars dead and another dying. As Amos Barrett recalled, "There were 8 or 10 that were wounded and a running and a hobbling about, looking back to see if we were after them." But then the rebels "saw the whole body coming out of town," and Buttrick ordered his troops "to lay behind a wall that run over a hill and when [Smith's grenadiers] got near enough, Maj. Buttrick said he would give the word fire."

Amos Barrett believed that had Buttrick given the order, "we would have killed almost every officer there was in the front." But the grenadiers halted, probably as Smith and Parsons conferred, and after about ten minutes they turned around and marched back to Concord, protecting Captain Laurie's retreat. [27] Who would protect Captain Parsons's retreat from Barrett's farm was another matter.

Captain Laurie reported his casualties at the North Bridge as three privates killed and four officers, a sergeant, and four other ranks — nine in all — wounded. These included Lieutenant Suther-land, who received a slight wound in his right breast. Among the rebels, Captain Isaac Davis and Abner Hosmer lay dead and Luther Blanchard wounded. "It is strange," Amos Barrett recalled, that "there were no more killed, but they fired too high."[28] Indeed, the mortal wounds to Davis and Hosmer were inflicted upon their heads.

The rebel dead were taken first to Major Buttrick's house, near the battlefield, and then to the Davis home in Acton, where Han-nah Davis saw to it that her husband, the captain, was "placed in my bedroom till the funeral. His countenance was pleasant, and seemed little altered."[29]

WATCHING THE REGULARS DISAPPEAR TOWARD Concord, the rebel militia — from Colonel Barrett and Major Buttrick down to the greenest recruit — appeared stunned by the exchange of fire that had just taken place and not sure of their next action. The smoke from the town that had sparked their initial advance had died down, suggesting there was no immediate rush to continue their advance. They were in possession of the North Bridge, which remained largely intact. No one seems to have given much notice to the troops of Parsons's companies in their rear.

"After a short time," recalled Solomon Smith of the Acton com-pany, "we dispersed, and, without any regularity, went back over the bridge." For a time, Thaddeus Blood confirmed, "every one appeared to be his own commander."[30]

Into this momentary confusion marched Captain Parsons and his men, fresh from Barrett's farm. The hairs on the backs of their necks must have been standing on end. There was no sign of Cap-tain Laurie and nary a redcoat in sight, only hundreds of rough-cut rebels with guns in their hands. Had Parsons halted his troops or commanded them to load, they might have all been killed or taken prisoner. But he simply kept them marching straight ahead.

"Notwithstanding" the casualties on both sides a few minutes before, Ensign Henry De Berniere, who had guided Parsons's detachment to Barrett's farm, expressed surprise that "they let Capt. Parsons with his three companies return, and never attacked us." Encountering the planks pulled up on the North Bridge, De Berniere assumed it was the work of the rebels, designed to impede the regulars' return, and not the work of his comrades. Despite the raised planks, "we got over," recorded De Berniere, but "had they destroyed it we were most certainly all lost." [31]

Minuteman Solomon Smith agreed. The regulars "passed us without molestation," and it was "owing to our want of order, and our confused state," recalled Smith, "that they were not taken prisoners." [32]

But the day's fight and casualties — on both sides — were far from over. Colonel Smith has faced pointed criticism from modern analysts for being slow to depart Concord. No doubt a small part of this apparent delay came from his usual deliberate manner of operation. But Smith also required time to re-form his widely scattered command. As Captain Laurie's beleaguered companies marched into the Concord town common with two companies of grenadiers covering their backs, Colonel Smith rode up the small rise of the cemetery hill north of the common to survey the scene.

Laurie's wounded were cared for, and horse-drawn chaises were appropriated from Concord stables to serve as makeshift ambulances. Major Pitcairn assembled the companies that had been searching Concord homes and buildings. Captain Mundy Pole was recalled from the South Bridge. Smith nervously watched both the road from the North Bridge — down which he expected Captain Parsons would come and from which he also perhaps feared an onslaught of rebels — and the road from Lexington, down which he desperately hoped to see some sign of the relief column he had requested of General Gage earlier that morning.

Smith couldn't believe his luck when he saw Parsons and his companies march over the North Bridge unopposed and arrive in town tired and thirsty but alive. There was no sign, however, of red-coated soldiers on the road from Lexington—only growing numbers of rebels in homespun filling the ridgelines and surrounding hills.

All this took time. Reverend William Emerson, watching from the ridge above Smith's position, recorded a scene of disarray and reported, "For half an hour ye Enemy by their Marches and counter Marches discovered great Ficklness and Inconstancy of Mind, sometimes advancing, sometimes returning to their former Posts, till at Length they quitted ye Town."[33]

A British history of the affair charged that Smith "delayed until noon; and those two hours were his ruin."[34] The latter proved correct, but the full two hours cannot be charged singularly to Smith's delay. By most accounts, the best estimate of the time of the encounter at the North Bridge was 10:00 a.m. Captain Parsons heard these shots while still at Barrett's farm. If he departed immediately—and it would have taken at least a few minutes to assemble his troops, as they were still searching the farm—it would have taken almost an hour to march the two miles from the farm, across the bridge, and into Concord, and it may well have taken longer. Given the necessity of awaiting the recall of Parsons's and Pole's troops, half an hour to prepare to march once they both arrived is much more likely. For Smith to have taken any less time to reorganize his column would have meant even more chaos on the road to Lexington than he was about to encounter.

Thus it was near high noon when Colonel Smith's column heard his command to march. Boston, depending on the route, was almost twenty miles away, and it had already been a long night and morning. Whatever his critics would say, Smith must have been eager to get out of Concord without further bloodshed on either side. It was clear from the activity on the surrounding hills that rebels were continuing to congregate. It was time to escape this melee and return to Boston—if they could.

Chapter 13

~

Retreat, If We Can

How was General Thomas Gage spending what would become such a momentous day? It had not started well. The general was awakened shortly after 5:00 a.m. on the nineteenth by the arrival of the messenger whom Colonel Smith had dispatched with a request for more troops even before Smith's column reached Lexington. Gage had gone to bed the night before quite confident that he had made arrangements for just such a contingency. In fact, the general may well have been planning all along to use a second force of overwhelming numbers to crush any rebel resistance that dared challenge Smith's advance.

Before retiring, Gage had issued orders to Lord Percy's brigade of three regiments and a battalion of Pitcairn's marines to be assembled and ready to march at four o'clock the next morning. All told, this amounted to about fifteen hundred officers and men and included such well-trained troops as those of the Fourth "King's Own" Regiment of Foot. Gage's first waking thought was that this force now stood ready to march. A quick inquiry showed otherwise.

Gage's orders—perhaps written by his confidential secretary, Samuel Kemble—were addressed to Lord Percy's brigade major, Captain Thomas Moncrieffe. In one of what a contemporary British history called "two stupid blunders we committed," they were delivered to Moncrieffe's quarters, but the captain was out for the evening. Moncrieffe later came home and went to bed oblivious of them. Consequently, as General Gage roused himself and heard Smith's recommendation for reinforcements, the troops of the First Brigade were sound asleep. Why Lord Percy himself, who had been with General Gage the evening before and supposedly reported to him that their plan against Concord was known, did not take steps to ensure that his brigade was at the ready is just another of the mysteries of that evening.

The second "stupid" blunder was even more incredible. As the regiments of the First Brigade hastily prepared to march, Percy waited expectantly for the battalion of marines. By the time his regiments were finally formed and squared away, it was well after 7:00 a.m. Still, there was no sign of the marines. With what seems like far too much patience considering the confusion that had befallen his own troops, Percy waited some more before finally sending an aide to determine their condition. The marines, too, were asleep. Their orders had been sent to Major Pitcairn's quarters and left there unopened, despite the fact that "the gentleman concerned in this business ought to have recollected that Pitcairn had been dispatched" with Colonel Smith. "This double mistake," the British history concluded, "lost us from four till nine o'clock, the time we marched off to support Col. Smith."[1]

Lord Percy took the route that Colonel Smith probably wished that he had taken instead of his watery crossing and slog through the marshes: south out of Boston by way of Boston Neck, westward through Roxbury, across the Charles River at the Cambridge bridge, and on through Cambridge toward Menotomy. Although it was midmorning, according to Percy, "all the houses were shut up, & there was not the appearance of a single inhabitant." Those who dared to peer out from shuttered windows saw a rather grand procession led by an advance guard of a captain and fifty men and two six-pound cannons—the latter calculated mostly for show, as Percy had declined to be encumbered with an ammunition wagon.

Consequently, the supply of six-pound shot was limited to what was held in the ammo boxes on the two gun carriages.

Behind this spear point marched the Fourth "King's Own" Regiment, Pitcairn's First Battalion of Marines, absent their commander, the Forty-Seventh Regiment, and the Twenty-Third "Royal Welch Fusiliers" Regiment, all trailed by a rear guard. All three regiments were missing their light infantry and grenadier companies, who were already out on the Lexington road with Colonel Smith. Though he was finally under way, Percy "could get no intelligence" concerning the fate of Smith's column until he "had passed Menotomy."[2]

Meanwhile, having dispatched Lord Percy to Smith's rescue, however belatedly, General Gage took time to answer two short letters from Lord Dartmouth. These had arrived on the sixteenth in the same pouch aboard the *Falcon* as Dartmouth's detailed instructions to strike a prompt and decisive blow. Both had been hastily written on the eve of the *Falcon*'s sailing from England, but they revealed Dartmouth's attention to North American details.

One letter suggested that British troops in Boston might routinely be supplied with coal from Cape Breton Island, thus avoiding the possibility that rebels might interrupt local deliveries. The other was a direct order for Gage to instruct the area commander at Saint Augustine, Florida, to deploy "not less than 100 Men and Officers in proportion to Savannah in Georgia." Gage, ever the loyal subordinate, assured Dartmouth that he would take the coal supply under consideration and that he had sent orders via Georgia's royal governor, Sir James Wright, to move the troops to Savannah.

When Wright received this letter from Gage several months later, however, the governor did not forward it to the Saint Augustine commander; Wright thought the presence of British troops in Savannah would only serve to excite public opinion in Georgia — exactly the situation Gage had been facing in Boston since 1768! The even greater irony is that Wright's reply to Gage was intercepted in Charleston, South Carolina, by the local committee of correspondence, and rebels ingeniously substituted a reply to the effect that everything was quiet in Georgia and there was no need to send troops.[3]

In his reply to Lord Dartmouth on April 19, General Gage made no mention of the day's brewing events.

LORD PERCY AND HIS MEN were not the only ones leaving Boston for Lexington that morning. Dr. Joseph Warren, who had sent Paul Revere and William Dawes riding to spread the alarm the prior evening, was now determined to get into the thick of the fighting. But how had Warren come to this decision? Warren's principal biographer notes, "A special messenger, early in the morning, brought to Warren the intelligence of the events that occurred in the morning at Lexington . . . and [Warren] directed [his student] to take care of his patients, mounted his horse, and departed for the scene of action."[4]

It is certainly possible that the rebel network slipped a messenger *into* Boston to report the Lexington news to Warren.[5] It is also possible that during this short night, Warren had planned all along to head for Lexington as soon as he could do so without raising undue suspicion. He was, after all, a member of the committee of safety, which was scheduled to meet again that day at the Black Horse Tavern in Menotomy. A more intriguing possibility, however, is that if Warren did indeed have an informant in General Gage's headquarters or household, might not the same report from Colonel Smith requesting reinforcements also have reached Warren and told him that something major was brewing?

In any event, Dr. Warren rode through Boston to the Charlestown ferry. That the guard upon it would have permitted so well known a rebel as Warren to pass out of Boston on this of all days reveals the depth of British ineptitude. The last person to whom Warren spoke on the Boston side reported him as saying, "Keep up a brave heart! They have begun it, — that either party can do; and we'll end it, — that only one can do."[6] Joseph Warren would never set foot in Boston again.

Somewhere between eight and ten o'clock that morning — reports differ as to the time — at least two Charlestown residents encountered the doctor "riding hastily out of town." By the time he reached Cambridge, Warren was behind Percy's relief column after it had crossed the Charles River bridge. As Warren reached Watson's Corner in North Cambridge (the intersection of present-day Rindge and Massachusetts Avenues), he encountered two stragglers from Percy's column who were attempting to steal an old man's horse. "The old man, with his cat and hat, [were] pulling one way, and the soldiers the other, [when] Dr. Warren rode up, and helped drive them off."[7]

Then Warren spurred his horse forward and attempted to make his way around Percy's column. He was stopped at the point of a bayonet and soon faced two officers who demanded, "Where are the troops?" Warren could justifiably say that he didn't know, and they left him alone. Warren appears to have followed Percy's column into Menotomy and then blended into the countryside as he sought out the committee of safety. Meanwhile, events had come to a head around Concord.

ALL EVENTS, BE THEY LARGE or small, have a tipping point. Two centuries after the battles at Lexington and Concord, American historian and novelist Wallace Stegner would refer to that tenuous balance as "the angle of repose." On April 19, 1775, about the stroke of noon, just such a point was reached somewhere on the hills surrounding the town of Concord. Having permitted Colonel Smith's reinforcement of grenadiers to cover Captain Laurie's retreat from the North Bridge without firing a shot, and also having allowed Captain Parsons's detachment to return unmolested from Barrett's farm, the rebel militia went from a posture of limited defense to a state of all-out attack.

Upon marching out of Concord, Colonel Smith once again deployed several light infantry companies as flankers along the ridge above the road leading eastward toward Lexington. The first major landmark en route was the crossroads of Merriam's Corner, where Bedford Road ran north. How the decision was made to oppose Smith's retreat and who made it are interesting questions.

The time-honored myth of a swarm of minutemen operating independently upon individual initiative has long been put to rest. Not only did minutemen and militia companies have different operational roles, there was also considerable command and control exerted at the company and regimental levels. At the North Bridge, Colonel Barrett and Major Buttrick each commanded a regimental structure. What was missing, as more and more companies and regiments converged on the Lexington-to-Concord corridor, was an overarching decision-making process and high command presence on the scene above the regimental level. This was not because one did not exist.

Just weeks before, the Massachusetts Provincial Congress had empowered its committee of safety to prosecute fully the defense of the colony—at least that portion of the colony with rebel sentiments. The committee had put a military command structure in place, incorporating the existing militia companies and regiments and their officers, and appointed six men of varying military abilities as generals. The difficulty on the morning of April 19 was in getting these general officers to a point on the battlefield where unified command decisions could be made and, as important, communicated to the various regimental commanders who were on the march.

Thus there was not one command decision by an individual or high-ranking group to move from tentative defense on Lexington Green and at Concord's North Bridge to a concerted, all-out attack.

But if command and control above the regimental level was lacking, the rumor grapevine was surprisingly speedy. The rebels' pause after the North Bridge skirmish and Colonel Smith's preparations to depart Concord gave time for the news of what had occurred on Lexington Green—including word that nine of their neighbors lay dead—to circulate among the rebel forces. Suddenly there was a pattern. The firings on the green and at the bridge melded from individual unfortunate events into what was quickly characterized as a concerted British effort to attack local residents and destroy their villages. In the emotion of the moment the day's occurrences took on the aura of a major invasion—something more than a foray or a raid.

There is something to be said for shock wearing off as well. No matter how well one is trained to prepare for combat, there is something about one's initial taste of battle that triggers a flood of emotions. Overlaying them is a degree of shock that takes some time to dissipate. The confusion and stupor among the rebels at the North Bridge as Parsons marched by is an example of this. But the news of bloodshed at Lexington was a tonic that sped renewed determination through all rebel ranks. Without an overarching directive, but with regimental and company control as the shock of what had transpired wore off, the rebels—under Barrett's and Buttrick's orders and those of other arriving regimental and company commanders—closed in on all sides of Smith's column and were susceptible to the nudge that broke the friction of the angle of repose.

This tipping point, this moment when armed frustration turned to outright vengeance and determined attack, occurred as the flanking companies of light infantry on the left of Smith's column closed with the main body to squeeze ahead of it and cross a small bridge over a fork in Mill Brook just beyond Bedford Road, at Merriam's Corner. No fifes and drums filled the air. The only music the column of regulars heard was the tramp, tramp, tramp of their tired feet. Edmund Foster, a twenty-year-old militiaman from Reading, who later became a minister, recalled that "silence reigned on both sides."[8]

Then, for the third time that day, a disputed shot resounded through the spring air. But unlike the first shots at Lexington and Concord, there was little argument over its origin. A preponderance of evidence suggests that it was fired from the rebel side, either intentionally or as an accidental discharge as someone stumbled in the rocks or climbed over a log. The result was that a company or two of the light infantry turned in the direction of the retort, presented their muskets, and fired a poorly aimed volley that by all accounts was once again high. But then the woods and fields erupted with the rattle of rebel musketry.

"Before we had gone ½ a mile," Lieutenant Barker of the King's Own recorded, "we were fired on from all sides, but mostly from the Rear, where People had hid themselves in houses 'till we had passed and then fired; the country was an amazing strong one, full of Hills, Woods, stone Walls, &c., which the Rebels did not fail to take advantage of, for they were all lined with People who kept an incessant fire upon us."[9]

Indeed, this action appeared to British regulars to be just the sort of fight that General Gage had predicted to Lord Dartmouth some six weeks before. "The most natural and eligible mode of attack on the part of the people," Gage wrote, "is that of detached parties of Bushmen who from their adroitness in the habitual use of the Firelock suppose themselves sure of their mark at a distance of 200 rods." Then, with the condescending air of superiority that so many British officers shared, Gage went on to say that, these tactics aside, he was "firmly persuaded that there is not a man amongst [them] capable of taking command or directing the motions of an Army."[10]

This, of course, was not true. There might have been a momentary lag in command and control above the regimental level, but this was no "wild and ungovernable" mob, as Gage predicted. Regimental and company leaders showed a remarkable sense of tactics and deployments as the British column sought to retreat. They had, after all, been using these tactics for generations against Indians and, more recently, against the French and their Indian allies. This was their type of warfare and terrain, and they would make the most of it.

THE LEXINGTON ROAD EAST OF Merriam's Corner was then a much more constricted route than it appears more than two centuries later. "The narrow road dropped at times into small ravines which were commanded by the hillsides above. At least two large sections of the route bent to the northward"—at what would be called Bloody Curve and Parker's Revenge—"with great trees on the west, and high bushes on the east." [11]

But first there was the challenge of passing Brook's Hill, also known as Hardy's Hill. Lieutenant William Sutherland, who appears

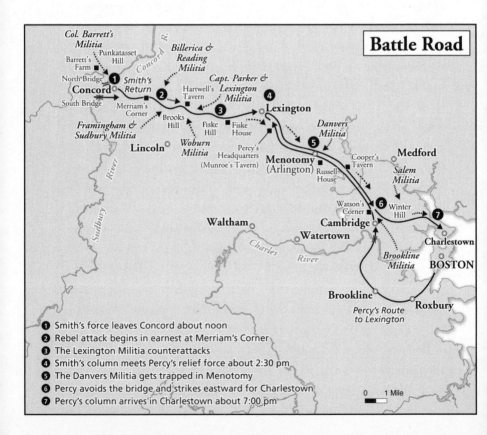

Battle Road

Col. Barrett's Militia
Barrett's Farm
Punkatasset Hill
Concord R.
Billerica & Reading Militia
North Bridge ① Smith's Return
Concord
② Hartwell's Tavern
Capt. Parker & Lexington Militia
South Bridge
Merriam's Corner
③ Lexington ④
Framingham & Sudbury Militia
Brooks Hill
Fiske Hill
Fiske House
Danvers Militia
Lincoln
Woburn Militia
Percy's Headquarters (Munroe's Tavern)
⑤
Menotomy (Arlington)
Russell House
Cooper's Tavern
Medford
Salem Militia
Waltham
Watson's Corner
⑥ Winter Hill ⑦
Cambridge
Watertown
Charles River
Charlestown
BOSTON
Brookline Militia
Brookline
Roxbury
Percy's Route to Lexington
Sudbury River
0   1 Mile

① Smith's force leaves Concord about noon
② Rebel attack begins in earnest at Merriam's Corner
③ The Lexington Militia counterattacks
④ Smith's column meets Percy's relief force about 2:30 pm
⑤ The Danvers Militia gets trapped in Menotomy
⑥ Percy avoids the bridge and strikes eastward for Charlestown
⑦ Percy's column arrives in Charlestown about 7:00 pm

not to have been seriously wounded at the North Bridge, recalled, "Here I saw upon a height to my right hand, a vast number of Armed men drawn out in Battalia [line of battle] order, I dare say near 1000 who on our coming nearer dispersed into the Woods & came as close to the road on our flanking partys as they possibly could." A little farther on, Sutherland observed another party to the left, and as the column of regulars moved through this gauntlet, the rebel fire "never Slackened." [12]

On the north side of the road, militia companies from Bedford, Billerica, and Chelmsford, as well as Edmund Foster's Reading company, fired from stands of trees that surrounded plowed pastures. The Chelmsford militia clustered around Sergeant John Ford, a grizzled veteran of the French and Indian War, and watched as Ford's musket brought down five British soldiers. But even Ford was surprised at the sudden intensity of the fighting. It was a day "full of horror," Ford recalled, and "the Patriots seemed maddened and beside themselves." [13]

There was equal rebel fury on the south side of the road. Here were at least nine companies of minutemen and militia that totaled about five hundred men and included units from Framingham and Sudbury, the former as far away as twenty miles to the south. News that the British were on the march for Lexington and Concord had reached Framingham before eight o'clock that morning, and within an hour the bulk of two companies of minutemen and one company of militia were hurrying northward for Concord. As a nineteenth-century history of Framingham recalled, barely had the men departed their town when "a strange panic seized upon the women and children" of the white households as someone started the rumor that "the Negroes were coming to massacre them all!" As the history concluded, "Nobody stopped to ask where the hostile Negroes were coming from; for all our own colored people were patriots." Indeed, Peter Salem, a twenty-five-year-old black slave, was one of the Framingham men assigned to Captain Simon Edgell's minute company. [14]

Edgell's company and that of Captain Micajah Gleason appear to have taken up positions "in the Lincoln woods" above Brooks Tavern and poured a deadly fire into the British column. Edgell and Gleason, along with Captain John Nixon of the West Sudbury minute company, which had been on the move since its appearance at the South Bridge, were all veterans of the French and Indian War, and they "acted in concert" to coordinate the attacks. It was reported that they "well knew the need of discipline in harassing a retreating enemy" and that "a single deliberate shot, from a man behind a safe cover, is effective, when a dozen hurried shots are harmless"[15] — further evidence that, far from being a disorganized rabble, the rebels were working together with deadly efficiency.

Colonel Smith and Major Pitcairn urged their column forward through this dangerous terrain, but there was worse up ahead. The narrow road dipped into the valley of Tanner's Brook and then began a strenuous climb up a higher hill on the other side. As it did so, the road made its first major swing to the north and entered a stand of timber. Not surprisingly, another ambush awaited. These were men from Woburn, seven or eight miles to the northeast. They had proceeded down the road in advance of the regulars, and when they came to the wooded knoll on the south side of the road, beyond the bridge at Tanner's Brook, their leader, Major Loammi Baldwin, recalled, "[We] then concluded to scatter and make use of the trees and walls for to defend us, and attack them."[16]

Edmund Foster's Reading militia company was among those shadowing Smith's column, and, seeing this same wood, it arrived on the north side of the road just as the regulars began to pass. The result, Foster reported, was that "the enemy was now completely between two fires, renewed and briskly kept up." The British force was likely Captain Lawrence Parsons's light infantry company from the Tenth Regiment, and he ordered flankers into the trees to rout the Reading men, but according to Foster, "they only became a better mark to be shot at."[17]

Now it was time to run. Exhausted though they were, the regulars advanced at the quick through what came to be called Bloody Curve, desperately trying to get ahead of the rebels outflanking them. The British officers were particularly hard-hit. The rebels undoubtedly targeted them, but in part that was because they were so conspicuous, brandishing their swords and exhorting their men. On the rebel side it was much more difficult to distinguish the officers from the rank and file, as they were mostly dressed alike and to a great extent hidden behind trees, stone walls, and rock outcroppings.

ONCE THE FRONT HALF OF Colonel Smith's riddled column was out of Bloody Curve, the deep ravines and dense woods gave way to plowed fields and open pastures, near the spot where Major Mitchell and his patrol had captured Paul Revere in the wee hours of that same day. The hurried pace took a terrible toll in fatigue—particularly among the flankers moving over rough ground—but the alternative was to slow down and become easier targets.

As it was, twenty-one companies marching in column by twos and makeshift ambulance chaises made for a procession almost half a mile long. Consequently, barely had the rear of Smith's column cleared Bloody Curve than his advance elements passed into a field of boulders, once again announcing more difficult terrain. Here the road curved south below a wooded ledge some forty feet high that bordered the road on the north. It ran along the road for about a hundred yards and sloped upward to the north along a low hill. This spot was on the boundary line between Lincoln and Lexington.

The flankers on either side of the British column, slowed by fatigue and the boulder field, had momentarily fallen behind. Blinded by the terrain and without protection on his flanks, Colonel Smith was very vulnerable despite his need for speed. Once again there was a unit of militia on hand to take full advantage of this, but unlike most of the other swarming rebels, these troops had already encountered Smith earlier that morning, and they were determined to avenge their dead neighbors who had fallen on Lexington Green.

Despite what in any other engagement would have been an

appalling dead-and-wounded casualty rate of 25 percent, out of the seventy-five-man contingent that assembled that morning, Captain John Parker had rallied his troops by ten o'clock and struck west from Lexington to await the return of Colonel Smith's force. To his subsequent chagrin, Parker had formed his troops in proper military order that morning. Now he would employ the Indian-style ambush attack that his men knew so well. And there was no better place to make it than this forested terrain on the Lincoln-Lexington line. They would still be defending their town.

Parker spread his men — reinforced by Lexington men who had lived too far away to respond that morning — along the wooded ledge above the road. This position offered a good view of the road to the west, and the ridge rising higher to the north offered a good defense against any flanking attempts. Their wait must have been filled with anxiety and a continued measure of disbelief over what had befallen them earlier. And, too, these Lexington men still had no concrete news about what had occurred at Concord.

Finally, about 1:00 p.m., after Smith had been under way from Concord about an hour, a rebel horseman galloped up to Parker and reported that the regulars had indeed fired on militia at Concord and were now attempting to escape back to Boston. As the sounds of battle came toward Parker's position, it reminded those who had been within earshot of the regulars' victory volley and the three cheers that had echoed across their green that morning after their neighbors lay dead and bayoneted.

With no flankers out front or to the sides, the first to ride into this waiting hornet's nest was Captain Parsons, with the ragged remains of his own company from the Tenth Regiment. These included Lieutenant Waldron Kelly, who had been wounded at the North Bridge, and Ensign Jeremy Lister, who had been so quick to volunteer the night before. Lister had been wounded in his right elbow during the exchange at Merriam's Corner. Smith rode just behind them, at the head of the main column, and his ample girth made for an easily recognizable target to those who had seen him in action that morning.

Behind them marched the light infantry company of the Fifth Regiment, followed by those of the Twenty-Third and Captain Walter Laurie's Forty-Third. Parker watched silently and with no small measure of satisfaction as these units hurried along his line of fire. When the first three companies were spread out below, the Lexington men unleashed a ferocious volley that slammed into the column along its left flank. Colonel Smith was among those hit. He suffered a wound in the thigh and dropped from his horse. Captain Parsons, so lucky in his return over the North Bridge, was wounded in the arm.

As Parker's men continued to fire, Major Pitcairn rode forward into this leadership void and directed a counterattack against the Lexington militia. He hurried companies of grenadiers from the rear of the column to assault Parker's right flank and sent the flankers who had been lagging on the right of the column around its head to harry Parker's left. Meanwhile, this action caused the following companies in the British column to begin to telescope inward upon each other along the road.

Parker's men continued to fire at will into the advancing British troops, but they were soon on the verge of being overrun. Jedediah Munroe, who had been wounded that morning on Lexington Green, was struck by another ball and this time fell mortally wounded. Parker had little choice except to withdraw from the location that is now called Parker's Revenge. As his men came off the hill, they scattered into the woods.

Pitcairn didn't dare follow. His objective was to clear their roadblock and urge the leading companies of the British column onward toward a small hill called the Bluff. Here he could defend the passage of the remainder of the column past Parker's abandoned position and also protect the route up the next obstacle, Fiske Hill. In desperation, Pitcairn turned to his own marines and ordered them to seize and hold the Bluff. His marines did so, and this gave Pitcairn time to reorganize the column before it fought its way up Fiske Hill.

But Parker's men had accomplished more than they knew. Their delay of Smith's column had given the companies of militia that had started the attack at Merriam's Corner time to leapfrog to the head of the British column and renew their attacks even as Pitcairn was riding madly about re-forming the head of his column. As these militia units took up positions along Fiske Hill, their volley fire again raked the British column. Pitcairn's horse was hit, and the major went sprawling in the dirt, irate but unhurt.

This new onslaught appeared to be the end of Smith's command. The road over Fiske Hill was steep and heavily wooded— another bloody box of rebel cross fire. For many a regular it was the end of any self-respect and discipline. As the advance companies of the column again appeared to stall on the hill, the following companies collided into them and in the melee all sense of order was lost. It quickly became every man for himself. This throng pushed past Fiske Hill but then was met with yet another obstacle— Concord Hill, on the outskirts of Lexington proper.[18]

"When we arrived within a mile of Lexington," Ensign Henry De Berniere recalled, "our ammunition began to fail, and the light companies were so fatigued with flanking that they were scarce able to act, and a great number of wounded scarce able to get forward . . . [and] we began to run rather than retreat in order."[19] What further peril awaited them at Lexington Green one could only guess.

To Lieutenant John Barker it appeared that their choices were that "we must have laid down our arms, or been picked off by the rebels at their pleasure."[20] As a last recourse, the few remaining officers who were not wounded "got to the front and presented their bayonets." They told the men that if anyone tried to flee, he would die.[21] To most, it mattered not whether they met their end from a rebel musket ball or a bayonet thrust by one of their own officers. It looked as if this was the end of Smith's column.

Chapter 14

~

Percy to the Rescue

As rebel minutemen and militia closed in for the kill on Colonel Smith's column just west of Lexington Green, an extraordinary thing happened. British soldiers who were being goaded by their officers to stand and fight looked beyond them toward Lexington and slowly began to raise a cheer. Their puzzled officers turned around and stared in disbelief. There on the rise beyond Lexington Green, where all this had started ten hours before, stood a thick line of red uniforms, dazzling in the afternoon sun. It was Percy.

Had Lord Percy's brigade gotten its wake-up call on time, his force of fifteen hundred men might have marched all the way to Concord and arrived about the time of the action at the North Bridge — perhaps in time to have dissuaded Colonel Barrett's men from marching down to the bridge. But that is conjecture. What is known is that about the time Colonel Smith departed Concord, Percy's force passed Menotomy, and shortly thereafter Percy "was informed by a person whom I met that there had been a skirmish between his Maj s troops & the rebels at Lexn, & that they were still engaged." [1]

Percy pressed on, and "in less than 2 miles we heard the firing very distinctly." It was at this point, as Percy claimed in the draft of his after-action report to General Gage, that he met Lieutenant Edward Gould of the light infantry company of the Fourth Regiment, who had been wounded in the foot at the North Bridge. Gould was riding in a commandeered chaise and had somehow managed to get ahead of Smith's column and avoid capture and further assault by the rebels. Gould told Percy that the grenadier and light infantry companies "were retiring, having expended most of their ammunition."[2] In his final report, Percy inserted the words "overpowered by numbers, greatly exhausted & fatigued" to describe their condition.[3]

Percy hurried his troops onward to the sound of the guns and "drew up the Brigade on a height" overlooking Lexington Green. Seeing the tangled column of Smith's men struggling toward him, he "immediately ordered the 2 field-pieces to fire at the Rebels." Percy claimed that the cannons, now being used for more than just show, "had the desired effect, & stopped the Rebels for a little time," while the grenadier and light infantry companies gratefully found refuge under Percy's protection.[4] "I had the happiness," Percy wrote his father the next day, "of saving them from inevitable destruction."[5]

Smith's column moved through the ranks of Percy's brigade and found shelter around Munroe's Tavern, east of the town green. With the bulk of Percy's regiments forming a shield and marksmen sniping away at rebels who ventured too close, Percy turned his attention to several houses that overlooked the British position and offered vantage points for rebel snipers. Colonel Smith probably reported to Percy that the rebels had already employed similar buildings for that use, and Percy ordered them razed.

Deacon Joseph Loring's house, barn, and corncrib were put to the torch, as were two more homes and workshops on the road closer to the tavern. Percy had his military reasons for undertaking this destruction, but it inadvertently triggered a disregard for private property among his rank and file. Soldiers whose comrades only a few hours before had been quite content to say "yes, ma'am" and respect any assertion of private property in the homes of Concord now helped themselves to plunder as they burned these homes and later drove rebel sharpshooters from others along the road to Menotomy. Such destruction served to infuriate the rebels all the more.[6]

By all accounts—including Percy's own—the one constant of calm and determination on the British side was Lord Percy. Oblivious to rebel fire, Percy rode among the battle-scarred troops of Smith's column and those of his own regiments and inspired a steady confidence that the situation was under control. It was—for the moment—but it still remained for this combined force to retire the remaining dozen or so miles to Boston. But first Percy permitted his troops to share their meager rations with Smith's beleaguered men and rest with them for half an hour along the roadside around Munroe's Tavern.

Meanwhile, Percy held a conference with Smith and Pitcairn and his regimental commanders and gave instructions for the order of march on the return to Boston. He wanted the companies of grenadiers and light infantry so recently engaged to move off first, and he "covered them with my Brigade." Smith in turn chose to put his grenadier companies, which had suffered less during the day than his light infantry, in the van. This meant that Captain Mundy Pole of the grenadier company of the Tenth Regiment would go first.

During the respite around Munroe's Tavern, the regiments of Percy's brigade afforded Smith's troops some measure of protection from rebel fire, but "as soon as they saw us begin to retire," Percy reported to General Gage, "they pressed very much upon our rearguard." And up ahead and on the flanks, Percy was obliged in "sending out very strong flanking parties, which were absolutely necessary, as there was not a stone-wall, or house, though before in appearance evacuated, from whence the Rebels did not fire upon us."[7]

ON THE REBEL SIDE ABOUT this same time, some small measure of command and control above the regimental level was introduced by the arrival of William Heath, one of the six generals recently appointed by the committee of safety. Heath was himself a member of the committee and had been a participant in its meeting at the Black Horse Tavern the day before. As Heath had returned to his home in Roxbury that evening, he had encountered Major Mitchell and his patrol moving along the Cambridge road.

Heath was thirty-eight and, by his own description, "of middling stature, light complexion, very corpulent, and bald-headed." From his childhood, Heath had been "remarkably fond of military exercises" and an avid reader of military treatises. Although he had no combat experience, this avocation placed Heath in good stead to serve as an officer in several militia units. These were initially loyal to the king but after 1770 took on an increasingly rebel nature. Heath was unanimously chosen captain of Roxbury's first company and then colonel of the first regiment of Suffolk County.[8]

General Heath awoke about daybreak at his home to the news that Colonel Smith's detachment had crossed the Charles River by boat and was marching on Concord. He set off to attend the day's meeting of the committee of safety and in so doing crossed the Charles River bridge en route from Roxbury to Cambridge. Given his later concern for this structure, it seems likely that it was Heath who ordered planks to be removed to impede just the sort of reinforcement that Percy was then belatedly organizing in Boston. But those performing the task piled the bridge planks neatly on the Boston side of the river, and Percy's advancing column had little difficulty replacing them on its initial crossing. This early rebel action under Heath's directive did, however, give Percy cause to worry as the day progressed about the condition in which he would find the bridge on his return march.

Heath met with the committee of safety—or at least some of its members. Exactly where this occurred is uncertain, because Elbridge Gerry and others had fled the usual meeting place at the Black Horse Tavern as Colonel Smith approached early that morning. Heath's memoirs, in which he refers to himself grandly in the third person as "our general," say only that "from the committee, he took a cross road to Watertown" and there found some militia "who had not marched" and were awaiting orders. By then, Percy's advancing regulars were, in fact, the troops Heath reported as "being in possession of the Lexington road."

Rather than rushing them directly against Percy, Heath dispatched the Watertown militia to Cambridge with directions to take up the planks on the Charles River bridge once again, barricade the south end of the bridge, and impede any and all British troops should they return that way to Boston. Heath then moved northward toward Lexington, and somewhere along the way he was joined by Dr. Joseph Warren, who had trailed Percy's column out of Cambridge searching for the committee of safety as it met on the run.

Heath arrived near Lexington shortly after Smith's column reached Percy's rescuers. He initially occupied himself with re-forming a rebel regiment that had been scattered by Percy's artillery, and then he and Joseph Warren followed Percy's combined column eastward as it made good Colonel Smith's escape. Warren had one close call, when a musket ball came so close to his head that it struck a pin holding a lock of his hair. He would not always be so lucky.[9]

HAVING HELD OFF THE REBELS converging on Lexington, Lord Percy adroitly protected his column with flankers beating the woods and fields alongside the road over the course of the three miles to Menotomy. He was beginning to think the worst was over. The tempo of the fight was slowing, and only a few scattered shots from flankers suggested continuing danger. The grenadier companies of Smith's force descended the grade of Peirce's Hill (now Arlington Heights) toward a point called Foot of the Rocks and looked with satisfaction over the relatively flat ground that stretched ahead on either side of the road for a distance of almost a mile.

Menotomy wasn't much of a place — it was more a collection of houses and buildings strung along the Lexington-to-Cambridge road than a town of residential blocks and cross streets. Though it lacked size and population, Menotomy sat at a major intersection of roads leading not only east to Cambridge and west to Lexington but also north to Woburn and Medford and south to Watertown and Waltham. As rebel militia were about to prove, it was easy to get to Menotomy from all points of the compass.

Colonel Smith and Captain Pole looked down Menotomy's one major street and saw frenzied activity. Just three hours before, Percy's relief column had marched through and encountered hardly a soul. The hairs on Smith's stout neck bristled as he and his few remaining officers—many of whom desperately wished that the rebels would form up on open ground and give what to them was a fair fight—now saw that once more they would be forced into a gauntlet of rebel fire. Percy had about two thousand rebels hounding his rear, and now—thanks to the road network converging on Menotomy—there were another two thousand or so armed men blocking the route through town. These were largely fresh troops from three regiments of minutemen and one regiment of militia augmented by scattered companies.

But some of the rebels made a critical mistake. Without any overall command and control and the intelligence that goes with it, each regimental commander—and sometimes each company commander—made his own decision about where to deploy his troops. Many chose to hunker down in houses, buildings, and yards along the road, assuming that Percy's column would come marching gaily along it. Percy was much too shrewd for this and had already had a taste of a town fight through the buildings on the outskirts of Lexington. Colonel Smith could only add his own deadly experiences.

The result was that Percy strengthened his flankers and sent them from house to house in advance of his main column. Given the narrow nature of the town strung along the road and the wide sweep that Percy ordered his flankers to take, some rebel units were trapped between the main British column and the flankers. It made for a fierce fight. In fact, of every place that saw action that day, this stretch of road through Menotomy was the most heavily contested, and casualties along it were the heaviest on both sides.[10]

As the Fourth Regiment's John Barker observed, "We were now obliged to force almost every house in the road, for the Rebels had taken possession of them and galled us exceedingly, but they suffer'd for their temerity for all that were found in the houses were put to death."[11]

Almost all. Joseph Adams was a deacon of the Second Precinct Church. For whatever reason, he had not mobilized with the local militia, perhaps because he was not a member or because his wife had just given birth to a little girl. When Adams saw Percy's column returning amid the firing, however, he had second thoughts about staying at home and took off running across the fields. Regulars fired a volley in his direction, but it missed. Adams took shelter in a nearby barn and hid under the hay. Some of the soldiers followed and repeatedly stabbed the hay in pursuit, but Adams managed to lie still and avoid their thrusts.

Other soldiers entered the Adams house and made their way to the bedroom, where Hannah Adams lay clutching her newborn daughter. They ordered Hannah out of the house so they could burn it. She rose and painfully made her way to an outbuilding, fearful for her five other children, who remained hidden under a bed. Thanks to the precocious nine-year-old who poked his head out from underneath and taunted the regulars, they were discovered and chased outside unharmed.

The soldiers finished ransacking the house, taking an heirloom clock and a silver tankard from a communion set among their bounty, and packed it off in the sheets from Hannah's bed. Before leaving, they dumped a basket of wood chips on the floor and set them on fire with a hot brand from the hearth. Hannah Adams need not have worried about her young brood, however. After the regulars moved on, her children made their way back into the house and put out the fire with a quantity of home-brewed beer.[12]

A little farther down the road, fifty-nine-year-old Jason Russell had a less pleasant experience. He and his family sought refuge away from their home, but after going with them some distance, Russell, who was partially lame, returned to look after the house. He piled wooden shingles up beside his gate as a makeshift breastwork and waited. A neighbor urged Russell to abandon his post, but Russell refused.

As the flankers approached the Russell house, a party of Danvers militia found themselves in danger of being trapped between the flankers and the main British column, and, despite its proximity to the road, they took shelter inside the Russell house. Blasted by a hail of British bullets, Russell followed them, but as Russell limped through the doorway, two bullets struck him down. The regulars rushed him and put eleven bayonet wounds in his body. Inside, seven of the Danvers men were killed. Other rebels took refuge in the cellar and shot a British soldier who attempted to descend the stairs. Another soldier died in the melee upstairs. When it was over, twelve lay dead in this one location alone: nine Danvers men (seven inside and two in the yard), Russell, and two British soldiers, making the Russell house the bloodiest site of the day.[13]

There is another oft-told story from the fight at Menotomy. Samuel Whittemore was an eighty-year-old former militia officer who lived with his wife, son, and grandchildren. After the continuing alarms and the passage of both Smith's and Percy's columns through town that morning, Samuel's wife, Elizabeth, made preparations to flee to the safety of another son's house, toward Medford. Elizabeth presumed that Samuel would accompany her until she found him oiling his musket and pistols and sharpening his sword. He refused to leave and sent Elizabeth off with their grandchildren.

Whittemore took up a position almost five hundred feet from the main road, being close enough for an effective shot but not so close as to get pinned by the roving flankers. When Percy's troops came into view, Whittemore fired a round from his musket and killed the soldier he aimed at. As flankers saw the puff of smoke and closed in on his hiding place, Whittemore fired his two pistols and killed two more, one instantly and another with a wound that would later prove fatal. But now the flankers had his range, and a musket ball struck the old man in his head and rendered him unconscious. Regulars rushed the spot and may have been surprised to discover Whittemore's white hair and grizzled age, but that did not stop them from clubbing him with their muskets and adding a few bayonet jabs for good measure.

By all accounts, the regulars left Samuel Whittemore for dead. The "incessant fire, which like a moving circle surrounded and followed us," as Percy described it, moved on with the British column. Residents who then gathered around Whittemore's body also presumed him dead. But his old heart was still beating. Less than optimistic, they carried him to Cooper's Tavern and summoned a doctor. The doctor pronounced it useless and a waste of time to dress his wounds because he would soon be dead. But that didn't happen. Not only did Samuel Whittemore survive, he lived to see the end of the Revolution and did not die until the age of ninety-eight. During his recovery, when Elizabeth, no doubt with a reproving frown, asked him if he did not now regret that he had not fled with his family, Whittemore supposedly replied, "No! I would run the same chance again."[14]

The same could not be said for two customers of Cooper's Tavern, which stood just east of the crossroads where Samuel Whittemore made his stand. Proprietors Benjamin and Rachel Cooper had already had one excitement that morning when a group of Menotomy men judged too old to mobilize with the town's militia nonetheless assembled at their tavern and then went off to capture a supply wagon that was lagging behind Percy's outbound column. These old-timers were so successful that they next captured the wounded Lieutenant Edward Gould after he parted from Percy and made his way toward Boston in his commandeered chaise ahead of Percy's column. None of this activity, however, kept Jason Winship and Jabez Wyman, two regular customers who were in their forties, from having their usual afternoon mug of flip at Cooper's.

Colonial flip was not for the faint of heart. Served in a large mug or pitcher, flip consisted of about eight ounces of beer, sweetened to taste with a quantity of sugar, molasses, or dried pumpkin, and then topped off with about a gill of rum—four ounces. The bartender stuck a red-hot iron poker into the mixture, and this produced a flurry of foaming and bubbling and gave flip its trademark burned and bitter taste.

In the manner of regular drinkers unperturbed by events around them, Winship and Wyman were sipping their flip, seemingly oblivious to the sounds of approaching musket fire, when British regulars stormed into Cooper's Tavern. They did not stop to notice that these patrons were unarmed and otherwise engaged. Benjamin and Rachel Cooper hid in the cellar, but according to the Coopers' subsequent testimony Winship and Wyman were repeatedly stabbed and horribly beaten, "their heads mauled, skulls broke and their brains dashed out on the floor and walls of the house." Later, more than one hundred bullet holes were counted in the tavern's walls. It was yet another indication of the growing savagery on both sides.[15]

That thirsty British soldiers undoubtedly helped themselves to the remaining flip and had been doing so with other beverages at taverns of convenience en route only served to increase the ferocity of their actions. Lord Percy and Colonel Smith didn't want to admit it, but they were losing control of their men. "The plundering was shameful," Lieutenant Barker, who had been all the way to the North Bridge, reported. "Many hardly thought of anything else; what was worse they were encouraged by some Officers."[16] Lieutenant Mackenzie, who marched with Percy, acknowledged, "many houses were plundered by the Soldiers, notwithstanding the efforts of the Officers to prevent it." Mackenzie speculated that this behavior "influenced the Rebels, and many of them followed us further than they would otherwise have done."[17]

THERE REMAINED ONE MORE MAJOR building to pass before Percy's column could rid itself of Menotomy. This was the Black Horse Tavern, at what is now the intersection of Massachusetts Avenue and Tufts Street. When it was finally cleared, the British troops were able to cross Alewife Brook and proceed toward Cambridge.

The fight at Menotomy had not only cost Percy valuable men but valuable time as well. It was well past five o'clock, and darkness would be upon his command within two hours. In Menotomy alone, the British lost forty men killed and about eighty wounded, about half their casualties for the entire day's fighting. On the rebel side, it was more difficult to assign figures to this piece of ground, but estimates totaled twenty-eight killed, at least ten wounded, and three captured.[18]

Now, with Cambridge looming up ahead, Percy faced perhaps his most important decision. Having just endured the passage through Menotomy, Percy worried that Cambridge, long a hotbed of rebel sentiment, might give him an even warmer reception. On its northern outskirts, two roads diverged. One was the route over which Percy had ridden so confidently at midday: through Cambridge, across the Charles River bridge, and back to Boston via Roxbury, Brookline, and Boston Neck. The rebels were expecting him to return by this route. The other led almost due east to Charlestown. Although this second route would not return his command to Boston proper, it was slightly shorter, and once in Charlestown, Percy would have both a strong, defensible line at the narrows of Charlestown Neck—in those days about as narrow as Boston Neck—and the protection of the British men-of-war guarding the Charlestown-to-Boston ferry crossing.

There was also the matter of the bridge over the Charles River. Percy simply could not be sure that it was intact. His column had found planks missing on its crossing that morning—thanks to General Heath's diligence. His men had encountered little difficulty repositioning them, but this slowed their supply wagons and may have contributed to one wagon being captured by the feisty old-timers of Menotomy.[19] Now, however, the Watertown militia had removed the bridge planks once again and taken up positions to defend the crossing.

There has been speculation as to whether Percy himself could see that the bridge was impassable and/or heavily defended—or at the very least whether he had scouting reports that it was — before he made his decision to detour around Cambridge and strike for Charlestown. If Percy sent his column cutting eastward in the vicinity of the back road of Kent Lane in Cambridge (south of the present-day Massachusetts Avenue and Somerville Avenue intersection), as seems likely, it would have been impossible for him to observe the bridge himself from that distance.[20]

In hindsight, Percy made the correct decision to bypass Cambridge, but he seems to have done so in order to avoid another Menotomy rather than because he knew for certain that the Charles River bridge was impassable. In fact, the draft of Percy's report to General Gage supports this: "We retired . . . under an incessant fire all round us, till we arrived at Chastown, wh road I chose to take, lest the rebels shd have taken up the bridge at Cambridge (wh I find was actually the case), & also the country was more open & the road shorter."[21]

It is certainly clear that Percy's sudden turn to his left flank momentarily disrupted the rebel strategy. "We threw them," Lieutenant John Barker later gloated, "and went on to Charles Town without any great interruption."[22] But it wasn't quite that easy. There was indeed a warm welcoming committee spread throughout Cambridge, and there likely would have been a pitched battle at the bridge. As it was, some militia once again moved rapidly to get in front of Percy's advance, taking up positions on Prospect Hill, a piece of high ground en route to Charlestown Neck. Percy was down to the last of his cannonballs, but he fired them to scatter the rebels until his troops could plod by. Even then, he might have been cut off from the safety of Charlestown Neck but for the inaction of militia from Salem, which would add one final controversy to the day's events.

ONE CAN SUPPOSE THE MEN of Salem felt both anger and a sense of obligation regarding the events of the prior February — anger at the British regulars who had then marched so boldly through their town and a sense of obligation to the minutemen from neighboring towns who had come so quickly to the town's aid. Twenty-nine-year-old Colonel Timothy Pickering commanded the Essex County regiment, composed of militia companies from Danvers, Salem, and Marblehead. This April morning, he was working quietly at his office in the Registry of Deeds at Salem when sixty-four-year-old Captain Daniel Epes of the Danvers company reported with news of the initial British march and asked for orders. Pickering and Epes agreed that because the Danvers company was already assembled and closer to the action, it would march and not wait for the rest of the regiment. This decision itself was to have major ramifications as Epes and his Danvers men rushed into the fight at Menotomy and suffered horrible casualties at the Russell house.

Meanwhile, Colonel Pickering's next move was to call a meeting of Salem's board of selectmen. Given the distance between Salem and Concord, and not yet knowing what would ensue on Percy's retreat through Menotomy, many militiamen in Salem assumed that the regulars would be safely back in Boston before they could take the field. But the public relations side of the equation prompted a show of support for their neighboring towns. Pickering formed his companies of Salem men, numbering about three hundred, or roughly half his regiment, and started west. The Marblehead company did not join this advance because many of its members were absent, having gone fishing, and the remainder were reluctant to leave their town unguarded with a British warship anchored in its harbor.

The subsequent controversy centered on the speed of Colonel Pickering's march. Had he delayed several hours at the start, he might not have been faulted, but to some his conduct appeared to be just fast enough to satisfy neighboring towns that Salem was doing its share but not so quick as to make a headlong rush into action. Like their British counterparts, the Salem men took refreshment along the way at the only places available: the roadside taverns. Twice Pickering ordered long rest stops near such establishments, each time in full expectation of receiving news of the British withdrawal. When none was forthcoming, it was the murmurs of his troops that encouraged him onward, not his own impatience.

Finally, Pickering received reports that far from being in a backwater, the Salem men were very close to the line of Percy's surprise withdrawal to Charlestown. Pickering finally quickened the pace, and as the Salem militia crested Winter Hill, near Charlestown Neck, they found Percy's column strung out below. Had Pickering instantly attacked, at the very least Percy would have had to fight one more bloody encounter as he pushed his beleaguered troops across the neck and onto the defensible heights of Bunker Hill. It is also possible that Pickering's strong fire on Percy's left would have delayed his advance and permitted the militia assembled in Cambridge to catch up and wreak more havoc, particularly as by all reports Percy's ammunition was almost exhausted.

But instead of attacking, Pickering sent a messenger in search of General Heath, asking for orders. According to Pickering, Heath responded "that the British had artillery in their rear, and could not be approached by musketry alone; and that he [General Heath] desired to see me." Percy's disposition of artillery had, of course, been the case all afternoon and had not dissuaded other attacks. Heath's memoirs recounted the arrival of "an officer on horseback"—perhaps Pickering himself—but did not recount any orders Heath gave in return, only the speculation that had the men from Salem "arrived a few minutes sooner, the left flank of the British must have been greatly exposed." The end result was that the Salem men did not fire on Percy's brigade, and his troops completed their withdrawal across Charlestown Neck.

Timothy Pickering went on to a far more successful career than William Heath, serving as the Continental Army's quartermaster general and much later as secretary of state. Although Heath was appointed a major general in the Continental Army, he botched actions during the Trenton and Princeton campaigns and was relieved of serious command. What brought this 1775 incident to the forefront years later were political claims made against Pickering when he was a senator from Massachusetts. Pickering was a dedicated Federalist, and some, including Mercy Warren, in her history of the Revolution, speculated that his delay in engaging Percy that day was "owing to timidity, or to a predilection in favor of Britain."[23] Regardless of Pickering's actions that evening of April 19, General Heath posted patrols on Charlestown Neck and ordered the remainder of his fledgling army into camp in Cambridge as Percy's troops moved into Charlestown.

Under threat of being bombarded by the British fleet and burned, Charlestown did not resist Percy's arrival. Instead, the selectmen assured Percy that if he would not attack the town, they would see that his troops were not molested and would do all in their power to get them across the ferry to Boston, but that did not keep Percy's frazzled soldiers from being edgy after the events of the day. As his men marched into town, a lad of fourteen perched in the window of his house to watch their procession. Having endured hostile fire from many such windows, soldiers let loose some shots and struck the unarmed boy dead.[24]

For all it had been a very long day. Its fury was evidence of the long-simmering frustrations on both sides. The rebels were sick of chafing under the yoke of what they considered second-class status, conferred by a repressive system. The regulars were just as fed up with their perceived roles as royal nursemaids to an ungrateful brood. According to historian Robert Middlekauff, the retreat from Lexington through a countryside in arms foreshadowed the reality that the British would face throughout the coming struggle: "how to subdue not just another army but a population in rebellion."[25]

As the twilight darkened and the moon once again rose over Boston Neck, there was many a British soldier who thankfully tumbled into the safety of his lodgings or tent and wondered what in the world had happened during that long, long day. On the rebel side, as these men also fell exhausted in homes, taverns, and on the roads leading toward Boston, there was a common refrain: "What have we done?"

Chapter 15

~

What Have We Done?

As both sides struggled to determine *what* each had done, on the rebel side the events of the day raised the broader question of *why* had they acted—not merely why they had fired on the king's troops, no matter which side shot first, but why they were pursuing a determined, armed resistance against the established government. There was no one answer, and whatever answers were given varied with the retelling of events and were influenced by the context of the times in which they were told. With that caveat, it is nonetheless instructive to recount the oft-told tale of Levi Preston of Danvers.

Preston was a young man of eighteen that spring, and his title of captain would come later. He was one of the Danvers militia who rushed headlong into the fight at Menotomy. Sixty-seven long years after that fight, when Preston was approaching ninety, Mellen Chamberlain, then a young man of about the same age as Preston had been in 1775, interviewed the old warrior.

"Capt[ain] Preston," Chamberlain asked, "what made you go to the Concord fight?"

The old man straightened in his chair and repeated the question. "What did I go for?"

"Yes," Chamberlain answered. "My histories all tell me you men of the Revolution took up arms against intolerable oppression. What was it?"

According to Chamberlain, Preston launched into disavowals that it hadn't been about stamps or tea or taxes or high-minded writings about the principles of liberty. "Well, then," queried Chamberlain again, "what was the matter?"

"Young man," bristled Captain Preston in reply, "what we meant in fighting the British was this: We always had been free and we meant to be free always!" [1]

It makes a patriotic story. It may well have been tempered by Preston's age and Chamberlain's retelling, but in almost two and a half centuries since that day on Lexington Green and in the fields and hills from Concord to Menotomy, Preston's reply became the most basic and cherished answer to the question, why did they do it?

ON THE MORNING OF APRIL 20, 1775, Boston and the towns of Charlestown and Cambridge, across the river, were scenes of chaos. Those British troops who had staggered home from Concord saw to their wounded and pondered what had happened to several trained regiments of one of the world's better armies. Loyalists were aghast at the rebels' determined show of force. And while a few rebels celebrated, most were as stunned by the violence as their loyalist neighbors were.

If, when he heard the first musket fire from Lexington Green, Samuel Adams indeed chortled and said to John Hancock that it was a great day for America, even Adams must have been horrified — or at the very least surprised — by the ferociousness of the fighting. The pent-up frustrations of a decade had exploded on both sides.

"You will easily conceive," Lord Percy wrote to an officer friend in England, "that in such a retreat, harassed as we were on all sides, it was impossible not to lose a good many men." [2] Reports of British casualties varied, but Ensign De Berniere recorded seventy-three dead, 174 wounded, and twenty-six missing. Of these, there were eighteen officers, including Lieutenant Edward Hull of the Forty-Third, mortally wounded at the North Bridge; the mercurial Lieutenant William Sutherland of the Thirty-Eighth, wounded slightly at the North Bridge; and Lieutenant Edward Gould of the Fourth, who was wounded and listed as missing after his capture outside Menotomy.

In his official report to General Gage, Percy speculated that the British casualties were much less than the number "I have reason to believe were killed of the Rebels." But the rebels actually fared considerably better. A total of fifty were killed or mortally wounded. Fewer rebels were wounded — thirty-nine compared to 174 for the British — because the protective cover of rocks, trees, fences, and buildings had shielded many of them. These rebel casualty counts did not include civilians, such as Jason Russell of Menotomy, but, significantly, they were spread over minuteman and militia units from twenty-three towns — stark evidence that Lexington and Concord's neighbors had rushed to their aid and that the Massachusetts alarm system was highly effective. Despite the carnage at Menotomy, the town of Lexington bore the highest number of rebel casualties for the day — ten killed and ten wounded.[3]

Among those rebels and regulars most critical of the expedition was Lieutenant John Barker of the Fourth "King's Own" Regiment. "Thus ended this Expedition," Barker wrote of his regiment's return to Boston, "which from beginning to end was as ill plan'd and ill executed as it was possible to be." The litany of failure in Barker's eyes was long: the three hours slogging around the Cambridge marsh, the consequent late arrivals in Lexington and Concord — all delays that gave rebel militia time to converge on Menotomy from as far as twenty miles away. And what had the British accomplished? "Thus for a few trifling stores," Barker wrote, summing up their bounty, "the Grenrs. And Lt. Infantry had a march of about 50 Miles (going and returning) through an Enemy's

Country, and in all human probability must every Man have been cut off if the Brigade had not fortunately come to their Assistance."[4]

Lord Percy was in no position to be so critical, but he could certainly express his surprise about the rebel resistance. "For my part," Percy wrote, "I never believed, I confess, that they wd have attacked the King's troops, or have had the perseverance I found in them yesterday." Gone was a great deal of Percy's smugness about British superiority and his disdain for the perceived lack of rebel command and control. "Whoever looks upon them as an irregular mob," Percy continued, "will find himself much mistaken. They have men amongst them who know very well what they are about."[5]

Other British officers found the rebel tactics of shooting from behind cover quite despicable and hardly worthy of His Majesty's troops. Captain W. G. Evelyn commanded a regular infantry company in the King's Own and marched with Percy to the rescue. Evelyn reported in a letter to his father back in Ireland that the "bickerings and heartburnings" with the rebels had come to blows "between us and the Yankey scoundrels." He found the rebels "the most absolute cowards on the face of the earth" because they would not fight in open fields by rank and file. But despite their lowly tactics, Evelyn worried that "they are just now worked up to such a degree of enthusiasm and madness that they are easily persuaded the Lord is to assist them in whatever they undertake."[6]

General Gage waited three days to receive full reports from Lord Percy and Colonel Smith before writing his own reports to his superiors in London. To Lord Dartmouth, Secretary of State for the Colonies, Gage first noted the receipt of Dartmouth's letters up to the one dated February 22, including the secretary's lengthy missive concluding that the time had come when His Majesty's government "must act with firmness and decision."[7] The originals of these dispatches had arrived on board the *Falcon* on April 16, and Gage evidently sought to assure Dartmouth that he had acted upon them promptly. Unfortunately for Gage, the result had been to no one's liking. In recounting the events of April 19, the only good news Gage imparted was that "too much Praise cannot be given Lord Percy for his remarkable Activity and Conduct" and his speculation that "the Loss sustained by those who attacked is said to be great." [8]

To Lord Barrington, the longtime secretary of war, Gage bookended the news about Lexington and Concord with mundane acknowledgments of promotions and recommendations for further promotions. He eased into the most important news with what in retrospect seems a decided understatement: "I have now nothing to trouble your Lordship with, but of an Affair that happened here on the 19th." To both Dartmouth and Barrington, Gage concluded with the obvious: "The whole Country was Assembled in Arms with Surprising expedition, and Several Thousand are now Assembled about this Town, threatening an Attack, and getting up Artillery; and we are very busy in making preparations to Oppose them." [9]

Then, either out of lackadaisical indifference or an outright attempt to downplay the importance of this news, Gage — or, more accurately, probably his secretary, Samuel Kemble, the younger brother of his wife, Margaret — affixed seals and entrusted both letters to the two-hundred-ton merchantman *Sukey* instead of to a faster dispatch ship of the Royal Navy. The *Sukey* cleared Boston Harbor and set sail for England on April 24.

GENERAL GAGE WAS CORRECT: THERE were many people flocking to Boston and its environs, but not all were rebels. There was also a rush of loyalists in the same direction. Their aim was to get into Boston and under General Gage's protection — however tenuous — before rebel siege lines rendered access difficult if not impossible. In the weeks ahead, these lines would expand to encircle Boston, with the goal of keeping General Gage and his troops penned up there.

Josiah Sturtevant, the local doctor in the town of Halifax, near Plymouth, who had long espoused "the cause of the king," galloped north in fear for his life as soon as word came of the fighting at Lexington and Concord. By one report, Dr. Sturtevant rode in such haste that he lost his saddlebags. General Gage rewarded him for both his effort and his loyalty. The doctor was commissioned a captain in the British army, and Gage gave him responsibility for the army hospital. But things didn't work out so well for Dr. Sturtevant. He became infected with smallpox and died four months later. His wife, Lois, was particularly bitter, writing upon his death, "My dear husband departed this life at Boston in his fifty-fifth year where he was driven by a mad and deluded mob for no other offence but his loyalty to his sovereign." [10]

Abijah Willard arrived in Boston to receive a similar reward with a better ending. Willard was a veteran of the French and Indian War and one of the wealthiest landowners in Lancaster, some fifty miles northwest of Boston. As one of the hated mandamus councilors, Willard endured several beatings and confinements. Although he then disavowed his royal appointment, his true allegiance remained uncertain—perhaps even to himself. On the morning of April 19, Willard was riding toward his farm with saddlebags filled with seeds for his fields when he encountered rebel militia marching toward Lexington and Concord. It was decision time. Willard might have joined them, but he turned instead in the opposite direction and rode for Boston. There he reported to General Gage and was promptly commissioned a captain in the Loyal American Association, a paramilitary union of loyalists. [11]

Truth be told, however, Boston quickly became an unpleasant place to be for anyone save perhaps those with an ample larder hidden away as rebel troops stopped deliveries of fresh produce from the countryside. "In the course of two days," recorded Ensign De Berniere after returning from Smith's Concord foray, "from a plentiful town, we were reduced to the disagreeable necessity of living on salt provisions, and fairly blocked up in Boston." [12] Most local farmers and dairymen were supporters of the rebel cause and all too glad to find new customers among the large numbers of rebel militia gathering in and around Cambridge.

But not everyone who wanted to leave Boston could. Sometimes, the issue caused marital strife. Sarah Winslow Deming acknowledged to her nephew in England that those British troops who had wintered in Boston "had not given us *much* molestation, but an *additional strength* [more troops] I dreaded and determined if possible to get out of their reach, and to take with me as much of my little life interest as I could. Your uncle Deming was very far from being of my mind from which has proceeded those difficulties which peculiarly related to myself.

"Many a time," Sarah Deming continued, "have I thought that could I be out of Boston together with my family and friends, I could be content with the meanest fare and slenderest accommodation. Out of Boston, out of Boston at almost any rate — away as far as possible from the infection of smallpox & martial musick as it is called and horrors of war — but my distress is not to be described." [13]

There were others — including merchant John Andrews, who had wished in the New Year hoping for any sign of moderation from the Crown — who were now forced to choose sides. On what he called "this fatal day," Andrews wrote his brother-in-law, William Barrell: "When I reflect and consider that the fight [at Lexington] was between those whose parents but a few generations ago were brothers, I shudder at the thought, and there's no knowing where our calamities will end." [14]

With an army of rebels surrounding Boston, General Gage feared insurrection from armed inhabitants inside the city. It was impossible to know which side some residents were on. After a series of tense town meetings that took the unprecedented step of continuing through a Sunday — April 23 — it was agreed that all Bostonians, whatever their political leanings, would deliver up their arms to the town selectmen, and in exchange General Gage would open the avenues and docks to permit those who wanted to leave town to do so. "If I can escape with the skin of my teeth," John Andrews told his brother-in-law, "[I] shall be glad as I don't expect to be able to take more than a change of apparel with me, as Sam. [possibly Andrews's nephew] and his wife with myself and Ruthy [Andrews's wife] intend for Nova Scotia."

But even with this accommodation for those who wished to depart, Gage could not be certain that rebel forces would not attempt to take Boston by force. "I expect to become a beggar ere long," Andrews continued, "as our own countrymen have not compassion, but persist in threatening the town with storming it, which pray God avert before I depart." [15]

ON THE REBEL SIDE, THERE was equal anxiety over what had just occurred and equal uncertainty as to the future. General Gage's nervousness aside, there was no immediate plan to push into Boston. Chaos reigned. Even Samuel Adams and John Hancock seemed out of the loop. Following their belated departure from the Clarke parsonage on the early morning of April 19, they momentarily took refuge in Woburn, to the northeast of Lexington, and then moved westward to Billerica, where they were rejoined by Hancock's aunt Lydia and his fiancée, Dorothy Quincy. Despite Dorothy's professed determination to return to Boston and see to the safety of her father, she and John finally agreed that given John's imminent departure for the Continental Congress in Philadelphia, the safest place for Dorothy and Aunt Lydia would be in Fairfield, Connecticut, at the home of Thaddeus Burr, an old family friend and Hancock's ally in both business and politics. [16]

Over the course of the next several days, Samuel Adams and the Hancock entourage worked their way westward to Worcester, Massachusetts, there to await the arrival of the other Massachusetts delegates — John Adams, Thomas Cushing, and Robert Treat Paine — and to travel on to Philadelphia together. From Worcester, on the evening of Monday, April 24, Hancock wrote a spirited though somewhat disjointed letter full of questions to the Provincial Congress then meeting in Watertown. "Gentlemen," began Hancock, "Mr. S. Adams and myself, just arrived here, find no intelligence from you and no guard." A passing express from the south had conveyed word of four more British regiments arriving in New York, and Hancock wondered, "How are we to proceed? Where are our brethren?"

Knowing little about the military situation in and around Boston, Hancock nevertheless urged, "Boston *must* be entered; the [British] troops *must* be sent away." Then, speaking more as a businessman than as a patriot, he complained: "I have an interest in that town; what can be the enjoyment of that to me, if I am obliged to hold it at the will of general Gage, or any one else?" [17]

Meanwhile, Samuel's cousin John had taken it upon himself to get a firsthand look at the carnage along what would come to be called Battle Road. John Adams's usually verbose diary is silent — or missing — after his return from the First Continental Congress, in November of 1774, until April 30, 1775. During much of that time, he was consumed by his responses to Massachusettensis. Only in his autobiography did Adams fill in his whereabouts for the ten days immediately following the events of April 19, which, he claimed, "changed the Instruments of Warfare from the Penn to the Sword."

A few days after the battle, Adams left his home in Braintree and rode to Cambridge, where he saw generals Artemas Ward and William Heath and what he called "the New England Army" — really still only those regiments of militia gathering there in the wake of the Concord fight. The scene was one of "great Confusion and much distress: Artillery, Arms, Cloathing were wanting and a sufficient Supply of Provisions not easily obtained." Nonetheless, Adams found that neither the officers nor their men were lacking in spirit or resolve.

From Cambridge, Adams rode on to Lexington "along the Scene of Action for many miles" and quizzed the locals about the circumstances of that day. What he heard in return did not diminish his enthusiasm for the cause in which he had been laboring and "on the Contrary convinced me that the Die was cast, the Rubicon Passed, and . . . if We did not defend ourselves they would kill us." [18]

John returned home to Abigail in Braintree with a fever and "alarming Symptoms." He was still feeling poorly when he was forced to depart Braintree again about April 26 in order to reach Philadelphia for the Continental Congress. Abigail was not pleased. "I feared much for your health, when you went away," she later wrote him. "I must entreat you to be as careful as you can consistently with the duty you owe your country. That consideration alone, prevailed with me to consent to your departure, in a time so perilous and so hazardous to your family, and with a body so infirm as to require the tenderest care and nursing." [19]

The portly Adams had been planning to ride horseback, but being indisposed, he hired two horses, a sulky, and a servant and set off to rendezvous with his cousin Samuel, John Hancock, and the other Massachusetts delegates. Because of his delays, they had proceeded without him beyond Worcester, and he caught up with them in Hartford, Connecticut. [20]

As the Massachusetts delegates gathered in preparation for their journey to the Continental Congress in Philadelphia, the Provincial Congress of Massachusetts found plenty to occupy its sessions. Meeting briefly at Concord on the morning of Saturday, April 22, the congress adjourned so that it could reconvene at 4:00 p.m. in Watertown, which was closer to the action in Cambridge. Many of its members were involved with the rush of military activities. The congress's committee of safety had been meeting almost nonstop since the afternoon of April 19, and the full congress had previously granted it powers as a de facto executive committee to oversee the defense of the province — and now, in light of events, to orchestrate what was quickly becoming a siege of Boston.

Reconvening in Watertown, the congress summoned the committee of safety to attend "with whatever plans they may have in readiness for us" and also requested absent members of the congress then in Cambridge to provide "their punctual attendance." The principal matter of business for the remainder of that evening was to appoint a committee of nine members, headed by Elbridge Gerry, to take sworn depositions from participants in and eyewitnesses to the April 19 actions and send the depositions to moderates in "England by the first ship from Salem." [21] This was no small matter. Each side was eager to cast blame on the other and spread its version of events.

Meeting on Sunday, April 23 — the exigencies of the moment having temporarily overshadowed established customs against conducting business on the Sabbath — the congress resolved "that 13,600 men be raised immediately by this province" to join a Continental Army of at least thirty thousand men; they also elected Joseph Warren president in place of the absent John Hancock. Then the members turned their attention again to the matter of public relations.

Having already ordered depositions taken, the congress appointed Elbridge Gerry and Thomas Cushing — the latter about to depart for Philadelphia — to work with a third member of the congress, who was not on the depositions committee, "to draw up a narrative of the massacre on Wednesday last." [22] By use of the word *massacre*, there was not much doubt as to how the rebel media would portray these events. The third member was the highly esteemed Dr. Benjamin Church Jr.

Born in Newport, Rhode Island, in 1734, Church was raised in Boston, where his father was an auctioneer and respected deacon in the congregation of the senior Mather Byles. Young Church graduated from Harvard in 1754 and went to London to study the medical profession, eventually returning to Boston with both medical training and an English-born wife. The doctor's talents included gifts for writing and speaking, and by the 1770s Church was an intimate member of Boston's rebel circle. His position was so respected that Samuel Adams tapped him to deliver the 1773 oration for the anniversary of the Boston Massacre. Church was a member of the committee of safety, and when it came to secrets and plotting, it could be argued that only Samuel Adams, John Hancock, and Joseph Warren were more involved than he. It seemed quite logical that Dr. Church would be asked to use his talents to spread the rebel position.[23]

But not everyone thought highly of Dr. Church. For example, Paul Revere, after he lugged John Hancock's trunk away from Buckman's Tavern in the nick of time on the morning of April 19, may have lingered on the sidelines about Lexington or possibly have been dispatched by Hancock on some other errand as they parted. By the following day, however, Revere was at Cambridge with the rapidly assembling rebel army. There he met Dr. Church, who showed Revere "some blood on his stocking, which he said spirted on him from a Man who was killed near him, as he was urging the Militia on." Revere had never been enamored of Dr. Church, despite their years together as members of the Sons of Liberty. Revere, in fact, doubted very much whether Church "was a real Whig." Nevertheless, Revere came away from this encounter persuaded that "if a Man will risque his life in a Cause, he must be a Friend to that cause."[24]

That same day, Revere met up with Dr. Joseph Warren, who had sped him on his mission out of Boston two nights before. Warren now asked Revere to perform messenger duties for the committee of safety as it met at the Hastings house in Cambridge prior to the call to join the entire Provincial Congress in Watertown. In this role, Revere was in and out of the committee's meetings. After sunset on Friday, April 21, as things were winding down for the day, Dr. Church suddenly rose from the conference and declared his intention to go into Boston the next day. The other committee members and Dr. Warren in particular were aghast. "Are you serious, Dr. Church?" Warren inquired. "They will Hang you if they catch you in Boston." Indeed, after the events of that week, hanging quite likely would have been the fate of any of the committee members should they have been so bold as to venture into the city.

Church replied that he was in fact very serious and determined to go no matter the objections. After considerable pleading, to which Church turned a deaf ear, Warren suggested that Church concoct a cover story that he was traveling in search of medical supplies to aid both rebel and British wounded officers. Church agreed and left early the next morning with seemingly no cares about his safety.

Indeed, by Sunday evening, April 23, Church was back in Cambridge no worse for the wear. Revere took him aside and asked how things had gone. Church reported that he had been made a prisoner as soon as he crossed over the lines at Boston Neck, taken before General Gage, and questioned by him. He was further detained in a barracks and only allowed one brief, supervised visit to his home. Revere nodded sympathetically. It all seemed quite plausible that Church would then have been released to return with the medical supplies that were part of his cover story.

But Dr. Church had also had two encounters while in Boston that he chose not to reveal to Revere or anyone else. Caleb Davis was a newly appointed deacon of the Hollis Street Church and a member of Boston's committee of correspondence. Davis was also a shopkeeper who had recently ordered a special buckle at the request of General Gage. On Saturday morning, April 22, Davis called on the general to deliver the buckle and was told that Gage was in private conversation and could not be disturbed. Davis chose to wait, and about half an hour later, the general emerged from his office in the company of Dr. Church. Far from appearing a prisoner, the good doctor was conversing with Gage "like persons who had been long acquainted." Although they were not intimates, Church and Davis immediately recognized each other, and Church "appeared to be quite surprised at seeing Deacon Davis." [25]

Circumstantial evidence suggests that Dr. Church also either called directly upon Rachel Revere, the widowed Revere's second wife, or somehow took receipt of a letter from her to be delivered to Paul. Rachel was not yet trying to get out of Boston — she had six stepchildren and a young son, Joshua, to look after — but she was definitely concerned for Paul's well-being, particularly in light of reports that he was "missing, supposed to be Waylaid and slain."[26]

Church probably told Rachel that Revere was safe in Cambridge, and she trusted Church, as an insider, to cross paths with him. If Church, upon his return to Cambridge, mentioned this meeting or the letter in his conversation with Paul, the latter did not include it in his recollection of Church's activities during those two days. More likely, Church himself never mentioned Rachel Revere's letter because Church never delivered it.

"My Dear by Doctr Church," Rachel had written, "I send a hundred & twenty five pounds and beg you will take the best care of yourself and not atempt coming into this town again and if I have an opportunity of coming or sending out anything or any of the Children I shall do it." Asking Paul to keep up his spirits and trust in "the hands of a good God," Rachel signed herself, "Love from your affectionate R. Revere."

But if Paul Revere did not receive this via Dr. Church or any other means, what did Church do with the letter and the referenced "hundred & twenty five pounds," a sum with a substantial value (approximately twenty thousand dollars by 2010 valuations)? In fact, this was such a considerable sum that Rachel's words may not have referred to money at all. Revere family letters from this period reveal that Paul and Rachel managed to exchange several letters discussing how to procure a pass that would allow Rachel, their children, and as many of their household goods and furnishings as possible to be taken across the Charlestown ferry to a house Paul would find for them in Cambridge. (Paul's oldest son, fifteen-year-old Paul junior, was to stay in Boston and mind the silversmith shop.)

In one letter, Paul advises Rachel, "If you send the things to the ferry send enough to fill a cart, them that are the most wanted."[27] It seems unlikely that Church would have taken Revere household goods with him, but would Rachel have had the modern-day equivalent of twenty thousand dollars accessible? This, too, seems unlikely, considering that in their exchange of letters, she apparently refers to having been unable to collect a debt of three pounds due them. Would she have worried about three pounds if she were able to send 125 pounds to Paul?

All of this—convoluted and filled with conjecture though it may be—would not be very germane to this story save for the fact that the letter from Rachel to Paul "by Doctr Church" was found 150 years later among the papers of General Thomas Gage.

There are no clear answers, but plenty of innuendo: Did Church deliver the letter to Gage instead of Revere? What happened to the money, if there was any?

It is not known how quickly Caleb Davis told others of his encounter with Dr. Church outside General Gage's private office. Nor, it appears, was there much contemporary scrutiny of the reliability of the doctor as a Revere family messenger. After his return to Cambridge, the Provincial Congress tasked Church with numerous committee assignments. He was at the center of everything.

Finally, Benjamin Church was given the ultimate mission: he was dispatched to Philadelphia as the Provincial Congress's most trusted and articulate spokesman to convey to that body Massachusetts's urgent request that the Continental Congress assume responsibility for the organizing of a continental army. The question that would soon be asked was, did Dr. Church make another visit to Boston before departing for Philadelphia—and to what purpose?[28]

Chapter 16

~

Spreading the News

A s uncertain and confused as things were on the rebel side in the first few weeks after April 19, rebel leaders recognized the importance of spreading the news of what had occurred at Lexington and Concord and putting a decidedly pro-rebel spin on it. There was no equivocation. The rebel story line was short and concise: British regulars had marched out of Boston in the dead of night and without provocation attacked well-intentioned, defensive militia. It needed to be told as quickly as possible.

Postal riders carried dispatches that came to be called the Lexington Alarm throughout Massachusetts and into neighboring New Hampshire, Connecticut, and Rhode Island almost before Lord Percy's brigade reached the relative safety of Charlestown. One such rider was Isaac Bissell, a twenty-seven-year-old post rider from Suffield, Connecticut. Bissell's regular route was along the Upper Post Road, which led directly west from Boston to Worcester and Springfield and then south to Hartford, Connecticut. This route was connected to the Lower Post Road, which ran along the coast, and the Middle Post Road, which ran in between them, by lesser north-south roads. These roads formed the infrastructure of a sophisticated communications network—compliments of Ben

Franklin's efforts years before — that tied the colonies together and facilitated relatively speedy delivery of "express" messages.

Colonel Smith's detachment of regulars was still maneuvering about Concord and the North Bridge when Joseph Palmer of the committee of safety, meeting on the run that day, handed Isaac Bissell a message for points south. It was dated "Wednesday Morning near 11 O'clock" on April 19 and addressed "To all friends of American liberty." Recounting what was then known about the British march on Lexington and Percy's advance with reinforcements, it noted Bissell's charge "to alarm the country quite to Connecticut" and asked all persons to assist him with fresh horses.[1]

Standard procedure called for these express circulars to be copied upon receipt and the copy endorsed by one or more members of the local committee of correspondence before the copy was sent on its way with the rider to the next town. This had several purposes. Multiple copies allowed the news to spread out from the post roads, and the names of the endorsers gave some measure of credibility as well as a chain of custody to the report when it arrived in the next town. The downside was that continued copying frequently introduced misspellings and other errors that were not in the original.

Isaac Bissell galloped into Worcester later that afternoon of April 19 and came to the proverbial fork in the road: the Upper Post Road, his usual route, led west toward Springfield; another road ran south toward New London, Connecticut, after crossing the Middle Post Road at Pomfret. Subsequent stories to the contrary, Isaac Bissell did not detour from his usual route. After copies of the dispatch were duly made and attested to by Nathan Baldwin, Worcester's town clerk, Bissell continued westward to complete his charge "to alarm the country quite to Connecticut."

But the committee of safety's Lexington Alarm was also sped south from Worcester into Connecticut by another rider, whose name appears lost to history — and therein lies the confusion that over the years has made for a great but totally false story. Because Isaac Bissell's name was in the original message, it was copied at each town along the routes and, as early as Worcester, appears to have been corrupted to "Israel" Bissell. This incorrect first name was repeated—as well as occasionally further distorted—and its appearance in copies strewn along the post roads from Boston to Philadelphia gave rise to the tale that a Bissell—be it Israel or Isaac—had singularly carried the Lexington Alarm all the way from Watertown to Philadelphia, a distance of about 300 miles.[2]

Rather, Isaac Bissell was one link in an established cadre of veteran postal riders who set a pace of three to four miles per hour depending on road conditions, weather, and the presence or absence of moonlight. As Bissell continued west from Worcester on the Upper Post Road on the morning of April 20, another rider carried the Lexington Alarm some twenty miles south to Brooklyn, Connecticut. Here another copy was made at 11:00 a.m. and endorsed accordingly.

Perhaps most important about this stop in Brooklyn was that the home of Israel Putnam stood nearby. Putnam was a tough veteran of the French and Indian War and arguably one of the most able of the rebel military leaders. When the postal rider shouted the news of the Lexington Alarm to him, Putnam was working in his field. He immediately dropped everything and set off for Connecticut governor Jonathan Trumbull's home in Lebanon, some twenty miles away, to consult with him on a plan of action. "He loitered not," Putnam's fifteen-year-old son later recalled, "but left *me*, the driver of his team, to unyoke it in the furrow."[3]

On through Norwich the news went to reach the Lower Post Road at New London. Fresh horses carried the rider westward from New London to Saybrook, Guilford, and Branford before arriving in New Haven sometime after midday on Friday, April 21. By then, the same news either had reached or soon would reach Hartford to the north via Isaac Bissell's route through Springfield on the Upper Post Road. Behind these advance riders came additional messengers with updates to the initial report. The first update appears to have caught up with the original message at Fairfield, Connecticut, and the home of John Hancock's friend

Thaddeus Burr. Meanwhile, post riders hurrying in the opposite direction carried the news to Portsmouth, New Hampshire, and eventually as far east as Machias, Maine, then still part of Massachusetts. When word reached Machias, it produced interesting results that, as we shall see, brought about what some would come to call the Lexington of the Seas.

Throughout Connecticut, the news of apparent war had a galvanizing effect. To be sure, there were loyalists in the colony, but the majority of Connecticut's population held rebel leanings. The colony's response — after Israel Putnam had conferred with Governor Trumbull — was to mobilize militia units and prepare to march for Boston.

But when the news reached New York City on Sunday morning, April 23, it was a different matter. Initial reports from Rhode Island and New London "that an Action had happened between the King's Troops and the Inhabitants of Boston" had not been given much credence that morning in New York, but then "about 12 o'Clock an Express arrived" with the original Watertown dispatch as well as two updates. The printers at the *New-York Gazette and Weekly Mercury* worked overtime to set the messages in type for publication in the weekly newspaper the following day.[4]

Thomas Jones, an attorney and staunch loyalist who later wrote a history of New York during the Revolution, was dismissive and snide in his characterization of the rebel response. "They had wished for it for a long time," Jones remembered, and "they received the news with avidity." Several rebel leaders, Jones said, "paraded the town with drums beating and colours flying, (attended by a mob of negroes, boys, sailors, and pickpockets) inviting all mankind to take up arms in defence of the 'injured rights and liberties of America.'"

These same rebel leaders, Jones maintained, "broke open the Arsenal in City Hall, and forcibly removed 1,000 stand of arms, belonging to the City Corporation, and delivered them out to the rabble.... The whole city became one continued scene of riot, tumult and confusion."[5]

But as New York reacted with turmoil, the news continued to race south as fast as the manner of the times could carry it. For the next leg, it traveled not by horse but by boat from the tip of Manhattan to Elizabeth, New Jersey. There, Elias Boudinot, who would go on to become president of the Continental Congress, heard the news on the evening of April 23.[6] Farther west, at Mount Kemble, his plantation near Morristown, one wonders how Peter Kemble heard the news and what thoughts he had for his children — Margaret, Stephen, and Samuel — whose lives were so entwined with the fate of General Gage in Boston.

Jemima Condict probably heard the news in Essex County, just north of Elizabeth, the same day. "As every Day Brings New Troubels," she recorded in her diary, "so this Day Brings News that yesterday [sic] very early in the morning They began to fight at Boston. The regulers We hear Shot first there; they killed 30 of our men And hundred & 50 of the Regulers."[7] Near and far, the rebel news of the fighting was already inextricably bound up with the idea that the British had fired first.

And onward the news ran. Committee members endorsed its receipt at New Brunswick at 2:00 a.m. on Monday, April 24; Princeton, at 4:00 a.m.; and Trenton at 9:00 a.m. before the Lexington Alarm arrived in Philadelphia at 5:00 p.m. on April 24. The big bell in the statehouse rang out to assemble a crowd to hear the news. It had taken five days and six hours for Joseph Palmer's message to travel the three hundred miles from Watertown to Philadelphia. (One can only imagine the physical condition of Isaac Bissell if indeed he had ridden that distance in this length of time.) Now the Continental Congress that was due to assemble at the Pennsylvania statehouse in little more than two weeks would have plenty on its plate.[8]

MEANWHILE, ACCOUNTS OF APRIL 19 began to appear in Massachusetts newspapers. The *Boston News-Letter* of April 20 reported first. This paper was decidedly pro-government and a veritable mouthpiece for General Gage. It acknowledged the departure of Colonel Smith's advance column and the subsequent march of Lord Percy's brigade, but thereafter, details got thin. "The reports concerning this unhappy Affair," the *News-Letter* concluded, "and the Causes that concurred to bring on an Engagement, are so various, that we are not able to collect any thing consistent or regular, and cannot therefore with certainty give our Readers any further Accounts of this shocking Introduction to all the Miseries of a Civil War." [9]

In the same issue, by order of General Gage, the *News-Letter* reminded Boston residents that "certain persons stiling themselves Delegates of several of his Majesty's Colonies in America" were assembling in Philadelphia, "without his Majesty's Authority," and all concerned were directed "to use your utmost Endeavours, to prevent such Appointment." [10]

Among other newspapers to report was the *Essex Gazette* of April 25. Editors Samuel and Ebenezer Hall were staunch Whigs, and they wasted no ink softening the rebel rhetoric. "Last Wednesday, the 19th of April, the Troops of his *Britannick* Majesty commenced Hostilities upon the People of this Province," the *Gazette* announced, "attended with Circumstances of Cruelty not less brutal than what our venerable Ancestors received from the vilest Savages of the Wilderness." The situation had introduced to the colonies "all the Horrors of a civil War," the paper declared.

While admitting to a "present confused State of Affairs," the *Gazette* nonetheless did not hesitate to describe atrocities, both real and imagined. "They pillaged almost every House they passed by, breaking and destroying Doors, Windows, Glasses, &c. and carrying off Cloathing and other valuable Effects." That much was true enough along the return route from Lexington through Menotomy, but "the savage Barbarity" reported to have been "exercised upon the Bodies of our unfortunate Brethren" was mostly a gross distortion — the civilian deaths at Cooper's Tavern notwithstanding. "Not content with shooting down the unarmed, aged and infirm," the paper claimed, "they disregarded the Cries of the wounded, killing them without Mercy, and mangling their Bodies in the most shocking Manner."

Forgetting (or unaware of) the hatchet incident at the North Bridge, the *Gazette* then boasted on behalf of the rebels, "We have the Pleasure to say, that, notwithstanding the highest Provocations given by the Enemy, not one Instance of Cruelty, that we have heard of, was committed by our victorious Militia." [11]

War, however, was not good for the newspaper business in Boston. Of five newspapers published in the city on April 1, 1775, only one was left in business six weeks later. Tory Thomas Fleet Jr.'s *Boston Evening-Post* reported on April 24: "The unhappy Transactions of last week are so variously related that we shall not at present undertake to give any particular Account thereof." [12] Nor did he ever. It was his last issue.

With similar sympathies, the *Boston Post-Boy* published its last issue on April 10. It wasn't that there was no news to report in and around Boston, but rather that so many of these newspapers' subscribers were unreachable beyond the siege lines of the growing rebel army. Only the Tory mouthpiece the *Boston News-Letter* survived, but even its proprietor, Margaret Green Draper, printed no paper between April 20 and May 19. [13]

On the rebel side, Isaiah Thomas closed up his *Massachusetts Spy* after the April 6 issue and moved his press to the safety of Worcester, quite presciently anticipating the chaos to come. By May 3, Thomas was up and running again, publishing no explanation for either the interruption of service or his change of venue. The situation at the *Boston Gazette* was more complicated. The *Gazette's* copublishers, Benjamin Edes and John Gill, had been the newsprint godfathers of every moment of rebel dissent in Boston since the Boston Tea Party was planned in the paper's back room. Edes and Gill published their last issue in Boston on April 17. While Edes loaded their press into a boat and rowed up the Charles River to Watertown, Gill remained in town and was arrested for treason. Edes was able to start publishing again on June 5.[14]

VIA CIRCULARS AND NEWSPAPERS, MORE news and rumors spread outward from Massachusetts. Some of these reports were purely propaganda and not even close to the truth. A circular dated April 28, 1775, addressed "To the Inhabitants of New York," was as incendiary as it was false. Signed only "An American," it claimed that in marching from Lexington to Concord, the British troops had "killed a man on horseback, and killed geese, hogs, cattle, and every living creature they came across." Before the regulars left Lexington, they reportedly surrounded the parsonage where Adams and Hancock had been staying and then "searched the house, and when they could not find them, these barbarians killed the woman of the house and all the children in cool blood, and then set the house on fire."[15] All this was untrue, save the escape by Adams and Hancock. In fact, British regulars had never appeared at the Clarke house—unless one counts Lieutenant Sutherland's solo bolt on his runaway horse.

But then came more provocative incriminations: "Alas!" the writer continued, "would not the heathen in all their savage barbarity and cruelty, blush at such horrid murder, and worse than brutal rage?" The answer was a call to arms that "every *American* hear and abhor; let every inhabitant consider what he is likely to suffer if he falls into the hands of such cruel and merciless wretches." The message was clear: hesitate to rally to the side of the rebels at your peril.[16]

But even the de facto government of Massachusetts—and the Provincial Congress was indeed now being looked to for leadership throughout the province, outside occupied Boston—was not above waving a bloody shirt to accomplish its goals. "The barbarous murders committed on our innocent brethren on Wednesday the 19th instant," the committee of safety stressed in a message to Massachusetts towns, "have made it absolutely necessary that we immediately raise an Army to defend our wives and children from the butcherying hands of an inhuman soldiery." Then, foreshadowing words that would soon appear on another document, the committee concluded, "We conjure, therefore, by all that is dear, by all that is sacred, that you give all assistance possible in forming the Army. Our all is at stake." [17]

NOWHERE WAS THAT STAKE JUDGED to be higher than in communications with moderates in Great Britain who were sympathetic to the rebel cause. The two dozen affidavits from the approximately one hundred participants and eyewitnesses whom the Provincial Congress scurried to assemble within days of the Lexington battles were distributed and published at least in part in numerous newspapers around the country, but the most important set was copied in total and put in a packet with a cover letter from congress president Joseph Warren. [18] This was entrusted to thirty-three-year-old Captain John Derby of Salem. His destination was England.

John Derby was the youngest son of Richard Derby Sr., a longtime Salem merchant and patriarch of a successful shipping firm (and the man who had sold the cannons that had been the aim of Colonel Leslie's raid). John's older brother, Richard junior, was soon to be a member of the third Provincial Congress. When the current congress resolved to report its side of the Lexington episode as quickly and directly to the English people as possible, all thoughts turned to the Derby family's fleet of ships.

On April 27, with the ink on the various affidavits and the cover letter barely dry, the committee of safety directed the junior Richard Derby "to make for Dublin or any other good port in Ireland, and from thence to cross to Scotland or England and hasten to London." This circuitous route was necessary, the orders explained, so Derby might elude "all cruisers that may be in the chops of the channel" to stop these communications from reaching the colonies' agent in London. As if Derby needed to be told the obvious, the committee added a postscript: "You are to keep this order a profound secret from every person on earth."[19]

Richard Derby gave this delicate assignment to his brother, John, who would prove more than a little daring in accomplishing it. The family ship that the brothers chose to outfit for the hurried voyage was the sixty-two-ton schooner *Quero*. Not much is known about the vessel, but in contrast to the heavy merchantman *Sukey*, via which General Gage had sent his dispatches to England, the *Quero* was light and fast, a veritable will-o'-the-wisp. With time of the essence and the Provincial Congress footing the bill, John Derby did not linger to load an outbound commercial cargo. Instead, he sailed with an empty hold, save for the requisite ballast.

Just how the *Quero* managed to slip out of Salem Harbor untouched by patrolling British ships is something of a mystery. The twenty-gun sixth-rate frigate HMS *Lively* was stationed off Marblehead Harbor, just to the south, immediately after April 19, and its duties included keeping a watch on nearby Salem and Beverly Harbors. In any event, no one knew these waters better than John Derby, and he seems to have made the most of his knowledge, probably slipping out of Salem on the night of April 28, four days after the *Sukey* sailed carrying Gage's rendition of events.[20]

The cover letter that Captain Derby carried from Joseph Warren, president of the Provincial Congress, was hardly a plea for reconciliation. Rather, despite its announced purpose to deliver "an early, true and authentic account of this inhuman proceeding," it read more like a partisan press release. After recounting the basic facts of Colonel Smith's advance and the rebel response, Warren and his coauthors acknowledged that giving "a particular account of the ravages of the troops . . . would be very difficult, if not impracticable." But then they proceeded to do just that, sometimes with a flagrant disregard for the truth.

"A great number of the houses on the road were plundered," Warren wrote. This was true, although perhaps what might be considered "a great number" was subjective. But when it came to asserting that "women in childbed were driven, by the soldiery, naked into the streets; [and] old men, peaceably in their houses, were shot dead," Warren's letter strained credulity.[21] Whom was he referring to?

Hannah Adams, while perhaps still weak from childbirth several weeks before, was, by her own daughter's account, fully clothed when she took her newborn from her house in the face of British troops.[22] If the "old men" shot dead in their homes were in fact the middle-aged Jason Winship and Jabez Wyman, who were unwilling to interrupt their afternoon pints at Cooper's Tavern despite the approaching sounds of gunfire, some might say they deserved the outcome. As for any other "old men," Samuel Whittemore, for one, was doing his best to shoot first.

But indeed there was no equivocation in these reports, and every measure of exaggeration was deployed on behalf of the rebels. With the letter and evidence dispatched, Joseph Warren and the Provincial Congress were counting on their colonial agent in London to distribute their version of events as quickly and widely as possible to the public in England. The man to whom John Derby was directed to deliver his package was Benjamin Franklin.

Since his chess-playing flirtations with Caroline Howe over the Christmas holidays, Franklin had grown increasingly exasperated by the state of affairs between Great Britain and its colonies. To be sure, there were many in England who sympathized politically with the plight of their American cousins and many others of the merchant and shipping classes who had economic reasons to worry. They feared what an open conflict with their best trading partner might do to their fortunes.

But to Franklin's chagrin, these were not the people making decisions of policy. The people calling the tune were among the close-minded, self-important inner circle of George III. Indeed, the nearer one was to the king, the more strident seemed to be his view about the audacity of colonials questioning anything His Majesty might ordain. They simply could not fathom that a viable threat to British power could come from upstarts an ocean away. France they feared, or at least respected after three centuries of dueling for dominance of Europe, but among King George's closest confidants, there was little or no respect for the abilities and resolve of the opposition in the colonies. In the end, that lack of respect and the arrogance that it bred would be their downfall.

But in the spring of 1775, Benjamin Franklin could do little more than sigh at this intransigence. Via Captain Derby, his friends in Massachusetts had again conveyed their confidence in his "faithfulness and abilities" and now asked him to publish and disperse the Lexington reports "throughout England to sway public opinion." In his heart, Franklin knew that their plea was genuine and correct: only "the united efforts of both Englands [Britain *and* North America] can save either," but that unity was not going to happen. Those with the power to make decisions in England were as unbending as those in North America were firm in their resolve. "Whatever price our breathren in the one [England] may be pleased to put on their constitutional liberties," the Provincial Congress wrote Franklin, "we are authorized to assure you, that the inhabitants of the other, with the greatest unanimity, are inflexibly resolved to sell theirs only at the price of their lives." [23]

There was one other problem. Benjamin Franklin was no longer in England. After considerable procrastination, he had finally sailed west from Portsmouth in the company of his fifteen-year-old grandson, Temple, on March 21. Somewhere off the coast of North America, inbound to Philadelphia, their ship, the *Pennsylvania Packet*, crossed paths with the outbound *Quero*.

Knowing quite well the importance and timeliness of his mission, John Derby now showed a full measure of Yankee brass. Rather than make for Dublin and undertake a clandestine journey by land across Scotland and England, as his instructions advised, Derby put the *Quero* on a direct course for the English Channel. After a speedy crossing, the *Quero* slipped unreported into a quiet anchorage on the Isle of Wight near the port of Southampton. Derby bundled up his dispatches, took the public ferry across to Southampton, and continued overland some seventy-five miles to London, arriving there on Sunday evening, May 28. Because it likely took Derby two or three days en route between the Isle of Wight and London, *Quero*'s crossing may have been as speedy as twenty-eight days. After that, the *Quero* became something of a ghost ship.

Once in London, Derby found Franklin absent and delivered his urgent dispatches, along with a copy of the April 25 issue of the *Essex Gazette*, to Arthur Lee, Samuel Adams's frequent correspondent and a ready stand-in for Franklin. Together, Derby and Lee enlisted the aid of John Wilkes, described as an "eccentric and fearless radical," who was the Lord Mayor of London and a strong supporter of the colonies. London was a rumor mill, and by the following day—thanks in part to some well-placed whispers by Wilkes—most informed citizens knew of the contest at Lexington and Concord and had been introduced to the rebel version of events.

Lord Dartmouth may have heard the news in some earlier fashion, but it is certain that Thomas Hutchinson, the ex-governor of Massachusetts so despised by Samuel Adams, carried the information to Dartmouth sometime on May 29. Having been effectively run out of Massachusetts for what many considered double-dealing, Hutchinson was nonetheless a darling of George III's inner circle and an unofficial adviser on North American affairs. Given Hutchinson's haughty personality and his unsuccessful tenure in Massachusetts, he was undoubtedly a poor choice for this role, but his presence was indicative of the less-than-balanced advice the king was receiving.

Hutchinson confided to his diary that Dartmouth was "much struck" with the news and that the first accounts "were very unfavourable" until they realized "that they all came from one side." There was little they could do except "wait with a greater degree of calmness for the accounts from the other side." [24] They could, however, question the veracity of the messenger and question not only the speed with which he had appeared in England but the whereabouts of his transport.

Horace Walpole, alluding to Derby's mysterious arrival, referred to him as the "Accidental Captain," and Dartmouth immediately began a search for the *Quero* both in the harbor at Southampton and among the coves of the Isle of Wight. Surprisingly enough, however, Dartmouth did not order Derby's arrest—suggesting that cherished principles of English law were still in place in England even as they were being bent in North America. [25]

What Dartmouth did do, however, was to issue an official statement on May 30 to inform the public that, recent reports from Massachusetts via Derby notwithstanding, Dartmouth had had no official communication from General Gage about the matter. Everyone should remain calm and without judgment until he had received Gage's report. That brought a salvo from Arthur Lee in the rebel-friendly newspapers the next day wherein Lee challenged anyone who doubted the veracity of Derby's account to inspect the affidavits in the custody of the Lord Mayor. [26]

Meanwhile, despite Derby's assertion that the *Sukey* had preceded him out of Boston by four days, there was no sign of the vessel and, with it, General Gage's account of events. Derby's mission in delivering the rebel version accomplished, the captain chose not to linger in London and risk a change in Dartmouth's adherence to English law. It might be better that he be long gone before Gage's official dispatches arrived. Accordingly, Derby left his lodgings in London on June 1 and melted into the countryside as stealthily as he had come. Some said they had heard that he was sailing for Spain with a cargo of fish, perhaps to buy arms and ammunition; others that he was going for a load of mules. Further inquiries into his whereabouts or those of the *Quero* at Southampton produced no information, and the collector of the port there disavowed any knowledge of the ship. [27]

That General Gage's account was not at hand caused more than a little apprehension with each passing day. Hutchinson, always a good friend of Gage, wrote him on May 31. "It is unfortunate to have the first impression made from that quarter," Hutchinson noted, referring to Derby's widely circulated account. "It is said your dispatches are on board Cap. Brown, who sailed some days before Darby [*sic*]. I hope they are at hand, and will afford us some relief." [28]

Dartmouth was even more perplexed about the delay, but all that he, too, could do was vent his frustrations in a letter to Gage the next day. Dartmouth did his best to speculate that Derby's reports must be wrong or, at the very least, greatly exaggerated: "There is the greatest Probability that the whole amounts to no more than that a Detachment sent by you to destroy Cannon and Stores collected at Concord for the purpose of aiding Rebellion, were fired upon, at different times, by the People of the Country in small Bodies from behind Trees and Houses, but that the Party effected the Service they went upon, & returned to Boston."

Yes, that was a fairly accurate reading of the story, although Dartmouth rushed on to gild the outcome: "I have the Satisfaction to tell you that the Affair being considered in that light . . . has had no other effect here than to raise that just Indignation which every honest Man must feel at the rebellious Conduct of the New England Colonies." All of this was just whistling in the dark, of course, and Dartmouth could not refrain from tweaking Gage just a little: "It is very much to be lamented," he told the general, "that We have not some account from you of this Transaction." [29]

Throughout the first week of June, there were rumors that Gage's report had finally reached England, but these proved unfounded. In the meantime, it only served to strain the public's nerves when other ships docked in England from North America with bits and pieces of information. Thomas Hutchinson caught the mood of many who remained optimistic. "Lord Gage called," Hutchison noted in his diary, in reference to the general's older brother, "who professes to believe nothing that is unfavourable, but appears very anxious notwithstanding." [30]

Finally, on June 9, a full thirteen days after the *Quero*'s arrival, the *Sukey* docked, apparently at Portsmouth, and a Royal Navy lieutenant hurried to Dartmouth's office in London by noon the next day with General Gage's belated dispatches. Hutchinson, ever the smug observer, noted he had "assured many gentlemen who would give no credit to Darby's [*sic*] account that it would prove near the truth," and it did. Indeed, Hutchinson could find that the only material difference between Derby's dispatches and Gage's account was Colonel Smith's assertion in the latter that the rebels had fired first. [31]

As the news spread in London and throughout England, the populace who had waited, as Dartmouth had advised, for the other side of the story were shocked and in "great grief." They had wished, one London newspaper reported, "that the fatal tale related by Captain Derby might prove altogether fictitious . . . [but] this is not the case." It was clear that Derby's mission to publicize the Massachusetts version had been successful. "The *Americans*," the newspaper noted wryly, "have given their narrative of the massacre; the favourite official servants have given a *Scotch* [meager] account of the skirmish." [32]

Only weeks later did Lord Dartmouth extend General Gage a rebuke over his speed of communication. Noting the obvious, Dartmouth told Gage that he had received his dispatches only after the general public had "received Intelligence by a Schooner, to all Appearances sent by the Enemies of Govt on purpose to make an Impression . . . in a light most favorable to their own Views." Their "Industry on this Occasion" in speedily dispatching Captain Derby had had its effect, Dartmouth complained, and he mentioned it to Gage "with a Hope that, in any future Event of Importance, it will be thought proper, both by yourself and the Admiral [Samuel Graves], to send your Dispatches by one of the light Vessels of the Fleet." [33]

And what of Captain Derby? He stole out of London unmolested and made his way by public postal chaise to Falmouth, on the western tip of Cornwall. The expense statement he later submitted to the Provincial Congress reported that he went by way of Portsmouth and covered 294 miles at a cost of eleven pounds, eight shillings. At Falmouth, the elusive *Quero* was waiting. Derby had shrewdly ordered the vessel to wait for him there, out of the hubbub of Southampton. Still carrying only ballast, the *Quero* slipped its moorings and sped west, back toward America.[34]

Meanwhile, there continued to be many reactions to the news of Lexington and Concord on both sides of the Atlantic, but perhaps the most succinct and prescient appraisal of the future came from the normally verbose pen of Edmund Burke. "The sluice is opend," Burke wrote to a friend. "Where, when, or how it will be stopped God only knows."[35]

PART III

~

DECISIVE DAYS

May–June 1775

The Day — perhaps, the decisive day — is come, on which the fate of America depends.

— Abigail Adams to John Adams, June 18, 1775

Chapter 17

~

Must We Stand Alone?

As initial reports of the confrontations at Lexington and Concord spread, the question arose in the minds of loyalists and rebels alike: Was this to be simply more evidence of Massachusetts's characteristic defiance or a call to arms to which rebels throughout the thirteen colonies would respond? In a few short weeks, the question would be no less perplexing in Charleston, South Carolina, than it was in Charlestown, Massachusetts, and it would divide neighbor from neighbor and even family from family.

FROM PHILADELPHIA, THE LEXINGTON ALARM continued south to Baltimore, where rebels promptly seized fifteen hundred stands of arms from the provincial armory. On Saturday, April 29, ten days after the Lexington fight, the news reached Williamsburg, Virginia. There it threatened to light a powder keg under a situation that was already volatile because of recent actions taken by Lord Dunmore, the royal governor.

In a mission quite similar to those General Gage had been attempting in Massachusetts, Lord Dunmore had ordered royal marines to confiscate a large quantity of gunpowder from the provincial magazine in Williamsburg in the dead of night and move it on board a Royal Navy ship. The following morning, Friday, April 21, as news of Lexington was making its way through Connecticut, an angry crowd of rebels confronted the Virginia governor and demanded the return of the powder. Dunmore muttered something about protecting the powder from a possible slave uprising, and the crowd dispersed at the urging of its leaders.

But news of what Dunmore had done—and a call for reinforcements to retake the powder—spread from Williamsburg just as the alarm had spread from Lexington. By Monday, April 24, it had reached as far north as Fredericksburg, one hundred miles distant, and relays of riders were carrying it onward to George Washington's plantation in Fairfax County. "This first publick insult is not to be tamely submitted to," a Fredericksburg committee told Washington, a colonel of the militia, as it asked permission to join those "willing to appear in support of the honor of Virginia, as well as to secure the military stores yet remaining in the Magazine."[1]

Throughout Virginia, citizens bristled at Dunmore's overt act and then became inflamed all the more after Dunmore vented his own anger at their initial defiance. If so much as a grain of powder was touched off against his authority, the governor vowed to turn slaves loose against the protesters and burn Williamsburg to the ground.[2] By Lord Dunmore's standards, General Gage looked quite moderate.

Peyton Randolph, about to set off from Williamsburg for the Continental Congress in Philadelphia, pleaded for some measure of Virginia moderation. If the gathering militias marched, Randolph warned, "violent measures may produce effects, which God only knows the consequences of."[3] But by the time Randolph's message of restraint reached Fredericksburg on April 28, more than one thousand men from fourteen militia companies had assembled and were brimming with confidence that they could set matters straight.

Then came the news about Lexington and Concord. Even among the saber rattlers in Fredericksburg, it had a sobering effect. It also put Randolph's plea for restraint in a new light. Bluster and verve was one thing, but here was direct evidence that considerable

bloodshed might be the consequence. The Fredericksburg companies decided to disperse temporarily but hold themselves in readiness to reassemble "at a moment's warning." Significantly, the
Fredericksburg resolution noted that they would do so "to defend
the laws, the liberty, and rights of this, or any sister colony, from
unjust and wicked invasion."[4]

But in Patrick Henry's Hanover County, north of Richmond,
there was to be no temporary stand-down. Firebrand Henry had
cheered Dunmore's seizure of the powder just as Samuel Adams
cheered Gage's thrust at Concord. According to his biographer,
Henry thought "it would rally the apathetic and rout the cautious."[5]
This news from Massachusetts only hardened his resolve.

In the early dawn of May 3, Henry led a contingent of about one
hundred men from Hanover County toward Williamsburg and that
evening camped on the grounds of Duncastle's Tavern, about
twelve miles from the capital. Now began a game of chicken. Henry
lacked the troops to seize the gunpowder outright, but Governor
Dunmore could not risk taking the field to dislodge him. Giving up
the gunpowder was out of the question for Dunmore, but Henry
needed something for his efforts.

A deal was finally brokered whereby the king's receiver general —
essentially the collector of rents on royal lands in the province —
produced 330 pounds in bills of exchange endorsed to Henry's
satisfaction "as a compensation for the gunpowder lately taken out
of the public magazine." Henry promised to deliver the bills of
exchange to the next provincial assembly so that they could be used
to purchase replacement gunpowder.[6]

Upon their return to Hanover County, Henry and his men were
cheered as heroes. Governor Dunmore took a different view and
promptly denounced Henry and his "deluded Followers" as rebels.[7]
Arresting Henry, however, was well beyond Dunmore's capabili-
ties, and, besides, Henry was soon on the road north to Philadelphia to take his own seat in the Continental Congress alongside
Virginia's other delegates. There was some question whether those

delegates, including George Washington and Richard Henry Lee, approved of Henry's boldness in the gunpowder episode, but according to James Madison, it gained Henry "great honor in the most spirited parts of the Country." Madison fretted, however, that the landed gentry in the Tidewater region of Virginia, whose property would be more exposed in the event of war, "were extremely alarmed lest Government should be provoked to make reprisals."[8]

MEANWHILE, THINGS IN BOSTON GREW worse under the tightening rebel siege. "Three days have now passed without communication with the country," a Royal Navy officer on board the transport *Empress of Russia* wrote from Boston on April 23; "three more will reduce this town to a most unpleasant situation." The town had been dependent on the surrounding countryside for daily provisions of eggs, milk, vegetables, and anything fresh. "That ceasing," the officer told his correspondent, "you may conceive the consequences. Preparations are now making on both sides [of] the Neck for attacking and defending."[9]

On April 30, the Provincial Congress, still meeting in Watertown, ratified the deal that had been brokered with General Gage. Those Boston residents who chose to leave town were permitted to do so with their personal effects, "excepting their fire arms and ammunition," and make their way into the country. Inhabitants of the province elsewhere were guaranteed safe passage in the opposite direction should they be inclined "to go into the town of Boston."[10] About the only people taking the latter route were loyalists who hoped to book quick passage out of Boston by ship.

But that was much easier said than done. John Andrews, who had earnestly told his brother-in-law of his desire to quit town as soon as possible, was still there. "You'll observe by this that I'm yet in Boston," Andrews glumly wrote on May 6, "and here like to remain." Merchant Andrews had tried to charter a ship for Halifax and load up a substantial quantity of his merchandise, but General

Gage, despite his accommodation for personal effects, "*absolutely*" forbade any merchandise to leave town. Given that choice, Andrews determined to stay and safeguard his property. "Of consequence," Andrews continued, "our eyes have not been bless'd with either vegetables or fresh provisions, how long we shall continue in this *wretched* state — God only knows." [11]

For the moment, Mather Byles Jr. was also remaining in Boston. A committee of vestrymen had terminated his position as rector of Christ Church (the Old North Church) the very day two lanterns were hung in the church's steeple. His loyalist politics aside, it appears that Byles was paid his outstanding salary despite his termination. His father was another matter. The Reverend Mather Byles Sr. was one of New England's best-known clergymen. At present he occupied the pulpit of the Hollis Street Church, a Congregational parish in the South End. Despite his son's Episcopal ordination and loyalist choices, Mather Byles Sr. professed rebel sympathies and refused to leave his post even as his son eventually sailed away to Halifax. [12]

Split allegiances also continued to beset the Josiah Quincy family. Young Josiah Jr. had gone to England the previous fall to argue the rebel cause but died of tuberculosis within sight of the Massachusetts shore upon his return, just after the battle of Lexington. Conversely, his older brother Samuel stood fast by his king and left Boston for London on May 25. Samuel never returned, and for all practical purposes it was the end of his marriage. Hannah Hill Quincy, who had long goaded Samuel to get on what she perceived to be the right side, stayed behind in Boston and never saw him again. [13]

In the Massachusetts towns surrounding Boston, there were more tender good-byes when husband and wife were staunchly on the same side, but that did not make them less anguished. Mercy Warren had accompanied her husband, James, on horseback as he rode from Plymouth to Providence, Rhode Island, to spread the alarm and coordinate the march of Rhode Island militia to Cambridge. Along the way, they found a safe house in Taunton where

Mercy and their boys might take refuge should the British strike at Plymouth.

Returning to Plymouth, James "made the best provision I could for the security of our Family" and then rode alone to take his place once again at the Provincial Congress in Watertown. Like Abigail Adams at John's departure for the Continental Congress in Philadelphia, Mercy Warren was most apprehensive as James left home, but they had talked the talk of freedom together for so long that his riding to effect it was a duty she could not question. This did not keep her, however, from suffering a severe bout of migraines that seemed to surface during periods of high stress.[14]

James wrote Mercy almost every day during these pivotal weeks of May, and mail between Watertown and Plymouth was usually a matter of next-day delivery. "What a Letter every day!" he scrawled in jest. "Was ever a Woman doom'd to such drudgery before to be obliged to read half a Sheet, and sometimes a whole one, full of Impertinence before dinner." But James presumed, quite rightly, that Mercy's "Love for reading, or affection for her Husband will secure a welcome to his Scribbles."[15]

FAR TO THE SOUTH, THE news of Lexington and Concord was finally reaching Charleston, South Carolina. In many respects, South Carolina appeared to have less reason to challenge Great Britain and more to lose if it did so than any of the other colonies. South Carolina's capital, Charleston, was a glittering hub of southern society and wealth. It had strong commercial ties throughout the British Empire. Rice, indigo, and other crops raised largely with slave labor left the docks of Charleston and made fortunes for their planters and shipping merchants alike. But here, too, just as in Massachusetts and other provinces, many citizens held a decided interest in self-government—an inclination to manage the colony's internal affairs without edicts from Parliament as to taxes, tariffs, and regulations.

After the royal governor dissolved the South Carolina legislature in January of 1775, most representatives of the lower house met again in a provincial congress similar to that organized in Massachusetts. By April, this body had become the de facto governing arm of the province. Its members were well aware — having received correspondence from Boston as well as news carried on board ships originating in England — that parliamentary debates brooked little chance of reconciliation.

Consequently, on April 17, two days before the Lexington action, a five-man committee of the South Carolina Provincial Congress took the unprecedented step of intercepting royal dispatches, intended for the acting royal governor, delivered from England on the packet *Swallow*. These documents made clear that the same force that General Gage had been directed to use against insurgents in Massachusetts was to be applied just as aggressively against rebels in South Carolina. In response, on the evening of April 21, rebels seized arms, ammunition, and gunpowder from three arsenals and magazines in and around Charleston, much as their New England brethren had already done in Portsmouth, Salem, and Concord.[16]

Any royal response to these seizures in South Carolina was muted both by the lack of sufficient force to confront the rebels and by the pending arrival of a new royal governor. It would not do to start something drastic before he arrived. Thus on May 3, much of rebel Charleston gathered festively on the docks to wish Godspeed to the colony's five delegates to the Continental Congress as they sailed for Philadelphia on the outbound packet.[17]

A few days later, Charleston learned the news of Lexington and Concord not from postal riders, who were still making their way south through the Carolinas, but from a copy of the *Essex Gazette* when it arrived in town on May 8 on board the brigantine *Industry*. This was the issue of April 25, which went to great lengths to characterize the cruel and savage atrocities of the British regulars and cast the Massachusetts response in the best possible light.[18]

Not only did these one-sided descriptions ring true to southern readers—as they did throughout the colonies—they also gave white South Carolinians particular pause as they confronted an ugly rumor that had been making the rounds. There appeared to be growing concerns about a British-inspired slave uprising throughout South Carolina of the kind Governor Dunmore had threatened in Virginia.

On the very day the South Carolina delegation sailed for the Continental Congress, a ship inbound to Charleston brought a letter from colonial agent Arthur Lee in London to Henry Laurens, one of the province's leading rebels. In it, Lee claimed to know of a plan hatched by Lord North's government "for instigating the slaves to insurrection." This was certainly not a new fear. Lee had written his brother Richard Henry Lee in Virginia about "a proposal for emancipating your Negroes by royal Proclamation & arming them against you" some six months before.[19]

But after the news of Lexington, South Carolina's rebel leaders, most of whom were slaveholders, were suddenly confronted with a triple threat. A subsequent proclamation described these threats as "the actual Commencement of Hostilities against this Continent— the Threats of arbitrary Impositions from Abroad—and the Dread of Instigated Insurrections at Home." If the British were capable of such atrocities as reported at Lexington and Concord, why would they hesitate to unleash a slave insurrection?[20]

What gave this rumored slave revolt further credence was the work of David Margrett (sometimes "Margate"), an itinerant free black preacher who had provoked considerable uproar the previous winter. Margrett had preached to slaves around Charleston that their predicament was akin to the Jews held in bondage in Egypt and that the brewing tensions between their masters and their masters' master in Great Britain would set them free. Margrett had been tending to a flock at an orphanage called Bethesda, near Savannah, Georgia, but given that the benefactress of Margrett's ministries was an English countess, it was not too much of a leap to suspect the hand of Lord North's government behind Margrett's evangelism.

Margrett's recent preaching, Arthur Lee's letter warning of a slave uprising, and the news of British aggressiveness at Lexington and Concord combined to cause white imaginations to run wild about what armed blacks might do. A party of rebels embarked for Georgia to seize Margrett and hang him for his contributions to the unrest. Whatever the rumors of insurrection, they insisted that Margrett was a key contributor. A friendly warning reached Margrett, and he escaped to England before he could be taken, but within weeks continuing fears of a slave revolt were to prove deadly for a free black named Thomas Jeremiah, who was one of Charleston's most accomplished harbor pilots.[21]

Little if anything is known of Jeremiah's early life. He may have been born of a free mother, been granted his freedom by his owner under special circumstances, or purchased his own freedom after receiving his owner's permission to work additional jobs. In Charleston, there were then perhaps only two hundred free blacks out of a black population approaching one hundred thousand across all of South Carolina. The first public notice of Jeremiah may have appeared in the *South-Carolina Gazette* in 1755, when it was reported that he had erroneously piloted the fourteen-gun sloop HMS *Jamaica* onto mudflats off the harbor entrance. He was still an apprentice, and Jeremiah weathered the mistake and a similar one the following year, and by 1775 he was known as "one of the best pilots in the harbor."[22]

Mastering the tides and currents, the shifting sandbars, and the labyrinthine twists and turns of the approaches to Charleston Harbor was no easy task. Those pilots who did so commanded top dollar and were held in considerable esteem—if they were white. Jeremiah nonetheless amassed substantial wealth, even if it came with little personal respect, and by some accounts, by 1775, he may have been "the richest man of African descent in British North America." Jeremiah owned his pilot boat and fishing boats and also engaged in merchant activities. He was also a slave owner, working them on board his various vessels. There is some evidence that Jeremiah took himself quite seriously and was justifiably proud in signing himself "Thomas Jeremiah, (a Free Negro)." To the white establishment, however, he was "Jerry the pilot" or "the Negro Jerry." [23]

Whether Thomas Jeremiah was the mastermind behind a southern slave uprising or merely a prominent black freeman in the wrong place at the wrong time is still a matter of debate. There is no question that throughout South Carolina in the spring of 1775, local militias were preparing to defend themselves against a loyalist-inspired slave revolt as much as they were preparing to fight British regulars to protest their own enslavement. Charleston merchant Josiah Smith Jr. confessed to a friend that his greatest fear was "hostile attempts that may be made by our domesticks, who of late have been taught to believe they will be all sett free on the arrival of our New Governer." Indeed, rumors were rampant that the new governor, Lord William Campbell, was soon to arrive on HMS *Scorpion* with fourteen thousand stands of arms to distribute to slaves and Indians. [24]

For Thomas Jeremiah, the wait for Governor Campbell would ultimately prove deadly. Jeremiah was arrested and charged with fomenting insurrection on the basis of rather dubious claims made by two slaves, one of whom may have been Jeremiah's brother-in-law. After an extended trial that at one point recessed for weeks so that the prosecution could gather more evidence, Jeremiah was judged guilty. His status as a freeman didn't do him any good, because South Carolina's Negro Act mandated that all blacks, once charged with crimes and offenses, were treated as if they were slaves. He was promptly hanged.

Newly arrived Governor Campbell had tried his best to save Jeremiah, but rebel Charleston was unsympathetic both to Campbell's royal position and Jeremiah's plight. Indeed, it appears that the rebels' real fear may have been that Jeremiah and Charleston's other black pilots "might prove valuable to an invading British fleet." [25]

Thomas Jeremiah's hanging was almost surely a miscarriage of justice, just one example of how the heated and emotional tenor of the times became particularly dangerous when one was a free black. According to historian William R. Ryan, many whites claimed that Jeremiah had "overstepped his bounds, exceeded his station, and conspired against provincial authority." [26]

BY NOW, THE NORTHERN FRONTIERS of the colonies were in arms, from New York's Adirondack Mountains all the way eastward through New Hampshire to the seaports of Massachusetts's territory of Maine. Here, too, as in the southern colonies, there was another threat besides British regulars. It did not come from black slaves. Prince Estabrook, Peter Salem, and others had just fought and bled on the rebel side with no guarantees of emancipation. Some northern slaves indeed curried British favor, but they lacked the numbers to pose a great danger. Lurking on the northern borders was a larger and potentially much more hostile enemy.

Relations between Native Americans and English colonists on the northern frontier had always been complex. There were certainly some Indian nations, particularly among the Iroquois Confederacy, who had historically allied themselves with the English against the French. But a great many more had long resisted British colonial expansion. It is perhaps an oversimplification to state it this way, but the very nature of the French colonial experience in North America — transitory trappers and traders moving through the country and bringing with them a mutually beneficial system of barter — tended to embrace and sustain indigenous lifestyles. The English, on the other hand, were largely settlers who came into the land, cut down trees, planted crops, and stayed. With France legally removed from Canada after 1763, British administrators were faced with the task of controlling both their historic Indian allies as well as their restless former enemies.

Early in 1775, General Gage advised the Crown's two principal Indian agents, Guy Johnson for the northern provinces and John

Stuart for the southern provinces, to ensure that those Indian nations within their jurisdictions reserved their loyalty for the Crown and were not won over by rebellious colonists. Gage gave no outright orders that these Indians should launch attacks in the event of open conflict by rebels, but he did advise that they should make themselves "ready to move against the frontiers in case the king should desire their assistance."[27]

That same winter, when Lieutenant Colonel John Caldwell, the commanding officer at Fort Niagara, reported to Gage that Indians in the vicinity of his post appeared to be itching for a fight, Gage gave Caldwell specific instructions that if they indeed felt compelled to attack, they should be encouraged to vent their frustrations on rebel frontiersmen and not the king's troops. If they showed such discretion, Gage told Caldwell, "they would continue to receive their supplies as in the past."[28]

By April, things were far more serious. Two days after the Lexington fight, Gage wrote Canadian governor Guy Carleton that a force of Canadians and Indians "would be of great use on the Frontiers of the Province of Massachusetts Bay Under the Command of a Judicious person."[29]

AFTER A FATEFUL FEW WEEKS, the answer to the Massachusetts question — "Must we stand alone?" — appeared to be that rebels throughout the thirteen colonies would stand together. But the rebels were harried on every side — by British regulars in their face, loyalist neighbors in their midst, the internal threat of a slave insurrection, and the external threat of a British-instigated Indian assault. Nowhere was this final threat more ominous than along the Canadian border, and it would encourage bold action in response.

Chapter 18

"In the Name of the Great Jehovah..."

As if the Massachusetts Provincial Congress did not have enough to occupy its attention that spring around Boston, there was animated talk about acquiring Canada. This was not a new thought. Despite two centuries of exploration and settlement by France, Canada had long been the object of British dreams of colonial expansion. The European wars of the earlier eighteenth century between Great Britain and France had always involved warfare along their tenuous colonial borders from the Great Lakes to Nova Scotia.

Many of those rebels now gathering around Boston who were middle-aged had received their military training in some manner or another during the French and Indian War. Some had sailed to Nova Scotia to storm Louisbourg with the dashing General Wolfe. Others had climbed with him onto the Plains of Abraham, outside Quebec. A great many more had battled in their own backyards, up and down the watery reaches of the Hudson River and Lake Champlain. Their sacrifices had helped Great Britain acquire Canada, and it was memories of those sacrifices that had further inflamed anti-British sentiments after the adversarial Quebec Act.

"Massachusettensis... threatens you with the vengeance of Great-Britain," John Adams warned, and added that the country would "support her claims by her fleets and armies, Canadians and Indians." [1] To many, the Canadian part of this vengeance appeared every bit as real as the Indian portion, and anyone with the slightest sense of geography knew very well the direct route from which it was likely to come.

The Hudson River, flowing south from the Adirondacks to the gateway of New York, and Lakes George and Champlain, draining north down the Richelieu River to the Saint Lawrence, had long been a path of migration, trade, and warfare. In the 1700s, this watery corridor was to colonial America what the Mississippi River and its many tributaries would become to American expansionism a century later. Control the Hudson-to-Champlain corridor and one controlled the most direct line between New York and Quebec; an adversary who did so might also neatly sever the limb of New England from the trunk of the other colonies.

The French had understood this well as they advanced southward from what they called Fort Carillon, at the southern end of Lake Champlain, in the summer of 1757. After the capture of Fort William Henry—made infamous by *The Last of the Mohicans*—the French chose to hunker down at Fort Carillon and make it a fortress, but this threat only intensified British efforts to capture it. Abercromby's ill-fated assault of 1758 failed miserably and cost the young Lord Howe his life, but the following year, the French blew up the fort rather than surrender it. General Jeffery Amherst renamed the post Ticonderoga and set about rebuilding it.

By the spring of 1775, absent any French threat from what was now British Canada, Fort Ticonderoga had fallen into a dismal state of disrepair. It was also severely undermanned. The prize of Ticonderoga, however, was not just its strategic location but also dozens of heavy cannons that had been dragged there two decades before by both the French and British. Many were aging relics, but given the meager resources of the yet-to-be-formed Continental Army, they would make a treasure trove of rebel artillery.

General Thomas Gage, well versed as he was in Britain's frontier

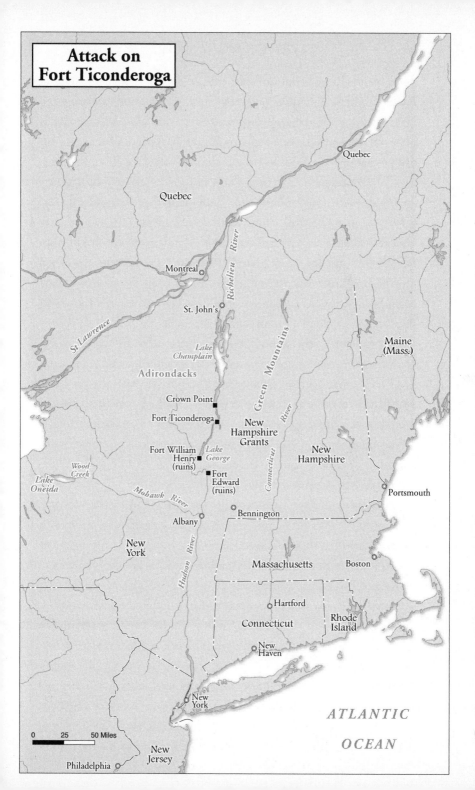

Attack on Fort Ticonderoga

Quebec

Quebec

Montreal

St. John's

Richelieu River

St. Lawrence

Lake Champlain

Maine
(Mass.)

Adirondacks

Crown Point

Fort Ticonderoga

Green Mountains

New
Hampshire
Grants

New
Hampshire

Fort William
Henry
(ruins)

Lake George

Connecticut River

Fort Edward
(ruins)

Wood Creek

Lake Oneida

Mohawk River

Albany

Bennington

Portsmouth

New
York

Hudson River

Massachusetts

Boston

Hartford

Connecticut

Rhode
Island

New
Haven

New
York

ATLANTIC

OCEAN

0   25   50 Miles

New
Jersey

Philadelphia

posts, was fully cognizant of this, and, in light of rebel campaigns at Portsmouth, Salem, and Concord to seize and stockpile weapons, he ordered Fort Ticonderoga's commander, Captain William Delaplace, to be especially on his guard. Delaplace's predicament was not unlike that of other British commanders spread throughout the colonies. He commanded a garrison best fit for caretaking, not fighting. At his disposal was one officer, Lieutenant Jocelyn Feltham, and forty-two men, half of whom were described as "old, wore out & unserviceable," along with about two dozen women and children. In fact, of this number, Lieutenant Feltham and a reinforcement of ten men had only recently arrived from Canada. Had Ticonderoga's garrison been at full strength, it would have boasted at least four hundred soldiers to man its cannons and defend its walls.[2]

Rebel leaders throughout the northern colonies were equally well versed in the importance of Fort Ticonderoga and its present poor condition. Samuel Adams saw the post as critical to holding open the New York–Quebec corridor, through which he hoped would flow a lifeline of men and supplies from Canadians friendly to the rebel cause. "We have lately opend a correspondence with Canada," Adams wrote Arthur Lee, "which, I dare say will be attended with great and good Effects."[3]

John Brown, a young lawyer then practicing in Pittsfield, Massachusetts, delivered Adams's entreaty to Canada — overly optimistic of support though it was — sometime in March of 1775, after a hard journey to Montreal over and around the ice-clogged waters of Lake Champlain. Brown was a delegate to the Massachusetts Provincial Congress and a member of its committee of correspondence with Canada. Ultimately, he was charged with determining whether the province of Quebec would work in concert with rebels in the other colonies.[4]

Brown found a general reluctance among Canadians — be they French-speaking inhabitants of long standing or more recent British arrivals — to get involved with family feuds south of their border. That was disconcerting, but more alarming to his colleagues was that Brown also reported that British troops in Quebec had been ordered "to hold themselves in readiness for Boston, on the shortest notice." This was evidence of precisely the sort of attack down the Hudson-Champlain corridor that many feared. (It was also the strategy that the British would clumsily employ in 1777 at Saratoga and again in 1814 at Plattsburgh.)

But Brown's arduous journey north, during which he reported "almost inconceivable hardships," had given him time to pause at Fort Ticonderoga in the role of an innocent wayfaring stranger, and he reported to Samuel Adams the obvious. "One thing I must mention," wrote Brown, "to be kept as a profound Secret [is that] the Fort at Ticonderoga must be seized as soon as possible, should hostilities be committed by the King's Troops. The people on New-Hampshire Grants have engaged to do this business, and in my opinion they are the most proper persons for this job. This will effectually curb this Province [Quebec], and all the troops that may be sent here."[5] In other words, seize Ticonderoga and block any British effort to strike from Canada and capture New York or sever New England from the rest of the colonies.

Brown made it sound as if the mission to capture Ticonderoga were already arranged, and indeed it may have been with "the people on New-Hampshire Grants," but his letter of March 29, 1775, from Montreal probably did not reach Adams and the Provincial Congress until after the hostilities at Lexington and Concord and after another effort to capture the fort had been set in motion. This meant that two polar opposites were about to converge on the shores of Lake Champlain and—although they were on the same side—almost come to blows with each other. Their names were Benedict Arnold and Ethan Allen.

SUBSEQUENT CONDEMNATION AND LEGEND HAVE frequently obscured the men Benedict Arnold and Ethan Allen were in the spring of 1775. Benedict Arnold was somewhat of a city slicker, an ambitious wheeler-dealer always eager to rush to the forefront. Rough-and-tumble Ethan Allen just naturally assumed that the forefront was wherever he happened to be. At a certain level, both were connivers. About the only other thing the two men had in common was that both had aspired to attend Yale but had been forced by family circumstances to forgo higher education.

Benedict Arnold was thirty-four that spring, and while late of New Haven he had been born in Norwich, Connecticut. When little more than a lad, Arnold had marched to Ticonderoga during the French and Indian War before taking turns as an apothecary, bookseller, horse trader, and shipowner. He was, as he would prove on Lake Champlain, an experienced sailor. He was also an avid reader of military history and, like so many others with a similar interest, immediately presumed himself a military tactician of some standing. A short while before, a good amount of Arnold's passion had been directed to New Haven's rebel network; he had served as captain of a company of its militia. Physically small in stature, he made himself noticed with his manner and dress.

A big bear of a man, Ethan Allen was three years older than Arnold and also a Connecticut native. Allen's French and Indian War experience lay with a company of Connecticut militia that had hurried to the aid of Fort William Henry but turned around after receiving word of the fort's capture. The country southeast of Lake Champlain held Allen's interest, however, and after working with his brothers in an iron foundry, he joined a group of settlers in the area who received land grants that later came to be called the New Hampshire Grants. Allen took an active role in early settlements, fending off competing claims to the area from New York and organizing a local militia. To his admirers, Allen and the men who congregated around him to do the dirty work of settling that rowdy frontier were the Green Mountain Boys. Others less impressed by their antics and crude methods—particularly New Yorkers competing for land in the grants—were more apt to call them the Bennington rioters.

Benedict Arnold could be smooth as silk, but there was a quality about him that made one uneasy. He was apt to undermine his opponents behind their backs. With Ethan Allen there was no question what was coming. He was the essence of in-your-face bluster and bravado. Yet there was also a quality about Arnold's and Allen's determined confidence that made men follow them with unquestioned loyalty and equal enthusiasm.

When Benedict Arnold heard about the confrontations at Lexington and Concord from the post rider who reached New Haven two days afterward, he immediately "rounded up sixty-three members of his Second Connecticut Company of Foot and ordered them . . . ready to march early the next morning." At dawn on April 22, while the New Haven board of selectmen debated a response to the Lexington Alarm, Arnold took the matter out of their hands by demanding the keys to the town's powder magazine. Armed and provisioned, his company of militia then followed him eastward toward Cambridge to offer its services to the budding Continental Army.[6]

Somewhere beyond Hartford, Arnold met up with Samuel Holden Parsons, a colonel in the Connecticut militia who would make a brief but important appearance as the third member of this unlikely trio.

Parsons was just turning thirty-eight, the oldest of the three men. Born in Lyme, Connecticut, he had gone to Harvard instead of Yale only because his parents were living at the time in Newburyport, Massachusetts. After graduating in 1756, he returned to Lyme to practice law and was soon elected to the Connecticut General Assembly at the age of twenty-five. Among his later legislative assignments was the committee advocating Connecticut's western land claims and Connecticut's standing committee of correspondence, in 1773.[7]

It would be fascinating if a transcript existed of the conversation between Benedict Arnold and Samuel Parsons on the road near Hartford. Each would later claim that the idea of attacking Fort Ticonderoga had been his and that he had sold the other on the plan. Nonetheless, even Parsons acknowledged, in a letter apparently written that same day, that Arnold "gave him an account of the state of Ticonderoga, and that a great number of brass cannon were there."[8] Arnold probably presumed to speak confidently in his role as military historian and also emphasized the fort's strategic importance.

The two men soon went their separate ways. Arnold continued east to Cambridge and, with his smooth salesmanship, regaled the committee of safety of the Massachusetts Provincial Congress with tales of the treasure of cannons and other arms at Ticonderoga. He also offered his opinion that the fort "could not hold out an hour against a vigorous onset." Parsons continued west to Hartford and had a similar conversation, but with an ad hoc group of militia leaders rather than any formal governmental body. In Parsons's words, he "first undertook and projected taking that Fort &c, and with the assistance of other persons procured money men &c."[9]

Parsons apparently remained in Hartford, but the band of adventurers he helped to organize headed north through Pittsfield, in western Massachusetts. As they did so, they encountered more men equally excited about the prospects of an expedition to Ticonderoga, including, probably, John Brown, fresh from his mission to Montreal for the Provincial Congress. Augmented by the Pittsfield contingent, this private army continued north.

Not surprisingly, as they passed north of Bennington, they ran into the "people on New-Hampshire Grants" who Brown had reported were "engaged to do this business" of reducing Ticonderoga. This, of course, was Colonel Ethan Allen and his Green Mountain Boys, who were indeed embarked upon the same purpose. The Massachusetts men seem to have immediately recognized that Allen was on his home turf; there was no question but that he would take command of the combined force.

MEANWHILE, THE COMMITTEE OF SAFETY of the Massachusetts Provincial Congress had debated granting Benedict Arnold full leave to capture Ticonderoga on Massachusetts's behalf. All agreed it was a fine idea, but Ticonderoga and the surrounding region of Lakes Champlain and George were contested ground. Whether the area belonged to New York or New Hampshire was of considerable debate, and the province of Massachusetts had little or nothing to do with it.

Consequently, the committee of safety decided to send a missive to New York noting the importance of Ticonderoga and hinting that New York might "give such orders as are agreeable to you" to effect its immediate capture. While coveting "the usefulness of those fine cannon, mortars, and field-pieces which are there," the Massachusetts committee assured its New York neighbors, "we would not, even upon this emergency, infringe upon the rights of our sister Colony."[10]

But then Massachusetts did just that. Recognizing that time was of the essence—just as it was in so many rebel decisions of late—the committee gave Benedict Arnold a temporary commission as colonel and authorized him to raise a force for the specific purpose of capturing Ticonderoga. Evidently suspecting that just such a force was already in the field because of his conversation with Samuel Parsons, Arnold delegated the raising of Massachusetts volunteers to others and hurried north to assume command of whatever troops might be in the field. The full irony of the commission he carried in the pocket of his tunic would not become clear until some months later. It had been signed for the committee of safety by one of its most trusted members, Dr. Benjamin Church.[11]

Arnold caught up with the combined Hartford, Pittsfield, and Green Mountain Boys contingent at the frontier town of Castleton, Vermont, about twenty miles southeast of Ticonderoga, near what is now the New York–Vermont border. Ethan Allen was farther ahead, scouting the approaches to the fort, but the reaction of his men was predictable when Arnold officiously waved his commission and announced that he was assuming command. There were a host of guffaws and chuckles and then so-what shrugs. Arnold could tag along if he wanted, but they would take their orders only from Ethan Allen.

The next day, Allen and Arnold met in person. A man of lesser backbone and force of personality than Arnold probably would have backed down, but Arnold stood his ground in the face of Allen's domineering presence. Capturing Ticonderoga might well be Arnold's path to sudden military celebrity in a continental army. He was not about to let some rough-cut frontiersman, whom he clearly viewed as beneath him — at least as a gentleman — interfere with the opportunity. Allen would have been quite satisfied to settle the matter with a duel, but Arnold instead played the role of charmer and with a certain amount of guile brought Allen under his spell. The result was an agreement to devise a plan of attack and share command, which in military situations is rarely, if ever, a good solution.

On the evening of May 9, these two polar opposites gathered their force — which still did not include any Massachusetts troops — of not quite three hundred men at Hand's Cove, on the eastern shore of Lake Champlain. Slightly up the lake, across about a mile of water, stood the massive walls and forbidding gun emplacements of Ticonderoga. But where were the boats that were supposed to transport them across the lake? Only one small skiff floated at the shore. No other boats were to be found, and as the night wore on, both Arnold and Allen worried that they would be discovered. Finally, in the early hours of May 10, a decrepit scow floated into view. Fearing that their element of surprise would be lost if they waited for better transport, Arnold and Allen for once agreed, and they set off for the opposite shore in the scow with less than a third of their men.

They almost didn't make it. A brisk wind kicked up whitecaps on the lake and rendered the heavily laden scow almost unmanageable. Waves broke over the gunwales and drenched the oarsmen, who desperately tried to make some headway. No one else stayed dry, either. The tattered sail was of no use and only served to make the vessel less stable. It looked as if at any moment eighty-three men would be thrown into the frigid spring waters of Lake Champlain and meet rapid death from hypothermia. Only after an excruciating ninety minutes did the scow touch on the western shore just north of the fort.

But upon landing, the first exchange of combat almost came between Arnold and Allen, as Arnold once again asserted his right to sole command. In one of those ridiculous episodes that leave later observers wondering what they could have been thinking, one of Allen's officers brokered a truce and sent the two leaders, looking like Mutt and Jeff—Allen the towering hulk of a bear and Arnold the diminutive spit-and-polish soldier—marching side by side through dense undergrowth to the gates of the fort.[12]

No warning shot sounded from the ramparts, and while the huge wooden gates were closed, the smaller wicket door stood open in apparent welcome. The lone guard in the sentry box brandished his musket and offered a tentative challenge, but then ran, shouting, into the fort's interior. Allen quickly brushed aside another sentry with his sword and followed. The ragged party formed on the parade ground, facing the two barracks, and according to Allen "gave three huzzas which greatly surprised" the sleeping British garrison.

Allen, with Arnold on his heels, made for the officers' quarters on the second level, where Lieutenant Jocelyn Feltham, the fort's second in command, confronted them. Feltham had stumbled out to inquire about the noise with a dazed look on his face and his breeches in his hand. Meanwhile, Captain Delaplace, the post's commander, refused to open the door to his quarters until he was properly attired. He may well have been having flashbacks to General Gage's letter urging him to be on guard against any unpleasant surprises.

Unpleasant as this was, and trying to buy time for his commander, Lieutenant Feltham demanded to know by what authority this band of rabble had entered His Majesty's fort. Allen's purported response would be repeated by rebels and published in dozens of newspapers throughout the colonies. Even if he didn't say it, the words made for marvelous press. Surrender, Ethan Allen declared, "in the name of the great Jehovah, and the Continental Congress."[13]

Allen himself eschewed organized religion, and the Continental Congress was as yet ignorant of his mission, but the words struck a chord and perfectly caught the tenor of the times—particularly in the retelling—by balancing God and country.

According to Lieutenant Feltham's subsequent report to General Gage, only Arnold's "genteel manner" prevented Allen from storming Captain Delaplace's quarters before the commandant was neat in his uniform with his sword at his side. When Delaplace finally appeared, he was left with little choice but to surrender to Allen and Arnold what only a few years before had been the most heavily defended and most important strategic position between Quebec and New York. Allen's men captured the nearby post of Crown Point and its eleven-man garrison with a similar lack of opposition the next day. Control of Lake Champlain would be more problematic but arguably more important.

On May 11, the day after taking Ticonderoga, Benedict Arnold and Ethan Allen each sat down and wrote separate reports to the Massachusetts Provincial Congress detailing the capture. It is understandable that Arnold, having received his commission from Massachusetts, would do so. But Allen seems also to have done so in an attempt to emphasize his own role in the venture and cloak it in the dubious authority of the Connecticut General Assembly. Although the two protagonists had not come to physical blows in the course of their short campaign together, these initial reports began a duel of letters that Arnold and Allen repeatedly fired off to various authorities in the neighboring colonies.

In his May 11 letter, Ethan Allen noted "with pleasure unfelt before" that "by order of the General Assembly of the colony of

Connecticut" he had taken "the Fortress of Ticonderoga by storm" with "about one hundred Green Mountain Boys and near fifty veteran soldiers" from Massachusetts. Allen made no mention of Benedict Arnold, but went on to report: "The soldiery behaved with such resistless fury, that they so terrified the King's Troops that they durst not fire on their assailants." Allen's short message ended with a plea that Massachusetts immediately assist "the Government of Connecticut in establishing a garrison in the reduced premises." [14]

Benedict Arnold had a great deal more to say, and much of it was about Ethan Allen and his Green Mountain Boys. Having already dispatched a short report on the day of the capture, Arnold then launched into a lengthy indictment of Allen and his methods as well as the manners of his men. Despite their agreement on a joint command, Arnold reported that Allen, "finding he had the ascendance over his people, positively insisted I should have no command," in part because Arnold had insisted on strict order. The result, Arnold claimed, was "near one hundred men, who are in the greatest confusion and anarchy, destroying and plundering private property, committing every enormity, and paying no attention to publick service." As for Allen himself, Arnold found him "a proper man to head his own wild people, but entirely unacquainted with military service." [15] Clearly there were different standards of conduct between New Haven and the New Hampshire Grants. Despite their differences, however, Arnold and Allen were soon involved in another military venture.

Sailor that he was, Benedict Arnold was convinced that the capture of Ticonderoga and Crown Point would not be complete until he controlled the waters of Lake Champlain. Amid a host of dugouts, skiffs, and bateaux, there were two major ships on the lake that could tip the balance of power. One was a schooner owned by loyalist Philip Skene, which had been captured at nearby Skenesborough by Allen's men on the same day as Ticonderoga. The other was the *George*, a British sloop of war. It was then at St. John's,

Quebec, on the Richelieu River near the outlet of the lake, about one hundred miles to the north.

As long as the *George* was at large, there was the threat of several hundred British troops sailing quickly up the lake and recapturing Ticonderoga and Crown Point. Arnold proposed arming Skene's captured schooner and sailing down the lake to surprise the *George* at St. John's before it could get under way with a relief expedition. Whether Ethan Allen embraced this plan at the time or subsequently, in light of its success, is a matter of some debate.

Allen's Green Mountain Boys were initially content to help themselves to whatever plunder Ticonderoga had to offer, and their actions, as Lieutenant Feltham wryly observed, were "most rigidly performed as to liquors." [16] The boys probably thought that Benedict Arnold's scheme to capture the *George* was just a little too far from home. But then the first complement of the Massachusetts men whom Arnold had been authorized to raise arrived on the scene, and this suddenly gave Arnold troops under his own command who held no loyalty to Ethan Allen. At the same time, once the liquor had quenched their thirst, many of Allen's men were ready to leave for their homes to put in spring planting. This was not out of selfishness but in recognition of frontier reality: one might fight for a cause, but one farmed for survival.

The end result was that Benedict Arnold took a complement of his own men on board Philip Skene's newly armed schooner, which Arnold renamed *Liberty*, and made a successful raid against St. John's that captured the *George*. Arnold returned toward Ticonderoga with his little fleet—he also gave the *George* the new name *Enterprise*, the first of a noble line of American warships to bear that name—only to find Ethan Allen and some of his men rowing north in a collection of bateaux. Whether Allen had had second thoughts about being left out of Arnold's attack or had in fact embarked simultaneously with him and been quickly outdistanced by the faster schooner is not entirely clear.

In his memoirs, Ethan Allen never mentioned Benedict Arnold

having been involved in the capture of the fort or anything else until this moment, when Allen's flotilla of bateaux met Arnold's schooner and captured sloop on the lake. According to Allen, Arnold "saluted me with a discharge of cannon, which I returned with a volley of small arms." Allen then joined Arnold aboard the *Enterprise*, "where several loyal Congress healths were drank." But such conviviality was fleeting.[17]

Ethan Allen was bound and determined to continue on and, by seizing and holding St. John's, win a measure of glory that would match what Arnold won with his capture of the *George*. Arnold had picked up intelligence while there that the British were indeed preparing a major counterattack, and he warned Allen that an extended occupation by Allen's men was far different from his hit-and-run raid to capture the sloop. Allen refused to hear such cautionary advice and rowed on toward St. John's. Arnold may have been secretly delighted, because it left him the undisputed commander of Ticonderoga in Allen's absence.

Ethan Allen's foray farther north ended as Benedict Arnold had predicted. British regulars and Canadian militia—the latter far from welcoming to the Americans, contrary to what Samuel Adams and others had hoped—surprised Allen's force just south of St. John's and sent it scurrying southward in a rout. Allen also failed to mention this episode in his memoirs. By May 21, he and his men were once more safely inside the walls of Fort Ticonderoga, where Arnold had taken advantage of Allen's brief absence to cement his own personal control.

MEANWHILE, PITTSFIELD ATTORNEY JOHN BROWN, who that spring had already traveled to Montreal, back to Massachusetts, and then north again to Ticonderoga to take part in the assault with Allen and Arnold, was riding hard to reach the Second Continental Congress in Philadelphia and announce the news of Ticonderoga's capture. After reporting first to Massachusetts while en route,

Brown arrived in Philadelphia on Wednesday night, May 17, and delivered letters from Allen and Arnold to Virginia's Peyton Randolph, the presiding officer. The next morning, Randolph apprised the members of this "important intelligence," had the letters read, and then summoned Brown to give a further account not only of the taking of the post and its importance but also of "the disposition of the Canadians" to help the rebel cause. To the latter, Brown could add no further insight beyond what he had already given to the Massachusetts Provincial Congress: any intervention from Canada was likely to come at the point of a British bayonet and not from legions of Canadians coming south to offer their support to the rebel cause.

After Brown left the assembly, its members began a heated debate. It might seem that Brown's news from Ticonderoga would have been met with wild jubilation in view of the strategic importance of the fort and the newly acquired artillery. But the Continental Congress was, if not deeply divided, at least still tentative on what its broader course of action should be. To be sure, there were avowed rebels on the floor, such as John Hancock and Samuel Adams and Virginia's Patrick Henry. The latter had taken his seat only that very morning, after his gunpowder confrontation at Williamsburg. But there were also some moderates intent on making one last stand for reconciliation with Great Britain.

The run-ins at Lexington and Concord had indeed shed blood between the mother country and its colonies, but many in the Continental Congress and throughout the colonies viewed those battles as defensive in nature — the natural reaction and right of the populace against armed incursion — a self-defense that the numerous affidavits given by rebel participants had gone to great lengths to claim.

The capture of Ticonderoga, clearly His Majesty's fort despite its disrepair, was, however, an entirely different matter. Ethan Allen and Benedict Arnold's cross-country dash — regardless of who was in command—was not an inadvertent clash of arms after someone discharged a weapon on a village green. If this overt act of aggression—tyranny, in the king's eyes—were not renounced, any remaining hope for reconciliation would be extinguished.

New England's representatives, generally recognizing the importance of the Hudson–Lake Champlain corridor and the looming threat not only of British regulars but also of Indians and Canadians sailing or marching along it, took the hard line: occupy the post and rejoice in its armaments. But others prevailed, and the Continental Congress passed a resolution that disingenuously couched the actions of Allen and Arnold as "a just regard for the defence and preservation of themselves and their countrymen" from a threatened invasion from Canada.

Without any mention of occupying the fort, the resolution went on to advise that the captured armaments should be removed from Ticonderoga, taken to the southern end of Lake George—a distance of some thirty-five miles—and kept in a secure post to be established there. "An exact inventory" was to be taken "of all such cannon and stores in order that they may be safely returned when the restoration of the former harmony between Great Britain and these colonies so ardently wished for by the latter shall render it prudent and consistent with the overruling law of self preservation." [18]

HAD COMMUNICATION BEEN TIMELIER, a howl of indignation would no doubt have echoed from the Green Mountains all the way to the Saint Lawrence even as President Randolph's gavel fell that day in the Continental Congress. When Ethan Allen, sitting at Crown Point, read what the Continental Congress had resolved, he could not believe it. When he had invoked its name in demanding surrender, he had expected stouter stuff.

By the time Allen put quill to parchment in response, he was calmer but no less outraged by the recommendation. Allen began by reiterating the facts to his advantage—as usual—and stating his belief that the Congress "approves of the taking the fortresses on Lake Champlain." Actually, the resolution didn't signal approval so much as reflect an effort to find a defensive excuse for actions already taken. Still, Allen charged onward: "I am nevertheless much surprised that your Honours should recommend it to us to remove the artillery to the south end of Lake George, and there to make a stand." Doing so, Allen maintained, would leave his people in the New Hampshire Grants exposed to attack and give up the newly won control of Lake Champlain.

Far from withdrawing from Ticonderoga and Crown Point, Allen urged an attack in force against St. John's and claimed that had he had five hundred men with him on his abortive raid— mentioned as though it had occurred at the same time as Arnold's successful capture of the *George*—he "would have advanced to Montreal." Still singing the refrain of the longed-for Canadian support, Allen somehow concluded that an invasion of Canada would be agreeable to both Canadians and Indians there. As for the British, "it is bad policy," Allen declared, "to fear the resentment of an enemy." [19]

Benedict Arnold expressed similar dismay in his own letter to the Continental Congress. Arnold strongly hinted that the congress was ignorant not only of his charge from the Massachusetts committee of safety but also of his success in taking total control of Lake Champlain. To reverse course now was unthinkable. "I must beg leave to observe, gentlemen," Arnold wrote, "that the report of Ticonderoga's being abandoned, have thrown the inhabitants here into the greatest consternation." [20]

Arnold also told the Massachusetts committee of safety that he was "equally surprised and alarmed" that the Continental Congress had recommended removing all the cannons and stores and evacuating Ticonderoga entirely. "You may depend, gentlemen," Arnold had assured the committee in an earlier communication, "these places will not be given up unless we are overpowered by numbers, or deserted by Providence, which has hitherto supported us."[21] Benedict Arnold and Ethan Allen might have their differences, but they could both agree that they would never voluntarily surrender their hard-won prizes.

Neither, as it turned out, would the colonial legislatures of Connecticut, New York, New Hampshire, and Massachusetts. Fight though they might among themselves over land claims, these colonies exchanged a flurry of letters designed to recruit troops, defend the posts, and keep control of the Hudson–Lake Champlain corridor. They would stand united in this mission as well as in their opposition to the recommendations of the Continental Congress. If nothing else, their independent resolve showed how far away those delegates assembled in Philadelphia were from crafting a strong central government that wielded any real power.

Massachusetts, having stirred the pot by sending Benedict Arnold north in the first place, also now sent a three-man commission to Ticonderoga, purportedly to investigate the Arnold-Allen feud and the general nature of Arnold's administration. This panel was given broad authority not only to review how well Arnold had "executed his Commission and instructions" but also, if necessary, to discharge him and order his return to Massachusetts. The man who moved the most aggressively to bestow these powers on the inquiry panel was the same person who had signed Arnold's commission in the first place—none other than Dr. Benjamin Church.

All of Massachusetts was increasingly preoccupied with events around Boston. Church twisted the facts somewhat and assured his fellow committee of safety members that Connecticut, about to march hundreds of its own troops to Ticonderoga, had demanded that one of its officers command the combined forces. This was not entirely true—command of its own troops, yes, but not of the combined force—and why Church took this position causes some speculation. He may have done so simply to rid Massachusetts of the distraction of a major role in a campaign so far afield from Boston, but quite possibly he had a more sinister motive.

Amid the whispers of a British spy inside the inner circle of the committee of safety, Dr. Church had always been above reproach. But was he? Benedict Arnold, despite what later shame would come to his name and despite his rows with Ethan Allen, had heretofore been highly effective at what he had attempted. By checking Arnold's authority, was Church trying to deprive the rebels of his leadership?

The three Massachusetts officials arrived at Crown Point on June 22, and rather than waste time observing Arnold's methods and evaluating his successes they rather unceremoniously informed him in his cabin onboard the *Enterprise* that he was immediately to turn over his command to Colonel Benjamin Hinman of Connecticut. Arnold, who had been planning a full-scale invasion of Canada, was dumbfounded.[22]

Benedict Arnold might well have stayed on as Hinman's deputy, but he was greatly upset and declared he would not be second in command to any person. The end result was that Arnold resigned his Massachusetts commission on June 24, taking from Ticonderoga a bad taste and a discontent that would only grow in the future. By the time he reached Massachusetts, he received more unwanted news. His thirty-year-old wife, Margaret, had died suddenly of unknown causes the same week as his dismissal, leaving him a widower with three young sons under the age of eight.

Ethan Allen, meanwhile, was faring only slightly better. Before Arnold's encounter with the Massachusetts investigators, Allen had left Ticonderoga in the company of his cousin and erstwhile lieutenant, Seth Warner, and headed for Philadelphia. He was determined to convince the Continental Congress of the wisdom of holding the Lake Champlain posts and present his own plan for invading Canada. The bustling city of Philadelphia would be a shock to Allen, who was more accustomed to New Hampshire villages.[23]

Chapter 19

~

Ben Franklin Returns

A s Ethan Allen and Seth Warner rode south with their frustrations, the Second Continental Congress had been meeting
since May 10 in the Pennsylvania State House in Philadelphia. Fired
by the events on Lexington Green and at Concord's North Bridge,
this gathering was to prove more assertive than the plodding session John Adams had bemoaned the previous fall. Still, there were
far more questions than answers about the course to be taken, and
some of the uncertainty was directed toward the oldest head in the
room. It had been a long time, but Ben Franklin was home.

Revered though he was by many on both sides of the Atlantic,
Benjamin Franklin was nonetheless something of an unknown quantity to the younger generation of rebels who now gathered around
him. At sixty-nine, he was far and away the oldest delegate. Despite
his reputation as a stalwart proponent of colonial rights, Franklin
had been away from the colonies for most of the last two decades.
Some couldn't help but wonder if the years in London had softened
his resolve. Especially among the most ardent of this crowd of young
Turks, who knew where Franklin's true loyalties lay?

Benjamin Franklin had arrived in Philadelphia on board the
Pennsylvania Packet on Friday evening, May 5. Ever the inquisitive
scientist, Franklin, with his fifteen-year-old grandson, Temple, had

recorded the differing water temperatures in the Atlantic to bolster his theory of the Gulf Stream during their crossing from London. The very next day, the Pennsylvania assembly voted to add Franklin's name and those of two others to the list of Pennsylvania delegates already approved the prior December.[1]

"Dr. Franklin is highly pleased to find us arming and preparing for the worst events," a private observer wrote in a letter that was given wide circulation in rebel newspapers. "He thinks nothing else can save us from the most abject slavery and destruction."[2] But in practice, during those first weeks in what would come to be known as Independence Hall, Franklin was far more reserved. John Adams recalled him "sitting in silence, a great part of the time fast asleep in his chair."[3] Others were more skeptical. Some of the delegates, Philadelphia printer William Bradford wrote James Madison, "begin to entertain a great Suspicion that Dr. Franklin came rather as a spy than as a friend, & that he means to discover our weak side & make his peace with the minister [Lord North] by discovering it to him."[4]

Madison did not give Franklin the benefit of the doubt. "Indeed it appears to me," Madison responded to Bradford, "that the bare suspicion of his guilt amounts very nearly to a proof of its reality. If he were the man he formerly was, & has even of late pretended to be," Madison continued, "his conduct in Philada. on this critical occasion could have left no room for surmise or distrust."[5]

Part of Franklin's reticence to engage in these early debates was a matter of style. He had always been one to brood and contemplate privately before uttering what in retrospect would appear as profound observations. But since he had missed the gathering of so many of these same men the prior fall, Franklin was also taking his time—in between naps—to be certain he understood the depth of their individual commitments.

By now the moderates, it appeared, had largely been sent packing. Even Franklin's friend and longtime ally in Pennsylvania politics, Joseph Galloway, had been swept aside. Despite his election as a delegate to this congress, Galloway asked that he be excused from serving. His moderation had failed, and even Franklin had criticized his compromise plan for a junior-level Parliament in North America. Galloway would soon take his place in the loyalist camp, and his friendship with Franklin would run its course.

But most trying to Franklin during these days was the matter of loyalties within his own family. Even as Franklin landed in Philadelphia, his son, William, was still the royal governor of New Jersey and going to great lengths to proclaim his loyalty to the king. With family confrontation quite likely, grandson Temple became a pawn between the grandfather he adored and the father he barely knew. (Siring illegitimate sons—such as William and Temple—was something of a Franklin family tradition.) Ironically, it was Joseph Galloway, with whom William Franklin had once studied law, who made a last-ditch effort to broker a family truce.

Galloway hosted the three generations of Franklins at Trevose, his magnificent country home just north of Philadelphia. To all appearances, Galloway had long been the lord and master of Trevose, but the vast estate was legally part of his wife's inheritance, a situation that would come to weigh heavily on Galloway's own family relationships as the divide widened between rebels and loyalists. But for now, his attention was focused on the Franklins.

Their reunion was cordial, but rather stiff and without mention of politics until a few glasses of Madeira managed to loosen their tongues. "Well, Mr. Galloway," the senior Franklin asked his host, "you are really of the mind that I ought to promote a reconciliation?" Galloway affirmed that he was, but Franklin had already heard that much and more from Lord Howe back in England. He responded with a litany of colonial complaints, which Galloway answered with his own list of affronts that included anonymous rebels sending him a noose: evidently his moderation in proposing to save the British union was intolerable to some of his countrymen.

As Galloway and Ben Franklin volleyed back and forth, William offered that it might be best for them all to remain neutral. To his father, such a course smacked of timidity rather than resolve, and one senses that Franklin would have had more respect for his son had William firmly staked out his position then and there, no matter how opposed it was to Franklin's own views. By the time they all parted, there could be no question in Galloway's mind or that of William where Benjamin Franklin stood. There could be no middle ground. He was for independence.

The one family matter that the Franklins resolved at Trevose was to agree that young Temple would spend the summer with his father in New Jersey before returning to Philadelphia to enroll in the University of Pennsylvania in the fall. William lobbied to send the lad to King's College (later Columbia College, then Columbia University) in New York City instead, but grandfather Benjamin vetoed that plan because New York had become "a hotbed of English loyalism." Poor Temple remained caught in the middle between his father and grandfather.[6]

Joseph Galloway would go on to assist the British in their administration of Philadelphia during the war. Years later, particularly bitter from the defeat of his moderate plan at the First Continental Congress, Galloway would claim that the rebel leaders had used "every fiction, falsehood, and fraud to incite the ignorant and vulgar to arms."[7]

When Galloway finally slunk away to England in exile as the British abandoned Philadelphia in 1778, his wife, Grace Growden Galloway, stayed behind to fight for her inheritance of Trevose even though she had two strikes against her — she was a woman and a loyalist. William Franklin continued to serve as the royal governor of New Jersey until the New Jersey Provincial Congress finally declared him "an enemy to the liberties of this country" and had him arrested. Later exchanged for a rebel prisoner, he then offered his services to the British in administering New York City.[8] Meanwhile, Benjamin Franklin went about building a new nation.

AMONG FRANKLIN'S FELLOW DELEGATES AT the Second Continental Congress were a high number of reappointees from the first session, held the previous September. The new man in the Massachusetts delegation was John Hancock, never one to shrink from any prominent role. Hancock's short-lived experience as president of the Massachusetts Provincial Congress and his habit of leading in any venue in which he found himself would stand him in good stead.

One of Samuel Adams's preoccupations upon arriving in Philadelphia was to outfit himself with new clothes befitting his role — perhaps at the dapper Hancock's urging. Adams had arrived in Philadelphia straight from Lexington with "only the Cloaths on my back, which were very much worn." With his customary casual approach to monetary matters, it was almost two years before Adams got around to billing the Massachusetts legislature for what he considered "a Necessity, of being at an extraordinary Expense, to appear with any kind of Decency for Cloathing & Linnen after my Arrival in this City."[9]

The five South Carolina delegates who had sailed so gaily from Charleston had arrived in Philadelphia in time, as had John Jay of New York and Caesar Rodney of Delaware. An assembly in Savannah, Georgia, declined to certify a slate of delegates, but St. John's Parish took exception and dispatched Dr. Lyman Hall on his way nonetheless. Hall was seated with the understanding that he would not vote upon matters "when the sentiments of the Congress were taken by colonies." Once the delegates had assembled, Peyton Randolph of Virginia was again elected president of the congress.[10]

Aside from an inordinate amount of fussing with parliamentary procedure and credentials, the Continental Congress addressed three issues of major and continuing importance during its first few weeks: publicity, money, and an army. John Hancock's first action as a delegate was to lay before the congress resolutions passed by Massachusetts in the wake of Lexington and Concord, along with the depositions taken from participants and Joseph Warren's fiery letter to British inhabitants, which had been sent to England aboard the *Quero*. Recognizing the importance of disseminating the rebel version of events throughout the colonies, the Continental Congress ordered that the same be published in as many newspapers as possible.[11]

Other requests from Massachusetts could not be accommodated so readily. Joseph Warren's most critical communication from the Massachusetts Provincial Congress proudly reported Massachusetts's "*unanimous* Resolve" to raise its own force of 13,600 men, but made clear that in the face of British reinforcements this would not be enough. The rest of New England was arming itself in similar proportions, but Warren warned that "a powerful Army, on the side of America" and under the direction of the Continental Congress, was the only means left "to stem the rapid Progress of a tyrannical Ministry."[12]

This was a big step, and the Continental Congress did what legislative bodies have always done with thorny issues: they referred it to a committee — in this case the entire congress sitting as a committee of the whole — for due consideration. But events were overtaking any semblance of measured debate. Rebels in New York sent the congress a missive similar to Warren's and asked what their response should be to the arrival of the fresh regiments of British troops that were expected any day in New York City. The congress encouraged New York to act only on the defensive, as long as they could do so "consistent with their safety and security." The British troops should be allowed to take up quarters in barracks "so long as they behave peaceably and quietly . . . [but] if they commit hostilities or invade private property, the inhabitants should defend themselves and their property and repel force by force."[13]

This defensive posture was similar to the position that Massachusetts maintained it had taken at Lexington and Concord — the vicious attacks on Percy's retreating column notwithstanding. But then came news via John Brown of Ethan Allen and Benedict Arnold's capture of Fort Ticonderoga. This act could hardly be considered "defensive," no matter how the Green Mountain Boys chose to portray it.

The Continental Congress vacillated and dispatched its wishy-washy response — advising the rebels to store captured property until it could be returned to the king — that so infuriated both Allen and Arnold. Benjamin Franklin at this point still seems to have been in his phase of brooding observation. Having recognized the threats from beyond the northern frontier and called for common defense as early as 1754, in his Albany Plan of Union, Franklin should have been a force who urged a concerted offensive. But Franklin wasn't quite ready to lead his fellow delegates off a cliff that could only end in independence or destruction.

Barely had the Continental Congress sent its Ticonderoga response north, however, than it addressed the situation in New York with more military vigor and passed resolutions concerning fortifications along the Hudson River and the arming and training of troops. Next came a letter to "the oppressed Inhabitants of Canada" drafted by New York's John Jay. It expressed hope that the recent forays around Ticonderoga had given Canadians "no uneasiness" and assured these northern neighbors, "We yet entertain hopes of your uniting with us in the defence of our common liberty." The missive was translated into French, and one thousand copies were printed and "sent to Canada, and dispersed among the Inhabitants there." [14]

Meanwhile, all this talk about armies was stirring the martial spirit in almost every delegate assembled, save perhaps Benjamin Franklin and Samuel Adams. Franklin had never held strong military ambitions, and Samuel Adams had long recognized that his place was among the plotters in legislative halls and not upon battlefields. But his cousin John couldn't help but be caught up in the glory of it. "Oh that I was a Soldier!" John Adams wrote Abigail. "I will be. — I am reading military Books. — Every Body must and will, and shall be a soldier." [15]

One of those who most wished for a military command was John Hancock. When Peyton Randolph, after only two weeks as the congress's president, decided that he must return immediately to Virginia, Hancock saw his opportunity to move to the forefront.

He turned to both John Adams and George Washington for assistance. These two men had begun to form close ties with each other that went well beyond their respective provincial boundaries. They were discussing the broader ramifications of continental union as opposed to mere independence. On May 24 with their support, Hancock was unanimously elected to succeed Randolph as president of the Continental Congress.[16] (Randolph was also speaker of the Virginia House of Burgesses, and Governor Dunmore had unexpectedly called it into emergency session. By midsummer, a young Thomas Jefferson would arrive in Philadelphia to replace Randolph as a member of the Virginia delegation.)

For the moment, Hancock's role was that of a civilian leader. Joseph Warren was adamant about the supremacy of civilian control of any military forces—"otherwise," as he wrote to Samuel Adams, "our soldiery will lose the ideas of right and wrong, and will plunder, instead of protecting the inhabitants."[17] But President Hancock clearly expected military lightning to strike him when the time was right. What Hancock apparently did not grasp was that when that time came, one of the brokers of his election as president of the congress would be his rival. George Washington had been wearing his resplendent colonial uniform to the sessions, and at forty-three it gave him an air of a battle-tested hero. Three days after Hancock's election as president, Washington was appointed to chair a committee of seven, which included Samuel Adams, to consider "ways and means to supply these colonies with Ammunition and military stores."[18]

The floodgates that had been holding back concerted military action were opening. It hadn't taken very long. On May 31, the congress received Benedict Arnold's warning that a force of four hundred British regulars—almost surely an inflated number—were gathering at St. John's and along with "a number of Indians" were expected to sail up Lake Champlain "with a design of retaking Crown-point and Ticonderogo." The congress quickly reversed its mild-mannered approach of only two weeks before and requested that Governor Trumbull of Connecticut send a strong reinforcement to garrison both forts and keep "so many of the cannon and other stores . . . as may be necessary for the immediate defence of those posts." New York was asked to furnish those troops with provisions and other necessary stores and also provide a sufficient number of bateaux for use on the lake.[19]

How to pay for all this was another matter. This was to be a leap of faith. During a Saturday session on June 3, the congress took the first step and resolved to empower the Pennsylvania delegation to borrow six thousand pounds, "the repayment of which with interest, the Congress will make full and ample provision." The intent was that the locals would knock on the doors of Philadelphia banks, obtain loans, and then apply the funds toward "the purchase of gunpowder for the use of the Continental Army."[20] Technically, there was not yet a Continental Army, but a strong plea to create one was on the table.

The day before, Dr. Benjamin Church had arrived in town and delivered the petition of the Massachusetts Provincial Congress, which had been entrusted to his special care and personal delivery. Church had been a very busy person—signing Benedict Arnold's original commission, dispatching the committee to investigate Arnold's leadership, and attending to myriad details for the committee of safety among the troops gathering about Cambridge. But in that critical month of May, with so much in flux on all sides, it is hard to imagine a more important or delicate assignment for Church than to convey to the Continental Congress the Massachusetts plea that it create a national army. "As the Army now collecting from different colonies is for the general defence of the right of America," the petition concluded, "we wd beg leave to suggest to yr consideration the propriety of yr taking the regulation and general direction of it, that the operations may more effectually answer the purposes designed."[21]

The words, signed by Joseph Warren as president of the Provincial Congress, were one thing, but Dr. Church was also counted on to lend a persuasive personal touch and credibility to the Massachusetts delegates and help them convince the other delegates of the exigencies of the moment. In the end, however, that diplomatic duty would fall to John Hancock and Samuel Adams, because deep down in his soul Benjamin Church was a very conflicted man.

On May 24, the day before he left Cambridge for Philadelphia—he may or may not have previously made another clandestine visit to Boston—Church had written a lengthy letter to someone who appears to have been a frequent recipient of his communications. "May I never see the day when I shall not dare to call myself a British American," Church confessed before getting to the nub of the matter: "I am appointed to my vexation to carry the dispatches to Philadelphia, & must set out tomorrow wh will prevent my writing for some time, unless an opportunity should be found thence by water." [22]

One hundred and fifty years later, this letter—along with Rachel Revere's undelivered note to her husband—would be found among the papers of Thomas Gage. When it was, it would become damning evidence that for at least two years, Dr. Benjamin Church, the insider's insider of the Massachusetts committee of safety, had been passing rebel information to General Gage.

But for the moment, Dr. Church was above suspicion. As he left Philadelphia about a week later to carry resolutions from the Continental Congress back to Massachusetts, no one among the rebel hierarchy doubted his allegiance to their cause. Only Church and General Gage knew the depth of his treachery. For Gage, it was simply a matter of military intelligence bought and paid for. As for Church, he had gladly taken the pieces of silver, but at a cost to himself that was much greater. "Oh for Peace & honor once more," Church lamented, but it was not to be. [23] Meanwhile, Benjamin Franklin, the man whose own loyalty some had questioned, was appointed to a committee charged with drafting yet one more last-ditch petition of reconciliation to George III. [24]

~

Chapter 20

Lexington of the Seas

While the Continental Congress and provincial congresses of the various colonies debated courses of action, the rebel noose around Boston grew tighter and tighter. With a cork in the bottle of Boston Neck, the only ingress and egress to and from Boston was via the surrounding waters of greater Boston Harbor. It was inevitable that watery conflicts would arise, and with the news of Lexington and Concord fresh on their minds, rebels did not hesitate to contest the power of the Royal Navy.

On May 11, 1775, HMS *Falcon*, the same fourteen-gun sloop that the month before had delivered the original copies of Lord Dartmouth's action orders to General Gage, was anchored in a cove off northern Martha's Vineyard, about seventy air miles south of Boston on the far side of the Cape Cod peninsula. Since its departure from England the previous February, the *Falcon* had been under the command of thirty-two-year-old John Linzee, an experienced master with somewhat of an aggressive reputation. *Falcon*'s assignment was to interdict ships attempting to circumvent the closures mandated by the Boston Port Act and land cargoes elsewhere in Massachusetts. About 6:00 p.m., Linzee sent the *Falcon*'s barge out to intercept a sloop returning from Nantucket Island on the pretense that it lacked proper clearance.

The suspect sloop was the property of Simeon Wing of Sandwich, sailing under the command of his son Thomas. For some years, the Wings had made regular trips to Nantucket with cargoes of wood, returning in ballast and squaring up with customs officials on an annual basis. Thomas Wing was brought aboard the *Falcon*, and Commander Linzee informed him that he and his ship would be released only if he provided information on nearby vessels recently arrived from the West Indies.

Wing initially pleaded ignorance, but one of his crew offered that a ship owned by Jesse Barlow was somewhere on the far side of Buzzards Bay near Fairhaven, offloading a cargo just arrived from the West Indies. Apparently its stay would be short, as Barlow was eager for it to return to the Indies and continue what appeared to be regular voyages. Thomas Wing may have finally confessed to this as well, but he paid for his earlier loyalty. Commander Linzee seized Wing's ship, armed it with fourteen of his crew under the command of midshipman Richard Lucas, and then ordered Lucas to sail Wing's sloop in search of Barlow's West India trader. Reports differ as to whether Wing went along with Lucas or was detained on the *Falcon* as a hostage, but subsequent events suggest the former.

Midshipman Lucas and Wing's sloop found Jesse Barlow's West India trader in a cove on the west side of Buzzard's Bay, where it had already landed its cargo. Lucas seized the Barlow sloop, and although he must have been getting short on men, he put a prize crew aboard it and started both ships back toward Martha's Vineyard. Lucas was feeling rather smug, but Jesse Barlow was furious and determined to strike back.

In the port of Fairhaven, on the western coast of Buzzards Bay, Barlow commandeered a forty-ton sloop—named, appropriately enough, *Success*—and appealed to the local militia to lend him officers and a crew of some thirty men. With militia captain Daniel Egery in command and Barlow footing half the cost of the outfitting, the *Success* stood out of Fairhaven Harbor in the early evening of

May 13 in search of what one newspaper report called "these *royal* pirates." The *Success* was only armed with two swivel guns, and it was clearly no match for the *Falcon*'s fourteen six-pounders should it come across Linzee's sloop. Encountering dense fog and light winds, the *Success* didn't get very far in its pursuit that evening, but those same conditions meant that Midshipman Lucas had been unable to return his two prizes to the protection of the *Falcon*, which Commander Linzee had rather nonchalantly kept anchored off Martha's Vineyard.

The result was that sunrise on May 14 found the *Success* in sight of one of the sloops, which was taken without firing a shot. While this vessel was sailed into Fairhaven, the *Success* located Lucas's second sloop trying to raise sail and get under way. This capture was to be more difficult, and the resulting gunfire gave rise to the claim that this action in Buzzards Bay was the Lexington of the Seas. As *Success* closed with the second sloop, "the pirates fired upon them; the fire was immediately returned, by which three of the pirates were wounded, among whom was the commanding officer." Once subdued, this sloop was also sailed into Fairhaven, and the rebels detained Midshipman Lucas and his original prize crew as prisoners. Commander Linzee, aboard the *Falcon*, was particularly irate when he heard the news.

Jesse Barlow and Thomas Wing, on the other hand, should have rejoiced and been pleased to have their vessels back, but it wasn't that simple. The townspeople in nearby Dartmouth told them that their ships would be released if Wing paid an eight-dollar fee; Barlow was assessed ten dollars. The two paid the fees, but then locals decided that they best refer the entire matter to the Provincial Congress, with the result that the ships remained tied to the wharf. Notwithstanding this referral, the price of freedom was now announced to be forty-five dollars more for both ships.

Wing and Barlow were also required to sign bonds to indemnify the locals. What they were indemnifying them from is not entirely clear. Perhaps the townspeople were merely looking for a ready source of income or covering themselves should Commander Linzee and the *Falcon* glide into their harbor looking for revenge. In any event, the two captured sloops, even though owned and manned originally by Barlow and Wing, who by all accounts manifested rebel leanings, were branded "British sloops." In 1927, the New Bedford chapter of the Sons of the American Revolution erected a marker at Fort Phoenix, off Fairhaven, that read: "On the waters of Buzzards Bay within sight of this spot the first naval battle of the Revolutionary War was fought on May 14, 1775. Twenty-five days after the battle of Concord and Lexington, a gallant force of Fairhaven men . . . in the sloop Success, captured two British sloops and their crews." [1]

AS THE NOOSE TIGHTENED AROUND Boston, fresh provisions for its soldiers and citizens, as well as fodder for its livestock, became increasingly scarce. General Gage turned his attention to the many islands that dotted the broader reaches of Boston Harbor. One of those was Grape Island, a rather innocuous dot roughly fifty acres in area. It rose to about seventy feet above sea level almost ten miles southeast of Boston, off Upper Neck Point and the towns of Weymouth and Hingham. Today, Grape Island is part of the Boston Harbor Islands National Recreation Area. In 1775, it was a lush haven of livestock and hay owned by Elisha Leavitt of nearby Hingham. By all accounts, Leavitt was a dedicated loyalist who had either sold or donated hay and livestock to the British in the past. General Gage was determined that the remainder of Leavitt's provisions be secured to the benefit of his forces.

Accordingly, on May 21, a Sunday morning—Gage could not seem to resist mounting such forays on the Sabbath—the Royal Navy dispatched three sloops and an armed schooner (the latter may have been the newly purchased HMS *Diana*) to procure cargoes of hay. About thirty regulars from the Forty-Third Regiment, under the command of Lieutenant Thomas Innis, went along to ensure their success. But as this little fleet of shoppers dropped anchor off Grape Island, rumors flew along the shore that their real target was nearby Weymouth and that the town was to be burned to the ground. The alarm spread to Braintree, where Abigail Adams, upon hearing the alarm guns, was immediately concerned for the safety of her children. "People, women, children . . . came flocking down this way," Abigail wrote John in Philadelphia, "every woman and child driven off from below my father's; my father's family flying." [2]

As the alarm spread, several thousand militiamen began to gather. They arrived with haste equal to that of the fleeing civilians. "The alarm flew like lightning," Abigail told John, and soon three companies were dispatched to the shore as an advance guard against a possible British landing. Their orders were merely to observe, but gathering close to the island they soon began to fire at the regulars across the water despite the fact that they were beyond range. One of the sloops fired a few rounds from its swivel guns in return, but the balls flew over the heads of the rebels. Meanwhile, Lieutenant Innis's men continued to load hay on board the ships.

By now it was late morning, and as the tide came in it floated several lighters that had been grounded near shore. Dozens of rebel militia swarmed on board and began to row for Grape Island. By the time this little force reached the island, on the point nearest the mainland, the regulars were hastily embarking for their ships from the opposite end. As the British vessels paraded past en route back to Boston, the sloops and schooner let loose some cannons, and the rebels replied with muskets. Meanwhile, the rebels burned whatever hay the British had not taken, set fire to Leavitt's barn, and removed the balance of his livestock. Casualties for the entire fray were but three British regulars wounded. [3]

Still, it was a lot of show for one or two tons of hay — the equivalent of about fifty bales. Lieutenant John Barker of the Fourth Regiment — never one to have much good to say about the efforts of his superiors — called the entire affair "the most ridiculous

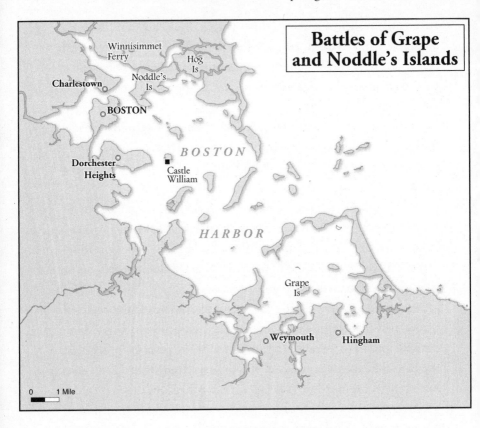

Battles of Grape and Noddle's Islands

Winnisimmet Ferry

Hog Is

Charlestown

Noddle's Is

BOSTON

BOSTON

Dorchester Heights

Castle William

HARBOR

Grape Is

Weymouth

Hingham

0   1 Mile

expedition that ever was plan'd." Barker thought there had been neither enough ships nor enough men for the job. On the rebel side, the angst of Abigail Adams and her neighbors aside, the response proved once again how quickly local militia could turn out to oppose a threat.[4]

But with the British regulars sailing back to Boston, how did the rebels of Hingham feel about their neighbor Elisha Leavitt, who was at least partially responsible for the intrusion into their Sabbath? By one anecdotal account from Hingham's history, an angry band of rebels set out for Leavitt's house, which was a rather grand structure. Instead of running, Leavitt and his wife, Ruth, appeared in their Sunday-go-to-meeting attire, set out a spread of crackers, cheese, and cake, and then cracked open a barrel of rum, "dispensing its contents liberally." Supposedly this calmed the crowd, and the so-called Battle of Grape Island ended with the civility of a garden party.[5]

THE MINOR AFFAIR OF GRAPE ISLAND was to be but a precursor to a much more involved confrontation one week later. Northeast of the North End of Boston in 1775 — generally in the direction that the Sumner and Callahan Tunnels run toward Logan Airport today — lay the expanse of Noddle's Island. Beyond Noddle's Island, in the same general direction, were Hog and Snake Islands. Hog Island had some low hills, but Noddle's Island was relatively flat and well suited to hay fields and livestock. At that point in time, though, anyone trying to tend either faced a quandary.

Those who sold their goods to the British faced the wrath of rebels — just as Elisha Leavitt did — and those who sold goods to the rebels faced the wrath of the British. One resident of Hog Island was duly warned that because "the people from the Men of War frequently go to the Island to buy fresh provision his own safety obliges him to sell to them [but] on the other hand the Committee of safety have threatened if he sells anything to the [British] army or Navy that they will take all the cattle from the Island and . . . handle him very roughly."[6]

The Massachusetts committee of safety was well aware of this quandary and determined to do something about it on behalf of the rebels. On May 24, it ordered all sheep and hay removed from Noddle's Island together with all livestock on the other two islands.[7] General Artemas Ward sent Colonel Ephraim Doolittle with a force of Massachusetts and Connecticut men from Cambridge to implement the committee's directive. Soldiers from Colonel John Stark's First New Hampshire Regiment, which was stationed in nearby Medford, reinforced them.

Despite the islands involved, this was hardly a naval exercise. The water between Chelsea, on the mainland, and Hog Island was only knee-deep at low tide and much the same in the channel called Crooked Creek, between Hog and Noddle's Islands. About midday on May 27, upwards of five hundred rebels waded across the Chelsea–Hog Island channel and began rounding up livestock on Hog Island. A smaller detachment of about thirty men continued on to Noddle's Island to corral other livestock and burn hay, but there they were not alone. The Royal Navy had recently occupied buildings on Noddle's Island in which to warehouse stores, and the army was also stockpiling hay there for its horses in Boston. By one account, there were about six hundred sheep and some cattle and horses on the island.[8]

By coincidence, the very day of the rebel incursion, Admiral Samuel Graves, commander in chief of the Royal Navy's North America squadron, was on his fifty-gun flagship, HMS *Preston*, celebrating his promotion to Vice Admiral of the White by receiving thunderous salutes from the ships of his squadron. Admiral Graves was not known for his dash or aggressive demeanor, and he seems to have been as intent on interservice fighting with General Gage as he was on subduing rebels.

Graves had begrudgingly arranged for the transport of Colonel Smith's Lexington force across the Charles, stood the *Somerset* and other warships off Charlestown to effect Percy's retreat, and generally been content, via his command of the seas, to keep Boston Harbor open—a relatively easy thing, since the rebels lacked any naval power. As the siege of Boston tightened and fresh produce and victuals of any kind became hard to come by, one suspects that Admiral Graves—thanks to his supplies on Noddle's Island—was eating far better than General Gage.

Amid the pomp of his promotion ceremony, Admiral Graves was aware of an urgent message from General Gage dated two days before, reporting that Gage had received intelligence that "the Rebels intend this Night to destroy, and carry off all the Stock & on Noddles Island for no reason but because the owners having sold them for the Kings Use." (Benjamin Church wasn't the only spy employed by Gage, and such intelligence may have come from any number of informants. Church himself was on the road to Philadelphia at that point.) Graves's response was typical. The admiral told the general that his patrol boats would keep the "strictest look out," but begged "leave to observe to your Excellency that in My opinion A Guard upon the Island is the Most probable Means of preserving the Hay from being destroyed"—intending to throw the issue back in Gage's lap.[9]

Now, as Graves looked in that direction, he did not need a telescope to see the billowing black clouds from the hay fires and know that something was amiss. His first reaction was to sigh and complain that Gage and the army had let him down again and that "assistance from the Army could not immediately be had." But with "no time to be lost," he swung into action. A small marine guard of forty men was already on Noddle's Island, and as it moved to engage the marauding rebels Graves ordered a larger force of marines to be landed in support. He also dispatched the small schooner HMS *Diana*, under the command of his nephew, Lieutenant Thomas Graves, to sail between Noddle's Island and the mainland as far as the depth would allow and frustrate the rebels' line of retreat.[10]

Armed with four six-pounders and a dozen smaller swivel guns, the *Diana* soon poured fire on the rebels on Noddle's Island while the larger force of marines splashed ashore from longboats. In the face of this assault, the Noddle's Island force slaughtered what livestock they had corralled, set fire to a farmhouse and barn, and retreated across Crooked Creek. About fifteen of them, including Private Amos Farnsworth of Groton, "Squated Down in a Ditch on the mash and Stood our ground" as a company of marines marched into view. "We had A hot fiar untill the Regulars retreeted," Farnsworth recalled. "But notwithstanding the Bulets flue very thitch yet thare was not A Man of us kild." On the British side, two marines were killed and two others wounded, one mortally.[11]

By then it was about 5:00 p.m. The *Diana* was in the shallows between Hog Island and the mainland, attempting to trap the rebels there until the high tide might strand them. But at the same time, with the tide still ebbing, it was dicey business for Lieutenant Graves and the *Diana*. The schooner exchanged heavy fire with the rebels on Hog Island and continued to do so as the rebels managed to escape the island and re-form on the Chelsea mainland. This left the rebels safe from the advancing marines on Noddle's, but as Lieutenant Graves tried to steer the *Diana* back to deeper waters and make his own escape, the wind died completely. The *Diana* became trapped and unable to maneuver in the shallow water. Graves put out the ship's boats in a hurried attempt to tow it to safety.

As more rebels congregated along the Chelsea shore, they poured fire into the *Diana*, a barely moving target. Admiral Graves dispatched eight to ten longboats to his nephew's assistance, but they rowed into an increasing fusillade of rebel fire as they attached towropes. For a time, the crews of the flotilla of longboats struggled to make headway as the guns of *Diana* returned the rebel fire.

All this made for quite a show along the Chelsea shore. By 9:00 p.m., with the sun setting, Israel Putnam and Joseph Warren arrived on the rebel side with two fieldpieces and still more men. Both were drawn to the sound of the guns. Putnam called out to the *Diana* to surrender and be given appropriate quarter, but Lieutenant Graves answered with two cannon shots. Putnam directed his two fieldpieces to respond, and despite one cannon later exploding and wounding four of its gun crew, this concentrated fire lasted two hours as the *Diana* slowly drifted along the shore.

Finally, the schooner caught on the ways of the Winnisimmet ferry. These ways were heavy wooden beams that ran like railroad tracks into the water to facilitate hauling boats ashore. For the *Diana*, they proved to be a spider's web. The schooner came fast aground and soon heeled over to the point that Graves and his crew could no longer stand on deck. They abandoned ship and were rescued by the nearby longboats well after midnight.[12]

By sunrise on May 28, the rebels had boarded the *Diana* and were making off with what plunder had survived the shelling, including the ship's cannons and swivel guns. A British sloop, the *Britannia*, tried to prevent this with another round of cannon fire, but the rebels on board the *Diana* responded in kind and then piled bales of hay under the vessel's stern and set it on fire. By 7:00 a.m. the *Diana* was a flaming wreck.

On the British side, Admiral Graves held the requisite court-martial for a commander who had lost his ship, but "the persever-ance and good Conduct" of his nephew were judged to be beyond reproach. As Lieutenant Graves and all his crew had "lost every thing they possess on Board her," Graves asked the Admiralty to indemnify them for their personal losses and termed the encounter "an Example to the whole Fleet to defend his Majesty's Ships and Vessels to the last Extremity." [13]

News of this encounter gave a huge boost to the morale of the rebel troops around Cambridge, who were in the doldrums of not having much to do. It had only been a small, lightly armed schoo-ner, but rebel forces — on land, of all places — had taken on the Royal Navy and left one of its ships ablaze.

THE NAVAL ACTION THAT TOOK place in and around the waters of Machias, Maine, in May and June 1775 was not so clear-cut as that off Noddle's Island. Instead, it showed just how convoluted things could become as rebels and loyalists maneuvered for power. Machias was about as far east as one could get and still be in Maine, then a district of Massachusetts. Established in 1763, Machias was a log-ging town. Its economy and the well-being of its one thousand or so inhabitants revolved around lumber that was shipped principally to Boston in exchange for just about everything the town needed. Among the leading players in this commerce were Morris O'Brien and his six sons, who owned one of the local sawmills, and Stephen Jones, who managed the local mercantile interests of his uncle, Boston merchant Ichabod Jones.

Machias was not immune from the political passions sweeping the rest of colonial America, but it had pressing matters of survival. The winter of 1774–75 had not been a good one. A severe drought the previous summer had decimated what local crops there were, and the closures mandated by the Boston Port Act meant that the normal flow of lumber and supplies between the town and Boston were interrupted. Ichabod Jones, who had passed the winter in Machias because of the growing unrest in Boston, determined to break this deadlock, and early in May of 1775 he sailed for Boston with his two vessels, the sloops *Unity* and *Polly*, loaded with lumber.

It seems likely that Jones sold the lumber to the British and then convinced General Gage — who was all too happy to receive it — that he should be permitted to return to Machias carrying not only certain provisions for the town but also a significant stash of merchandise from his Boston warehouses — exactly the sort of transaction that Gage had been strenuously forbidding. In order to protect himself on both ends, Jones had obtained an assurance from Admiral Graves — because this involved the sea approaches to Boston — that anyone carrying much-needed provisions such as lumber would be free to arrive and depart without being molested or detained. But Jones also approached the rebels on Boston's board of selectmen and got their promise to the people of Machias — whose welfare the board had in mind — that Jones should be allowed to return to Boston for further trading. Upon pondering whether Jones might be in danger from local rebels upon reaching Machias, or wondering whether Jones really intended to return to Boston, Admiral Graves, at General Gage's request, decided to order the schooner *Margueritta* to sail with Jones's convoy, which had grown to include three other vessels besides his two sloops.

The fifty-ton *Margueritta* was hardly a powerhouse, but it did make an impression against unarmed merchant vessels. The schooner was armed with twelve swivel guns and carried a crew of twenty under the command of midshipman James Moore. It appears that as a secondary assignment to keeping tabs on Mr. Jones, Admiral Graves ordered Moore to attempt to salvage guns from the British schooner *Halifax*, which had been wrecked near Machias the previous year. Graves and Gage feared that these, like other armaments throughout the colonies, had fallen or were about to fall into rebel hands.[14]

On June 2, Jones's convoy, shepherded by the *Margueritta*, dropped anchor off Machias, and the next day Jones went ashore to begin his final negotiations. He thought it would be simple: in exchange for much-needed supplies, all a citizen had to do was sign a paper indulging "Capt. Jones in carrying Lumber to Boston" and promising "to protect him and his property, at all events." But suddenly, the townsfolk of Machias showed a good deal of rebel resolve even as the Boston board of selectmen had been concerned about their welfare. Few, if any, were willing to sign Jones's safe conduct decree if it meant trading with the British in Boston.

By the time Ichabod Jones called a town meeting, which assembled on June 6, Machias residents realized that Jones had them over a barrel. To date, their pleas to the Massachusetts Provincial Congress for assistance had gotten lost in the exigencies around Boston. They could starve or they could give Jones a short leash. He was the only game in town. Accordingly they agreed that, while "averse to the measures proposed," they would permit Jones to carry lumber to Boston and purchase from him those provisions with which he returned. Those who thought they were being blackmailed were certain of it when they left the meeting and saw that Midshipman Moore had quietly sailed the *Margueritta* closer to town and anchored it in an intimidating position. Meanwhile, Moore found four of the cannons from the *Halifax* and put them aboard his ship.

However Ichabod Jones had managed it, it now appeared as if he had the town's acquiescence: he could go about his business as one of the few merchants in America trading in British-held Boston. The *Unity* and the *Polly* tied up at the town wharf and began to offload much-needed supplies and take on cargoes of lumber. But then Jones showed his true colors. Annoyed at the strength of the rebel opposition in town, he decided to distribute supplies only to the loyalist portion of the population—identified as those who had voted in favor of his carrying lumber to Boston. This goaded the rebel faction into action. They collected near the town meeting-house on Sunday morning, June 11, and determined to capture Ichabod and Stephen Jones and Midshipman Moore as they attended church services.

The upshot was that Moore saw an armed band of about thirty men coming toward the meetinghouse and eluded capture by jumping out a window and making his way back to the *Margueritta*. Stephen Jones was captured, but Ichabod Jones escaped into the nearby woods. Once Moore was on board the *Margueritta*, he beat his crew to quarters and demanded the Joneses' safe passage to his ships, threatening to burn the town if his orders were not followed.[15]

This was something of an idle threat, because his ship's swivel guns were hardly heavy enough ordnance to cause much damage. Rebel action against Ichabod Jones's two sloops was another matter. They were anchored in the Machias River some distance from the *Margueritta*, one above it and the other below it. The rebels fell first on the sloop anchored upstream—it has never been categorically established whether this was the *Polly* or the *Unity*—stripping sails and rigging and plundering the remainder of its cargo. Then they turned to the *Margueritta* and ordered Midshipman Moore to strike his colors. Moore declared he "would defend the Vessel as long as he lived and would fire on the Town" unless they gave up Jones's sloop.[16]

An exchange of small-arms fire went on for about fifteen minutes, until Moore slipped his anchor cables and drifted downriver. But meanwhile, a second band of rebels had gone farther downriver in three small boats, boarded Jones's other sloop, and begun to bring it upriver. By now it was near sunset as Moore, putting some distance between the *Margueritta* and his antagonists on shore, floated down the river and came upon the second sloop moving upstream under rebel control.

Seeing the *Margueritta* advancing downriver as if to attack, the rebels on the second sloop drove it ashore. Moore evidently now intended its capture, and he brought the *Margueritta* within fifteen yards. This set off a flurry of musketry from the shore and renewed calls for Moore to surrender. Supposedly he replied that he "was not ready yet," and once again the *Margueritta*'s swivel guns blazed away to the accompaniment of small-arms fire on both sides.[17]

Attempts by the rebels to board the *Margueritta* were turned back after a brisk action. Dawn on June 12 found four small boats, abandoned and riddled with holes, stuck on the mudflats of the river as the tide went out and Moore still in possession of the *Margueritta*. Miraculously, for all the firepower, it appears that the only casualty to that point after a long day of gunfire was one wounded British sailor.[18]

But the fight was not over. Moore brought the *Margueritta* alongside yet another sloop new to the action and pressed its captain to pilot both vessels into the open sea. As they sailed down the river, rebel fire continued from the riverbank. Moore even hailed a sloop inbound from Nova Scotia and appropriated some needed rigging and supplies. Meanwhile, the rebels were far from abandoning the chase. About forty men took over what long tradition maintains was the sloop *Unity* with Captain Jeremiah O'Brien in command. Enlisting the aid of a small schooner to accompany them, they got under way in pursuit of the *Margueritta*.

Seeing this pursuit, Moore finished his repairs and provisioning from the other vessels and made for the open sea with *Unity* close behind. Near a small island at the mouth of the river, the *Unity* came within hailing distance of the *Margueritta*, and Moore let loose with the swivels on its stern. The British schooner was clearly the slower vessel, and Moore saw that he had no chance to outrun the *Unity*. He luffed his sails and turned to present a broadside, but since his ship had no carriage guns, this amounted to no more than his swivels and small arms.

The rebels closed, and once again a fusillade of musket balls followed. This time there were more serious casualties. Midshipman Moore was hit in the chest and abdomen; he would die of his wounds. His second in command was also wounded; one marine was killed, and two other marines, along with two sailors, were wounded. With Moore stricken, resistance paled, and the rebels boarded the *Margueritta* and took control of the ship. This part of the two-day battle had lasted just over an hour. Reports differ, but it appears that the rebel force incurred about the same number of casualties as the British: two killed and five wounded.[19]

When the *Margueritta* and Jones's two sloops were returned upriver to Machias — Ichabod Jones was apparently still hiding in the woods — there was a momentary celebration among the rebels, but it quickly turned to Machias's version of "What have we done?" Anticipating a reprisal from the Royal Navy, the town organized its own committee of safety and decided to arm one of Jones's sloops, the *Polly,* giving Jeremiah O'Brien command.

The Machias committee sent a report to the Provincial Congress asking for assistance and direction. But by the time the congress, meeting near Boston, received the request it was occupied with much graver news closer to home. Nonetheless, the final encounter between the *Margueritta* and the *Unity* would be celebrated as Maine's version of the Lexington of the Seas.[20]

Chapter 21

~

Three Generals and a Lady

Two days before the destruction of the *Diana* off Noddle's Island, the twenty-eight-gun frigate HMS *Cerberus* sailed into Boston Harbor with three very special passengers on board. It was one of those small ironies of history that the ship was named for the three-headed dog of Greek and Roman mythology said to guard the gates of hell. One of the three passengers did not reference that mythic beast in his writing, but nonetheless unabashedly referred to himself and his two companions as a "triumvirate of reputation." [1]

The truth of the matter was, however, that none of these three men was particularly pleased to be sailing into the cauldron of occupied Boston. The fact that King George III had dispatched three major generals to North America on the same ship was evidence of his government's determination to impose a military solution on the errant colonies as well as a less-than-sterling confidence in General Gage. However high their individual opinions of themselves, William Howe, Henry Clinton, and John Burgoyne were to have their hands full.

Dark-complexioned and good-looking, with a martial air, Sir William Howe was the ranking member of the trio. Over time, his girth had slowly expanded as his penchant for high living, women, and gambling increased. He was the younger brother of Lord

George Howe, who had given his life on the shores of Lake George during the French and Indian War, and Admiral Richard Howe, who along with their sister had attempted to recruit Benjamin Franklin to the role of peace mediator.

Howe was the only one of the three arriving generals to have previously served in North America. In command of a special unit of light infantry, he had led the way at Quebec as Wolfe's troops climbed onto the Plains of Abraham. A longtime member of Parliament, Howe had promised his Whig-leaning constituents during the 1774 election campaign that "if he were appointed to a command against the Americans he would refuse." But when his orders came, Howe went anyway, telling one local critic who hoped his mission would fail, "I was ordered, and could not refuse." [2]

Next in order of rank was Henry Clinton, who may have been born in Newfoundland, where his admiral father was for a time the local governor. Those records are sparse and conflicting, but young Clinton later spent considerable time growing up in New York, where his father was again the governor. Sensitive to criticism, stoic in his demeanor, Clinton may have been the best soldier of the three, at least in that he lacked the distractions of Howe's indulgences and Burgoyne's flair for theatrics.

Clinton was small of stature and fair-haired. While he lacked the flamboyance to match his scarlet complexion, he had earned a reputation on European battlefields as a brave and skillful soldier who had a particular eye for detail. There was at least one aspect of his career in which he wholeheartedly agreed with William Howe. "I was not a volunteer in that war," Clinton later wrote of his deployment to North America. "I was ordered by my Sovereign and I obeyed." [3]

That left John Burgoyne—the most junior of the threesome in rank but the oldest in age because of his circuitous career path. After early service in the army, Burgoyne eloped with the daughter of the eleventh Earl of Derby, and the couple spent years estranged in poverty on the Continent. After they finally reconciled with her family, Lord Derby used his influence to make up for the time Burgoyne had lost in his army career. Witty and charming, Burgoyne soon commanded a regiment of dragoons, won glory in a cavalry action against Spain near the end of the Seven Years' War, and after the war's conclusion continued his seat in Parliament.

Postwar England suited Burgoyne, and he joined London clubs, did his own share of gambling, and even dabbled in literature by writing a play that David Garrick produced in London. When debate in the House of Commons turned to repeal of the tea tax, Burgoyne was firm but hardly a saber rattler. Saying that he looked upon America as a child "we have already spoiled by too much indulgence," he nonetheless "wished to see America convinced by persuasion, rather than the sword."[4]

Among the three generals, it was Burgoyne who had the least ties to or sympathy for America. But Burgoyne was definitely not pleased with the prospect of being the lowest-ranking general in a small headquarters overflowing with them. Before sailing from England, Burgoyne made the rounds among George III, Lord North, and others and suggested that the best use of his skills in North America would be not to sit fourth or fifth chair to Gage in Boston but rather to take command himself in New York, which was expecting reinforcements recently embarked from Ireland. It soon appeared that Howe coveted the New York command for himself, but Burgoyne left England with some assurance from the king that if he were not given an independent command he would be allowed to return to England before the winter.[5]

For all the criticism and infamy that would later be heaped upon John Burgoyne after his service in North America, his stint in Boston would best be remembered for a boastful comment he made as the three generals stood by the rail of the *Cerberus* and learned from a passing ship several days out of Boston that Gage and his troops were besieged on Boston's promontory. "Well, let us in," Burgoyne is said to have exclaimed, "and we shall soon make elbow-room."[6] The phrase would come back to haunt Burgoyne on more than one occasion.

*   *   *

GENERALS HOWE, CLINTON, AND BURGOYNE had not necessarily been sent to Boston to critique Gage, but neither had they been expected to praise him. It was obvious to any informed observer on both sides that General Gage's days as commander in chief in North America were numbered. What he might have done differently since returning from England the previous May is open to speculation. The general failures of his forays into the countryside had only stiffened rebel resolve and proven that even a scorched-earth campaign against selected rebel hotbeds was likely to do nothing more than stoke an equally repulsive retaliation—quite likely against Gage's own headquarters in Boston.

It would be fascinating to have a transcript of the first meeting between General Gage and this "triumvirate of reputation." When the pleasantries were over, there must have been tough talk about what was to be done and how best to accomplish it. Transports full of troops were arriving, and more were on the way. In fact, just four days after the major generals arrived in Boston, Gage asked Admiral Graves to dispatch a ship to intercept the transports bound from Ireland to New York and direct them instead to Boston as additional reinforcements. So much for Burgoyne's plan of an independent command in New York!

William Howe seems to have settled into Boston—rough though its conditions were—and been content to await orders from Gage. Henry Clinton and John Burgoyne were antsier. Clinton found "nothing but dismay among the troops on my arrival." He couldn't believe that so little was known about the countryside beyond Boston, despite a number of marches into the territory. The detailed tactician in Clinton immediately focused on the heights at Charlestown, to the north across the Charles River, and at Dorchester, to the south beyond Boston Neck. They were essential, Clinton thought, to the safety of Boston and any effort "to have an Entrey into the Country." An attack in either direction or both directions would, Clinton believed, "shake those poor wretches and probably dislodge them totally, and possibly disperse them for a time." [7]

Burgoyne was inclined to agree on both counts. He described an army whose troops were "still lost in a sort of stupefaction which the events of the 19th of April had occasioned." They were alternately filled with frustrations of "censure, anger, or despondency." [8] There was no élan or esprit de corps among these troops, as there had been among the dragoons who had charged behind him on the Iberian Peninsula. But they would follow orders. What Burgoyne realized all too quickly was that among the abundance of generals he would neither be giving those orders nor be responsible for implementing a goodly portion of Gage's—in other words, he was in the situation he had dreaded upon leaving England. Consequently Burgoyne reverted to his part-time avocation—writing.

Rather harmlessly, Burgoyne wrote letters to Lord North, Lord Barrington, and others in England reminding all of the king's promise that he be allowed to return before winter. Rather creatively, he even suggested to Lord North that along the way he might be permitted to detour to New York and/or Philadelphia "as an individual member of Parliament" to somehow advance the by now largely abandoned "work of conciliation." [9] It would have made for high drama had John Burgoyne showed up in Philadelphia and marched into the Continental Congress to confront Samuel Adams and John Hancock, but that didn't happen.

More ominously for the state of affairs on both sides, what did happen is that Burgoyne also turned his pen to crafting a proclamation for General Gage's signature. While Henry Clinton eyed the rebel positions beyond Boston and considered the tactics necessary to dislodge them, John Burgoyne simply summoned up the power of his pen and proceeded to attempt to hurry them from those positions with words alone.

Just why Gage gave Burgoyne such free rein is open to question. Gage was certainly not inarticulate, but he may well have thought that he had already tried just about everything else, and no doubt

Burgoyne was persuasive in offering his assistance. The resulting proclamation of June 12, 1775, was not Thomas Gage's finest hour. If it was meant as reconciliation, it did nothing more than drive a wedge deeper between rebels and loyalists. If it was meant as intimidation, its pomposity produced nothing short of guffaws from the rebels it sought to frighten. Even upon its arrival in England, the proclamation was met with chuckles and derision, particularly among Whigs who recognized Burgoyne's part in it.

"Whereas the infatuated multitude, who have long suffered themselves to be conducted by certain well known incendiaries and traitors, in a fatal progression of crimes against the constitutional authority of the State, have at length proceeded to avowed Rebellion; and the good effects which were expected to arise from the patience and lenity of the King's Government have been often frustrated, and are now rendered hopeless, by the influence of the same evil counsels; it only remains for those who are invested with supreme rule, as well as for the punishment of the guilty, as the protection of the well-affected, to prove they do not bear the sword in vain." [10]

And those one hundred–plus words were just the opening paragraph. Those who read beyond it and could decipher Burgoyne's haughty prose found three salient points: first, Gage offered a full pardon to all persons who would lay down their arms and "return to their duties of peaceable subjects." The only exceptions to this general amnesty were Samuel Adams and John Hancock, whose "offences" Gage and Burgoyne judged to be "of too flagitious a nature to admit of any other consideration than that of condign punishment." (No record remains if Joseph Warren, arguably the third member of the triad, felt slighted by his exclusion from accusations of flagitiousness.)

Second, having been given full warning, all persons after the date of the proclamation who took up arms or otherwise aided and abetted the rebel cause in any way, even if only by a single secret correspondence, were to be judged "Rebels and Traitors" and treated as such. Finally, Gage declared martial law, citing the provision in the Massachusetts Royal Charter of which Lord Dartmouth had reminded him some months before.[11] As might have been expected, Gage's proclamation landed with a thud.

Damning his new superior with faint praise, Burgoyne wrote to a member of the cabinet that it was no reflection on Gage "to say he is unequal to his present situation, for few characters in the world would be fit for it." Nevertheless, Burgoyne went on, Gage should have seized Adams and Hancock when he had the chance, adapted his troops to the American style of fighting he knew so well from the French and Indian War, and fortified the high ground above Charlestown and at Dorchester Heights long before Clinton arrived on the scene to scrutinize the matter.[12]

Meanwhile, even before any communications from Howe, Clinton, or Burgoyne made their way back to England, Thomas Gage was increasingly being found wanting on that side of the Atlantic as well. Lord George Germain, who was about to replace Lord Dartmouth as Secretary of State for the Colonies, wrote Lord Suffolk, who was Britain's Secretary of State for the Northern Department (essentially Europe), with a candor that Suffolk had demanded. "I must lament," Germain told him, "that General Gage, with all his good qualitys, finds himself in a situation of too great importance for his talents."

As yet knowing only of the carnage during the retreat from Concord, Germain, who had served with both distinction and controversy during the Seven Years' War, was firm in his opinion that the looming war required "more than common abilities" and that "the distance from the seat of Government necessarily leaves much to the discretion and the resources of the general." Germain doubted "whether Mr. Gage will venture to take a single step beyond the letter of his instructions, or whether the troops have that opinion of him as to march with confidence of success under his command."[13] For General Thomas Gage, it appeared as though time was running out.

*　　*　　*

DESPITE THE INCREASED TEMPO THAT events around Boston and the arrival of Generals Howe, Clinton, and Burgoyne seemed to demand, two questions that traced their roots back to the night of April 18 shadowed Thomas Gage: Was he betrayed in his Concord plans, and was his wife, Margaret, somehow involved? The first question is more difficult to answer even if the marital intrigue of the second has long made a better story.

As previously noted, Gage's reported admission to Lord Percy late on the night of April 18 — that "his confidence had been betrayed, for he had communicated his design to one person only besides his lordship" — was not recorded until Charles Stedman's British history of the Revolution was published in 1794. If such a conversation indeed occurred, neither Gage nor Percy chose to mention it in their subsequent writings. Gage might well have done so in a self-exculpatory fashion in his after-action reports to Dartmouth or Barrington. Percy, who was low-key and discreet in any written criticism of Gage, was nonetheless prone to candor and might have mentioned it in his many letters to his father and other highly placed correspondents in England. The question must be asked again, did such a *solitary* confidant exist?

It seems unlikely. Gage may well have thought he was keeping a secret, but circumstantial evidence suggests that it was widely recognized by many people on both sides that a British march of some magnitude was about to get under way. Beyond a *solitary* confidant, if there were someone in Gage's inner circle who overtly betrayed the general's plans to the rebels, the potential list is long. It may well have been someone named Kemble: Gage's adjutant, Stephen Kemble, or his private secretary, Samuel Kemble. It may have been the messenger who did such an incompetent if not almost treasonous job of alerting Lord Percy's brigade and Major Pitcairn's marines to be prepared to march in support of Colonel Smith. It may have been a domestic staff member in the general's household who overheard Gage dictating Smith's orders. And it may have been no one at all.

But does Margaret Kemble Gage belong on the list of potential suspects? In the interest of inclusiveness, perhaps, yes, but there is little circumstantial evidence and certainly no direct evidence to keep her there. All the reports branding Margaret Gage a rebel informant come from secondary sources relying on hearsay. The first published indictment seems to be Samuel Adams Drake's account in the *Boston Sunday Herald* of July 6, 1879, published more than a century after the events. Drake took an obscure footnote in a book recently published from the letters and papers of John Burgoyne and made it his text.

"He was an amiable well-meaning man of no military or administrative capacity," Edward de Fonblanque wrote of Gage in that note, "and of a weak character." Well-meaning, yes, and far from a military genius, but to say after three major campaigns and fifteen years in command of Great Britain's far-flung outposts throughout North America that Gage lacked military or administrative ability is simply wrong. But then de Fonblanque stuck the fork in: "Among other complaints made against [Gage] was that of being so completely under the influence of his wife as habitually to confide in her his local projects and correspondence with the ministry, which she, it was alleged, as habitually confided to his enemies." [14]

This allegation was repeated in two biographies of Paul Revere, Charles Ferris Gettemy's *The True Story of Paul Revere*, published in 1905, and Elbridge Henry Goss's *The Life of Colonel Paul Revere,* first published in 1891. Goss repeated Drake's error of adding Stedman's secondary account of the Gage-Percy conversation and Gordon's description of a "daughter of Liberty" and categorically assuming, in Goss's words, that "this 'daughter of Liberty' was undoubtedly the wife of General Gage." [15] Gettemy went to some lengths to debunk this myth, at one point calling the tale "the most romantic theory that has been advanced to account for the foreknowledge possessed by the patriots relative to the British movements." [16]

If such a circuitous and shadowy trail of dubious facts got Margaret Gage on the list of suspects, what evidence exists to exonerate her? Even the historian David Hackett Fischer, so meticulous and careful in so many things, rather cavalierly brushed off any chance of her innocence by citing "much circumstantial evidence" of her guilt, including "her husband's decision to send her away from him after the battles, and the failure of their marriage." [17] Neither of those points stands up very well under scrutiny.

Margaret Gage's departure from Boston for England on board the *Charming Nancy* in mid-August was hardly banishment. Thomas Gage wrote to his brother, Lord Gage, as early as May 13, saying that it was his intention to send Margaret and his children home to England. [18] Given Thomas and Margaret's pleasant year together in England and the grueling year just passed in Boston, who could blame either of them? Boston was full of people — rebels, loyalists, and British soldiers — who could think of little else but escaping its confines and its harsh living conditions. Duty, it is safe to say, was the only thing keeping General Gage himself in town.

At the time Gage wrote his brother of his plans for Margaret's return, the trio of Howe, Clinton, and Burgoyne had not quite arrived in Boston, but Gage was well aware from Dartmouth that they were coming. And he was far too experienced an officer not to know that their appearance was strong evidence that his own days as commander in chief were numbered. It was for Margaret's well-being and that of their children that he wanted them out of the turmoil of Boston and safely across the Atlantic before the gales of another winter. He knew that he would follow them in due course; indeed, he appears to have heartily wished for that end.

There is no hint in any record that Margaret was anything but relieved to go. The truth of the matter was that the lifestyle to which she had been born and to which she was accustomed was far more readily had in England, particularly as it seemed increasingly likely that her husband would inherit his childless brother's peerage. To be sure, there were many rebels who chose liberty's cause over such earthly considerations, but there is nothing in Margaret Kemble Gage's past to suggest that she might embrace that kind of sacrifice even if she had been so inclined politically. Without a doubt, she was anxious to reunite her children, three of whom she had left in school in England the previous summer as she had followed the general back to Boston. One of those, eleven-year-old William, had died in the interim.

And what of the reported failure of their marriage? Once again, David Hackett Fischer, despite what reservations he may have had, nonetheless summarized the speculation of earlier secondary sources by writing of Gage's later years, "His shattered marriage with Margaret Gage was never repaired."[19] There is, however, no direct evidence that it was ever shattered, and circumstantial evidence supports just the opposite.

After leaving Boston, Thomas and Margaret Gage had two more children. Daughter Emily was born in London on April 25, 1776, eight months after Margaret sailed on the *Charming Nancy*. The timing is such that probably neither Thomas nor Margaret yet knew she was pregnant as they parted, but Margaret was no stranger to childbearing and may have had an inkling. Providentially for her, the *Charming Nancy* made the eastbound crossing in the very fast time of only twenty-four days.

Their last child, William Hall Gage, was born in England on October 2, 1777, when Margaret was forty-three.[20] (As a captain in the Royal Navy during the Napoleonic Wars and later an Admiral of the Fleet, William Hall Gage would become arguably a greater military commander than his father.) Childbearing is certainly not dispositive of marital bliss; however, short of questioning Margaret's fidelity, these children are evidence of their continuing intimacy just prior to Margaret's leaving Boston and well after Thomas returned to England.

There is one further point often raised by those who would condemn Margaret as a rebel spy in General Gage's bedchamber: a dubious report of Gage's philandering after he returned to England.

This came, some years after the birth of their last child, in the pages of the *Town and Country Magazine*, a publication best described as one of the leading scandal sheets of the day — one that in later times might have printed headlines proclaiming that aliens rode with Paul Revere. *Town and Country*'s subtitle termed itself a "universal repository of knowledge, instruction, and entertainment." Indeed, the story in question spends pages recounting the favors that a fallen young woman bestowed on various military types before her liaison with an older gentleman called "the lenient commander" and presumed by some to be Gage.[21]

Finally, however, Margaret Kemble Gage held the general's love and esteem — and by all accounts returned it — to their dying days. After Gage died on April 2, 1787, Margaret and the general's brother, Lord Gage, were named coexecutors of his will. After distributions to their surviving children, Gage left "a considerable part" of his estate "in a trust for his widow during her life." Margaret outlived the general by almost thirty-seven years, never remarried, and died on February 9, 1824, near the age of ninety years old.[22] That Margaret Kemble Gage, glamorous American-born wife of the British commander in chief, should have betrayed her husband and her loyalist upbringing in the rebel cause makes a great story, but it does not hold up under careful scrutiny.[23]

Chapter 22

~

What Course Now, Gentlemen?

As Margaret Gage packed her trunks and prepared to leave Boston, the deliberations of the Second Continental Congress continued in Philadelphia. President John Hancock was feeling increasingly comfortable in the presiding chair, but then again Hancock rarely felt uncomfortable anywhere. Some of the delegates were on a fast track to declaring independence; others still harbored hopes for reconciliation or at least a peaceful parting. Hancock's task was to keep a steady rein on the body and maintain some sense of unity and cooperation among all factions. It was, as John Adams remembered, like driving "a Coach and six — the swiftest Horses must be slackened and the slowest quickened, that all may keep an even Pace." [1]

Two matters continued to command the attention of all delegates: an army and the means to pay for it. On Monday, June 12, in recognition of "the present critical, alarming and calamitous state of these colonies," the congress voted July 20 to be "a day of public humiliation, fasting and prayer" and "recommended to Christians, of all denominations, to assemble for public worship, and to abstain from servile labour and recreations." Then it resolved itself into a committee of the whole to "take into consideration the ways and means of raising money." [2]

These matters occupied the attention of the congress during the following two days, and at the day's adjournment on June 14, it was ordered that consideration of the ways and means of raising money "be a standing order, until the business is compleated." But even if they were not yet agreed on how to pay for it, the delegates also authorized "six companies of expert riflemen, be immediately raised in Pennsylvania; two in Maryland, and two in Virginia." John Adams went to some length to explain to Abigail that the difference between smoothbore muskets and rifled bores made these men "the most accurate Marksmen in the World." Each company was to consist of eighty-one men—a captain, three lieutenants, four sergeants, four corporals, a drummer or trumpeter, and sixty-eight privates. As soon as it was formed, each unit was to march to Boston for service as light infantry. Perhaps somewhat optimistically, the term of enlistment was to be one year.[3] At the time, few could imagine a longer conflict.

These ten companies, totaling slightly more than eight hundred men, were hardly an army, but added to the provincial troops in the field around Boston—the leaders of which were clamoring for some sort of continental structure—they were proof that the Continental Congress was slowly but surely assuming a national role. Who was to command this assemblage was another matter.

In making this decision, the congress faced its strongest test of colonial unity since the economic sanctions it had passed the previous fall. From New Hampshire to South Carolina and initially reluctant Georgia, there were men on the same page for revolution, but would Virginia or Maryland soldiers take orders from a Massachusetts general and vice versa?

On June 15, the congress debated the matter at length and resolved "that a General be appointed to command all the continental forces, raised, or to be raised, for the defence of American liberty."[4] This description of the proceedings in the journal of the Continental Congress is almost maddening in its brevity. The truth is, there had already been a flurry of private conversations—

"canvassing this Subject out of Doors," as John Adams termed it — and Adams and his Massachusetts comrades were well aware that a commander in chief of a Continental Army from Massachusetts would be met with "a Jealousy" by the southern colonies.

Adams, his cousin Samuel, and John Hancock were equally aware at the political level that binding Virginia and the southern colonies to Massachusetts and the rest of New England was in their long-term interests. If John Adams's later recollections are to be taken at face value — he did have a tendency in retrospect to place himself at the center of every event — Adams promoted a Massachusetts-Virginia accord and particularly ingratiated himself with Virginia's George Washington. John Hancock had already been the beneficiary of this Massachusetts-Virginia alliance when Adams helped to broker Hancock's election as president to succeed Peyton Randolph. Now that it was time to appoint a commander in chief, many reasoned it was Virginia's turn.

"Whether this Jealousy was sincere, or whether it was mere pride and a haughty Ambition, of furnishing a Southern General to command the northern Army," Adams recalled, "the Intention was very visible to me, that Col. Washington was their Object, and so many of our staunchest Men were in the Plan that We could carry nothing without conceeding to it."[5]

A further wrinkle was John Hancock's aspirations to be appointed commander in chief himself — or at least to have the opportunity to decline the honor of the position. John Adams was polite enough to term Hancock "an excellent Militia Officer" for his showy service with Boston's First Corps of Cadets, but Adams found Hancock's "entire Want of Experience in actual Service" to be a decisive objection to him.[6]

Once again, John Adams claimed that he took a walk with his cousin Samuel "for a little Exercise and fresh Air" to ponder this situation and propose a plan. Samuel was noncommittal, but John nonetheless returned to the session and called for the appointment of a commander in chief, further declaring that he "had but one

Gentleman in my Mind for that important command." According to Adams's recollections, which are not readily supported by other participants, John Hancock's ears perked up at this, and he waited expectantly for Adams to put forth his name. But the name that rolled off the tongue of Hancock's fellow Massachusetts delegate was that of "a Gentleman from Virginia who was among Us and very well known to all of Us." According to John Adams, when George Washington heard his name mentioned in this manner, he rose from his seat and with "his Usual Modesty darted into the Library Room" to escape attention.[7]

John Hancock just as quickly was said by John Adams to have undergone a "sudden and sinking Change of Countenance" that covered his face with "Mortification and resentment." If this was indeed the case, it added insult to injury that Hancock's mentor, Samuel Adams, quickly seconded his cousin's motion to appoint a commander in chief and said nothing to detract from the suggestion that, once the position was created, Washington should be the obvious choice to fill it.[8]

The congress then passed the resolution to appoint a commanding general and provide five hundred dollars per month for his pay and expenses. Next, Thomas Johnson of Maryland, a lawyer whom George Washington would one day appoint to the Supreme Court, rose to nominate the Virginian for the position. In spite of some lingering sentiments in favor of appointing a New Englander, Washington appears to have been unopposed and "was unanimously elected."[9]

Eliphalet Dyer of Connecticut wrote home to his future son-in-law, Joseph Trumbull, that Washington had received "the Universal Voice of the Congress." Dyer speculated that Washington would be "Very agreable to our officers and Soldiery" and called him a gentleman "highly Esteemed by those acquainted with him." As to Washington's military service, Dyer didn't believe that "he knows more than some of ours" but was satisfied that his appointment "removes all jealousies [and] more firmly Cements the Southern to the Northern."[10]

If he did indeed carry some of the resentment that John Adams later attributed to him, John Hancock certainly did not show it when he notified Joseph Warren of Washington's appointment. "He is a gentleman who all will like," Hancock assured his Massachusetts friend. "Pray do him every honor." [11]

The day after his election, forty-three-year-old George Washington, who as yet had somewhat of a dubious military record, rose to accept his appointment. "Tho' I am truly sensible of the high Honour done me, in this Appointment," Washington began, "yet I feel great distress, from a consciousness that my abilities and military experience may not be equal to the extensive and important Trust." [12] Perhaps Washington was merely being modest, but perhaps he was also truthfully remembering his surrender of Fort Necessity in the opening days of the French and Indian War, his role in Braddock's Defeat the following year, and his less-than-enthusiastic participation in the retaking of Fort Duquesne as a disgruntled subordinate under General John Forbes. [13]

"Lest some unlucky event should happen, unfavourable to my reputation," Washington continued, "I beg it may be remembered, by every Gentleman in the room, that I, this day declare with the utmost sincerity, I do not think myself equal to the Command I am honored with." But he would accept it, of course, and take pains to assure the congress that, "as no pecuniary consideration could have tempted me to have accepted this arduous employment, at the expence of my domestic ease," he would serve without compensation, save for his expenses, which he was never shy about submitting. [14]

Congress officially passed Washington's commission as "General and Commander in chief, of the army of the United Colonies," and the new general sat down to write a lengthy letter to his wife. For reasons known best to her, Martha Washington burned most of the letters she received from her husband. The one he wrote from Philadelphia two days after accepting command of the Continental Army survives as an exception. Saying that he was writing on a subject that filled him "with inexpressable concern," Washington acknowledged in his first sentence that this concern was "greatly aggravated and Increased" by "the uneasiness I know it will give you."

Telling Martha that duty required him "to proceed immediately to Boston," Washington tried to assure her "that, so far from seeking this appointment I have used every endeavour in my power to avoid it, not only from my unwillingness to part with you and the Family, but from a consciousness of its being a trust too far great for my Capacity." [15]

Here again was a shade of modesty, perhaps, but far from evidence of genuine reluctance on Washington's part, this letter was much more the careful communication of a husband to a wife assuring her that he had at least tried to avoid a situation where he would be both in danger and away from her for an extended period. His requisite modesty and spousal attentiveness aside, Washington had accepted command of Virginia militia units and routinely worn his military uniform to sessions of the congress. He may have been somewhat humbled when the moment came, but it was a role he welcomed.

The congress went on to appoint two major generals, including Artemas Ward as first major general, eight brigadier generals, and assorted officers to staff the new army. And there would be funds with which to fight a war. The ways and means debate resulted in an agreement to issue the sum of two million dollars (almost sixty million in 2010 dollars) in bills of credit—essentially continental paper currency—that were due in seven years. These were backed by all the colonies, except Georgia, in proportion to the number of inhabitants in each colony: thus New York was on the hook for a much larger share of the debt than tiny Delaware. [16]

On Tuesday, June 20, the congress gave Washington his marching orders. He was "to repair with all expedition to the colony of Massachusetts bay and take charge of the army of the united colonies." [17] That same morning the man who was now *General* Washington reviewed about two thousand troops from nearby militias, including Philadelphia's artillery company and a troop of light horse assembled on the town common. They were said to have gone through the manual of arms and various maneuvers "with great Dexterity and exactness."[18] The next day, Washington left Philadelphia for Boston not knowing that several days earlier a bloody battle had occurred on the hills above the town.

MEANWHILE, AS MUCH AS DELEGATES to the Second Continental Congress accomplished in those hectic days of May and June, 1775, there was no attempt—and apparently little, if any, discussion on the matter—to broaden the reach of their cherished concepts of liberty and freedom to a wider segment of the population. There were white males in low social and economic classes who were accorded lesser rights than men of property, but the major categories of people who had little hope of achieving equality were women and slaves. It is difficult to say which group then stood the better chance.

As early as 1771, after abolitionists had introduced an antislavery bill into the Massachusetts legislature, James Warren told John Adams that if it was passed, "it should have a bad effect on the union of the colonies." How could Warren and the Adams cousins court Virginia and South Carolina to their cause against Great Britain, Warren asked, if they allowed slavery to become "a disruptive side issue?"[19] Their answer was to ignore it, even as men of color and servitude, including Prince Estabrook and Peter Salem, were regularly drilling with their militia units. (At some point, it appears, both Estabrook and Salem were granted their freedom in return for their military service.)

Looking for ways to bolster their fledgling provincial forces, the Massachusetts committee of safety drew a distinction between free men of color and slaves. The discussion was less about race than about the members' underlying concept of freedom—however misguided in retrospect. Since the colonies were fighting Great Britain over their "liberties and privileges," committee members considered the recruitment of slaves "into the army now raising" to be "inconsistent with the principals that are to be supported, and [would] reflect dishonor on this colony." Consequently, they agreed "that no slaves be admitted into this army upon any consideration whatever."[20] Nothing was said about free men of color.

This is not to say that abolition was not a topic of discussion in both the northern and southern colonies. In the northern provinces, particularly among the Quaker enclaves of Philadelphia, rural New Jersey, and coastal Rhode Island, some took the matter into their own hands and quietly emancipated their slaves by ones, twos, or threes. Other owners simply refused to purchase replacement slaves or to break up family units with further trading. Rarely, others, such as the Quaker merchant Joshua Fisher, embarked on quests to track down slaves he had previously sold, repurchase them, and grant them their freedom.[21]

Even in Virginia, where Lord Dunmore was threatening to employ the slave population against the rebels, there had been some discussion of limiting slavery. Thomas Jefferson, who arrived in Philadelphia to take Peyton Randolph's seat in the Second Continental Congress the same day that George Washington departed for Boston, was on record as asserting that "the abolition of domestic slavery is the great object of desire in those colonies where it was unhappily introduced in their infant state." Jefferson wrote this in 1774 in the context of an example of George III's heavy-handedness — in this case his government's refusal to pass laws banning the slave trade despite the wishes of some colonies. Jefferson's prohibition against the importation of new slaves — "No person hereafter coming into this country shall be held in slavery under any pretext whatever" — survived into the early drafts of Virginia's 1776 constitution, though it would be dropped from the final version.[22]

As noble talk about freedom and individual rights trickled down and spread among New England domestics and Carolina field hands, those slaves who understood came to take the words even more personally than whites did. But short of individual efforts, such as those of Prince Estabrook and Peter Salem, or a mass insurrection of slaves on behalf of the British Crown, slaves lacked enough political allies to effect a change in their status. Women, on the other hand, had earned some measure of political influence by their aggressive support of the nonimportation and nonconsumption measures that traced their roots to the original boycotts of the mid-1760s.

This emerging influence may have encouraged Abigail Adams and Mercy Otis Warren to participate in political debates—even if only with other women or within family circles—but it did not begin to grant them the independent equality so fervently sought by their husbands. John Adams was particularly adamant on that point. The most documented and pointed exchange between John and Abigail on the subject would not occur until the spring of 1776, but there is no reason to suspect that the feelings they each expressed then had not been ingrained in John or bubbling in Abigail years before.

How real was the "passion for Liberty" among those who kept fellow humans enslaved? Abigail wondered. Then she turned her attention to the predicament of her own sex. Noting that she assumed John was at work on a legal code in the congress, Abigail beseeched him to "remember the Ladies, and be more generous and favourable to them than your ancestors." As if to underscore the seriousness of her charge, Abigail, only partially in jest, went on to assert: "If perticular care and attention is not paid to the Laidies, we are determined to foment a Rebelion, and will not hold ourselves bound by any Laws in which we have no voice or Representation."[23] Her words intentionally echoed those her husband and his rebel friends had been spouting for years.

"I cannot but laugh," John Adams told her in reply. Then, alluding to potential unrest among children, workers, Indians, and slaves, John went on to say that Abigail's letter was his first intimation "that another Tribe more numerous and powerfull than all the rest were grown discontented." This was "rather too coarse a

Compliment," he told her, "but you are so saucy, I wont blot it out."[24] Abigail's response was to withhold her normal reply to John for longer than usual and vent her frustrations in a letter to Mercy Otis Warren instead.

As for John, he was adamant in cautioning James Sullivan, a Massachusetts lawyer, that no good could come from enfranchising more Americans no matter what the category. "Depend upon it, sir," Adams told Sullivan. "It is dangerous to open So fruitfull a Source of Controversy and Altercation, as would be opened by attempting to alter the Qualifications of Voters. There will be no End to it. New Claims will arise. Women will demand a Vote. Lads from 12 to 21 will think their Rights not enough attended to, and every Man, who has not a Farthing, will demand an equal Voice with any other, in all Acts of State. It tends to confound and destroy all Distinctions, and prostrate all Ranks to one common Levell."[25] It remained to be seen if the rebel cause would be successful, but even if it was, the fruits of liberty were to be heavily restricted.

MEANWHILE, MANY LOYALISTS IN BOSTON remained focused on just one goal: to get out of town as quickly as possible. Some believed they would soon return and "left friends or relatives behind to guard their abandoned homes or businesses." Others were certain that a chapter of their lives — perhaps an entire volume — was closing. In Boston, acrimony among former neighbors and friends divided by political loyalties reached as high a level as anywhere in the colonies. As loyalists continued to depart, one rebel ditty ran: "The Tories with their brats and wives, have fled to save their wretched lives."[26]

Where they would go was another matter. Increasingly, throughout the late spring and summer of 1775, Halifax, Nova Scotia, became the first port of refuge. It was convenient and more a matter of expedience than of choice. In time, some fleeing loyalists would stay there or make their way farther into Canada, to

England, or to other parts of the British Empire. For most, their lives would never be the same. Anglican clergy, who were almost all loyalists, did not find a warm welcome in the greater Church of England. The Reverend Henry Caner, the seventy-six-year-old rector of King's Chapel, was among the loyalists to leave Boston. He recalled that upon his arrival in England, he heard considerable expressions of compassion from the archbishop of Canterbury and bishop of London but received no offer of an appointment to an English parish. "We can't think of your residing here," Caner was told. "We want such men as you in America." [27] America, of course, had thrown them out.

The exodus of loyalists was not confined to Boston, and those who felt forced to leave their homes and hometowns did so with a decided taste of bitterness. Thomas and Mary Robie of Marblehead didn't want to go, but being closely allied with former governor Hutchinson and as such in the decided minority in pro-rebel Marblehead, they had little choice. Sailing first for Nova Scotia, they would eventually end up in England. As they were rowed from the dock in Marblehead to their ship anchored in the harbor, they were jeered by loud catcalls from an assembled group of rebels. Far from being cowed, Mary Robie looked shoreward from the rowboat and shouted back: "I hope that I shall live to return, find this wicked Rebellion crushed, and see the streets of Marblehead run with Rebel blood." [28]

IN THE SHORT TERM, PERHAPS the most consequential discussions of what course to take occurred between General Gage and his newly arrived triumvirate of reputation. On the grand scale, General Howe advocated a plan to reduce Boston to a mere garrison and move the principal thrust of British military operations to New York and the Hudson River Valley. No doubt swayed by his oldest brother's colonial experience as well as his own, Howe recognized the strategic importance of the New York–Champlain corridor.

Boston was New England's major seaport, but it led nowhere and had become a vortex sucking in resources. The Hudson River corridor led to Canada and could sever radical New England from the other colonies.

Howe speculated that such an effort would require nineteen thousand troops in addition to a strong force of Canadians and Indians. (It is interesting that both sides anticipated an outpouring of men and assistance from Canada that never materialized.) Such large numbers — roughly three times the number of troops that Gage now had in Boston after reinforcements had arrived — appalled Lord North's government, but Howe presciently advised, "With a Less Force than I have mentioned, I apprehend this war may be spun out untill England shall be heartily sick of it." [29]

England's dismay would indeed come to pass, but Howe's cohorts, Clinton and Burgoyne, were preoccupied with more immediate concerns. The initial shock that had gripped the survivors of Lord Percy's retreat from Lexington was ebbing. Bolstered by reinforcements, there was a renewed sense of confidence among the regulars that a lesson must and could be taught to these upstart rebels. Clinton and Burgoyne agreed and urged General Gage to undertake operations that would secure some of Burgoyne's desired "elbow room." Given the largely unsuccessful forays at Grape and Noddle's Islands, they recommended seizing the heights across the Charles River at Charlestown and those adjacent to Roxbury at Dorchester. The question that must be asked, however, is why General Gage hadn't done something about these heights long before this.

According to the memoirs of Admiral Samuel Graves, on the evening of April 19 or shortly thereafter, as Lord Percy's beleaguered column hunkered down in Charlestown and began its evacuation across the Charles River, Graves went to General Gage and proposed a plan that in retrospect seems quite out of character with the normally disinclined admiral. Graves "advised the burning of Charlestown and Roxbury, and the seizing of the Heights of Roxbury and Bunkers Hill." [30]

Doing so would have left the rebels—short of an amphibious assault, for which they were not readily equipped—only two narrow and heavily defended routes against Boston had they opted to make such an attack. But Admiral Graves was certainly not thinking about the safety of Boston and General Gage's army. The admiral was chiefly concerned about his fleet. Rebel cannons placed either above Charlestown or near Roxbury would be within range of his ships.

According to Graves, General Gage replied that his forces were far too weak for such ventures, even after the admiral's offer of marine reinforcements from the fleet. That was possibly true about an advance south from Boston Neck to Roxbury and Dorchester Heights, given the openness of the terrain there. But on the Charlestown peninsula, the geography was reversed, and Charlestown Neck afforded a defensive strongpoint against rebels attacking from the mainland. In fact, fearing just such an assault against the retreating British column on the evening of April 19, Captain John Montresor of the engineers had begun work on fortifications on Bunker Hill that faced away from Boston and commanded the approaches across Charlestown Neck.

Even if Gage was correct in his fear of spreading his forces too thin at Roxbury—at that point he had yet to broker the agreement with the Boston citizens in his midst to turn in their arms—the Charlestown situation was entirely different. British troops already controlled that ground; the populace was preparing to abandon the town, and there was little concern for a successful rebel attack from Cambridge, particularly given Admiral Graves's warships at anchor in the Charles River. But Gage said no. He dismissed the admiral's plans as "too rash and sanguinary" and proceeded to complete the Charlestown evacuation and hunker his troops down in Boston proper—which was, of course, the condition Howe, Clinton, and Burgoyne found upon their arrival.[31]

In the meantime, however, Admiral Graves remained worried about the safety of his fleet—in part because the larger ships of his line could only maneuver easily at high tide. He was particularly concerned about the seventy-gun *Somerset*, which Paul Revere had rowed past on the evening of April 18 and which still stood guard near the Charlestown ferry crossing. Consequently, on April 23, Graves received permission from Gage to place a battery of twenty-four-pound cannons from his ships atop Copp's Hill in the North End, almost in the shadow of the Old North Church. This battery looked out across the Charles River at Charlestown and was about the same height as the hills above the town. It provided a stout backup to the *Somerset* and other vessels and was under the navy's direct control.

Army officers made an immediate joke about the effort, and even Admiral Graves recounted their reaction with humor. "The erection of this battery by the Commander at Sea afforded much pleasantry to the Garrison," Graves acknowledged — "particularly among those who did not readily perceive the intent; it was christened soon by the name of the Admiral's battery and always spoke of with a smile." [32]

As it turned out, Admiral Graves almost got to unlimber those guns a few days before Howe, Clinton, and Burgoyne sailed into town. There were commanders on the rebel side just as anxious for action as Clinton and Burgoyne, and one of them was that old Connecticut firebrand Israel Putnam. The man couldn't be idle, and he didn't expect his troops to be, either. Idleness was an enemy. Putnam may have been the original proponent of the old army saw that it was "better to dig a ditch every morning and fill it up at evening than to have the men idle." [33]

One May afternoon Putnam apparently took it upon himself to lead a ramble from Cambridge to Charlestown. With fifes blaring and drums beating, a column of some 2,200 men followed Putnam across Charlestown Neck, over the heights behind the town, and then down to the waterfront at the ferry landing. They did so, according to one Connecticut volunteer, "to Shoe themselves to the Regulars." [34] They were certainly seen, but it provoked no response.

Lieutenant John Barker of the Fourth Regiment heard the rebels give a war whoop opposite the anchored *Somerset* and expected them to fire on the ship. When they didn't, Barker wished that they had, because the *Somerset* "had everything ready for Action, and must have destroyed great numbers of them besides putting the Town in Ashes."[35]

The admiral's battery on Copp's Hill would have likely joined in the cannonade, but no commands to fire were given on either side. Putnam was only making a demonstration, and those in command on the *Somerset* and atop Copp's Hill evidently lacked the authority to engage unless fired upon. If nothing else, the absence of an exchange shows that there was still some tentativeness to this entire drama on both sides.

Putnam returned his men to Cambridge without firing a shot, but he had caused quite a stir among loyalists in Boston. "This movement," James Warren wrote Mercy, "produced a Terror in Boston hardly to be described."[36]

Such terror aside, the heights above Charlestown and at Dorchester remained unoccupied when Howe, Clinton, and Burgoyne sat down with General Gage to devise a course of action to seize them. "Why a situation, from which the town of Boston was so liable to be annoyed, was so long neglected," British historian Charles Stedman wrote critically a few years later, "it is not easy to assign a reason." But at that point, according to Burgoyne, "my two colleagues and myself . . . never differed in one jot of military sentiment" and formed the plan "in concert with General Gage." They proposed to begin with the Dorchester front because, with the support of Admiral Graves's fleet, "it would evidently be effected without any considerable loss."[37]

Howe, as the senior man of the trio, would lead the assault. On June 12 — by coincidence the very day that Gage's proclamation was nailing shut the last door of local reconciliation — Howe wrote his brother Richard, the admiral, the broad outline of the plan. Under the guns of the Royal Navy, Howe's troops would make an amphibious landing on Dorchester Neck and secure the heights. Then, pivoting to the west and joining forces with more troops, who would emerge from Boston via Boston Neck, they would sweep through the rebel lines at Roxbury and be poised to advance upon Cambridge from the south.

Once the Dorchester attack was assured of success, Clinton would lead a similar assault "with all we can muster" to take the heights above Charlestown. From there, Clinton would "either attack the Rebels at Cambridge" directly or encircle that post, perhaps linking up with Howe in a great pincerlike movement. "In either case," Howe wrote his brother, "I suppose the Rebels will move from Cambridge, And that we shall take, and keep possession of it."[38]

The opening assault was planned against Dorchester on the morning of June 18 — once again a Sunday. Given Howe's confidence in the matter, no one on the British side seems to have been terribly concerned about what the rebels might be doing in the interim. Much would later be made of various reports that reached Cambridge about the British plan. One came in a roundabout way from the New Hampshire committee of safety. It forwarded a warning from "a gentleman of undoubted veracity" who had left Boston even before Gage and his generals drafted their plan. After reinforcements arrived, the informant reported, Gage was expected to "secure some advantageous posts near Boston, viz: Dorchester and Charlestown." The friendly New Hampshire missive went on to say: "We are unacquainted with the importance of those posts, but if this hint should be in any degree useful, it will give us pleasure."[39]

Of course, just about everyone within a hundred miles of Boston was well acquainted with the importance of those posts, even if to date both sides had been frozen in any attempt to occupy them. On the very day the New Hampshire warning was written, the Massachusetts committee of safety noted that "it is daily expected that General Gage will attack our Army now in the vicinity of Boston, in order to penetrate into the country" and warned that the army should therefore "be in every respect prepared for action."[40] And one of the officers of a New Hampshire regiment stationed near Cambridge wrote home that while "it is still times with the Regular Troops at present; we expect they will make a push for Bunker's Hill or Dorchester Neck very soon."[41]

It was indeed obvious to any informed observer that something major was about to happen either in the direction of Dorchester or Charlestown or both. Despite this, one twenty-first-century writer pulled Margaret Gage into this matter, too, and claimed the rebels learned of the British plan because the general's "American wife probably again leaked the information."[42] It makes great fiction, but it didn't take spies or clandestine reports to confirm the obvious. Boston remained the leaky sieve of information it had always been, and with the town swelling with reinforcements something was going to happen.

Like the British, the rebels had also recognized the importance of the hills above Charlestown and Dorchester, but except for Israel Putnam's parade through Charlestown they had been as slow to act as General Gage. The first call for action came from a joint committee organized to reconnoiter "the Highlands in Cambridge and Charlestown." On May 12, after its examination, the committee recommended erecting breastworks flanking the Cambridge-to-Charlestown road on the Cambridge side of the neck and building redoubts with "three or four nine-pounders planted there" atop Winter Hill on the Cambridge side of the neck and Bunker Hill on the Charlestown side of the neck. "A strong Redoubt raised on Bunker's Hill" was calculated "to annoy the enemy coming out of Charlestown, also to annoy them going by water to Medford." The report concluded with the prediction that "when these are finished, we apprehend the country will be safe from all sallies of the enemy in that quarter."[43]

The breastworks were soon erected — perhaps as part of Putnam's "keep 'em busy" digging campaign — but the larger redoubts recommended on Winter Hill and Bunker Hill were not. In part this was attributable to limited time and resources, but there was also a difference of opinion about putting forces in an exposed forward position on Bunker Hill. The firebrands, including Putnam and Colonel William Prescott of Massachusetts, were all in favor and sought to provoke the British into coming out of Boston and fighting rather than settling in for a protracted siege.

General Artemas Ward and Joseph Warren were among those who thought the army's resources too limited to maintain so extended a post. With long-range military concerns in mind, Ward and Warren weren't eager to bring on a general action until the colonial army might be better organized and supplied. For one thing, there never seemed to be enough gunpowder. Warren reportedly told Putnam that he thought the plan to build a redoubt on Bunker Hill was "a rash one." Nevertheless, Warren vowed, "If the project be adopted, and the strife becomes hard, you must not be surprised to find me near you in the midst of it."[44]

This difference of opinion on the rebel side continued until June 15, by which time an avalanche of information signaled that Gage was preparing for imminent action. That day, as the full body of the Massachusetts Provincial Congress agreed to pay for the removal of the Harvard College library to the safety of Andover, its committee of safety issued direct orders about the heights at both Charlestown and Dorchester. Citing the "importance to the safety of this Colony, that possession of the hill called Bunker's Hill, in Charlestown, be securely kept and defended," the committee recommended that it be "maintained by sufficient force being posted there." Of Dorchester Heights, the committee had less detailed knowledge, and it merely ordered officers to Roxbury to reconnoiter the situation there.[45]

It has never been answered with absolute certainty whether the Charlestown action was simply a long-overdue rebel move to fortify Bunker Hill or an attempt to forestall the anticipated British move against Dorchester with a more ominous threat to Boston than seizing Dorchester Heights would have been. Charlestown was less than a mile from Boston's North End and the Royal Navy ships in the Charles, whereas Dorchester Heights was a good two miles from Boston Harbor. The rebel decision was likely a combination of those goals — clear action on Charlestown and a distraction from Dorchester.

There is a report by Artemas Ward's principal biographer that the rebel general himself hurried to Bunker Hill about noon on June 16 with members of his staff.[46] This may or may not have been the case, but the result of rebel reconnaissance was that Colonel William Prescott was given command of three regiments, several companies from Putnam's Connecticut regiment, and an artillery company — a total force of about twelve hundred men — and ordered to march to Bunker Hill and construct fortifications. The march as well as the work was to be undertaken after dark so as not to alarm the British in Boston or on the ships in the Charles. Significantly, Ward also ordered that a relief party of a like number of men — three regiments and another two hundred of the Connecticut troops — be ready to march the following evening "with two days provisions and well equipped with arms and ammunition" to relieve Prescott's command.[47]

That evening, Friday, June 16, the bulk of Prescott's command assembled in Cambridge. "We were orderd to parade at six 'o Clock," a company clerk named Peter Brown later wrote to his mother, "with one days provision and Blankets ready for a March somewhere, but we knew not where but we readily and cheerfully obey'd."[48]

But there was no rush to march off immediately. The long midsummer evening would last another three hours, and it allowed ample time to view the assemblage. This was still less an army than a loose band of partisans "hearty in the cause," as Peter Brown termed it. Few had uniforms; most were in everyday work clothes; all carried muskets they had brought from home. Some of the weapons dated from before the French and Indian War and were older than the men who shouldered them. Almost no one had bayonets. Picks, shovels, and other entrenching tools suggested a full night's work.

Reverend Samuel Langdon, the president of Harvard College, his library secure, offered a lengthy prayer over the assembled troops. Then, as the twilight finally turned murky, Colonel Prescott and two sergeants carrying lanterns led the column east out of town. That night, the fifes and drums would be silent. Secrecy was of the utmost importance.

The column walked quietly over the wooden bridges that spanned several branches of Willis Creek and met the two hundred Connecticut men under the command of Captain Thomas Knowlton. Nearby stood the earthworks where Putnam had kept them busy digging and filling and digging. Might they be doing some more digging for Old Put? But onward Prescott and the two flickering lanterns led until they came to the crossroads at the western end of Charlestown Neck. As Prescott turned to the right, their destination suddenly became obvious to Private Brown and his comrades. The left-hand fork led back toward Winter Hill and Medford. The right-hand fork led east across the neck toward Bunker Hill.

~

Chapter 23

"The White of Their Gaiters"

It is perplexing to stand on the heights of Charlestown almost two and a half centuries later and fully appreciate the geography at work there in 1775. So much changed as the peninsulas of both Boston and Charlestown swelled with landfills. The distance in 1775 between Copp's Hill in northern Boston and the town wharves of Charlestown—essentially the route of the Charlestown ferry—was then about twelve hundred feet, slightly more than the distance it is today over the Charlestown Bridge.

The Charlestown peninsula was almost a small-scale mirror image of Boston but with a narrow neck, low rolling hills, and an ever-expanding girth as one moved southeast from the neck to the point where the Charles River separated the peninsula from Boston. This ground was a little over a mile in length and varied in width from mere yards at the neck to roughly three-quarters of a mile between the Charlestown wharves and the Mystic River to the northeast.

The neck, or isthmus, connecting Charlestown to the mainland was so low in elevation that it was occasionally awash at high tide. But just southeast of it on the Charlestown side, the ground rose to a series of hills that peaked and then stepped downhill toward Boston. The first of these was "a round, smooth hill" about 110 feet in

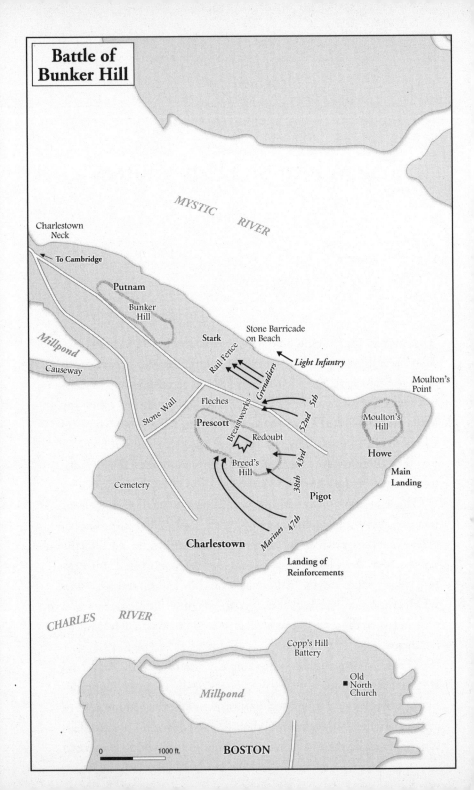

height that sloped steeply toward the waters of the Mystic River to the northeast and a millpond off the Charles River to the south-west. This was Bunker Hill, and there was no question about its name. It was well documented in public records and readily recognized in common usage.

From Bunker Hill, the spine of the ridge descended down the first step to a lower, broader hill. Its name was more problematic. While it would later be called Breed's Hill, there is no evidence that the name was affixed to it in 1775. Some simply thought that it was part of Bunker Hill. Others called the hilltop and surrounding area by the names of the owners of the pastures into which it was divided. Neat and orderly, as was New England custom, these fields were partitioned by stone walls and rail fences that could be counted on to impede any line of advancing infantry. The easterly portions of these hills were used chiefly for hay fields and pasturing; the westerly portions contained orchards and gardens.

The high point of this second hill rose sixty-two feet above sea level and divided brick kilns, clay pits, and some marshy ground on the Mystic River side from the core of Charlestown's buildings on the Charles River side. Charlestown had about four hundred buildings and, before Lord Percy's disruption on the evening of April 19, had been home to several thousand people. By June, however, with Admiral Graves's guns staring at it across the water from Copp's Hill, much of the town had been abandoned.

The final step of high ground before one reached the saltwater estuaries was Moulton's Hill, thirty-five feet tall and commanding the easternmost point of the peninsula above Moulton's (sometimes reported as "Morton's") Point. The main road extended from the neck across the summit of Bunker Hill, around the eastern side of the as-yet-unnamed Breed's Hill, and between it and Moulton's Hill to reach the Charlestown wharves. Smaller roads ran from the Bunker-Breed saddle down to Charlestown proper and along the millpond between Charlestown and the neck. All in all, the Charles-town peninsula was a relatively compact area of irregular terrain, the shoreline of which was heavily impacted by the ebb and flow of the tides. [1]

Whatever else might be said about nomenclature, it was clear to any trained observer that—as General Henry Clinton had noted within hours of his arrival in Boston—whoever controlled the heights of the Charlestown peninsula controlled much of Boston. Those parts of Boston not within cannon range from Charlestown's heights, including the wharves on the seaward side, were within range from the heights at Dorchester to the south. Seize both these positions, and Boston was squeezed like a lemon.

What followed became known to history as the Battle of Bunker Hill. Trivia buffs have long been quick to correct and say, ah, but it was fought on Breed's Hill. But since the name Breed's Hill was apparently not known in 1775, it seems correct to say that the Battle of Bunker Hill was indeed fought on the broader slopes of what everyone at the time thought was Bunker Hill. The crest at the center of the action only became known as Breed's Hill shortly thereafter. Regardless of names, General Gage's regulars and Colonel Prescott's rebels were about to fight one of the most deadly battles of what would become a seven-year war.

THE MOON WAS WANING THAT night, but it was only three days past full. It rose in the east and began to shed light on the hills above Charlestown. Colonel Prescott sent Captain John Nutting and a company from his regiment along the shore road past the millpond toward Charlestown. They were to act as an advance patrol and spread the alarm should they encounter any sign that the rebel movement across the neck had been detected.

Prescott and the bulk of his men continued up the slopes of Bunker Hill and soon came to the rudimentary works that Captain Montresor had thrown up at Lord Percy's direction on the evening of April 19. These were a start, and they might have been expanded. Admittedly, the works faced away from Charlestown, but they dominated all approaches to the neck and protected a backdoor exit from the peninsula to the Cambridge mainland. The other sides of the oval-shaped crest of Bunker Hill commanded the remainder of the peninsula as it sloped downhill toward Charlestown proper. Short of cannon fire against the neck from Royal Navy ships in the Mystic or Charles Rivers, there was no easy avenue by which these heights might be surrounded and cut off.

But as in the question of whether or not to occupy these highest heights in the first place, there now occurred a heated debate about where to dig a defensive perimeter. The three men involved in the decision were Colonel William Prescott, Colonel Richard Gridley—a sixty-five-year-old engineer whose service went back to the 1745 campaign against Louisbourg—and Colonel Israel Putnam. A complete account of what happened among them will never be known. There is no surviving record in writing—no formal version and no scribbling in orderly books. Any piecing together of contemporary evidence was stymied in the generation or so after the battle by dueling descendants and supporters of both Prescott and Putnam.

But this much can be surmised: Colonels Prescott and Gridley favored digging a redoubt and trench works on the crest of Bunker Hill. For Prescott, it was an easy decision: he was the one with the orders from General Ward, and they very plainly said, "Bunker Hill," the location of which was not in doubt. Gridley, as an engineer, likely favored Bunker Hill for its commanding geography. Colonel Putnam, however, led the trio down the ridge toward the lower knoll, which was closer to Boston. According to the late historian Allen French, it lacked "every advantage of the higher hill" and "commanded neither the water nor its own wide and gentle flanks: troops could be marched around it, or sent in boats to land in its rear."[2] In other words, it was an exposed position from which there were tenuous avenues of retreat. Indeed, its only advantage appeared to be that even small cannons along its crest could threaten Boston and shipping in the Charles River. That, of course, was exactly what Putnam was after. Faced with such a challenge, General Gage and his army would have to come out and fight.

Why Prescott and Gridley acceded to Putnam's aggressive stance is a matter of debate. Putnam was nominally a brigadier general of Connecticut forces, but that carried little weight among Massachusetts men. Besides, Colonel Prescott, who was almost Putnam's equal in military experience and age, if not quite in temperament, had been given command of the force. Putnam's role was less formal. He may have wrangled Captain Knowlton's two hundred men from his own Connecticut regiment into the expedition just so he had an excuse to tag along. In the end, however, Putnam's force of personality prevailed. Gridley proceeded to lay out a redoubt and exterior lines on Breed's Hill well below the Bunker Hill summit. About midnight, Prescott's men began to dig.

The redoubt dug on Breed's Hill was relatively small—by one account about 130 feet on each of four sides. If it could be said to have a "front," this was the side that projected outward in a V-shaped redan and faced directly toward the Charlestown ferry crossing and Copp's Hill. This made sense if the redoubt's most menacing feature was to be the cannons firing at Boston. It also presupposed that any counterattack would come directly from Charlestown. The construction did not, however, take into account the open slopes on the left, which dropped gently toward Moulton's Hill and the Mystic River. (On higher Bunker Hill, these slopes were more precipitous and thus more easily defended.[3])

All through the short night, as his troops dug and dug, Prescott was nervous that sentries on board Royal Navy ships in the Charles would raise a cry of alarm. At one point, he may have ridden to the shore to listen, but there was no sound except the reassuring routine calls of "all's well." Near dawn, Prescott ordered Captain Nutting's patrol to withdraw from the Charlestown road and join his other forces.

Even if the sentries on Admiral Graves's ships thought all was well, there was one sharp-eared individual in Boston who was not so sure. Just what Major General Henry Clinton was doing out and about in the late hours of June 16 is a matter of conjecture. According to Clinton's notes, later found among his papers, "In the Evening of ye 16th I saw them at work, reported it to Genls Gage and Howe and advised a landing in two divisions at day brake." Clinton claimed that Howe approved the plan, "but G Gage seemed to doubt their intention."[4]

Whether this encounter with Gage and Howe indeed happened that night or was simply Clinton's way of disassociating himself from events after the fact is not known. Howe, without mentioning Clinton's report, made a similar statement some days later and claimed "the Centrys on the Boston side had heard the Rebels at work all Night, without making any other report of it, except mentioning it in Conversation in the Morning."[5]

This left the first full-blown report of rebel activity above Charlestown to come from the guns of HMS *Lively*. The twenty-gun sloop was anchored in the middle of the Charles River, having recently replaced the *Somerset* at the Charlestown ferry station. The morning was moderate and fair. At 4:00 a.m., a lookout on the *Lively* heard sounds coming from the heights about half a mile away and, either by the light of the moon as it sank toward the west or by the first rays of the sun lighting the eastern horizon, he looked up to see fresh mounds of dirt heaped along the slope of Breed's Hill. As the ship's log succinctly recorded it, he "discover'd the Rebels throwing up a Redoubt on a Hill at the Back of the Charles Town. Began to fire upon them as did the Battery of Copps Hill."[6] Prescott heard the whistle of the *Lively*'s first nine-pound cannonball and knew for certain that he had been discovered.

There is some question about the ability of the *Lively* to elevate its guns high enough to reach the rebel works, but this is where Admiral Graves's battery on Copp's Hill became important. To the admiral's chagrin, it was no longer under the navy's direct command. Previous snickering aside, the army had come to realize how useful it might be against any force assembled in Charlestown or on the heights above the town. General Gage had prevailed upon Admiral Graves to turn its control over to the army. "Insensibly," the admiral later complained, "it lost its original nickname, and instead thereof was called by the army from hence forward Copeshill Battery."[7]

By whatever name it was known, this battery, along with high-angled mortars on floating gun platforms in the river, poured a regular fire against the rebel works as dawn revealed the stark reality of Colonel Prescott's situation. The Breed's Hill position was every bit as exposed as he had feared. His right flank could be somewhat protected as long as skirmishers could be hidden in the outlying buildings of Charlestown. From there, they could harry infantry advancing directly up the slopes toward his position. His left flank, however, was entirely open, and Prescott set his men to work extending a breastwork from the redoubt northward for about one hundred yards. This led to the vicinity of some marshy ground that offered some impediment to attacking troops.

While Prescott was thus occupied, Colonel Putnam seems to have spent a good deal of time reinforcing Bunker Hill and belatedly starting entrenchments along its crest. Historian Allen French suspects that the morning light showed Putnam the tenuous nature of the Breed's Hill position and that Putnam was trying to redeem his error in urging Prescott to the forward position.[8] This is certainly possible, but Putnam must surely have had a good idea of the limitations of Breed's Hill from his Charlestown march a month earlier. Perhaps more likely is that Putnam had long planned the Breed's Hill location as bait and intended that Prescott make an orderly retreat up Bunker Hill once the British had been lured out of Boston. It is even possible that Prescott initially agreed to this, which is why he went about the Breed's Hill fortifications.

But as the skies lightened and cannonballs continued to rain down, some of Prescott's men indeed felt like sacrificial lambs. They found themselves "against Ships of the Line, and all Boston fortified against us." Peter Brown, the company clerk in Prescott's regiment, later wrote what many were thinking: "The danger we were in made us think there was treachery and that we were brought there to be all slain, and I must and will say that there was treachery, oversight or presumption in the Conduct of our Officers."[9]

Soon Brown was not the only one looking over his shoulder. Colonel Prescott was, too. The men from his regiment were standing firm, mostly out of loyalty to him, but troops from the other two regiments slowly began to melt away and make their way up to higher Bunker Hill. For a time, the British cannon fire stopped, and there was an eerie silence broken on the rebel side by the sound of picks and shovels throwing dirt ever higher. Then, about eleven, recalled Brown, the British cannons "began to fire as brisk as ever, which caus'd many of our young Country people to desert."[10]

There was also an ongoing tug-of-war between Prescott and Putnam. Prescott wanted to keep digging and strengthening his forward position. Putnam wanted tools and workers to improve the Bunker Hill crest. Prescott claimed that if men moved back with tools to assist Putnam, they would never return to the redoubt on Breed's Hill, and he was right. In addition, there seemed to be no agreement — perhaps there was not even discussion — about what order of withdrawal might be undertaken when the British attacked. Having become invested in the Breed's Hill redoubt and trenches, Prescott now seems to have become the stubborn one. With no senior officer to direct the larger scope of the battle and order Prescott and Putnam otherwise, their actions toward one another's positions continued to be tentative: Prescott was not inclined to withdraw from Breed's Hill, and Putnam was not rushing reinforcements to Prescott's position to support him.[11]

MEANWHILE, GENERAL GAGE AND HIS three major generals were having their own discussions about what should be done. There was complete agreement about one thing. Despite their own plans to attack Dorchester the next day, the rebels' action in seizing the

Charlestown heights had preempted that. "It therefore became necessary," according to Burgoyne, "to alter our plan, and attack on [the Charlestown] side."[12] How to do it was another matter.

Clinton's reported plea for an attack at "day brake" was already out of the question—if, in fact, by "day brake" Clinton meant the morning of June 17, as has traditionally been assumed. But by the time Clinton conferred with Gage, Howe, and Burgoyne on the morning of the seventeenth, "day brake" that day had already passed. It may well be that by "tomorrow morning at day brake" Clinton really meant the morning of June 18, the date targeted for an assault on Dorchester. This would have kept assault preparations on schedule and given Clinton time to organize the additional logistics for the kind of enveloping attack he proposed.[13]

His plan was to take five hundred men and land them at "the Jews burying ground where," he said, he "would have been in perfect security and within half gun shot of the narrow neck of communication of the Rebels." Exactly where this landing site was is uncertain. It is equally uncertain whether Clinton initially meant to land on the Charles or Mystic side of the Charlestown peninsula.

However, if one assumes that "the Jews burying ground" was in some proximity to the Phipps Street Burying Ground, Clinton's geography works from the Charles River side. His force would have been behind Prescott's position on Breed's Hill and about half a cannon shot from Charlestown Neck in the other direction via the millpond road. This is supported by Clinton's further claim that his troops "marching through the town might have taken possession of the neck, and thus finished the affair." Howe, meanwhile, would land with the main force at some point between Charlestown and Moulton's Point and effect an enveloping, pincerlike movement. However, "my advice," remembered Clinton, "was not attended to."[14]

Whether the objection to Clinton's plan came from both Gage and Howe or Howe alone as the field commander is not certain. If it was Howe alone, he likely did not favor splitting his forces: Clinton's troops would be in potential danger of being cut off and sur-rounded until they could effect a linkup. Or possibly Howe may have underestimated the rebel resolve and assumed that one frontal show of force was all that was needed to send the rebels fleeing.

Instead of listening to Clinton, Howe planned to make a landing and an assault "as soon as the troops and boats could be got in readi-ness for that purpose." And he meant to do it on that same day, regardless of what Clinton meant by "day brake." This was clearly speeding up the timetable for the contemplated Dorchester assault the next day. Because the shore was very flat and the water quite shallow near Moulton's Point, where Howe had judged it was "most proper to land," it would be necessary to be ready to land with the next high tide—between two and three o'clock that afternoon.[15]

Clinton may have been beside himself, but he made no outward objection. Howe might have landed his troops on the Charlestown wharves without regard to the tide and fought his way through the largely abandoned town against whatever skirmishers Prescott might have deployed. Landing there in force would also have put Howe in good position to sweep along the millpond road and cut off the rebel redoubt, as Clinton had proposed. But perhaps because of the tales of Menotomy, Howe decided to steer clear of Charles-town's buildings and fight to the east, on the open ground, where European-style warfare was more effective.[16]

Time would tell whether or not this was a mistake, but in order to accommodate this schedule, there was quite a flurry of activity that morning among Howe's troops. The planned expedition against Dorchester had been calculated to keep men in the field at least sev-eral days before camp equipment could be landed. Howe did not alter this calculation even as the timetable was sped up and the tar-get switched from Dorchester to Charlestown. Consequently his troops were ordered to assemble "at Half after 11 o'clock, with their Arms, Ammunition, Blanketts and the provisions Ordered to be Cooked this Morning." This meant that "the bread must be baked, the meat boiled, and the whole served out before the troops could parade." More important, it also meant that they would be carrying considerable weight in their haversacks as they went ashore in heavy woolen uniforms in the heat of a midsummer's day. It might have been more expeditious and prudent to dispatch an agile force to secure the field rather than make a march in grand formation with cumbersome packs, but that is what Howe ordered.[17]

There is a tale that is perhaps apocryphal, but it nonetheless captures the mentality of the British high command concerning the rebels' resolve. One of General Gage's loyalist advisers was Abijah Willard, the former mandamus councilor late of Lancaster who had sought refuge in Boston immediately after the Lexington fight. Atop Copp's Hill, Gage—or, as reports vary, perhaps it was Howe—handed his telescope to Willard and asked if he recognized anyone among the rebels on Breed's Hill who might be in command. Willard did. On the hillside across the Charles River, easily recognizable in his floppy hat and loose white coat, stood Colonel William Prescott. He was not only Willard's friend and fellow soldier from the colonial wars but also his brother-in-law. "Will he fight?" demanded Gage. Willard was not happy to make his reply. He could not answer for the colonel's men, Willard said heavily, but "Prescott will fight you to the gates of hell!"[18]

THERE WAS ANOTHER MAN AS determined as Colonel Prescott to be present on Breed's Hill: Joseph Warren. Even in these very early days of the fledgling American nation, it was unusual for a man of Warren's position to ride to the front. John Adams mused about taking the field, but had never done so in practice. John Hancock ranted about his thoughts of military glory, but Samuel Adams placed a restraining hand on his shoulder and steered him elsewhere. Samuel Adams himself was never inclined to the military side of matters—viewing them simply as necessary work to be done by others to fulfill his political agenda. Given all this, it was exceptional for the man who was president of the Massachusetts

Provincial Congress and chairman of its committee of safety to take the field, but that is what Warren did.

To be sure, Joseph Warren had always been quick to ride to the sound of the guns. He left Boston for Lexington and Concord early on the morning of April 19. He showed up on the shore after the Grape Island raid and tried to get into the Noddle's Island fray. Just three days before the Bunker Hill battle, on June 14, the Massachusetts Provincial Congress voted to commission Warren a major general.[19] Admittedly, the congress was awarding general officer commissions based almost as much on political skills as military prowess. Warren desperately wanted to be directly involved on the military side, so he used his political clout to obtain the commission.

There is no better evidence of the esteem in which his fellow Massachusetts leaders held Joseph Warren than their having elected him president of the Provincial Congress in John Hancock's stead. One might speculate that Warren lobbied for the major general commission out of a desire to retain strong civilian control over the budding military. Warren had in fact written to Samuel Adams just days before, worrying about this very issue. "The continent must strengthen and support with all its weight the civil authority here," Warren urged Adams. "Otherwise . . . we shall very soon find ourselves involved in greater difficulties than you can well imagine."[20]

But that speculation seems to be a reach. As a major general, Warren would be part of the military establishment, and his inexperience would have been glaring. Warren was only thirty-four, had no military training, and was suddenly senior to grizzled veterans of the French and Indian War who were old enough to be his father—Putnam and Prescott among them. With this commission, Warren would be senior to all Massachusetts officers except Artemas Ward and John Thomas, a doctor and veteran militia officer. One may speculate that Warren got the number three position only with the expectation that he would function as an adjutant general to bring order out of the chaos until a continental commander could arrive. But if so, why did Warren show up in the front lines on Breed's Hill and then fail to provide Prescott and Putnam — the latter still not likely to be impressed by a Massachusetts commission — with some overarching direction?

By all accounts, Warren presided over a session of the Provincial Congress in Watertown until late on the evening of Friday, June 16. At some point, the session adjourned until eight o'clock the following morning, but Warren would not be there. He may have spent the night in Watertown or gone into Cambridge — the record is not clear — and if he did the latter, he may or may not have arrived in time to see Prescott's column march off at dusk. What is abundantly clear, however, is that he declared his intention to share the coming peril with his countrymen. His good friend Elbridge Gerry, with whom he had boarded in Watertown, tried to dissuade him, but Warren could not be restrained.

On the morning of the seventeenth, Warren stopped at General Ward's headquarters in Cambridge, but the general was not in. Warren opened express messages from John Hancock in Philadelphia regarding progress on forming a Continental Army, and then, suffering from an acute headache, he collapsed on a bed to rest. A short time later, a horseman galloped up with news that the British were landing at Charlestown.

As chairman of the Massachusetts committee of safety, Warren held civilian control over the Massachusetts military. But as a newly minted major general, he was junior to General Ward. Warren left Cambridge without seeing Ward or receiving any instructions, but in Ward's absence, at both the civilian and military levels, there should have been no question of Warren's authority. Yet upon his arrival at Bunker Hill in midafternoon, he did all he could to refrain from taking command. Supposedly Putnam recognized Warren's recent commission and offered him command. Warren refused, claiming that his commission was not yet official. Instead, he asked Old Put where the hottest action was likely to be, and Putnam nodded down the slope toward Prescott's redoubt on Breed's Hill.

Warren went there next and had a similar conversation with

Prescott. Once again, if the story is to be believed, a seasoned colonel on the brink of battle offered to turn over his command to an inexperienced, shiny new major general half his age. And once again, Warren refused, citing his unofficial commission. And yet: Putnam and Prescott must have known the Provincial Congress had approved Warren's commission on June 15 or they would never have offered Warren command. What "official" notice was lacking? Was Warren merely seeking an excuse not to be pushed to the forefront? It must have been an awkward situation for all concerned. Saying no more, Joseph Warren, wearing clothes more suited for presiding over a legislature than hunkering down in a newly dug trench, took up a position in Prescott's redoubt. He would indeed be on the front line.[21]

ON THE BRITISH SIDE, AFTER the bread was baked and the meat boiled, it was Major General William Howe who would be on the front lines. General Gage may or may not have put in an appearance on Copp's Hill. There is some evidence that he had agreed among his generals that he would not venture from his headquarters at Province House in the event that the rebels tried simultaneously to force the Roxbury lines at Boston Neck. Lord Percy was in command there, and later Percy would say that nothing had happened on that front except "a pretty smart cannonade, wh[ich] we kept up from there upon Roxbury, in order to amuse the Rebels on that side." This left Generals Burgoyne and Clinton to take up stations at the battery on Copp's Hill and watch Howe's troop movements.[22]

If pageantry alone could win battles, Howe was the victor even before his first troops embarked from Boston. His order of battle called for the Fifth and Thirty-Eighth Regiments, along with the ten senior companies of grenadiers and light infantry, to depart from the Long Wharf. Once again, as at Lexington and Concord, these men would bear the brunt of the attack. The Forty-Third and Fifty-Second Regiments marched to the North Battery, just east of

Copp's Hill, to embark from there. The remaining companies of grenadiers and light infantry, as well as the Forty-Seventh Regiment and Major Pitcairn's First Battalion of Marines, were to be held in reserve and ready to embark as necessary. Three of these regiments comprised Brigadier General Robert Pigot's Second Brigade, and Howe designated him second in command of the assault.[23]

Because of the limited number of small boats, Howe landed his troops in two waves. Those 1,100 troops assembled at the Long Wharf went first. Once they were ashore on the Charlestown side near Moulton's Point, the flotilla of wooden craft rowed the short distance back to the North Battery, and 450 additional men clambered into them for the second wave. Both landings were accomplished without opposition, mostly because the rebels were not inclined to waste precious gunpowder at long range or venture forward from the relative safety of their entrenchments and breastworks.

Meanwhile, the sloops *Lively*, *Glasgow*, and *Falcon* paraded back and forth off the beachhead, spouting cannon fire. The *Symmetry*, an armed transport of shallow draft, joined this effort by cruising off the millpond and lobbing shells onto Charlestown Neck from the Charles River side. A smaller armed sloop and five floating batteries added their firepower to the bombardment, which, Howe reported, "they executed very effectually."[24] It evidently did not occur to Howe, however, that some of this firepower might be better positioned on the Mystic River side of Charlestown Neck—decidedly *behind* the rebel positions visible from Boston.

Howe and Brigadier Pigot went ashore with the second wave, followed by some field artillery. They formed their troops in three lines on the rise of Moulton's Hill, about one hundred yards inland from the beach. But now, as Howe watched his regiments dress their ranks, he saw something that gave him pause. From Moulton's Hill, he got his first good look at the Mystic side of the Charlestown peninsula—the side that was not visible from Boston. The rebels had indeed been successful—over the course of one night and morning, and under sporadic fire—in pushing the breastworks on their left flank downhill from the redoubt. Beyond the marshy area, another defensive line ran down the slope toward the beach along the Mystic River. Howe couldn't be certain, but it looked as though these were substantial works, part of which he would later call "cannon proof."[25] But there was more bad news.

From this vantage point, the general could also look past the rebel redoubt on Breed's Hill to higher Bunker Hill and see quite a conglomeration of men. Howe had no way of knowing that Prescott and Putnam had not come up with much of a battle plan and that command and control was lacking. But what he saw was enough to give him pause. Colonel John Stark's First New Hampshire Regiment—likely about four hundred men—was moving through the confusion and making its way down the slopes toward what Howe thought was an "earthwork" above the Mystic River. In truth, it was only a reinforced rail fence covered with newly mown hay to give it an earthy tone.

Stark's regiment had been quartered in Medford, about four miles away, and had received its orders to march about ten o'clock that morning. Being as short of ammunition and powder as most units were, Stark formed his men in front of a temporary arsenal "where each man received a *gill cup* full of powder, fifteen balls and one flint." Given the hodgepodge of firearms, "there were scarcely two muskets in a company of equal caliber," and "it was necessary to reduce the size of the balls for many of them."[26]

By the time Stark led his companies to the Cambridge side of Charlestown Neck, he found two regiments halted and blocking the way because of the fire being poured on the neck by the *Symmetry* from across the millpond. Stark's adjutant went forward and said to their commanders that "if they did not intend to move on, he [Colonel Stark] wished them to open and let our regiment pass." This they gladly did.

Henry Dearborn, who would go on to less-than-glorious service throughout the Revolution and during the War of 1812, was then a captain commanding the advance company of Stark's regiment as it started across the neck. Stark led the way at "a very deliberate pace," despite the British cannon fire. Should they not quicken the march, Dearborn asked, in order that they might sooner get across the exposed ground? Stark, the French and Indian War veteran, looked over at Dearborn with steadied New Hampshire calm and replied, "'Dearborn, one fresh man in action is worth ten fatigued ones' and continued to advance in the same cool and collected manner."[27]

Stark found Putnam atop Bunker Hill, but as he looked down the slope toward Moulton's Point, it was obvious what needed to be done. After "a short but animated address," to which his men gave three cheers, Stark led his regiment into the gap between Captain Thomas Knowlton's men at the rail fence and the Mystic River. A smaller New Hampshire regiment, commanded by Colonel James Reed, arrived at about the same time and joined the line. In this way, the vulnerable left side of the rebel line came to be reinforced with men as hard as New Hampshire granite.

But as Howe's troops prepared to move forward, Stark saw one other weakness from his position at the fence. The rail fence ran down the slope toward a small bluff but then stopped where the slope dropped the last dozen feet to the beach. Even at high tide, there was ample passage at the base of the bluff for troops to flank the fence. Stark immediately directed several of his companies to pile stones between the base of the bluff and out into the water and to take up positions behind what became essentially a continuation of the rail fence.[28]

Seeing this increasing array of firepower forming on the left of the rebel line, Howe may have wished that he had worked with Admiral Graves to deploy the navy differently and/or that he had heeded Clinton's advice about a landing to the rear of the rebel line. He could see that a pounding from a ship or two in the Mystic, as the *Symmetry* was delivering off the millpond and as the *Lively*, *Glasgow*, and *Falcon* were engaged in on the Charles, might discourage Knowlton's, Reed's, and Stark's men at the rail fence and the hastily erected stone wall. Howe ordered two floating batteries that were firing off the millpond to move around to the Mystic side, but time and tide were against them, and they never got into position.[29]

Meanwhile, the left side of the British line, where Brigadier General Pigot was stationed as second in command, was coming under attack from rebel skirmishers firing from buildings in Charlestown. Pigot faced one of his regiments in that direction and returned ineffective volleys. Watching this harassment, Admiral Graves, who to his great credit "went ashore in person to be near General Howe," now made the same suggestion to Howe that he had made to General Gage on the evening of April 19: burn Charlestown. Howe readily agreed, and the admiral signaled his ships as well as the Copp's Hill battery to fire incendiary carcasses into the town. According to Graves, the town "was instantly set on fire in many places, and the Enemy quickly forced from that station." It didn't happen all that quickly, of course, and it is likely that some of Pigot's men on the shore finished the task with torches. In any event, the result was that most of the rebel skirmishers withdrew from the burning buildings, and Pigot secured his left flank for the coming assault up the hill.[30]

But Howe was clearly worried by the many signs of rebel activity. "From this appearance," the general recalled, "as well as our observation that they were assembling with all the force they could collect, I applied to General Gage for a reinforcement of troops."[31] These were the remaining troops assembled at the North Battery — the companies of light infantry and grenadiers remaining in Boston, along with the Forty-Seventh Regiment and Pitcairn's First Battalion of Marines.

By the time these reinforcements of the Forty-Seventh Regiment and the First Marines joined with those of the first and second waves, Howe had about 2,200 men in the field, divided between the right division, under his personal command, which would attempt to flank Breed's Hill by going through Stark's line at the rail fence, and Pigot's left division, which would march straight up the hill against Prescott's redoubt and principal earthworks.

Upon receiving these additional troops, Howe rearranged his command into two lines instead of the original three at Moulton's Point and "began the attack by a sharp cannonade from our field pieces and two Howitzers." In between the cannon blasts, Howe's entire formation — the right side of which was spread out some five hundred yards in front of the rebel left at the rail fence — began a slow but steady advance, "frequently halting to give time for the artillery to fire."[32]

But the field artillery action that day proved a comedy of errors on both sides. Rather than cannonading the rebel positions from his initial deployment on Moulton's Hill — which might well have proven that the rail fence was far from "cannon proof" — Howe ordered his meager artillery forward with his battle line. All that did was to stutter-step his advance and give the rebels more time to get into position to counter his thrust. Even then, the cannons bogged down in marshy ground on the rebel side of Moulton's Hill. To add insult to injury, a snafu in the supply department resulted in twelve-pound balls being delivered to the six-pound fieldpieces, forcing them to fire grapeshot, which had to cease once the troop lines moved forward of their mired positions.

Rebel artillery didn't fare much better. Four artillery pieces made their way to the crest of Breed's Hill early that morning, but according to Peter Brown of Prescott's regiment, "the Captn of which fir'd a few times [at Boston] then swung his Hat three times round to the enemy and ceas'd to fire." By the time Howe's troops started to land, these pieces were ordered to repulse the landing, but their commander, Captain John Callender, chose to withdraw to the safer heights of Bunker Hill instead.[33]

There Callender encountered an enraged Colonel Putnam on horseback. What did Callender think he was doing? Old Put sputtered. Callender claimed he was out of powder cartridges, but Putnam quickly dismounted and examined the ammunition boxes to find that was a lie. Putnam ordered Callender to return with his guns to support Stark's left flank. Callender himself quickly disappeared, but Putnam personally directed the redeployment of his cannons.[34]

So onward Howe's lines came. It was a pretty sight, but Howe, who had once led the way for General Wolfe's troops onto the Plains of Abraham, should have remembered his mentor's tactics: *speed* and *by column* were the operative words. There certainly was no speed to this advance, and rather than arrowlike columns, Howe had deployed most of his troops in long lines across the open ground. "If an intrenchment is to be attacked," Wolfe had written in 1755, in a set of instructions to young officers, "the troops should move as quick as possible towards the place, not in a line, but in small firing columns of three or four platoons in depth."[35]

The only column in the attack was formed by Howe's companies of light infantry that were sent along the beach against Stark's men at the stone barricade. These nimble troops were to turn the end of the rebel line and press it with a pincerlike movement against the grenadier companies and the Fifth and Fifty-Second Regiments advancing up the open slope. Incredibly, the British had not loaded their muskets. This was to be a bayonet charge.

But except for the light infantry along the beach, there was no dash to the maneuver. "The intermediate space between the two armies," Howe complained, "was cut by fences, formed of strong posts and close railing, very high, and which could not be broken readily."[36]

On the British left, Pigot was planning a similar encirclement. He had three companies of light infantry and three of grenadiers, along with the Thirty-Eighth, Forty-Third, and Forty-Seventh Regiments and the marine battalion led by Major Pitcairn. With his left flank skirting the burning buildings of Charlestown, Pigot intended to sweep up the hill and encircle the redoubt on the left while his center and right attacked it head-on.[37]

By now it was well after three in the afternoon. An after-action report by the Massachusetts Provincial Congress termed the British advance "a very slow march towards our lines."[38] General Clinton, still watching from Copp's Hill, termed it "exceedingly soldierlike" and, whatever misgivings he may have had, nonetheless called Howe's disposition "perfect."[39]

For one last fleeting moment, the difference between Lexington and Concord and what was about to occur below Bunker Hill stood in stark relief. This could not be called an accident or the result of a lack of intelligence by either side. As General Howe's troops advanced toward Prescott's and Stark's positions late on the afternoon of June 17, 1775, it was very clear to any observer from Copp's Hill to Cambridge that the outcome would be a pitched battle.

All afternoon, as Howe finessed his formations and moved his troops forward with all the speed of tentative pawns in a casual chess match, the bulk of the American line had remained silent. Rebel commanders, fully aware of their limited quantity of gunpowder, continually admonished their men to hold their fire and reminded them that when the order finally came, they were to aim low, a lesson learned from the errant volleys of the British regulars along the Concord road.

The famous line most associated with the Battle of Bunker Hill is, "Don't fire until you see the whites of their eyes." Who uttered it, if anyone did, is uncertain. The likely candidates are Israel Putnam, as he hurried Callender's cannons into place, William Prescott, as he peered out from the redoubt into Pigot's advancing lines, or John Stark, as he steadied his men along the rail fence. Given that the line was already somewhat of a military staple that originated in earlier European wars, all three men may have shouted some version of it.

According to James Wilkinson, who visited the battlefield as a young man a year later and who later still would become a scoundrel in the Burr conspiracy, Colonel Stark directed his men along the rail fence and behind the stone wall not to fire until they could see the enemy's white-colored half gaiters. Given the terrain, this would have been at a distance of about fifty yards. "From this it would seem," Wilkinson claimed, "that the often quoted order, 'Don't fire until you see the white of their eyes,' was more nearly, 'Don't fire until you see the white of their gaiters.'"[40]

As the rebels held their fire, onward the front line of Howe's regulars came, resplendent in their red uniforms. Then, at perhaps fifty yards, the command to fire came, and the entire rebel line exploded with a roar of thunder and a profusion of smoke.

Chapter 24

～

"A Dear Bought Victory"

A nd now," wrote Major General John Burgoyne with his usual dramatic flair, "ensued one of the greatest scenes of war that can be conceived: if we look to the height, Howe's corps ascending the hill in the face of intrenchments, and in a very disadvantageous ground, was much engaged; to the left the enemy pouring in fresh troops by thousands, over the land; and in the arm of the sea our ships and floating batteries cannonading them; straight before us a large and noble Town [Charlestown] in one great blaze — the church-steeples being timber, were great pyramids of fire above the rest; behind us, the church-steeples and heights of our own camp [Boston] covered with spectators of the rest of our Army which was engaged; the hills round the country covered with spectators; the enemy all in anxious suspense; the roar of cannon, mortars, and musketry." Perhaps the worst part, Burgoyne concluded, was the reflection that a defeat here would be "a final loss to the *British Empire in America*." [1]

GENERATIONS OF ARMCHAIR STRATEGISTS WOULD later fault General Howe for sending his troops to slaughter by marching them in two long lines up Breed's Hill. It wasn't quite that simple, and that frontal maneuver in and of itself was certainly not Howe's initial intent. To be sure, his advance was slow and not in column, save for the light infantry companies on the beach, but by all accounts Howe placed great faith in his light infantry's ability to turn the end of the rebel line and create havoc along it. After that, the grenadier companies, supported by the Fifth and Fifty-Second Regiments, would bulldoze through the rebel left with bayonets fixed and trap Prescott's men in the redoubt.[2]

On the rebel right, Brigadier General Pigot was trying somewhat the same maneuver on a more limited scale — given the narrow confines between the redoubt and Charlestown as opposed to the wide ground in front of Howe. Thus this was not an overconfident frontal assault — even if it turned out that way — but a calculated thrust designed to turn the rebel flanks and roll up the entire lot of them *behind* Prescott's redoubt. If that had indeed happened, it is interesting to speculate what action, if any, Colonel Putnam might have taken from atop Bunker Hill. Instead, the result was that Colonel John Stark and his New Hampshire men stood firm on the beach and at the rail fence and thwarted Howe's flanking attempt.

Eleven companies of light infantry, comprising about 350 men and led by the company from the Twenty-Third Regiment — the Royal Welch Fusiliers — rushed headlong in a column of fours against Stark's hastily erected rock piles on the Mystic beach. The first volley from the rebel line decimated this advance company. The second company in the column, that of the Fourth "King's Own," confidently moved forward to take its place, expecting to reach the defenders and rout them with bayonets. Stark's men, however, were positioned three deep, and before the attackers could gain more than a few yards, another ragged volley rent the air and ripped apart the men from the King's Own. Onward the column of light infantry came, but the New Hampshire lads continued to put up a hail of fire, and "as the broken lines of each company gave way, the successor pressed forward, only in turn to be shattered."[3]

The grenadier companies and regiments marching in two lines on the slope above the beach heard these musket volleys without being able to ascertain the results. They likely expected to hear a cheer as their light infantry comrades swept around the end of the rebel line and its defenders fled before them. But there was no cheer from the beach. Even more ominously, there was no movement from the rebel line behind the rail fence.

Howe had indeed intended that the grenadiers and men of the Fifth and Fifty-Second Regiments would sweep through the rebel line at the rail fence with bayonets alone — hard steel driven home. But as the coordinated light infantry attack collapsed on the beach, these advancing troops were thwarted in a bayonet charge both by the terrain — the difficulty in climbing over and through other fences en route — and by the heavy fire from the American line, which had in no way been abated by the light infantry attack.

"As fast as the front man was shot down," one rebel report claimed, "the next stepped forward into his place, but our men dropt them so fast, they were a long time coming up." What was most surprising to this observer was how the British regulars "would step over their dead bodies, as though they had been logs of wood."[4]

As Howe told the story, the grenadiers made the attack with "a laudable perseverance, but not the greatest share of discipline," because rather than pushing the bayonet charge they took time to load and "began firing, and by crowding fell into disorder, and in this State the 2d Line mixt with them." The only thing worse was what was happening on the beach to the companies of light infantry. "The Light Infantry at the same time being repulsed," wrote Howe, "there was *a Moment that I never felt before*."[5]

Pigot's attack on the American right and the redoubt met with similar failure, but just how aggressive Pigot was in pushing this first wave on his side of the battlefield has always been a matter of debate. Howe and Pigot may well have agreed that Pigot would make a feint in strength on the American right to distract Prescott's men while Howe swept around the left flank. Pigot would not charge the redoubt itself until Howe's troops were circling behind it. It's also quite possible that having encountered fences impeding their orderly advance, and still taking some fire from the outskirts of burning Charlestown, Pigot's advance bogged down in the face of fire from Prescott's lines in much the same manner as Howe's did.

Faced with the collapse of the light infantry's flanking attack, Howe's advance of the grenadiers and supporting regiments indeed took on the look of an ill-advised frontal attack. Their now-ragged lines were subjected to rebel fire from the breastworks extending from the redoubt and all along the main rail fence. There was apparently also rebel fire from a trio of hastily erected fleches, or angled fieldworks, that were constructed by unknown troops—perhaps part of Knowlton's command—between the redoubt breastworks and the rail fence. In the face of this concentrated fire, the British lines ground to a halt and then broke and fled back toward Moulton's Hill. Their officers tried in vain to halt the retreat. "Many of our men," recalled one rebel report, "were for pursuing, [but by] the prudence of the officers they were prevented leaving so advantageous a post."[6]

General Howe now faced a crucial decision. He could withdraw his troops and avoid more slaughter, or he could re-form his command and attack again. In practice, there was really no decision to be made. Howe's next act was preordained and unequivocal. He had no alternative but to order his men back up the hill to dislodge the rebels. To do anything less—particularly with Clinton and Burgoyne watching his every movement from Copp's Hill—would have been unthinkable. Howe was less than enthusiastic about taking on his American cousins, but once he embarked from Boston and became committed to the field on this mission, he had no choice—short of utter shame—than to prosecute it to a decisive conclusion.

SO THE BRITISH LINES MOVED forward once again. Whether this was a completely new assault separated in time and space or merely a continuation of the first advance after some regrouping has always been a matter of debate. On the field itself, it was difficult if not impossible to get a clear picture of what was happening. Events tended to telescope together in the observer's mind. The best view and tactical understanding may have been with Generals Clinton and Burgoyne as they watched this drama unfold from the battery on Copp's Hill. Even Clinton and Burgoyne, however, could not see far enough around Moulton's Point to observe the complete disaster of the light infantry companies on the Mystic beach. Nonetheless, what they could see of Pigot's unsuccessful advance left little doubt that this was a disaster in the making.

As the third-ranking major general on the scene, John Burgoyne indeed had little to do except mind the artillery and form the mental picture from which he would write his vivid description of the battle. General Gage had charged Henry Clinton, however, with hastening Howe's reserve — the Forty-Seventh Regiment and First Marines — into action from the North Battery should Howe call for it or should Clinton "observe the smallest occasion to reinforce him."[7] This Clinton had done before the first assault, but seeing the attack collapse, he now determined to join the battle personally.

"On seeing our left give totally away," Clinton recalled, "I desired G[eneral] B[urgoyne] who was with me to save me harmless to G[eneral] G[age] for going without his orders and went over to join with H[owe]."[8] At some point, Clinton also acknowledged Howe's request for *reinforcements* — as opposed merely for his *reserve*, which was already committed — and dispatched the Sixty-Third Regiment and the Second Marines from the North Battery, although neither would arrive in time for much action. Clinton, however, would soon be in the thick of things.

Meanwhile, the Americans in Prescott's redoubt could not afford even the hint of a victory celebration. To be sure, they had as yet lost few men and had broken the British advance, but they had done so with repeated firings. Their gunpowder supply was nearly as exhausted as they were after a sleepless night of digging and a hot day under frequent bombardment. From Colonel Prescott down to the greenest private, the men remaining in the redoubt and adjacent breastworks alternated glances between the British lines massed to their front and the conglomeration of fresh colonial troops waiting expectantly at their rear. Who would be the first to reach their position? Where was Colonel Putnam? Where was General Ward?

At best, history would pay Artemas Ward little mind, and he would be the largely unknown and unsung commander in chief of the rebels. At worst, Ward would be remembered as the general who never left his headquarters in Cambridge — which is probably not true — while all hell broke loose around Bunker Hill. That Ward didn't provide adequate command and control to Putnam and Prescott is a certainty, but whether he should have ridden to the sound of the guns, as Joseph Warren did, is debatable. The Massachusetts committee of safety charged General Ward with protecting the rebels' encirclement of Boston, including their supply center in Cambridge. Given the uncertainty about the number of troops Howe had deployed against Charlestown, Ward's broader mission was to guard against simultaneous attacks at Roxbury via Boston Neck — should Lord Percy do more in that direction than exercise his cannons — or directly across the Charles River at Lechmere Point, as Colonel Smith had done on the night of April 18. Indeed, Ward had no way of knowing the full extent of the British attack until quite late on the afternoon of June 17. Whatever happened on the heights above Charlestown, Ward's first duty was to keep Cambridge secure.[9]

That said, Ward seems to have conferred with Putnam at least once that morning as Putnam dashed back and forth between Cambridge and Bunker Hill. These conversations, or Ward's independent actions, resulted in Stark's New Hampshire men eventually making their way to the rail fence. What Ward evidently didn't do was provide Putnam much direction as to whether he should reinforce Prescott in force on Breed's Hill, hold Bunker Hill itself, or organize a withdrawal from the entire Charlestown peninsula.

Artemas Ward has long been a convenient scapegoat. But from his plans on the evening of June 16 for rotating troops to relieve Prescott's command to his sending additional regiments to the Charlestown peninsula—as the number of Howe's attacking troops suggested that his was to be the one and only thrust of the day— Ward acted with some degree of operational clarity and competence. The weak link was his inability to implement his directives at the regimental level. In great measure this was because Ward had very little staff and no brigade or division command structure between his headquarters and the individual regiments. (Such a hierarchy would not be formally established until George Washington arrived on the scene.) Regiments of three or four hundred men attempting to maneuver as units over narrow roads and unfamiliar terrain further muddied the situation.[10]

This chaos aside, what was Colonel Putnam doing with the troops he did have in the field? Exhorting them to fight, to be sure, but again, any measure of command and control over the disparate regiments and their fragmented companies was fleeting at best. Then, too, there is evidence that Putnam became occupied with the continuing saga of the rebel artillery. Certainly he pushed at least several pieces into the critical gap between the breastwork extending from the redoubt and the rail fence. Some reports even have him stopping to lend a hand with placement and firing. It was an example of selflessly doing what needed to be done, but in the broader view, this did little to reinforce Prescott or deploy arriving troops.

Captain John Chester's company of Spencer's Connecticut Regiment made it into the field, but their experience was indicative of the broader command problems. Early that afternoon, Colonel Putnam's son Daniel galloped into Cambridge with shouts that the British were landing at Charlestown and told Chester, "Father says you must all meet, and march immediately to Bunker Hill to oppose the enemy." Chester roused his men from the church where they were billeted and then stopped short as his eyes beheld their splendid blue uniforms with red facings. His company was one of the few among the continentals even to have uniforms. Such a display wouldn't do, Chester decided, and he ordered his men to put their "frocks and trowsers" on over their uniforms because "we were loath to expose ourselves by our dress."

Chester then led his men at a fast march across the neck and up to the crest of Bunker Hill. It was chaos—that was one thing upon which all reports agree. "When we arrived," Chester recalled, "there was not a company with us in any kind of order, although, when we first set out, perhaps three regiments were by our side." All around them, men were scattered behind rocks and small hay piles; thirty men clustered behind an apple tree. Others, to Chester's chagrin, were retreating, "seemingly without any excuse." Chester asked why and was given a lengthy list of reasons, from lack of "officers to head them" to the fact that "they had been all night and day on fatigue, without sleep, victuals, or drink."

But then Chester spied an entire company marching along in rank and file bound away from the British advance. He accosted the officer in command and asked why he was retreating. When the officer made no answer, Chester halted his own men "and told him if he went on it should be at his peril." Chester ordered his own company to make ready and declared to this flighty bunch that his men would fire if he so ordered. "Upon that they stopped short, tried to excuse themselves," but Chester ordered them to about-face, and momentarily they followed his company down off the crest of Bunker Hill toward Prescott's redoubt.[11]

Another of those rushing into action was fifteen-year-old John Greenwood, a fifer with Captain Theodore Bliss's company of Patterson's Massachusetts Regiment. Having had permission to be in Cambridge earlier that day, Greenwood crossed the neck and hastened up Bunker Hill, looking for his company. Uneasy without his comrades, Greenwood was petrified by the scene and recalled that he "could positively feel my hair stand on end." As he got near the crest, he met a black man who was wounded in the back of his neck coming toward him. Greenwood "saw the wound quite plainly and the blood running down his back." He asked the man if it hurt, and "he said no, that he was going to get a plaster put on it, and meant to return." That show of resolve gave young Greenwood a shot of encouragement, and he "began to feel brave and like a soldier from that moment." Greenwood went on to find his company and went into action with them "on the road in sight of the battle, with two field-pieces." [12]

On the slopes below, Howe and Pigot were preparing for yet another assault. Their second attempt—or perhaps it was a grim continuation of the first advance—had also fallen short. Seeing the absolute carnage that Stark's men had visited on his grenadiers and light infantry, Howe now angled his right flank toward the redoubt and its breastworks in an attempt to take them directly and avoid coming within deadly range of the rail fence. His battered companies of light infantry made a feint in Stark's direction to hold the colonel's troops in position, but the bulk of Howe's next advance was in concert with Pigot against Prescott's positions in and around the redoubt. [13]

Given the slow but steady withdrawal of his troops, Colonel Prescott was down to about 150 men in the redoubt. "The enemy advanced and fired very hotly on the fort," Prescott reported to John Adams afterward, "and meeting a warm reception, there was a very smart firing on both sides." Finding their gunpowder and musket balls "almost spent," Prescott ordered a short pause in the firing from the redoubt. If this momentary silence heartened the advancing regulars, they were soon blasted by the fury of Prescott's remaining volleys. [14]

Now the British front ranks were at the base of the redoubt. John Waller, the adjutant of Pitcairn's marines, reported that they encountered "the severe fire of the enemy, but did not retreat an inch." Major John Pitcairn, twenty-nine-year veteran of His Majesty's service and recent participant in the Concord raid, had been hoping that this campaign in North America would be his last. It was. As he led his men at the redoubt, he was shot in the head.

Legend has it that he fell into the arms of his son William. Certainly it was William Pitcairn who tended to his father as he was evacuated to Boston, where he died soon afterward. The other piece of the legend of the Pitcairn death is that Peter Salem, the black freeman from Framingham who had been at Concord, fired the shot that killed him. Perhaps. It was simply impossible to tell, but the fact that Salem's role was captured in John Trumbull's painting of Pitcairn's death — however dramatized the moment — is a testament to the hundred-some African Americans estimated to have fought on the rebel side. On Bunker and Breed's Hills that day, there was equality — for a fleeting moment.

With Pitcairn struck down close by, and a captain, a subaltern, and a sergeant also slain, Adjutant Waller ran across the hillside and commanded the men to stop firing so that they might advance into the redoubt with bayonets. "Had we stopped there much longer," Waller maintained, "the enemy would have picked us all off." Instead he got his men into "tolerable order," and they "rushed on, leaped the ditch, and climbed the parapet, under a most sore and heavy fire."[15] Confessed Waller, "I did not think, at one time, that I should ever have been able to write this, though in the heat of the action I thought nothing of the matter."[16]

As Major Pitcairn fell, Joseph Warren became the high-profile casualty on the American side. Warren's actions that day would also become the stuff of legend, but one must wonder if he did not harbor some fixation on having a martyr's death. There would be many who would give their lives for the rebel cause unselfishly and without much thought in the years ahead, but Warren seems to have been at the other extreme — one who made a needless sacrifice to satisfy no cause but his own desire to be in the thick of the action.

Joseph Warren's presence on Breed's Hill, however praised in patriotic telling, seems only to have confused the rebel chain of command. Particularly with Samuel Adams and John Hancock occupied in Philadelphia, one cannot help but wonder if Warren's higher duty lay in keeping a steady hand on the work of the committee of safety in Cambridge. So high were the contemporary compliments of his skills that had Warren survived he might well have come to occupy an even greater position in the republic born from his efforts. But Warren rushed to the field and was struck down by a British musket ball in the last bloody fighting at the redoubt.

Having turned the front of his assault away from the rail fence and aimed it squarely toward the redoubt, Howe was now able to aim his bogged-down cannons to the left and fire down the line of the breastworks below the redoubt. This use of artillery and the advancing ranks of infantry drove the American defenders from that line. Most of these men retreated toward the higher end of the rail fence. A few unlucky ones sought shelter in the redoubt.[17]

What ended the American resistance in the redoubt was neither a lack of courage nor unstoppable British resolve but rather the absence of rebel gunpowder. The acute awareness of dwindling powder supplies had hastened the exodus from Prescott's ranks as Pigot's troops advanced yet again. Prescott directed his men to hold steady for one final fusillade, but with few bayonets and spears among the remaining defenders, once their gunpowder was expended there was nothing they could do but flee.

British bayonets ran through those who did not do so with enough dispatch. After the rebels were surrounded, it was over in seconds. Even Lieutenant Waller admitted that the bayonet work of the regulars was shocking. "I cannot pretend to describe the Horror of the Scene within the Redoubt when we enter'd it," he wrote a friend four days later. "'Twas streaming with Blood & strew'd with dead & dying Men the Soldiers stabbing some and dashing out the Brains of others was a sight too dreadful for me to dwell any longer on."[18]

According to a British history written soon after the war, "the British soldiers, stung with the reflection of having given way before an enemy whom they despised, now returned with irresistible impetuosity, forced the intrenchments with fixed bayonets, and drove the provincials from their works."[19] General Howe merely noted that after the burning of Charlestown "relieved Pigot from the difficulty upon his left...he carried the Redoubt in a very handsome manner, at the second onset, tho' it was most obstinately defended to the last, thirty of the rebels having been killed by bayonets within it."[20]

Peter Brown, who had stood firm all day despite misgivings, was one of the lucky ones who escaped the redoubt. "I was not suffered to be toutched," Brown reassured his mother, "altho I was in the fort when the Enemy came in, and jumped over the walls, and ran half a mile where Balls flew like Hailstones, and Canons roared like Thunder."[21]

This rapid rout from the redoubt did not, however, signal panic or a mass retreat along the rebel lines—far from it. Captain John Chester's company of Connecticut men had taken up a position at a stone wall somewhere below the crest of Bunker Hill overlooking the redoubt. "Here," Chester reported, "we lost our regularity, as every company had done before us, and fought as they did, every man loading and firing as fast as he could." The stone wall was only two or three feet high, and bullets came through it with ease. "Good God, how the Balls flew," remembered Chester's lieutenant, Samuel Blachley Webb; "I freely Acknowledge I never had such a tremor come over me before." But for about six minutes, Chester's company stood firm and covered Prescott's retreat "till they came up with us by a brisk fire."[22]

And so the redoubt and main rebel breastworks were carried by the regulars' attack, but far from jubilation, there spread through the British ranks a dazed sense of disbelief. The carnage was almost unpalatable. The slope below the redoubt was a field littered with the red uniforms of the dead and the dying. From officers to the lowest private, no one appeared more dazed than General Howe himself. To his great credit, Howe had not hunkered down in the rear but led from the front. Somehow, despite a disproportionately high loss of officers, Howe came through without a physical scratch. His emotional toll would take some time to determine. The blood of his troops streaked his white gaiters, and the red of his uniform hid the dark blotches of much more.

Henry Clinton, after scurrying up the hill behind Pigot's troops, found Howe in this state and offered to take the lead in pressing the attack home toward Cambridge. "All was in Confusion," according to Clinton. "Officers told me that they could not command their men and I never saw so great a want of order." Howe thanked Clinton for his service in crossing from Boston to join the battle and appeared to acquiesce to Clinton's advance. But then he called Clinton back and told him to make dispositions for the night and to protect the neck but not advance across it.

Clinton continued up Bunker Hill and soon overtook General Pigot. What Clinton saw of the colonial troops gave him pause and may have made him glad that Howe did not want him directing an all-out continuation of the attack. Stark's men at the rail fence on the rebel left had given way, but they were retreating "in good order as soon as the men from the redoubt had passed them." It was definitely a fighting withdrawal and not a panicked rout. This impressed Clinton as well as the British rank and file. The rebels "continued a running fight from one fence, or wall, to another, till we entirely drove them off the peninsula of Charlestown." [23]

Even then, Clinton was anxious about what he would find on the Cambridge side of Bunker Hill. "I proceed," Clinton's notes read, "expecting that the redoubt made by us on the 19 was occupied, and for that I assembled all I could, but found hardly to be believed that they had left it in a state serviceable only to us I mean as a breast work against them." [24]

Some of the troops with Clinton at this point were those of the Fifty-Second Regiment. They took up positions on the Mystic side of Bunker Hill and dug crude earthworks facing the neck. The Forty-Seventh Regiment took up a similar station on the Charles side and secured both the shore road leading back to burning Charlestown and the access road across the millpond dam. After giving these regimental commanders advice on how best to defend their positions, Clinton, "having been there as a Volunteer," as he said, "returned to Boston."[25] The reported times of all actions throughout the day varied greatly, but according to one source that attempted an accurate timetable, the landing and assault were accomplished in about four hours, the regulars "having entire possession of the Neck by six o'clock."[26]

On the American side, there was to be one more significant casualty. Major Andrew McClary, who had served with John Stark in Rogers' Rangers, was the adjutant of Stark's First New Hampshire Regiment. McClary had cleared the way for Stark's regiment to advance through the chaos at the neck only hours before. Having covered a major part of the rebel retreat, Stark's regiment was now safely back across the neck, but McClary watched with concern as Clinton's forces clustered at the earthworks on Bunker Hill. McClary worried that the British might attempt to carry the neck and threaten Cambridge — indeed Clinton had considered doing just that. So McClary went back across the neck to reconnoiter the British positions. Satisfying himself that Clinton was holding his position and hunkering down, McClary was returning across the neck when one of the last cannon shots from the British ships in the Charles struck him down. It was a grisly end.[27]

Despite the losses on the American side and the stigma of having abandoned the field, there was no panic or pell-mell rush to Cambridge. The line of retreat "proceeded no farther than to the next hill." This was Winter Hill, from which Colonel Pickering and his Essex County men might have ambushed Percy's column on April 19 if they had taken action. Colonel Putnam had already constructed some entrenchments there as part of his "keep 'em busy" digging operations, and now he ordered more to be dug.

The sounds of picks and shovels broke the evening twilight as the midsummer night descended, but it was the continuing cries of the wounded that made the colonists' blood run cold. Behind the moans came the dull thudding of cannon fire from across the Back Bay. It was Percy's artillery, still firing on the Roxbury lines. Gunpowder was one thing the British had in ample supply.[28]

GENERAL HOWE WAS IN A state of denial and likely remained so for the rest of his military career, if not the rest of his life. He had won the field, of that there was no doubt, but at a staggering cost. The Battle of Bunker Hill was, Henry Clinton opined, "A dear bought victory, another such would have ruined us."[29]

In retrospect, there were many things that General Howe might have done differently or to greater effect. The extreme left of the rebel line at the rail fence was anchored, however tenuously, to the shoreline. Had the British sent one of their sloops or the transport *Symmetry* up the Mystic River, "one charge on their uncovered flank," one contemporary British historian noted, "might have dislodged them in a moment." Maybe or maybe not, given the granite resolve of John Stark and his men. But landing British troops in force to the rear of the rebel line, as General Clinton had proposed, might have been more effective than simply marching across an open field against entrenched troops. Such an encircling attack in the American rear would have rendered the breastworks largely useless and forced the rebels to fight their way past British lines to effect a withdrawal.[30]

From the American side, a better command and control system between General Ward and the regimental level might have avoided the forward position on Breed's Hill in the first place, or resulted in a determined reinforcement of it from fortifications atop Bunker Hill. Whatever the Americans might have done wrong, however, Stark and his compatriots' stand at the rail fence is the action that cost the British dearly and saved the rebel lines from an early rout.

What was undeniable were the casualties, bad enough on the American side but horrific to the British, particularly among the officer ranks. General Gage reported his losses as 226 killed and

828 wounded, an appalling casualty rate approaching 50 percent of those engaged. As many as 250 of the wounded may have died in the weeks that followed, and many others were maimed for life. Some companies of forty-odd men, particularly the grenadier and light infantry units that assaulted the rail fence, had less than ten men alive, let alone fit for duty.[31]

Loyalists in Boston had cheered when they saw the red lines crest the hills and the rebels flee over Charlestown Neck, but it was not long before the cost of this action was brought home. "We were exulting in seeing the flight of our enemies," Ann Hulton wrote, "but in an hour or two we had occasion to mourn and lament. . . . In the evening the streets were filled with the wounded and the dying; the sight of which, with the lamentations of the women and children over their husbands and fathers, pierced one to the soul."[32]

Ensign Jeremy Lister of the light infantry company of the Tenth Regiment, who was wounded in the arm during the retreat from Concord and thus mercifully avoided duty on the Mystic beach, watched as his wounded comrades were returned to Boston. He soon learned that Lieutenant Waldron Kelly of his company, who had also been at the North Bridge, "was wounded and suppos'd Mortally." Lister carried the news to Kelly's wife, "who for some time sat motionless with two small Children close by her." Summoning up her courage, she went to meet her husband, "who was brought home scarcely alive," but in time he recovered from his wounds.[33]

On the American side, the loose nature of the units engaged and the incompleteness of their muster rolls left some doubt as to the exact number of casualties. General Ward's orderly book recorded 115 killed, 305 wounded, and thirty captured. Many of these casualties occurred during the final British assault on the redoubt. About a month after the battle, George Washington put American losses at 138 killed and 276 wounded, which probably accounted for some who died of their wounds.[34]

Much as they had done in the aftermath of Lexington and

Concord, rebel leaders put forward a stream of propaganda favorable to their version of the battle. They couldn't claim victory, but the dead and dying in Boston were proof that neither had the day been an out-and-out loss. "The particulars of the late battle on Bunker's Hill have been differently represented," Rhode Island's Nathaniel Greene wrote his brother, "[but] upon the whole, I think we have little reason to complain." [35]

Being only generally aware of the cost of Great Britain's self-proclaimed victory, the rebels once again focused on British atrocities. This time it was the burning of Charlestown. "You may easily judge what distress we were in to see and hear Englishmen destroying one another," wrote Reverend Andrew Eliot of Boston, "and a Town with which we have been so intimately connected, all in flames." [36] What was not mentioned, of course, was that most of Charlestown had been abandoned and that Colonel Prescott's men had turned it into a military target by using the buildings as cover from which to harry Pigot's flank.

James Warren, distraught over the death of Joseph Warren, minced no words in his report to Mercy. "With a Savage Barbarity never practised among Civilized Nations," James told his wife, "they fired and have Utterly destroyed the Town of Charlestown." James had never been impressed with Artemas Ward, and he would become a harsh critic of the general in the days ahead, but in his "inexpressible Grief" over the death of "my Friend Doctor Warren," he was already holding Joseph Warren up to sainthood. The doctor "was killd it is supposed in the Lines on the Hill at Charlestown," James told Mercy, "in a Manner more Glorious to himself than the fate of Wolfe on the plains of Abraham." Professing his enduring love to Mercy, James concluded, "I will see you as soon as possible; can't say when." [37]

On the British side, the charred chimneys of Charlestown became a symbol of a different kind. "I am just now encamped on the heights of Charles-town, or Bunker's Hill, the scene of action on the 17th of June," Captain W. Glanville Evelyn of the Fourth

"King's Own" Regiment reported to his father. "We expect to be pretty late in the field this year," he continued, "and... I hope before the end of it to be able to tell you that Boston, New York, Philadelphia, and all the capital towns on the Continent, are but stacks of chimneys like Charlestown here."[38]

General Howe was not so optimistic. "My corps is now encamped upon these Heights, in a very strong situation," he told his brother Richard, the admiral, "but I much doubt whether we shall get much farther this Campaign, the rebels, on this side, having entrenched themselves very judiciously, about two miles in our front." Until he got more reinforcements, Howe said, "we shall not do more than to possess these Heights."[39]

In writing Lord George Germain, soon to be Lord Dartmouth's replacement as Secretary of State for the Colonies, General Burgoyne was more complimentary of Howe's efforts as well as his results. The only satisfactory feature of his own tenure in Boston to date, Burgoyne told Germain, was "the victory obtained at Charlestown by the conduct and spirit of my friend Howe, and the exemplary, I might say, unexampled bravery of the officers under him." The result, Burgoyne maintained, was to reestablish "the ascendancy of the King's troops in public opinion."

Truth be told, that was a bit of wishful thinking. Burgoyne was also quick to acknowledge that the rebels, though undisciplined, "are expert in the use of firearms, and are led by some very able men." Among those Burgoyne did not number was Samuel Adams, whom he called "as great a conspirator as ever subverted a state." And just to show that not all his enmity was directed against Adams and his cohorts, the general managed an interservice swipe at Admiral Graves and the Royal Navy. "It may perhaps be asked in England, what is the Admiral doing?" Burgoyne noted. "I wish I was able to answer that question satisfactorily. But I can only say what he is *not* doing."[40] Admiral Lord Richard Howe would soon be sent to North America to replace Graves.

The British official who was slow to claim victory and report its casualties to his superiors in Great Britain was General Gage. No matter what Howe felt on the field of battle, or what Clinton and Burgoyne opined from their vantage points, Thomas Gage was still the commander in chief of British troops in North America and the royal governor of Massachusetts, although for weeks his domain had been reduced to a besieged Boston. Ultimately, success or failure was his responsibility.

Gage delayed eight days, until June 25, to write his report to Lord Dartmouth. He waited for General Howe's report, which he seems to have incorporated almost verbatim, but there is no hint that he hurried Howe along. Margaret Gage was readying herself and her children to leave Boston, and after the carnage on Bunker Hill there was no doubt in Gage's mind that he would soon follow her to England. Only the slowness of transatlantic communications would delay his departure.

After reciting Howe's account of the battle, including his assertion that part of the rail fence was "Cannon proof," Gage concluded, "This Action has shewn the Superiority of the King's Troops, who under every disadvantage Attacked and defeated above three times their own Number, strongly posted, and covered by Breast works."[41] Those were hardly the odds, but this version was for public consumption.

In an accompanying private letter to Dartmouth, Gage was more frank and unguarded. In assuring Dartmouth that the battle was "very Necessary in our Situation," Gage nonetheless wished "most sincerely that it had not cost us so dear." His casualties were greater than "our Force can afford to lose," but even more ominous was his assessment of his opponents. "The Tryals we have had," Gage confessed, "shew that the Rebels are not the despicable Rabble too many have supposed them to be, and I find it owing to a Military Spirit encouraged amongst them for a few years past, joined with an uncommon Degree of Zeal and Enthusiasm that they are otherwise."[42]

"I think it my Duty to let your Lordship know," Gage concluded, "the true Situation of Affairs, that Administration may take Measures accordingly." Lord North and George III's government would indeed take measures, but after the reports of Bunker Hill, their actions would be to order Dartmouth to recall Gage to England and within months to replace Dartmouth with Lord George Germain.

Having sent Lord Barrington, the secretary of war, the perfunctory return of the killed and wounded, Gage also wrote a private letter to him. "These People," Gage warned, referring to the rebels, "Show a Spirit and Conduct against us, they never showed against the French." And then, with a frustration that went far deeper than military analysis, Gage said of Boston, "I wish this Cursed place was burned, the only use is its harbor, which may be said to be Material; but in all other respects its the worst place either to act Offensively from, or defencively."[43]

When Gage finally received the summons recalling him to England via HMS *Scarborough* on September 26, it was reportedly to confer about plans for major operations in North America during 1776. But Gage knew full well that he would not return to North America. He had spent the better part of his military career there. There would be other British defeats in North America, but for shock and loss of life, it is hard to name two more significant than those that bookended Thomas Gage's career on that continent: Braddock's Defeat and the Battle of Bunker Hill. Without pomp or ceremony, Gage sailed from Boston on October 11, 1775.[44] For better or worse, William Howe assumed command of the British troops in Boston.

If the confrontations at Lexington Green and Concord's North Bridge were the sparks that lit the fuse to the powder keg of war, Bunker Hill was the great explosion. After Bunker Hill, there was no doubt on either side that this was all-out war. Whatever bonds had tied the two sides together were severed.

Some historians suggest that the military importance of Bunker

Hill is overstated. Yet American history celebrates it—and the public at large recognizes it—with the same reverence and special awe accorded to Yorktown, Gettysburg, and Pearl Harbor. If one only counted control of the battlefield, Bunker Hill was a British victory, but in the rebel psyche in 1775, the battle was a huge morale booster. As the first major clash between rebel forces and British regulars, it proved that the rebel resistance at Lexington and Concord had legs and that troops who would increasingly be called American could hold their own. The American Revolution was not begun at Bunker Hill; it certainly was not decided at Bunker Hill; but Bunker Hill proved that the drive for independence, and the formal makings of the nation itself, were truly begun in the American spring of 1775.

Epilogue

~

Monday, July 3, 1775

The Battle of Bunker Hill—whether one chooses to characterize it as an American or British victory—had one immediate
and undeniable impact on the fledgling Continental Army. After
hearing the results of the battle and judging it an American opportunity, if not a victory, the Continental Congress authorized the
invasion of Canada. Rebel overtures of alliance and mutual support
north of the border earlier that spring had fallen on deaf ears, but
on June 23 Ethan Allen and Seth Warner finally arrived in Philadelphia. They made their case for keeping Fort Ticonderoga and
Crown Point and urged an invasion north from there. On June 27,
the Continental Congress authorized Major General Philip Schuy-
ler to "take possession of St. Johns, Montreal, and any other parts
of the country, and pursue any other measures in Canada." [1]

A heroic campaign against Montreal and Quebec late in 1775
was nearly successful. The failed effort ultimately sapped the
strength of American efforts around Boston, but Canada would
remain the object of American desires for another century. During
the War of 1812, acquiring Canada would be the focal point of three
years of unsuccessful invasion attempts by the United States. The
lust for Canada continued through the American Civil War, after
which some Unionists demanded Canada as compensation for Great
Britain's pro-Southern activities.

In July of 1775, as one last sop to moderates, the Continental Congress would pass what came to be called the Olive Branch Petition. Drafted in part by Benjamin Franklin and sent to George III, it may have helped assure even the most vocal of those crying for independence that they had done all they could to avoid an all-out war. As the delegates did so, however, they also set forth a lengthy litany of every perceived British wrong to America since 1763. This Declaration of the Causes and Necessity of Taking Up Arms foreshadowed in every respect the more famous declaration that would be signed the following year. After the spring of 1775, the dreams of most patriots were unequivocally clear. No matter how difficult the road ahead, the only acceptable destination was independence and a new nation.

Those firebrands in the group did not have to worry about the king accepting the olive branch. George III remained as immovable on the subject of his royal prerogatives as he always had been. As the Olive Branch Petition was being debated an ocean away in Philadelphia, well before he learned the news from Bunker Hill, George III wrote the Earl of Sandwich thanking him for passing on letters from Major John Pitcairn about the Lexington and Concord action. "That officer's conduct seems highly praiseworthy," the king noted, not knowing that Pitcairn now lay dead. "I am of his opinion that when once those rebels have felt a smart blow, they will submit; and no situation can ever change my fixed resolution, either to bring the colonies to a due obedience to the legislature of the mother country or to cast them off!"[2]

THE EVENTS OF THE SPRING of 1775 shaped not just the future of a country that was in open rebellion but also the lives of its citizens, whether rebel, loyalist, or still trying to decide. A great many would live to see the result of what started on Lexington Green. Others would not.

Captain John Parker, who had done his duty by assembling his neighbors on Lexington Green, succumbed on September 17, 1775, to the consumption he was battling that April morning. Jemima Condict, who expressed such trepidation about matrimony, finally married her first cousin in 1779, when she was twenty-five. She died in childbirth later that year. Peter Salem was discharged from the Continental Army at the end of 1779 after almost five years of service. He married Katy Benson, built a cabin near Leicester, Massachusetts, and worked as a cane weaver. He died in poverty in Framingham in 1816. In one of history's little ironies, John Derby, who had carried the news of Lexington and Concord to England on the *Quero*, brought the news of the Peace of Paris, which ended the Revolutionary War, to Boston in 1783 on board the twenty-gun privateer *Astrea*.

Of the three British major generals who arrived in Boston with so much swagger, all eventually came to grief in North America. William Howe abandoned Boston in March of 1776 and conducted inconclusive campaigns around New York and Philadelphia before resigning his command in 1777. John Burgoyne got his much-sought independent command but ended up surrendering his army at Saratoga in October of 1777. Henry Clinton succeeded Howe as commander in chief for North America in 1778, but aside from a campaign by sea against Charleston, South Carolina, he spent much of the war in New York, until Cornwallis's surrender at Yorktown in 1781. Lord Percy served under Howe until 1777, when he became disillusioned with Howe's conduct of the war. He resigned his command and returned to England, where he inherited his father's dukedom.

As to the British army, never again in a principal battle during the American Revolution would they suffer as high a casualty rate — calculated as a percentage of those engaged — as they did at Bunker Hill, particularly among officers. Indeed, the British army would not suffer a defeat of similar proportions in North America until the Battle of New Orleans in 1815, when General Edward Pakenham seems to have forgotten the Battle of Bunker Hill and charged Andrew Jackson's entrenched rabble across an open field.

Benjamin Franklin never reconciled with his loyalist son. He soon showed that any criticism of his reticence during the first few weeks of the Second Continental Congress was misplaced. After signing the Olive Branch Petition as a measure of continental unity, Franklin proceeded to resurrect his plan for Articles of Confederation and Perpetual Union, which he had first proposed at Albany in 1754. "The suspicions against Dr Franklin have died away," William Bradford assured James Madison. "Whatever was his design at coming over here, I believe he has now chosen his side, and favors our cause."[3] Franklin would soon return to Europe and mastermind the alliance with France that would ensure American independence.

Israel Putnam and William Prescott continued their military service, but their later exploits paled beside their actions — whether right or wrong — that night and day on Breed's and Bunker Hills. Putnam held commands in the Hudson Valley before suffering a stroke in December of 1779, and Prescott commanded a regiment in the new Continental Army. Their descendants and supporters would long argue about who deserved the greater laurels.

John Stark, who arguably stopped an American rout at Bunker Hill, went on to play a prominent role in the Battle of Bennington, which led to Burgoyne's isolation at Saratoga. Stark is one of the Granite State's honorees in the National Statuary Hall in the United States Capitol.

John Hancock presided over the Continental Congress until October of 1777. He routinely signed his name to acts first, and in large letters, but his most famous occasion for doing so would be the adoption of the Declaration of Independence on July 4, 1776. Hancock returned to Massachusetts and spent liberally of his fortune to resurrect Boston from the depths into which it had fallen. In 1780, he was elected the first governor of Massachusetts.

About the only tribute that John Hancock did not garner was to become one of Massachusetts's two honorees in Statuary Hall. That accolade went to Samuel Adams. There is ample evidence that Adams knew what he was getting into when he teamed up with

Hancock, but in the end Adams came to resent Hancock's ostentatious ways and expectations of deference. This did not keep him from serving as Hancock's lieutenant governor for four years and then governor in his own right. One can only wonder whether Joseph Warren would have been his competition for Statuary Hall had Warren lived.

Architect though he later claimed to be of George Washington's appointment as commander in chief, Samuel's cousin John Adams became something of a critic as Washington parried one British military threat after another during the following years without achieving a knockout blow. In time, Adams would serve as Washington's two-term vice president and then president himself for one term. Abigail Adams never shied away from speaking her mind, but women would wait until the Nineteenth Amendment, passed in 1919, gave them the right to vote nationally — a right she thought they deserved in 1775.

After Joseph Warren died on Bunker Hill, the Massachusetts Provincial Congress elected James Warren its president. After losing a reelection bid in 1777, Warren eschewed other appointments and spent most of the war serving on the Continental Navy Board. When he died, in 1808, he and Mercy had been married fifty-four years.

Mercy Otis Warren continued writing poetry and satire and went on to complete a three-volume history of the Revolution. Published in 1805 under her own name, *History of the Rise, Progress and Termination of the American Revolution* was the capstone of her career, but it was only marginally successful and caused a tiff with one of her earliest and biggest fans. John Adams took exception to some of her characterizations of his role, particularly assertions such as "His prejudices and passions were sometimes too strong for his sagacity and judgment."[4] She may well have been correct, but her candor did not sit well with her longtime friend. Eventually they reconciled.

The ultimate scoundrel, of course, proved to be Dr. Benjamin

Church. The man whom many had once considered the insiders' insider among the rebels was finally exposed as a traitor and a spy when a coded letter detailing rebel positions around Boston was intercepted and given to George Washington. The Massachusetts Provincial Congress arraigned Church on November 2, 1775. James Warren presided over his trial. As one patriot leader put it, "Dr. Church, who could have thought or even suspected it, a man who seemed to be all animation in the cause of his country...."[5] Tried and condemned, Church was imprisoned but then released on parole. He sailed from Boston in 1778, bound for exile on Martinique, on a ship that was never heard from again.

HAVING HEARD THE NEWS OF Bunker Hill in New York City while en route north from Philadelphia, General George Washington and his small staff continued toward Boston with growing trepidation. Washington's military instincts told him that it was best to arrive in Cambridge as expeditiously as possible and take stock of the situation, but his political savvy was sensitive to the need to please the New England populace. Just the fact that a Virginian would ride into New England as commander in chief of the Continental Army—however understaffed and undersupplied—was a huge boost to morale. Massachusetts and its neighbors were not alone: the colonies north and south would indeed stand together.

So everywhere he went, George Washington graciously acknowledged the cheers: from Yale students in New Haven and from rebels at Springfield, Worcester, and Watertown. At Watertown, James Warren asked Washington to address a session of the Provincial Congress. Washington thanked the delegates "for your declaration of readiness, at all times, to assist me in the discharge of the duties of my station."[6]

The next morning, July 2, Washington and his entourage, including General Charles Lee, rode the three miles into Cambridge. General Artemas Ward was waiting for him with far more relief than jealousy. Three days earlier, Ward had surreptitiously celebrated news of Washington's pending arrival by making *Washington* and *Virginia* the challenge and countersign of the day. Ward also took pains to sharpen up the demeanor of his army. His orders demanded that barracks be swept clean and tidy, soldiers watch their language, and all lewd women be removed from camp.

Upon Washington's arrival, around noon, Ward had planned a grand review, complete with twenty-one drummers and twenty-one fifers. There would not, however, be any salutes with musketry or cannons — the supply of gunpowder was far too short for that. But then the afternoon rains came. Before the assembled troops could pass in review, they were quickly dismissed so they could take shelter. They would try again the next day.

So, it was Monday, July 3, 1775, on a pleasant summer morning that General George Washington took formal command of the Continental Army in the field. Both astride his horse and standing before the assembled troops, he was easily recognizable by his height and his demeanor. He made a short speech that went largely unremembered and then took a small book from his pocket and read Psalm 101, including its second verse, which proclaims, "I will behave myself wisely in a perfect way." There was little if any cheering, and except among those on the parade ground, little notice was taken of the new commander.[7]

Among the rank and file, George Washington was still an unproven commodity — a name but little else. It would take some time; it would call for all his determination, diplomacy, and faith; but in the end he would lead them to victory and ensure that the promise of this American spring was fulfilled.

ACKNOWLEDGMENTS

~

At first blush it may seem redundant to add yet another book to the crowded field of Revolutionary War literature. As always, my overriding goal has been to tell a good story that makes these times more accessible to the general reader. But my secondary goals in focusing on this critical six-month period were two-fold and largely derived from perspectives more than 225 years apart.

First, I wanted to return to the original affidavits, correspondence, and remembrances of the participants and see the times and events through their lives as they lived them — before two centuries of reinterpretation clouded their words. Second, I wanted to incorporate into this fresh telling a flavor of the outpouring of academic research that has occurred during the last twenty years on frequently overlooked aspects of those days. These have included the roles of women, African Americans, Native Americans, and loyalists who were given little notice in so many earlier histories.

I appreciate the landmark studies — albeit half a century apart — of Allen French and David Hackett Fischer and am particularly grateful to those historians who commented on portions of the manuscript or offered advice: J. L. Bell, John Branson, Paul Lockhart, Nancy Rubin Stuart, and Harlow Giles Unger. David Lambert remains my go-to guy for crafting great maps, and I am once again in his debt.

I have nothing but deep thanks and high praise for the team at Little, Brown, who embarked on this project after launching *The Admirals:* first and foremost, my insightful editor and chief supporter, John Parsley, as well as Malin von Euler-Hogan, Carrie Neill, Michael Noon, and copyeditor Barbara Clark.

As should be clear to all after our seven books together, my greatest debt is to my stalwart friend and faithful agent, Alexander C. Hoyt. Alex has never failed to go above and beyond.

As always, I enjoyed my time walking the ground of these events with my wife, Marlene, from the streets of Boston — and a tavern or two — to Bunker Hill and on to Lexington, Concord, and Battle Road, as well as Salem, Fort Ticonderoga, Independence Hall, and Williamsburg. I never tire of experiencing firsthand the preserved vestiges of our country's past.

NOTES

~

Prologue: Tuesday, December 13, 1774

1. "From a gentleman in Boston, to Mr. Rivington, in New York, December 20, 1774," *AA4* 1:1053–54. There was some precedent for the seizure by colonials. On December 5, 1774, a little over a week before, the assembly of Rhode Island ordered that the powder and shot in Fort George, off Newport, be confiscated. The weather for Revere's ride is from the meteorological register in the *New-Hampshire Gazette*, January 6, 1775.
2. Wentworth to Gage, December 14, 1774, *AA4*, 1:1041–42.
3. Enlistment order, December 15, 1774, *Documents and Records Relating to the Province of New-Hampshire from 1764 to 1776* (Nashua, N.H.: Green C. Moore, State Printer, 1873), 7:421.
4. Gentleman in Boston to Rivington, December 20, 1774, *AA4*, 1:1054.

Chapter 1 — New Year's Day 1775

1. During 1774, Boston recorded 590 burials, of which 540 were listed as "whites" and fifty as "blacks." Recorded baptisms totaled 521. *Boston News-Letter*, January 5, 1775. Town population estimates from John A. Garraty, *The American Nation* (New York: Harper & Row, 1966), 48.
2. *Boston Evening-Post*, January 2, 1775.
3. *Boston Gazette and Country Journal* (hereinafter *Boston Gazette*), January 2, 1775.
4. *Boston Gazette*, January 2, 1775.
5. *Boston News-Letter*, January 5, 1775.
6. *Boston Post-Boy*, January 2, 1775.
7. *Boston Evening-Post*, January 2, 1775.
8. Andrews to Barrell, January 1, 1775, "Letters of John Andrews, Esq. of Boston, 1772–1776," *Massachusetts Historical Society Proceedings* 8 (1864–65), 392.
9. Nancy Rubin Stuart, *The Muse of the Revolution: The Secret Pen of Mercy Otis Warren and the Founding of a Nation* (Boston: Beacon Press, 2008), 68–69.

10. Diary of Jemima Condict Harrison, October 1774, North American Women's Letters and Diaries: Colonial to 1950 (subscription only), http://solomon.nwld.alexanderstreet.com/cgi-bin/asp/philo/nwld/getdoc.pl !S34-D025, accessed January 3, 2012, hereinafter "Jemima Condict Diary." This has also been published as *Jemima Condict: Her Book, Being a Transcript of the Diary of an Essex County Maid during the Revolutionary War* (Newark, N.J.: Carteret Book Club, 1930).

11. "several of whom," *Boston Evening-Post*, January 2, 1775; "Nothing remarkable," Elizabeth Ellery Dana, ed., *The British in Boston: Being the Diary of Lieutenant John Barker of the King's Own Regiment from November 15, 1774 to May 31, 1776; with Notes* (Cambridge, Mass.: Harvard University Press, 1924), 18, entry dated January 1, 1775.

12. For early Massachusettensis letters, see, for example, *Boston Post-Boy*, December 19, 1774, and January 2, 1775.

13. Alice M. Hinkle, *Prince Estabrook: Slave and Soldier* (Lexington, Mass.: Pleasant Mountain Press, 2001), 14, 25–29, 75. Benjamin Estabrook was born December 21, 1729; additional Estabrook information at http://nationalheritagemuseum.typepad.com/learning/, accessed August 22, 2012.

14. *Boston Gazette*, January 2, 1775.

15. *New-York Gazette and Weekly Mercury*, January 2, 1775.

16. *New-York Gazette and Weekly Mercury*, January 9, 1775.

17. Washington to McMickan, January 7, 1775, Jared Sparks, ed., *The Writings of George Washington* (Boston: Charles Tappan, 1846), 3:256.

18. Washington to Cleveland, January 10, 1775, *Writings of Washington*, 3:256.

19. *Boston News-Letter*, January 5, 1775.

20. Franklin to William Franklin, May 7, 1774, *Franklin Papers*.

21. William Franklin to Franklin, December 24, 1774, *Franklin Papers*.

22. "Journal of Negotiations in London," Franklin to William Franklin, March 22, 1775, *Franklin Papers*.

23. "to cement," "Franklin's Proposals to Lord Howe for Resolving Crisis," December 28–31, 1774, *Franklin Papers*; "threatens to be attended," Lord Howe to Caroline Howe, January 2, 1775, *Franklin Papers*.

Chapter 2 — Drumbeats of Dissension

1. Francis Bernard, *Select Letters on the Trade and Government of America* (London: Bowyer and Nichols, 1774), 9.

2. Henry Mayer, *A Son of Thunder: Patrick Henry and the American Republic* (New York: Grove Press, 1991), 85–87, 485n86. Mayer considers it very unlikely that Henry ever uttered this phrase, particularly that early in his career.

3. Thomas Fleming, *Liberty! The American Revolution* (New York: Viking, 1997), 61.

4. L. H. Butterfield, ed., *Diary & Autobiography of John Adams* (New York: Atheneum, 1964), 1:284, entry dated January 1, 1766.

5. Edward Sears Morgan and Helen M. Morgan, *The Stamp Act Crisis: Prologue to Revolution* (Chapel Hill: University of North Carolina Press, 1995), 93.

6. John C. Miller, *Origins of the American Revolution* (Boston: Little, Brown, 1943), 339.

7. Robert Middlekauff, *The Glorious Cause: The American Revolution, 1763–1789* (New York: Oxford University Press, 1982), 222–23.

8. *Boston Evening-Post*, October 25, 1773.

9. John Hancock oration, March 5, 1774, in H[ezekiah]. Niles, ed., *Principles and Acts of the Revolution in America* (Baltimore: W. O. Niles, 1822), 16.

10. "there was nothing," Middlekauff, *Glorious Cause*, 226; for Hancock's and Samuel Adams's personal involvement, see, for example, Miller, *Origins*, 348; "This destruction," *Diary & Autobiography of John Adams* 2:86, entry dated December 17, 1773.

11. "blocking up," Farmington Resolves, May 19, 1774, *AA4*, 1:336; "unconstitutional; oppressive," Niles, *Principles and Acts of the Revolution*, 179.

12. "Resolution of the House of Burgesses Designating a Day of Fasting and Prayer," May 24, 1774, Barbara B. Oberg and J. Jefferson Looney, eds., *The Papers of Thomas Jefferson Digital Edition* (subscription only) (Charlottesville: University of Virginia Press, Rotunda, 2008), main ser., 1:105, accessed December 16, 2012, http://rotunda.upress.virginia.edu/founders/TSJN -01-01-02-0082; "For my own part," Washington to Fairfax, August 24, 1774, Jared Sparks, ed., *The Writings of George Washington* (Boston: Charles Tappan, 1846), 3:242.

13. Adams to Warren, June 25, 1774, *Works of John Adams*, 9:339.

14. Page Smith, *A New Age Now Begins: A People's History of the American Revolution* (New York: McGraw-Hill, 1976), 431.

15. Miller, *Origins*, 382–83.

16. *JCC*, 1:32 (September 17, 1774).

17. Miller, *Origins*, 374.

18. Lord North comments, May 17, 1775, *The Parliamentary History of England from the Earliest Period to the Year 1803* (London: T. C. Hansard, 1813), 18:681.

19. *JCC*, 1:39 (September 17, 1774).

20. *Diary & Autobiography of John Adams*, 2:134 (September 17, 1774).

21. *Diary & Autobiography of John Adams*, 2:136 (September 22, 1774).

22. Miller, *Origins*, 385–86.

23. Clarence H. Vance, ed., "Letters of a Westchester Farmer (1774–1775)," *Publications of the Westchester County Historical Society* 8 (1930), 61–62.

24. Linda K. Kerber, *Toward an Intellectual History of Women* (Chapel Hill: University of North Carolina Press, 1997), 76.

25. *JCC*, 1:67–68 (October 14, 1774).

26. "I expect no redress," Miller, *Origins*, 392; "We must fight," Hawley to Adams, undated, *Papers of John Adams* 9, app. A ("Broken Hints, to Be Communicated to the Committee of Congress for Massachusetts"); "By God," Mayer, *Son of Thunder*, 229.

27. "if these Resolves," Peter Orlando Hutchinson, ed., *The Diary and Letters of His Excellency Thomas Hutchinson, Esq* (London: Sampson Low, Marston, Searle & Rivington, 1883), 284; "actual Revolt," Dartmouth to Gage, January 27, 1775, Clarence Edwin Carter, ed., *The Correspondence of General Thomas Gage with the Secretaries of State, and with the War Office and the Treasury, 1763–1775* (Hamden, Conn.: Archon Books, 1969), 2:180.

28. George III to Lord North, November 18, 1774, W. Bodham Donne, ed., *The Correspondence of King George the Third with Lord North, 1768 to 1783* (London: John Murray, 1867), 1:214–15.

Chapter 3 — Who Would Be True Patriots?

1. *Works of John Adams*, 4: 6–8.

2. Josiah Quincy, *Memoir of the Life of Josiah Quincy Jun.* (Boston: Cummings, Hilliard, 1825), 5–7, 160.

3. Abigail Adams to John Adams, September 16, 1774, Charles Francis Adams, ed., *Letters of Mrs. Adams, the Wife of John Adams* (Boston: Wilkins, Carter, 1848), 17.

4. *Massachusetts Gazette and the Boston Post-Boy and Advertiser*, February 7, 1774.

5. *Connecticut Journal*, January 4, 1775.

6. "Extract of a letter from Boston to a Gentleman in New York, January 26, 1775," *AA4*, 1:1178.

7. *New-York Gazetteer*, February 9, 1775.

8. *New-York Gazetteer*, February 9, 1775.

9. Gage to Dartmouth, January 27, 1775, Clarence Edwin Carter, ed., *The Correspondence of General Thomas Gage with the Secretaries of State, and with the War Office and the Treasury, 1763–1775* (Hamden, Conn.: Archon Books, 1969), 1:391.

10. Selectmen to Gage, February 7, 1775, *AA4*, 1:1218–19.

11. Marshfield town meeting, February 20, 1775, *AA4*, 1:1249–50.

12. Massachusetts Provincial Congress, February 15, 1775, *AA4*, 1:1341; County of Plymouth delegate list at p. 1326.

13. *AA4*, 1:1262–63.

14. *AA4*, 1:1263.

15. *AA4*, 1:1263.

16. For biographies of John Hancock, see William M. Fowler, Jr., *The Baron of Beacon Hill: A Biography of John Hancock* (Boston: Houghton Mifflin, 1980), and Harlow Giles Unger, *John Hancock: Merchant King and American Patriot* (New York: John Wiley, 2000).

17. Adams to Tudor, June 1, 1817, *Works of John Adams*, 10:259.

18. Unger, *John Hancock*, 48.

19. Unger, *John Hancock*, 59, quoting J. Hancock to T. Hancock, January 14, 1761.

20. Fowler, *Baron of Beacon Hill*, 46.

21. Unger, *John Hancock*, 66–68.

22. A particularly insightful look at Samuel Adams and his character remains Pauline Maier, "Coming to Terms with Samuel Adams," *American Historical Review* 81, no. 1 (February 1976), 12–37.

23. William M. Fowler, Jr., *Samuel Adams: Radical Puritan* (New York: Longman, 1997), 21–24; Unger, *John Hancock*, 84.

24. Adams diary, June 27, 1770, *Works of John Adams*, 2:238.

25. Unger, *John Hancock*, 89–90.

26. Unger, *John Hancock*, 91.

27. Adams to Tudor, February 9, 1819, *Works of John Adams*, 10:364.

28. Ira Stoll, *Samuel Adams: A Life* (New York: Free Press, 2008), 87. There is at least some evidence that Hancock either gave or loaned Adams a portion of the funds to square Adams's tax collector debts.

29. Unger, *John Hancock*, 100.

30. Adams to Tudor, June 1, 1817, *Works of John Adams*, 10:260.

31. *Pennsylvania Gazette*, February 27, 1766.

32. "I fancy the merchants," Washington to Dandridge, September 20, 1767, Jared Sparks, ed., *The Writings of George Washington* (Boston: Charles Tappan, 1846), 2:344; "that not a man," Unger, *John Hancock*, 99.

33. W. T. Baxter, *The House of Hancock: Business in Boston, 1724–1775* (Cambridge, Mass.: Harvard University Press, 1945), 260.

34. Adams to Tudor, June 1, 1817, *Works of John Adams*, 10:260.

35. *Boston Post-Boy and Advertiser*, May 26, 1766.

36. Adams diary, September 1, 1774, *Works of John Adams*, 2:361.

Chapter 4 — Volleys of Words

1. [Harrison Gray], *A Few Remarks upon Some of the Votes and Resolutions of the Continental Congress Held at Philadelphia in September and the Provincial Congress Held at Cambridge in November 1774* (Boston, 1775), 8–9.

2. *Boston Gazette*, January 30, 1775.

3. *Works of John Adams*, 4:9.

4. Carol Berkin, "Leonard, Daniel," *American National Biography Online* (subscription only), February 2000, accessed January 23, 2012, http://www.anb.org/articles/0101-00513.html.

5. Eric Burns, *Infamous Scribblers: The Founding Fathers and the Rowdy Beginnings of American Journalism* (New York: Public Affairs, 2006), 166–67.

6. *Massachusetts Gazette and the Boston Post-Boy and Advertiser*, December 5, 1774. Beginning on April 26, 1773, the masthead of the *Gazette* gave inclusive dates — e.g., "From Monday, December 5, to Monday, December 12, 1774." The first date of publication is used throughout.

7. *Massachusetts Gazette and the Boston Post-Boy and Advertiser*, December 5, 1774.

8. *Massachusetts Gazette and the Boston Post-Boy and Advertiser*, December 28, 1774.

9. *Massachusetts Gazette and the Boston Post-Boy and Advertiser*, January 9, 1775.

10. *Boston Gazette*, January 23, 1775.

11. *Massachusetts Gazette and the Boston Post-Boy and Advertiser*, January 23, 1775.

12. *Boston Gazette*, February 6, 1775.

13. *Boston Gazette*, January 23, 1775.

14. Nancy Rubin Stuart, *The Muse of the Revolution: The Secret Pen of Mercy Otis Warren and the Founding of a Nation* (Boston: Beacon Press, 2008), 6–19.

15. Stuart, *Muse of the Revolution*, 20.

16. Abigail Adams to Mercy Warren, December 5, 1773, H. C. Lodge, et al., eds., *Warren-Adams Letters, Being Chiefly a Correspondence among John Adams, Samuel Adams, and James Warren* (Boston: Massachusetts Historical Society, 1917), 18–19.

17. Stuart, *Muse of the Revolution*, 66.

18. Warren to Macaulay, December 29, 1774, in Elizabeth F. Ellet, *Women of the American Revolution* (New York: Baker & Scribner, 1849), 79.

19. *Massachusetts Spy*, March 26, 1772; Stuart, *Muse of the Revolution*, 48–49.

20. *Boston Gazette*, May 24, 1773; Stuart, *Muse of the Revolution*, 51.

21. Warren to Adams, February 27, 1774, L. H. Butterfield, et al., eds., *Adams Family Correspondence*, vol. 1, *December 1761–May 1776* (Cambridge, Mass.: Belknap Press of Harvard University Press, 1963), 99; *Boston Gazette*, March 21, 1774.

22. Warren to Adams, August 9, 1774, *Adams Family Correspondence*, 1:139.

23. *Boston Gazette*, January 23, 1775.

24. Stuart, *Muse of the Revolution*, 67–68.

25. Bernard Bailyn, ed., *Pamphlets of the American Revolution, 1750–1776*, vol. 1, *1750–1765* (Cambridge, Mass.: Belknap Press of Harvard University Press, 1965), 420.

26. Stuart, *Muse of the Revolution*, 67; *Boston Gazette*, January 23, 1775; the first two acts also appeared in the *Massachusetts Spy*, January 26, 1775.

27. *Essex Journal and Merimack Packet*, August 17, 1774.

28. Abigail Adams to John Adams, September 22, 1774, Charles Francis Adams, ed., *Letters of Mrs. Adams, the Wife of John Adams* (Boston: Wilkins, Carter, 1848), 24.

Chapter 5 — "Fire, If You Have the Courage"

1. The standard biography of Gage remains John Richard Alden, *General Gage in America: Being Principally a History of His Role in the American Revolution* (Baton Rouge: Louisiana State University Press, 1948).

2. Walter R. Borneman, *The French and Indian War: Deciding the Fate of North America* (New York: HarperCollins, 2006), 50–55, 131–36.

3. "The Kemble Papers," *Collections of the New-York Historical Society for the Year 1883* (New York: New-York Historical Society, 1884), 2:xiv–xviii.

4. Alden, *General Gage in America*, 159.

5. Gage to Barrington, September 26, 1768, Clarence Edwin Carter, ed., *The Correspondence of General Thomas Gage with the Secretaries of State, and with the War Office and the Treasury, 1763–1775* (Hamden, Conn.: Archon Books, 1969), 2:488.

6. Donald Jackson and Dorothy Twohig, eds., *The Diaries of George Washington*, vol. 3, *1771–75; 1780–81* (Charlottesville: University Press of Virginia, 1978), 182, entry dated May 27, 1773.

7. Alden, *General Gage in America*, 10, 194–95, 200–204.

8. Gage to Dartmouth, September 25, 1774, *Correspondence of Gage*, 1:377.

9. Gage to Dartmouth, November 15, 1774, *Correspondence of Gage*, 1:384; proclamation of November 10, 1774, in *AA4*, 1:973–74.

10. Gage to Dartmouth, December 15, 1774, *Correspondence of Gage*, 1:387.

11. Gage to Dartmouth, January 18, 1775, *Correspondence of Gage*, 1:390.

12. Dartmouth to Gage, December 10, 1774, *Correspondence of Gage*, 2:178.

13. Gage to Brown and De Berniere, February 22, 1775, *AA4*, 1:1263.

14. "Narrative of Ensign De Berniere," *AA4*, 1:1263–67.

15. *Essex Gazette*, February 28, 1775.

16. "Mr. William Gavett's Account," *Proceedings of the Essex Institute*, vol. 1, *1848–1856* (Salem, Mass.: Ives and Pease, 1856), 126. See also pages 104–35 for other accounts of the Salem raid.

17. *Essex Gazette*, February 28, 1775.

18. *Essex Gazette*, March 7, 1775.

19. "Gavett's Account," *Proceedings*, 127.

20. *Proceedings*, 115.

21. "Gavett's Account," *Proceedings*, 128.

22. *Essex Gazette*, February 28, 1775.

23. "Gavett's Account," *Proceedings*, 128. This episode was not reported in the *Essex Gazette* and was embellished over time. It carries a ring of Barbara Fritchie's stand in the face of Stonewall Jackson's troops in Frederick, Maryland, during the Civil War.

24. "not less than," *Essex Gazette*, March 7, 1775; "immediately dispatched," *Essex Gazette*, February 28, 1775.

25. *Essex Gazette*, February 28, 1775.

26. John Trumbull, *M'Fingal: An Epic Poem* (New York: American Book Exchange, 1881), 65.

27. "Mrs. Story's Account," *Proceedings*, 135.

Chapter 6 — Boston in the Bull's-Eye

1. For differing contemporary accounts, see the loyalist *Massachusetts Gazette and the Boston Post-Boy and Advertiser* and the rebel *Boston Gazette*, both March 12, 1770. On May 4, 1970, at the height of protest over the Vietnam War and, specifically, an incursion into Cambodia, Ohio National Guard troops fired on protesting Kent State University students, killing four and wounding nine.

2. Gage to Hillsborough, April 10, 1770, Clarence Edwin Carter, ed., *The Correspondence of General Thomas Gage with the Secretaries of State, and with the War Office and the Treasury, 1763–1775* (Hamden, Conn.: Archon Books, 1969), 1:250.

3. *Boston Gazette*, March 12, 1770.

4. Adams diary, March 5, 1773, *Works of John Adams*, 2:317.

5. *Boston Gazette*, September 10, 1764.

6. Adams to Lee, March 4, 1775, Harry Alonzo Cushing, ed., *The Writings of Samuel Adams* (New York: G. P. Putnam's Sons, 1907), 3:196.

7. *Massachusetts Spy*, March 17, 1775.

8. *Massachusetts Spy*, March 17, 1775.

9. *Rivington's New-York Gazetteer*, March 23, 1775.

10. *Massachusetts Spy*, March 17, 1775.

11. *Rivington's New-York Gazetteer*, March 23, 1775.

12. *Rivington's New-York Gazetteer*, March 16, 1775.

13. Barker diary, March 6, 1775, Elizabeth Ellery Dana, ed., *The British in Boston: Being the Diary of Lieutenant John Barker of the King's Own Regiment from November 15, 1774 to May 31, 1776; with Notes* (Cambridge, Mass.: Harvard University Press, 1924), 26.

14. Viator [pseud.], *The Thoughts of a Traveller upon our American Disputes* (London: J. Ridley, 1774), 19–20. This quote was a paraphrase of the oft-quoted original in Plutarch's *Lives*.

15. Adams to Lee, March 4, 1775, *Writings of Samuel Adams*, 3:197; number of regiments in David Hackett Fischer, *Paul Revere's Ride* (New York: Oxford University Press, 1994), 309.

16. Adams to Lee, March 4, 1775, *Writings of Samuel Adams*, 3:198.

17. Page Smith, *A New Age Now Begins: A People's History of the American Revolution* (New York: McGraw-Hill, 1976), 462.

18. Debate in House of Lords, March 16, 1775, *AA4*, 1:1681–83.

19. Pitcairn to Sandwich, February 14, 1775, G. R. Barnes and J. H. Owen, eds., *The Private Papers of John, Earl of Sandwich, First Lord of the Admiralty, 1771–1782* (London: Naval Records Society, 1932), 1:58.

20. Pitcairn to Sandwich, March 4, 1775, *Earl of Sandwich Papers*, 1:60–61.

21. Adams to Archer, et al., February 1, 1775, *Writings of Samuel Adams*, 3:174.

22. Adams to Randolph, February 1, 1775, *Writings of Samuel Adams*, 3:175–76.

23. A. W. Farmer [Samuel Seabury], *The Congress Canvassed: Or, an Examination into the Conduct of the Delegates, at the Grand Convention Held in Philadelphia, Sept. 1, 1774* (London: Richardson and Urquhart, 1775), 33.

24. Adams to Black, March 2, 1775, *Writings of Samuel Adams*, 3:192–93.

25. *Boston Gazette*, March 27, 1775.

26. Adams to Lee, March 4, 1775, *Writings of Samuel Adams*, 3:195–97.

27. Percy to Duke of Northumberland, July 27, 1774, Charles Knowles Bolton, ed., *Letters of Hugh Earl Percy from Boston and New York, 1774–1776* (Boston: Charles E. Goodspeed, 1902), 29–30.

28. Percy to Reveley, August 8, 1774, *Letters of Percy*, 30–31.

29. Percy to Duke of Northumberland, September 12, 1774, *Letters of Percy*, 37–38, 47.

30. *Boston Gazette*, January 30, 1775.

31. Percy to Harvey, February 9, 1775, *Letters of Percy*, 47–48.

32. Percy to Duke of Northumberland, January 25, 1775, *Letters of Percy*, 47.

Chapter 7—Independence or Reconciliation?

1. *Boston Gazette*, March 6, 1775.

2. Provincial Congress resolution, March 24, 1775, published in *Boston Gazette*, March 27, 1775.

3. Washington to John Washington, March 25, 1775, Jared Sparks, ed., *The Writings of George Washington* (Boston: Charles Tappan, 1846), 2:404–5. On March 17, 1775, the independent company of Richmond County, Virginia, unanimously chose Washington as its commander. He had already been chosen to command the Prince William independent company and later was chosen to command the Fairfax, Albemarle, and Spotsylvania companies.

4. Henry Mayer, *A Son of Thunder: Patrick Henry and the American Republic* (New York: Grove Press, 1991), 244–45; "*American* Continental Congress" reported in *AA4*, 2:167.

5. Debate on Bill for Administration of the Government of Massachusett's Bay, May 2, 1774, *The Parliamentary History of England from the Earliest Period to the Year 1803* (London: T. C. Hansard, 1813), 17:1314.

6. *Parliamentary History*, 17:1315–16.

7. Adams to Lee, March 4, 1775, Harry Alonzo Cushing, ed., *The Writings of Samuel Adams* (New York: G. P. Putnam's Sons, 1907), 3:196.

8. *Parliamentary History*, 18:149, 151, 153–54, 156.

9. *Parliamentary History*, 18:499.

10. *Parliamentary History*, 18:505.

11. *Parliamentary History*, 18:535–36.

12. *Parliamentary History*, 18:540.

13. *Boston Gazette*, April 3, 1775.

14. Farmar to Halroyd, February 17, 1775, in "Letters of Eliza Farmar to Her Nephew," *Pennsylvania Magazine of History and Biography* 40, no. 2 (1916), 202.

15. Diary of Jemima Condict Harrison, February 1775, North American Women's Letters and Diaries: Colonial to 1950 (subscription only), accessed January 3, 2012, http://solomon.nwld.alexanderstreet.com/cgi-bin/asp/philo/nwld/getdoc.pl!S34-D025.

16. Diary of Jemima Condict Harrison, February 1775.

17. Ricord, Frederick W., and William Nelson, eds., *Documents Relating to the Colonial History of the State of New Jersey*, vol. 10, *Administration of Governor William Franklin, 1767–1776* (Newark, N.J.: Daily Advertiser Printing House, 1886), 504.

18. Franklin to Galloway, February 25, 1775, William B. Willcox, et al., eds., *The Papers of Benjamin Franklin*, vol. 21, *January 1, 1774, through March 22, 1775* (New Haven: Yale University Press, 1978), 509.

19. "The People," Page Smith, *A New Age Now Begins: A People's History of the American Revolution* (New York: McGraw-Hill, 1976), 470–71; "the conflict," Henry Steele Commager and Richard B. Morris, eds., *The Spirit of 'Seventy-Six: The Story of the American Revolution as Told by Participants* (New York: Harper & Row, 1958), 733.

20. *Massachusetts Gazette and Boston Post-Boy and Advertiser*, March 27, 1775.

21. *Boston Evening-Post*, April 10, 1775.

22. James Warren to Mercy Warren, April 6, 1775, H. C. Lodge, et al., eds., *Warren-Adams Letters, Being Chiefly a Correspondence among John Adams, Samuel Adams, and James Warren* (Boston: Massachusetts Historical Society, 1917), 44.

23. *Massachusetts Gazette and Boston Post-Boy and Advertiser*, April 10, 1775. The same issue of the *Boston Gazette* announced the publication in pamphlet form of Mercy Warren's latest literary satire: "This Day Published, And Sold by the Printers hereof: (Price Nine Coppers) The GROUP" (*Boston Gazette*, April 10, 1775).

24. *Massachusetts Spy*, April 6, 1775. This was probably in reference to General Sir William Howe, younger brother of Lord Richard Howe, the admiral who had sought out Benjamin Franklin.

25. Lord Percy to Thomas Percy, April 8, 1775, Charles Knowles Bolton, ed., *Letters of Hugh Earl Percy from Boston and New York, 1774–1776* (Boston: Charles E. Goodspeed, 1902), 48.

26. Given the uncertainty of cross-Atlantic travel, Lord Dartmouth routinely sent multiple copies of dispatches to General Gage and other royal governors in North America. There is some uncertainty as to whether Gage first learned of his January 27, 1775, orders from Dartmouth via Captain Oliver De Lancey arriving in Boston on board HMS *Nautilus* or from the *Falcon*. Likewise, there is some question of the exact dates of each vessel's arrival during the second week of April, although Gage later reported to Dartmouth that the *Nautilus* arrived on April 14 and the *Falcon* on April 16 (Gage to Dartmouth, April 22, 1775, Clarence Edwin Carter, ed., *The Correspondence of General Thomas Gage with the Secretaries of State, and with the War Office and the Treasury, 1763–1775* (Hamden, Conn.: Archon Books, 1969), 1:396).

Chapter 8 — The General's Dilemma

1. Lord Percy to Thomas Percy, April 8, 1775, Charles Knowles Bolton, ed., *Letters of Hugh Earl Percy from Boston and New York, 1774–1776* (Boston: Charles E. Goodspeed, 1902), 49; "the cruelest month" is from the opening line of T. S. Eliot's "The Waste Land" (1922).

2. Gage to Hillsborough, August 17, 1768, Clarence Edwin Carter, ed., *The Correspondence of General Thomas Gage with the Secretaries of State, and with the War Office and the Treasury, 1763–1775* (Hamden, Conn.: Archon Books, 1969), 1:184.

3. Gage to Barrington, July 6, 1770, *Correspondence of Gage*, 2:547.

4. "On Conciliation with America," March 22, 1775, W. M. Elofson and John A. Woods, eds., *The Writings and Speeches of Edmund Burke*, vol. 3, *Party, Parliament, and the American War, 1774–1780* (Oxford: Clarendon Press, 1996), 130.

5. Dartmouth to Gage, January 27, 1775, *Correspondence of Gage*, 2:179–183.

6. Jerome Carter Hosmer, ed., *The Narrative of General Gage's Spies* (Boston: Bostonian Society, 1912), 31–33.

7. Allen French, *General Gage's Informers: New Material upon Lexington & Concord* (Ann Arbor: University of Michigan Press, 1932), 17.

8. French, *General Gage's Informers*, 22.

9. French, *General Gage's Informers*, 25–26, 29.

10. French, *General Gage's Informers*, 31–32.

11. David Hackett Fischer, *Paul Revere's Ride* (New York: Oxford University Press, 1994), 87.

12. Richard Frothingham, *History of the Siege of Boston, and of the Battles of Lexington, Concord, and Bunker Hill* (Boston: Charles C. Little and James Brown, 1849), 56–57.

13. "Deposition of Elijah Sanderson" in Elias Phinney, *History of the Battle at Lexington, on the Morning of the 19th April, 1775* (Boston: Phelps and Farnham, 1825), 31.

14. Frederick Mackenzie, *Diary of Frederick Mackenzie* (Cambridge, Mass.: Harvard University Press, 1930), 1:18, entry dated April 18, 1775.

15. "I dare say," Barker diary, April 15, 1775, Elizabeth Ellery Dana, ed., *The British in Boston: Being the Diary of Lieutenant John Barker of the King's Own Regiment from November 15, 1774 to May 31, 1776; with Notes* (Cambridge, Mass.: Harvard University Press, 1924), 29; French, *General Gage's Informers*, 36n.

16. The full congress adjourned at Concord on April 15. The most recent biography of Joseph Warren, which engages in some speculation about Dr. Warren's romantic pursuits, is Samuel A. Forman's *Dr. Joseph Warren: The Boston Tea Party, Bunker Hill, and the Birth of American Liberty* (Gretna, La.: Pelican Publishing, 2011).

17. Fischer, *Paul Revere's Ride*, 96.

18. Jeremy Belknap, "Journal of My Tour to the Camp and the Observations I Made There," October 25, 1775, *Proceedings of the Massachusetts Historical Society* 4 (1860), 84–86.

19. C[harles]. Stedman, *The History of the Origin, Progress, and Termination of the American War* (London, 1794), 1:119.

20. Richard Frothingham, *Life and Times of Joseph Warren* (Boston: Little, Brown, 1865), 454–56.

21. William Gordon, *The History of the Rise, Progress, and Establishment, of the Independence of the United States of America: Including an Account of the Late War; and of the Thirteen Colonies, from Their Origin to That Period* (London, 1788), 476–77.

22. Peter Orlando Hutchinson, ed., *The Diary and Letters of His Excellency Thomas Hutchinson, Esq* (London: Sampson Low, Marston, Searle & Rivington, 1883), 497–98, entry dated July 27, 1775.

Chapter 9 — Two Lanterns

1. "putting their hands," Jeremy Belknap, "Journal of My Tour to the Camp and the Observations I Made There," October 25, 1775, *Proceedings of the Massachusetts Historical Society* 4 (1860), 85; "equip themselves," Margaret Wheeler Willard, ed., *Letters on the American Revolution, 1774–1776* (Boston: Houghton Mifflin, 1925), 197; weather information in David Hackett Fischer, *Paul Revere's Ride* (New York: Oxford University Press, 1994), 310–11.

2. Belknap, "Journal of My Tour," 85.

3. Fischer, *Paul Revere's Ride*, 114.

4. For a detailed analysis of units and troop strength, including varying estimates over the years, see Fischer, *Paul Revere's Ride*, appendixes F and K, 309, 313–15.

5. Gordon to gentleman in England, May 17, 1775, *AA4*, 2:626.

6. Barker diary, April 19, 1775, Elizabeth Ellery Dana, ed., *The British in Boston: Being the Diary of Lieutenant John Barker of the King's Own Regiment from November 15, 1774 to May 31, 1776; with Notes* (Cambridge, Mass.: Harvard University Press, 1924), 31; for general confusion, see also Frederick Mackenzie, *Diary of Frederick Mackenzie* (Cambridge, Mass.: Harvard University Press, 1930), 1:18.

7. Barker diary, April 19, 1775, *The British in Boston*, 31; Allen French, *General Gage's Informers: New Material upon Lexington & Concord* (Ann Arbor: University of Michigan Press, 1932), 35–36.

8. Fischer, *Paul Revere's Ride*, 117–18.

9. Fischer, *Paul Revere's Ride*, 121.

10. "were obliged to wade," *Diary of Frederick Mackenzie*, 24; "at first through," French, *General Gage's Informers*, 40.

11. French, *General Gage's Informers*, 40.

12. Paul Revere, Letter to Jeremy Belknap, circa 1798, p. 2, Massachusetts Historical Society, http://www.masshist.org/database/img-viewer.php ?item_id=99&mode=small&img_step=2&tpc=&pid=#page2, accessed March 14, 2012. Given the British army's penchant for putting almost everything in writing, it seems unlikely that Gage repeated his orders to Smith verbally. Written orders to Major Mitchell apparently do not survive, but it seems most likely that if orders to capture the rebel leaders were given, they directed Mitchell's more clandestine and smaller-scale operation to hold them until the arrival of Smith's column.

13. Revere to Belknap, circa 1798, p. 2.

14. Revere to Belknap, circa 1798, p. 2.

15. William W. Wheildon, *History of Paul Revere's Signal Lanterns, April 18, 1775, in the Steeple of the North Church* (Concord, Mass., 1878), 45n.

16. Pulling on enemies list, Fischer, *Paul Revere's Ride*, 306.

17. Robert Newman Sheets, *Robert Newman: The Life and Times of the Sexton Who April 18, 1775 Held Two Lanterns Aloft in Christ Church Steeple, Boston* (Denver, Colo., 1975), 3–4; for moonlight see Fischer, *Paul Revere's Ride*, appendix 1, 312; for an analysis of the likely parties involved, see Fischer, *Paul Revere's Ride*, 100–101 and corresponding footnotes.

18. Fischer, *Paul Revere's Ride*, 103–5.

19. Revere to Belknap, circa 1798, p. 1.

20. Sheets, *Robert Newman*, 6; "Events of April 18, 1775," The Old North Church: Christ Church in the City of Boston (Old North Church website), http://www.oldnorth.com/history/april18.htm, accessed March 25, 2012. This window is now known as the Newman Window. Above it is a replica of Newman's lanterns that was lit by President Gerald Ford on April 18, 1975, in celebration of the bicentennial.

21. Revere to Belknap, circa 1798, p. 2.

Chapter 10 — Lexington Green

1. Jonas Clarke, *Opening of the War of the Revolution, 19th of April 1775, A Brief Narrative of the Principal Transactions of That Day* (Lexington, Mass.: Lexington Historical Society, 1901), 2. Today, the street running past the Hancock-Clarke house is called Hancock Street; what is now Bedford Street did not exist in 1775.

2. Elias Phinney, *History of the Battle at Lexington, on the Morning of the 19th April, 1775* (Boston: Phelps and Farnham, 1825), 31, 33.

3. Richard Frothingham, *History of the Siege of Boston, and of the Battles of Lexington, Concord, and Bunker Hill* (Boston: Charles C. Little and James Brown, 1849), 57.

4. "female connections," James Warren to Mercy Warren, April 7, 1775, postscript, H. C. Lodge, et al., eds., *Warren-Adams Letters, Being Chiefly a Correspondence among John Adams, Samuel Adams, and James Warren* (Boston: Massachusetts Historical Society, 1917) 45; Clarke, *Opening of the War*, iii.

5. Phinney, *Battle at Lexington*, 16–17.

6. Frederick Mackenzie, *Diary of Frederick Mackenzie* (Cambridge, Mass.: Harvard University Press, 1930), 1:24.

7. Frank Warren Coburn, *The Battle of April 19, 1775 in Lexington, Concord, Lincoln, Arlington, Cambridge, Somerville and Charlestown Massachusetts* (Lexington, Mass.: Lexington Historical Society, 1922), 55.

8. Elizabeth Baigent, "Pitcairn, John," *Oxford Dictionary of National Biography*, www.oxforddnb.com/view/printable/53715, accessed February 17, 2012. Charles Cochrane was later beheaded by a cannonball while standing beside Cornwallis at Yorktown.

9. Coburn, *Battle of April 19, 1775*, 58.

10. Paul Revere, Deposition, fair copy, circa 1775, Massachusetts Historical Society, www.masshist.org/database/img-viewer.php?item_id=98&img _step=1&tpc=&pid=&mode=transcript&tpc=&pid=#page1, accessed March 12, 2012.

11. Sanderson deposition, Phinney, *Battle at Lexington*, 32.

12. "I must do you," Phinney, *Battle at Lexington*, 32; Paul Revere's deposition, circa 1775.

13. Clarke, *Opening of the War*, 3.

14. "a great tall man," Coburn, *Battle of April 19, 1775*, 60; Elizabeth S. Parker, "Captain John Parker," *Proceedings of Lexington Historical Society and Papers Relating to the History of the Town* (Lexington: Historical Society, 1890), 1:42–47.

15. "Robert Munroe," *Proceedings of Lexington Historical Society*, 1:38–40.

16. Clarke, *Opening of the War*, 4.

17. W. Munroe deposition, Phinney, *Battle at Lexington*, 34.

18. W[illia]m H. Sumner, "Reminiscences by Gen. Wm. H. Sumner," *New England Historical and Genealogical Record* 8 (1854), 187–88.

19. Paul Revere's deposition, circa 1775, and Paul Revere, Letter to Jeremy Belknap, circa 1798, p. 2, Massachusetts Historical Society, http://www .masshist.org/database/img-viewer.php?item_id=99 &mode=small&img_step=2&tpc=&pid=#page2, accessed March 14, 2012; Clarke, *Opening of the War*, 4–5; Coburn, *Battle of April 19, 1775*, 62; "the art of military," David Hackett Fischer, *Paul Revere's Ride* (New York: Oxford University Press, 1994), 181.

20. Paul Revere's deposition, circa 1775.

21. *JCC*, 1:61–62 (October 11, 1774).

22. "Stand your ground," Coburn, *Battle of April 19, 1775*, 64.

23. Coburn, *Battle of April 19, 1775*, 64.

24. Sanderson deposition, Phinney, *Battle at Lexington*, 32.

25. Robbins deposition, April 24, 1775, *AA4*, 2:491.

26. Parker deposition, April 25, 1775, *AA4*, 2:491.

27. Fischer, *Paul Revere's Ride*, 401n.

28. Draper deposition, April 25, 1775, *AA4*, 2:495.

29. Fessenden deposition, April 23, 1775, *AA4*, 2:496.

Chapter 11 — On to Concord

1. "saw, & heard," Paul Revere, Letter to Jeremy Belknap, circa 1798, p. 6, Massachusetts Historical Society, http://www.masshist.org/database/img -viewer.php?item_id=99&mode=small&img_step=2&tpc=&pid =#page2, accessed March 14, 2012; "When one gun," Paul Revere, deposition, fair copy, circa 1775, Massachusetts Historical Society, www.masshist .org/database/img-viewer.php?item_id=98&img_step=1&tpc=&pid=& mode=transcript&tpc=&pid=#page1, accessed March 12, 2012.

2. Parker deposition, April 25, 1775, *AA4*, 2:491.

3. Robbins deposition, April 24, 1775, *AA4*, 2:491.

4. Smith deposition, April 25, 1775, *AA4*, 2:494.

5. John Pitcairn, "Major John Pitcairn's Report to General Gage, April 26, 1775," Digital History, "Explorations of the Revolutionary War," http:// www.digitalhistory.uh.edu/learning_history/revolution/account3_lex ington.cfm, accessed January 9, 2013.

6. Barker diary, April 19, 1775, Elizabeth Ellery Dana, ed., *The British in Boston: Being the Diary of Lieutenant John Barker of the King's Own Regiment from November 15, 1774 to May 31, 1776; with Notes* (Cambridge, Mass.: Harvard University Press, 1924), 32.

7. William Sutherland and Richard Pope, *Late News of the Excursion and Ravages of the King's Troops on the Nineteenth of April, 1775* (Cambridge, Mass.: Harvard College, 1927), 17.

8. Sutherland, *Late News*, 17; see also the version in Allen French, *General Gage's Informers: New Material upon Lexington & Concord* (Ann Arbor: University of Michigan Press, 1932), 58–61.

9. Tidd and Abbott deposition, April 25, 1775, *AA4*, 2:492.

10. "meanwhile the second officer," Fessenden deposition, April 23, 1775, *AA4*, 2:496; "The second of these," Jonas Clarke, *Opening of the War of the Revolution, 19th of April 1775, A Brief Narrative of the Principal Transactions of That Day* (Lexington, Mass.: Lexington Historical Society, 1901), 6.

11. David Hackett Fischer, *Paul Revere's Ride* (New York: Oxford University Press, 1994), 402n.

12. W. Munroe deposition, March 7, 1825, Elias Phinney, *History of the Battle at Lexington, on the Morning of the 19th April, 1775* (Boston: Phelps and Farnham, 1825), 34.

13. Edward Gould deposition, April 25, 1775, *AA4*, 2:501. It is interesting to consider the effects of both the differing political climate and the intervening span of years on memory, especially as reflected in the difference between those depositions taken within a week or so of the battle in 1775 and those set down in 1825. By then, the United States had not only won its independence during the American Revolution but also was heady over Andrew Jackson's victory over these same British regulars at New Orleans at the close of the War of 1812.

14. J. Munroe deposition, December 28, 1824, Phinney, *Battle at Lexington*, 35.

15. Richard Frothingham, *Life and Times of Joseph Warren* (Boston: Little, Brown, 1865), 459.

16. "the smoke prevented" and "then loaded my gun," J. Munroe, December 28, 1824, in Phinney, *Battle at Lexington*, 35–36; "the balls flew," E. Munroe deposition, April 2, 1825, Phinney, *Battle at Lexington*, 37.

17. W. Munroe deposition, March 7, 1825, Phinney, *Battle at Lexington*, 34.

18. J. Munroe deposition, December 28, 1824, Phinney, *Battle at Lexington*, 36.

19. Clarke, *Opening of the War*, 8; British casualties at Frederick Mackenzie, *Diary of Frederick Mackenzie* (Cambridge, Mass.: Harvard University Press, 1930), 1:24.

20. Sutherland, *Late News*, 18; "We then formed," Barker diary, April 19, 1775, *The British in Boston*, 32.

21. French, *General Gage's Informers*, 60, 62.

22. *Diary of Frederick Mackenzie*, 24–25.

23. Clarke, *Opening of the War*, 9.

24. Lemuel Shattuck, *A History of the Town of Concord* (Boston: Russell, Ordiorne and Company, 1935), 103–4.

25. Amelia Forbes Emerson, ed., *Diaries and Letters of William Emerson, 1743–1776* (Boston: Thomas Todd, 1972), 71–72.

26. Amos Barrett, "Concord and Lexington Battle," in Henry True, *Journal and Letters of Rev. Henry True, of Hampstead, New Hampshire: Also an Account of the Battle of Concord by Captain Amos Barrett, a Minute Man and Participant* (Marion, Ohio, 1900), 31.

27. Emerson, *Diaries and Letters*, 72.

28. French, *General Gage's Informers*, 104–5n. The light infantry company of the Twenty-Third was also reported by Captain Laurie to have belatedly come

on the scene and followed Parsons. For company displacements, see also Barker diary, April 19, 1775, *The British in Boston*, 33. For company strength, see Fischer, *Paul Revere's Ride*, 314.

29. Henry De Berniere, "Narrative of Occurrences, 1775," *Collections of the Massachusetts Historical Society*, 2nd ser., 4 (1816), 216; Fischer, *Paul Revere's Ride*, 208.

30. J. H. Temple, *History of Framingham, Massachusetts* (Framingham, Mass.: Town of Framingham, 1887), 276.

Chapter 12 — By the Rude Bridge

1. Jeremy Lister, *Concord Fight, Being So Much of the Narrative of Ensign Jeremy Lister of the 10th Regiment of Foot as Pertains to His Services on the 19th of April, 1775, and to His Experiences in Boston during the Early Months of the Siege* (Cambridge, Mass.: Harvard University Press, 1931), 25.

2. "exceedingly vexed" and "to give me 2 men," William Sutherland and Richard Pope, *Late News of the Excursion and Ravages of the King's Troops on the Nineteenth of April, 1775* (Cambridge, Mass.: Harvard College, 1927), 19; "still approached" and "Luckily for us," Lister, *Concord Fight*, 26.

3. Sutherland, *Late News*, 20.

4. Sutherland, *Late News*, 20.

5. David Hackett Fischer, *Paul Revere's Ride* (New York: Oxford University Press, 1994), 209.

6. Deposition of Amos Baker, April 22, 1850, in Josiah Adams, *Letter to Lemuel Shattuck, Esq. of Boston* (Boston: Damrell & Moore, 1850), 21.

7. Lemuel Shattuck, *A History of the Town of Concord* (Boston: Russell, Ordiorne and Company, 1935), 107–8.

8. Shattuck, *History of Concord*, 108–9.

9. Shattuck, *History of Concord*, 107.

10. Richard Frothingham, *History of the Siege of Boston, and of the Battles of Lexington, Concord, and Bunker Hill* (Boston: Charles C. Little and James Brown, 1849), 369–70. A year later, Mrs. Moulton petitioned the Massachusetts legislature for compensation for her services, citing her old age and poverty, and was awarded three pounds, then equal in purchasing power to about $450 in 2010.

11. Shattuck, *History of Concord*, 111. The additional words "stand here" were quoted by Amos Baker in his deposition of April 22, 1850, in Adams, *Letter to Shattuck*, 21.

12. D. Michael Ryan, "White Cockade: A Jacobite Air at the North Bridge?" https://www2.bc.edu/~hafner/Imm/music-articles/white_cockade _ryan.html, accessed March 22, 2012.

13. Hannah Leighton deposition, August 14, 1835, Adams, *Letter to Shattuck*, 19.

14. See differing versions in Shattuck, *History of Concord*, and the Acton response praising Captain Davis in Adams, *Letter to Shattuck*.

15. Allen French, *General Gage's Informers: New Material upon Lexington & Concord* (Ann Arbor: University of Michigan Press, 1932), 80.

16. Sutherland, *Late News*, 20–21: French, *General Gage's Informers*, 80.

17. Amos Barrett, "Concord and Lexington Battle," in Henry True, *Journal and Letters of Rev. Henry True, of Hampstead, New Hampshire: Also an Account of the Battle of Concord by Captain Amos Barrett, a Minute Man and Participant* (Marion, Ohio, 1900), 33.

18. "to march to," James Barrett deposition, April 23, 1775, *AA4*, 2:499; "quickened our pace," Thomas Thorp deposition, July 10, 1835, Adams, *Letter to Shattuck*, 15.

19. "a ball strike," Thorp deposition, Adams, *Letter to Shattuck*, 15; "saw where," Thaddeus Blood, "Statement on Battle of April 19," www.nps.gov/mima/forteachers/upload/Thaddeus%20Blood.pdf, accessed June 27, 2012.

20. For further analysis of this, see Fischer, *Paul Revere's Ride*, 406n41.

21. French, *General Gage's Informers*, 97.

22. Sutherland, *Late News*, 21.

23. Thorp deposition, Adams, *Letter to Shattuck*, 15.

24. Solomon Smith deposition, July 10, 1835, Adams, *Letter to Shattuck*, 17; "had worried him," Charles Hadley deposition, December 1, 1835, Adams, *Letter to Shattuck*, 18.

25. Shattuck, *History of Concord*, 109.

26. French, *General Gage's Informers*, 80.

27. Amos Barrett, "Concord and Lexington Battle," *Journal and Letters of Rev. Henry True,* 33.

28. Amos Barrett, "Concord and Lexington Battle," *Journal and Letters of Rev. Henry True,* 33.

29. Hannah Leighton deposition, Adams, *Letter to Shattuck*, 19.

30. Smith deposition, Adams, *Letter to Shattuck*, 17; Thaddeus Blood, "Statement."

31. Henry De Berniere, "Narrative of Occurrences, 1775," *Collections of the Massachusetts Historical Society*, 2nd ser., 4 (1816), 216.

32. Smith deposition, Adams, *Letter to Shattuck*, 17.

33. Amelia Forbes Emerson, ed., *Diaries and Letters of William Emerson, 1743–1776* (Boston: Thomas Todd, 1972), 72.

34. George Otto Trevelyan, *The American Revolution, Part I, 1766–1776* (New York: Longmans, Green, 1899), 306–7.

Chapter 13 — Retreat, If We Can

1. *The Detail and Conduct of the American War under Generals Gage, Howe, Burgoyne, and Vice Admiral Lord Howe* (London: Richardson and Urquhart, 1780), 10.

2. Percy to Gage, April 20, 1775, Charles Knowles Bolton, ed., *Letters of Hugh Earl Percy from Boston and New York 1774–1776* (Boston: Charles E. Goodspeed, 1902), 50; march order in Frederick Mackenzie, *Diary of Frederick Mackenzie* (Cambridge, Mass.: Harvard University Press, 1930), 1:19.

3. coal and "not less than," Dartmouth to Gage, January 28, 1775 (two letters), Clarence Edwin Carter, ed., *The Correspondence of General Thomas Gage with the Secretaries of State, and with the War Office and the Treasury, 1763–1775* (Hamden, Conn.: Archon Books, 1969), 2:183–84; Gage to Dartmouth, April 19, 1775, *Correspondence of Gage*, 1:395; Wright to Gage, June 27, 1775, *AA4*, 1:1109–10.

4. Richard Frothingham, *Life and Times of Joseph Warren* (Boston: Little, Brown, 1865), 456–57.

5. There is a report that a messenger arrived in Boston from the country about eight o'clock. John Andrews wrote his brother-in-law: "The first advice we had was about eight o'clock in the morning, when it was reported that the troops had fir'd upon and killed five men in Lexington — previous to which an officer came express to his Excellency Governor Gage..." Andrews to Barrell, April 19, 1775, in "Letters of John Andrews, Esq. of Boston, 1772–1776," *Massachusetts Historical Society Proceedings* 8 (1864–65), 404.

6. Frothingham, *Life of Warren*, 457.

7. Frothingham, *Life of Warren*, 457.

8. Richard Frothingham, *History of the Siege of Boston, and of the Battles of Lexington, Concord, and Bunker Hill* (Boston: Charles C. Little and James Brown, 1849), 73.

9. Barker diary, April 19, 1775, Elizabeth Ellery Dana, ed., *The British in Boston: Being the Diary of Lieutenant John Barker of the King's Own Regiment from November 15, 1774 to May 31, 1776; with Notes* (Cambridge, Mass.: Harvard University Press, 1924), 35.

10. Allen French, *The Day of Concord and Lexington: The Nineteenth of April, 1775* (Boston: Little, Brown, 1925), 57–58.

11. French, *Day of Concord and Lexington*, 220–21.

12. William Sutherland and Richard Pope, *Late News of the Excursion and Ravages of the King's Troops on the Nineteenth of April, 1775* (Cambridge, Mass.: Harvard College, 1927), 22.

13. Ellen Chase, *The Beginnings of the American Revolution* (New York: Baker and Taylor, 1910), 3:64.

14. J. H. Temple, *History of Framingham, Massachusetts* (Framingham, Mass.: Town of Framingham, 1887), 275, 278. Peter Salem was not alone in his service. A recent detailed study suggests that at least twenty-one men of color from twelve different companies representing eleven different towns took part in the fight along Battle Road. See George Quintal Jr., *Patriots of Color — 'A Peculiar Beauty and Merit': African Americans and Native Americans at Battle Road & Bunker Hill* (Division of Cultural Resources, Boston National Historical Park, 2004), 21–36.

15. Temple, *History of Framingham*, 275.

16. David Hackett Fischer, *Paul Revere's Ride* (New York: Oxford University Press, 1994), 224.

17. Frothingham, *Siege of Boston*, 73.

18. John R. Galvin, *The Minute Men: The First Fight: Myths and Realities of the American Revolution* (Washington, D.C.: Brassey's, 1996), 178–85.

19. Henry De Berniere, "Narrative of Occurrences, 1775," *Collections of the Massachusetts Historical Society*, 2nd ser., 4 (1816), 217.

20. Barker diary, April 19, 1775, *The British in Boston*, 37.

21. De Berniere, "Narrative of Occurrences," 217.

Chapter 14 — Percy to the Rescue

1. Draft of Percy's report to Gage, April 20, 1775, Charles Knowles Bolton, ed., *Letters of Hugh Earl Percy from Boston and New York, 1774–1776* (Boston: Charles E. Goodspeed, 1902), 51.

2. Draft of Percy's report to Gage, April 20, 1775, *Letters of Percy*, 51.

3. Percy to Gage, April 20, 1775, *Letters of Percy*, 50.

4. Percy to Gage, April 20, 1775, *Letters of Percy*, 50.

5. Percy to Northumberland, April 20, 1775, *Letters of Percy*, 54.

6. John R. Galvin, *The Minute Men: The First Fight: Myths and Realities of the American Revolution* (Washington, D.C.: Brassey's, 1996), 199.

7. Percy to Gage, April 20, 1775, *Letters of Percy*, 50.

8. William Heath, *Memoirs of Major-General William Heath* (New York: William Abbatt, 1901), 1–3.

9. Heath, *Memoirs*, 5, 7.

10. Galvin, *The Minute Men*, 212–17.

11. Barker diary, April 19, 1775, Elizabeth Ellery Dana, ed., *The British in Boston: Being the Diary of Lieutenant John Barker of the King's Own Regiment from November 15, 1774 to May 31, 1776; with Notes* (Cambridge, Mass.: Harvard University Press, 1924), 36.

12. Frank Warren Coburn, *The Battle of April 19, 1775 in Lexington, Concord, Lincoln, Arlington, Cambridge, Somerville and Charlestown Massachusetts* (Lexington, Mass.: Lexington Historical Society, 1922), 137–38.

13. Coburn, *Battle of April 19, 1775*, 139–40.

14. "incessant fire," Percy to Harvey, April 20, 1775, *Letters of Percy*, 52; Coburn, *Battle of April 19, 1775*, 141–42.

15. Depositions of Benjamin Cooper and Rachel Cooper, May 10, 1775, *Journals of the Provincial Congress of Massachusetts in 1774 and 1775, and of the Committee of Safety, with an Appendix* (Boston: Dutton and Wentworth, 1838), 678. Cooper's Tavern was located at the intersection of present-day Massachusetts Avenue and Medford Street.

16. Barker diary, April 25, 1775, *The British in Boston*, 39.

17. Frederick Mackenzie, *Diary of Frederick Mackenzie* (Cambridge, Mass.: Harvard University Press, 1930), 22, entry dated April 19, 1775.

18. Galvin, *The Minute Men*, 222–23.

19. Coburn, *Battle of April 19, 1775*, 116.

20. David Hackett Fischer, *Paul Revere's Ride* (New York: Oxford University Press, 1994), 259–60, 414n.

21. Draft of Percy's report to Gage, April 20, 1775, *Letters of Percy*, 51.

22. Barker diary, April 19, 1775, *The British in Boston*, 36.

23. Allen French, *The Day of Concord and Lexington: The Nineteenth of April, 1775* (Boston: Little, Brown, 1925), 261–64; Octavius Pickering and Charles W. Upham, *The Life of Timothy Pickering* (Boston: Little, Brown, 1867), 1: 69–72; Heath, *Memoirs*, 8–9; Mercy [Otis] Warren, *History of the Rise, Progress and Termination of the American Revolution* (Boston: E. Larkin, 1805), 1:187–88.

24. Heath, *Memoirs*, 9; Henry De Berniere, "Narrative of Occurrences, 1775," *Collections of the Massachusetts Historical Society*, 2nd ser., 4 (1816), 218; Richard Frothingham, *History of the Siege of Boston, and of the Battles of Lexington, Concord, and Bunker Hill* (Boston: Charles C. Little and James Brown, 1849), 372.

25. Robert Middlekauff, *The Glorious Cause: The American Revolution, 1763–1789* (New York: Oxford University Press, 1982), 273.

Chapter 15 — What Have We Done?

1. Mellen Chamberlain, "Why Capt. Levi Preston Fought," *The Historical Collections of the Danvers Historical Society* 8 (1920), 69–70. Chamberlain also told a different version of this story, ending with Preston's assertion "that their religious liberties were indissolubly connected with their civil liberties, and, therefore, that it was a religious duty to resist aggressions on

their civil rights; that a man could not be a good Christian who was not a true patriot."

2. Percy to Harvey, April 20, 1775, Charles Knowles Bolton, ed., *Letters of Hugh Earl Percy from Boston and New York, 1774–1776* (Boston: Charles E. Goodspeed, 1902), 52.

3. Percy to Gage, April 20, 1775, *Letters of Percy*, 50; Henry De Berniere, "Narrative of Occurrences, 1775," *Collections of the Massachusetts Historical Society*, 2nd ser., 4 (1816), 218–19; David Hackett Fischer, *Paul Revere's Ride* (New York: Oxford University Press, 1994), 320–21.

4. Barker diary, April 19, 1775, Elizabeth Ellery Dana, ed., *The British in Boston: Being the Diary of Lieutenant John Barker of the King's Own Regiment from November 15, 1774 to May 31, 1776; with Notes* (Cambridge, Mass.: Harvard University Press, 1924), 37.

5. Percy to Harvey, April 20, 1775, *Letters of Percy*, 52–53.

6. G[ideon]. D[elaplaine]. Scull, ed., *Memoir and Letters of Captain W. Glanville Evelyn, of the 4th Regiment, ("King's Own,"), from North America, 1774–1776* (Oxford: James Parker, 1879), 53.

7. Dartmouth to Gage, January 27, 1775, Edwin Carter, ed., *The Correspondence of General Thomas Gage with the Secretaries of State, and with the War Office and the Treasury, 1763–1775* (Hamden, Conn.: Archon Books, 1969), 2:183.

8. Gage to Dartmouth, April 22, 1775, *Correspondence of Gage*, 1:396.

9. Gage to Barrington, April 22, 1775, *Correspondence of Gage*, 2:673–74.

10. Thomas Weston, *History of the Town of Middleboro, Massachusetts* (Boston: Houghton Mifflin, 1906), 239.

11. Thomas B. Allen, *Tories: Fighting for the King in America's First Civil War* (New York: Harper, 2010), 67, 72.

12. De Berniere, "Narrative of Occurrences," 218.

13. Deming to Coverley, April 1775, "Journal of Sarah Winslow Deming," *American Monthly Magazine* 4 (January–July 1894), 46.

14. Andrews to Barrell, April 19, 1775, "Letters of John Andrews, Esq. of Boston, 1772–1776," *Massachusetts Historical Society Proceedings* 8 (1864–65), 405.

15. Andrews to Barrell, April 24, 1775, "Letters of John Andrews," 405.

16. Harrow Giles Unger, *John Hancock: Merchant King and American Patriot* (New York: John Wiley, 2000), 199.

17. Hancock to Provincial Congress, April 24, 1775, *Journals of the Provincial Congress of Massachusetts in 1774 and 1775, and of the Committee of Safety, with an Appendix* (Boston: Dutton and Wentworth, 1838), 170.

18. L. H. Butterfield, ed., *Diary & Autobiography of John Adams* (New York: Atheneum, 1964), 3:314.

19. Abigail Adams to John Adams, June 15, 1775, Charles Francis Adams, *Letters of Mrs. Adams, the Wife of John Adams* (Boston: Wilkins, Carter, 1848), 36.

20. Butterfield, *Diary & Autobiography*, 2:161.

21. *Journals of the Provincial Congress*, April 22, 1775, 147–48.

22. *Journals of the Provincial Congress*, April 23, 1775, 148–50.

23. Allen French, *General Gage's Informers: New Material upon Lexington & Concord* (Ann Arbor: University of Michigan Press, 1932), 147–49.

24. Paul Revere, Letter to Jeremy Belknap, circa 1798, p. 6, Massachusetts Historical Society, http://www.masshist.org/database/viewer.php?item _id=99&mode=large&img_step=6#page6, accessed March 14, 2012.

25. Revere to Belknap, circa 1798, pp. 7–8.

26. *New-York Gazette and Weekly Mercury*, May 1, 1775.

27. Paul Revere to Rachel Revere, undated, Elbridge Henry Goss, *The Life of Colonel Paul Revere* (Boston: Howard W. Spurr, 1906), 262–63.

28. French, *General Gage's Informers*, 170–71; see *Journals of the Provincial Congress*, May 16, 1775, p. 229, for Church's instructions to Philadelphia.

Chapter 16—Spreading the News

1. There are many versions of this dispatch, but this copy is from Henry Steele Commager and Richard B. Morris, eds., *The Spirit of 'Seventy-Six: The Story of the American Revolution as Told by Participants* (New York: Harper & Row, 1958), 90–91.

2. For a thorough analysis of the Bissell story in legend and fact, see Lion G. Miles, "The True Story of Bissell's Ride in 1775," iBerkshires.com, July 21, 2004, http://www.iberkshires.com/printerFriendly.php?story _id=15001, and Robert L. Berthelson, "An Alarm from Lexington," at the Connecticut Society of the Sons of the American Revolution, http://www .connecticutsar.org/articles/lexington_alarm.htm, accessed August 14, 2012; see also J. L. Bell's *Boston 1775* blogs pertaining to Bissell: http:// boston1775.blogspot.com/2010/05/legend-of-israel-bissell.html; http:// boston1775.blogspot.com/2010/05/true-story-of-isaac-bissell.html; http://boston1775.blogspot.com/2010/05/comparing-bissell-and -revere.html; http://boston1775.blogspot.com/2010/05/to-alarm-country -quite-to-connecticut.html, all accessed August 14, 2012. To add further confusion to the Bissell story, there was an Israel Bissell, who was born in East Windsor, Connecticut, in 1752, and who lies buried in Hinsdale, Massachusetts. He is frequently celebrated in error as the post rider.

3. William Farrand Livingston, *Israel Putnam, Pioneer, Ranger, and Major-General, 1718–1790* (New York: G. P. Putnam's Sons, 1901), 193.

4. *New-York Gazette and Weekly Mercury*, April 24, 1775.

5. Thomas Jones, *History of New York During the Revolutionary War* (New York: New-York Historical Society, 1879), 39–40.

6. Elias Boudinot, *Journal of Events in the Revolution* (Trenton, N.J.: Traver, 1899), 1.

7. Diary of Jemima Condict Harrison, April 1775, North American Women's Letters and Diaries: Colonial to 1950 (subscription only), http://solomon.nwld.alexanderstreet.com/cgi-bin/asp/philo/nwld/getdoc.pl!S34-D025, accessed January 3, 2012.

8. One might imagine that General Gage would have done his best to impede the spread of this news via what was ostensibly still a royal postal system. In truth, the network of postal riders had been heavily tied to rebel committees of correspondence and associated groups for years. The conversion from the king's system to a wholly colonial one took place with almost lightning speed. "We have the Pleasure to acquaint the Public," the *Connecticut Courant* reported as early as May 8, "that a constitutional Post-Office is now rising on the Ruins of the parliamentary One, which is just expiring in Convulsions." In just one example of this, Connecticut officials, encouraged by the Friends of Liberty at New York, "engaged a faithful Rider to proceed . . . with the Eastern Mails for Philadelphia and Colonies Southward" (*Connecticut Courant*, May 8, 1775).

9. *Boston News-Letter*, April 20, 1775.

10. *Boston News-Letter*, April 20, 1775.

11. *Essex Gazette*, April 25, 1775.

12. *Boston Evening-Post*, April 24, 1775.

13. Mary Farwell Ayer, *Check-List of Boston Newspapers, 1704–1780*, vol. 9 of *Publications of the Colonial Society of Massachusetts* (Boston, 1907), 11, 433.

14. Ayer, *Check-List of Boston Newspapers*, 449.

15. An American to Inhabitants of New York, April 28, 1775, *AA4*, 2:428.

16. An American to Inhabitants of New York, April 28, 1775, *AA4*, 2:428.

17. Committee of Safety to Several Towns of Massachusetts, April 28, 1775, *AA4*, 2:433.

18. This count of depositions and deponents (some of whom signed more than one affidavit) is from *Journals of the Provincial Congress of Massachusetts in 1774 and 1775, and of the Committee of Safety, with an Appendix* (Boston: Dutton and Wentworth, 1838), 661ff.

19. Committee of Safety to Derby, April 27, 1775, *Journals of the Provincial Congress*, 159.

20. Robert S. Rantoul, "The Cruise of the *Quero*," *Essex Institute Historical Collections* 36 (1900), 18–19; for confirmation of HMS *Lively* being on station, see also *Essex Gazette*, April 25, 1775.

21. Provincial Congress to Inhabitants of Great Britain, April 26, 1775, *Journals of the Provincial Congress*, 154–55.

22. Arthur B. Tourtellot, *Lexington and Concord: The Beginning of the War of the American Revolution* (New York: Norton, 1959), 232. This story became more gory and incredulous the further it spread. By the time Mercy Warren passed it on to Sarah Bowen, the wife of a Rhode Island rebel, Warren had it thirdhand from "a gentleman who conversed with the brother of a woman cut in pieces in her bed with her new born infant by her side." Taking the report at face value, Warren asked Bowen, "Are these the deeds of rationals?" See Nancy Rubin Stuart, *The Muse of the Revolution: The Secret Pen of Mercy Otis Warren and the Founding of a Nation* (Boston: Beacon Press, 2008), 74.

23. Provincial Congress to Franklin, April 26, 1775, *Journals of the Provincial Congress*, 153–54.

24. Peter Orlando Hutchinson, ed., *The Diary and Letters of His Excellency Thomas Hutchinson, Esq* (London: Sampson Low, Marston, Searle & Rivington, 1883), 455, entry dated May 29, 1775.

25. Rantoul, "Cruise of the *Quero*," 4.

26. Rantoul, "Cruise of the *Quero*," 6–7.

27. Hutchinson, *Diary and Letters of Thomas Hutchinson*, 464 (June 3 and 4, 1775).

28. Hutchinson to Gage, May 31, 1775, Hutchinson, *Diary and Letters of Thomas Hutchinson*, 456.

29. Dartmouth to Gage, June 1, 1775, Edwin Carter, ed., *The Correspondence of General Thomas Gage with the Secretaries of State, and with the War Office and the Treasury, 1763–1775* (Hamden, Conn.: Archon Books, 1969), 2:198.

30. Hutchinson, *Diary and Letters of Thomas Hutchinson*, 465, entry dated June 8, 1775.

31. Hutchinson, *Diary and Letters of Thomas Hutchinson*, 466, entry dated June 10, 1775.

32. Rantoul, "Cruise of the *Quero*," 13.

33. Dartmouth to Gage, July 1, 1775, *Correspondence of Gage*, 2:199–200.

34. Rantoul, "Cruise of the *Quero*," 23.

35. Burke to O'Hara, circa May 28, 1775, George H. Guttridge, *The Correspondence of Edmund Burke* (Cambridge: Cambridge University Press, 1961), 3:160.

Chapter 17—Must We Stand Alone?

1. Mercer et al. to Washington, April 25, 1775, *AA4*, 2:387.

2. John Pendleton Kennedy, ed., *Journals of the House of Burgesses of Virginia, 1773–1776* (Richmond, Va., 1905), 231.

3. Randolph to Page, Willis, and Grymes, April 27, 1775, Robert L. Scribner, ed., *Revolutionary Virginia: The Road to Independence*, vol. 3, *The Breaking Storm and the Third Convention, 1775: A Documentary Record* (Charlottesville: University Press of Virginia, 1977), 63–64.

4. Fredericksburg Committee Pledge, April 29, 1775, *Revolutionary Virginia*, 70–71.

5. Henry Mayer, *A Son of Thunder: Patrick Henry and the American Republic* (New York: Grove, 1991), 252.

6. Henry to Corbin, May 4, 1775, *Revolutionary Virginia*, 87–88; Mayer, *A Son of Thunder*, 254–57.

7. Dunmore proclamation, May 6, 1775, *Revolutionary Virginia*, 100–101.

8. Madison to Bradford, May 9, 1775, J. C. A. Stagg, ed., *The Papers of James Madison Digital Edition* (subscription only), Charlottesville: University of Virginia Press, Rotunda, 2010, congressional ser., 1, 144–45, http://rotunda .upress.virginia.edu/founders/JSMN-01-01-02-0044, accessed December 16, 2012.

9. Crozier to Rogers, April 23, 1775, Henry Steele Commager and Richard B. Morris, eds., *The Spirit of 'Seventy-Six: The Story of the American Revolution as Told by Participants* (New York: Harper & Row, 1958), 77–78.

10. *Journals of the Provincial Congress of Massachusetts in 1774 and 1775, and of the Committee of Safety, with an Appendix* (Boston: Dutton and Wentworth, 1838), 172–73, entry dated April 30, 1775.

11. Andrews to Barrell, May 6, 1775, "Letters of John Andrews, Esq. of Boston, 1772–1776," *Massachusetts Historical Society Proceedings* 8 (1864–65), 405–6. See, for example, the *Boston News-Letter* of May 19, 1775, reporting, "The Inhabitants of this Town continue daily to move out with their Effects, Merchandize, Ammunition and Provision excepted." Despite his attempts to escape Boston, John Andrews never succeeded in leaving. He was still in town when the British evacuated the city in March of 1776. Given that his motives were always more economic than political, he managed subsequently to embrace the rebel cause and was among those welcoming General George Washington.

12. For the Byles family, see Arthur Wentworth Hamilton Eaton, *The Famous Mather Byles* (Boston: W. A. Butterfield, 1914).

13. James H. Stark, "Samuel Quincy, Solicitor General," 8n, *The Loyalists of Massachusetts* (1910), http://www.robertsewell.ca/loyalmass.htm#_ftn8 .accessed August 30, 2012.

14. "made the best provision," Warren to Adams, May 7, 1775, H. C. Lodge, et al., eds., *Warren-Adams Letters, Being Chiefly a Correspondence among John Adams, Samuel Adams, and James Warren* (Boston: Massachusetts Historical

Society, 1917), 46; for Providence ride and migraines, see Nancy Rubin Stuart, *The Muse of the Revolution: The Secret Pen of Mercy Otis Warren and the Founding of a Nation* (Boston: Beacon Press, 2008), 73–74, 77.

15. J. Warren to M. Warren, May 18, 1775, *Warren-Adams Letters*, 49.

16. John W. Gordon, *South Carolina and the American Revolution: A Battlefield History* (Columbia: University of South Carolina Press, 2003), 19–20.

17. *South-Carolina and American General Gazette*, May 5, 1775.

18. *South-Carolina and American General Gazette*, May 12, 1775, quoting *Essex Gazette* of April 25, 1775.

19. J. William Harris, *The Hanging of Thomas Jeremiah: A Free Black Man's Encounter with Liberty* (New Haven, Conn.: Yale University Press, 2009), 84, 184n.

20. Harris, *Hanging of Thomas Jeremiah*, 86–87.

21. Harris, *Hanging of Thomas Jeremiah*, 84–86.

22. Harris, *Hanging of Thomas Jeremiah*, 93–94, 186n; *South-Carolina Gazette*, February 13, 1755, and May 7, 1756. The other recent biography of Jeremiah is William R. Ryan's *The World of Thomas Jeremiah: Charles Town on the Eve of the American Revolution* (Oxford: Oxford University Press, 2010).

23. Harris, *Hanging of Thomas Jeremiah*, 96.

24. Harris, *Hanging of Thomas Jeremiah*, 88.

25. Harris, *Hanging of Thomas Jeremiah*, 131, 134, 144.

26. Ryan, *The World of Thomas Jeremiah*, 157.

27. John Richard Alden, *General Gage in America: Being Principally a History of His Role in the American Revolution* (Baton Rouge: Louisiana State University Press, 1948), 228.

28. Gage to Caldwell, March 4, 1775, Alden, *General Gage in America*, 228.

29. Gage to Carleton, April 21, 1775, Allen French, *The First Year of the American Revolution* (Boston: Houghton Mifflin, 1934), 407.

Chapter 18 — "In the Name of the Great Jehovah…"

1. *Boston Gazette*, February 13, 1775.

2. Edward P. Hamilton, *Fort Ticonderoga: Key to a Continent* (Boston: Little, Brown, 1964), 103; Gage to Delaplace, March 8, 1775, in John Richard Alden, *General Gage in America: Being Principally a History of His Role in the American Revolution* (Baton Rouge: Louisiana State University Press, 1948), 228.

3. Adams to Lee, March 4, 1775, Harry Alonzo Cushing, ed., *The Writings of Samuel Adams* (New York: G. P. Putnam's Sons, 1907), 3:197; the committee's letter to Quebec, "begging you would be assured that we have our mutual Safety and Prosperity at heart," is at p. 182.

4. Archibald M. Howe, *Colonel John Brown, of Pittsfield, Massachusetts, The Brave Accuser of Benedict Arnold* (Boston: W. B. Clarke, 1908), 5–6.

5. Brown to Adams, March 29, 1775, at Fort Ticonderoga website, http://www.fortticonderoga.org/learn/re-enactors/1775-capture/re-enactor/brown, accessed June 7, 2012.

6. Willard Sterne Randall, *Ethan Allen: His Life and Times* (New York: Norton, 2011), 28.

7. Charles S. Hall, *Life and Letters of Samuel Holden Parsons* (Binghamton, N.Y.: Otseningo, 1905), 6, 8, 13, 19–21.

8. Parsons to Trumbull, April 26, 1775, in Hall, *Parsons*, 24.

9. "could not hold out," Arnold to committee of safety, April 30, 1775, *AA4*, 2:450; "first undertook," Hall, *Parsons*, 24.

10. Warren to McDougall, April 30, 1775, *AA4*, 2:450.

11. Hamilton, *Fort Ticonderoga*, 105.

12. For various versions of the crossing and the Arnold-Allen feud, see Hamilton, *Fort Ticonderoga*, 110–11; Willard Sterne Randall, *Benedict Arnold: Patriot and Traitor* (New York: William Morrow, 1990), 90–94; Randall, *Allen*, 306–9; and Page Smith, *A New Age Now Begins: A People's History of the American Revolution* (New York: McGraw-Hill, 1976), 588. Whether there was one scow or two and whether there was one or two crossings are matters of some dispute.

13. Ethan Allen, *A Narrative of Colonel Ethan Allen's Captivity* (Burlington, Vt.: H. Johnson, 1838), 17; Feltham to Gage, June 11, 1775, Henry Steele Commager and Richard B. Morris, eds., *The Spirit of 'Seventy-Six: The Story of the American Revolution as Told by Participants* (New York: Harper & Row, 1958), 101.

14. Allen to Massachusetts Congress, May 11, 1775, *AA4*, 2:556.

15. Arnold to Massachusetts Congress, May 11, 1775, *AA4*, 2:557.

16. Feltham to Gage, June 11, 1775, Commager, *Spirit of 'Seventy-Six*, 102.

17. Allen, *Narrative*, 19–22. Despite this account in his memoirs, Allen reported to the New York committee of safety on May 11: "Colonel Arnold entered the fortress with me side by side" (*AA4*, 2:606).

18. *JCC*, 2:55–56 (May 18, 1775).

19. Allen to Continental Congress, May 29, 1775, *AA4*, 2:732–33.

20. Arnold to Continental Congress, May 29, 1775, *AA4*, 2:734–35.

21. "equally surprised," Arnold to Massachusetts committee of safety, May 29, 1775, *AA4*, 2:735; "You may depend," Arnold to Massachusetts committee of safety, May 23, 1775, *AA4*, 2:694.

22. Randall, *Arnold*, 126–32.

23. Randall, *Allen*, 337–38.

Chapter 19—Ben Franklin Returns

1. For arrival, see *Pennsylvania Packet*, May 8, 1775, and *Pennsylvania Gazette*, May 10, 1775; delegate resolutions, *JCC*, 2:17–18, May 11, 1775.

2. *Essex Gazette*, May 12, 1775.

3. Walter Isaacson, *Benjamin Franklin: An American Life* (New York: Simon & Schuster, 2003), 292.

4. Bradford to Madison, June 2, 1775, J. C. A. Stagg, ed., *The Papers of James Madison Digital Edition* (subscription only), Charlottesville: University of Virginia Press, Rotunda, 2010, congressional ser., 1, 149, http://rotunda .upress.virginia.edu/founders/JSMN-01-01-02-0046, accessed December 16, 2012.

5. Madison to Bradford, June 19, 1775, Stagg, *James Madison Digital Edition*, 1, 151, http://rotunda.upress.virginia.edu/founders/JSMN-01-01-02-0048, accessed December 16, 2012.

6. Isaacson, *Benjamin Franklin*, 292–94, 546n.

7. T. H. Breen, *American Insurgents, American Patriots: The Revolution of the People* (New York: Hill and Wang, 2010), 132.

8. Thomas B. Allen, *Tories: Fighting for the King in America's First Civil War* (New York: Harper, 2010), 300–301; Beverly Baxter, "Grace Growden Galloway: Survival of a Loyalist, 1778–79," *Frontiers: A Journal of Women Studies* 3, no. 1 (spring 1978), 62–67.

9. Adams to Warren, February 10, 1777, Harry Alonzo Cushing, ed., *The Writings of Samuel Adams* (New York: G. P. Putnam's Sons, 1907), 3:355.

10. List of delegates and their credentials in *JCC*, 2:11–21, 44, 50.

11. *JCC*, 2:24, May 11, 1775, 44, May 13, 1775; one such printing appeared in the *Pennsylvania Packet*, May 15, 1775.

12. *JCC*, 2:25, May 11, 1775.

13. *JCC*, 2:52, May 15, 1775.

14. *JCC*, 2:59–60, May 25, 1775, 68–70, May 29, 1775.

15. J. Adams to A. Adams, May 29, 1775, L. H. Butterfield et al., eds., *Adams Family Correspondence*, vol. 1, *December 1761–May 1776* (Cambridge, Mass.: Belknap Press of Harvard University Press, 1963), 207.

16. *JCC*, 2:58–59, May 24, 1775. Randolph would return to Philadelphia later that fall, but he died suddenly on October 23, 1775, no doubt in part worn out from his hectic travel schedule.

17. Warren to Adams, May 26, 1775, Richard Frothingham, *Life and Times of Joseph Warren* (Boston: Little, Brown, 1865), 495.

18. *JCC*, 2:67, May 27, 1775; John Adams is among those who mentions Washington wearing his uniform (see J. Adams to A. Adams, May 29, 1775, above).

19. *JCC*, 2:73–74, May 31, 1775.

20. *JCC*, 2:79, June 3, 1775.

21. *JCC*, 2:78, June 2, 1775.

22. Church to Gage?, May 24, 1775, Allen French, *General Gage's Informers: New Material upon Lexington & Concord* (Ann Arbor: University of Michigan Press, 1932), 156–57.

23. Church to Gage?, May 24, 1775, French, *General Gage's Informers*, 157.

24. *JCC*, 2:80, June 3, 1775.

Chapter 20 — Lexington of the Seas

1. "Journal of His Majesty's Sloop *Falcon*, John Linzee, Commanding," *NDAR*, 1:311–12; *Massachusetts Spy*, May 24, 1775; "Nathaniel Freeman to the Massachusetts Provincial Congress," *NDAR*, 1:558–59; Kenneth Kellow, "Recapture of the *Falcon*'s Prizes: The First Naval Encounter of the War, 14 May 1775," American War of Independence at Sea, at http://www.awiatsea .com/incidents/14%20May%201775%20Recapture%20of%20Falcon's% 20Prizes.html#B000048T. For more information about the *Falcon* and its captain, see a contemporary reenactment site: https://sites.google.com/ site/hmsfalcon/about-us.

2. A. Adams to J. Adams, May 24, 1775, Charles Francis Adams, *Letters of Mrs. Adams, the Wife of John Adams* (Boston: Wilkins, Carter, 1848), 33.

3. "*New England Chronicle*, Thursday, May 25, 1775," *NDAR*, 1:522.

4. Barker diary, May 21, 1775, Elizabeth Ellery Dana, ed., *The British in Boston: Being the Diary of Lieutenant John Barker of the King's Own Regiment from November 15, 1774 to May 31, 1776; with Notes* (Cambridge, Mass.: Harvard University Press, 1924), 49.

5. Thomas Tracy Bouvé, et al., *History of the Town of Hingham, Massachusetts* (Cambridge: Cambridge University Press, 1893), 1:288; see also Christopher Klein, "A Forgotten Battle," PatriotLedger.com, May 17, 2008, http://www.patriotledger.com/opinions/x1880506383/A-FORGOT TEN-BATTLE#ixzz26wxvoZjc, accessed September 19, 2012.

6. Mellen Chamberlain, et al., *A Documentary History of Chelsea Including the Boston Precincts of Winnisimmet, Rumney Marsh, and Pullen Point, 1624–1824* (Boston: Massachusetts Historical Society, 1908), 431.

7. Chamberlain, *History of Chelsea*, 431.

8. "A Circumstantial Account of the Late Battle at Chelsea, Hog Island &c.," and "Report to the Massachusetts Committee of Safety of the Battle on Noddle's Island," *NDAR*, 1:544–46; animal count from Graves to Stephens, June 7, 1775, *NDAR*, 1:622–23.

9. Gage to Graves, May 25, 1775, and Graves's response to Gage of the same date, "at Night," *NDAR*, 1:523–24.

10. Graves to Stephens, June 7, 1775, *NDAR*, 1:622.

11. "Amos Farnsworth's Diary," *Proceedings of the Massachusetts Historical Society* 12 (1899), 80–81; "A Circumstantial Account," *NDAR*, 1:544–45.

12. Graves to Stephens, June 7, 1775, *NDAR*, 1:622–23, and "Report to the Massachusetts Committee of Safety," *NDAR*, 1:545–46.

13. Graves to Stephens, June 7, 1775, *NDAR*, 1:623. The National Park Service recently awarded Massachusetts a grant to help preserve the Chelsea Creek battle site and possibly find remnants of the *Diana* (*Boston Globe*, July 20, 2009). Losing his first ship did not affect the career of young Thomas Graves. He went on to become an admiral and serve as Nelson's second in command at the Battle of Copenhagen.

14. Graves communications, *NDAR*, 1:537–39.

15. "James Lyons, Chairman of the Machias Committee, to the Massachusetts Provincial Congress," June 14, 1775, *NDAR*, 1:676.

16. "Deposition of Jabez Cobb Regarding the Loss of the Schooner *Margaretta*," *NDAR*, 1:757–58.

17. "Pilot Nathaniel Godfrey's Report of Action between the Schooner Margueritta and the Rebels at Machias," *NDAR*, 1:655.

18. "Godfrey's Report," *NDAR*, 1:656.

19. "Godfrey's Report," *NDAR*, 1:656; "Lyons Report," *NDAR*, 1:677.

20. South Carolina and Georgia had their own "Lexington of the Seas" some weeks later. After hearing news of Lexington and Concord, the South Carolina Provincial Congress ordered a forty-man force of volunteers to take up positions on Daufuskie Island, off Hilton Head, where it could observe ship traffic in and out of Savannah via Tybee Roads—the area where the Savannah River meets the ocean. Savannah was then the capital of Georgia, and in addition to rumors of slave uprisings its rebels were anxious over reports that British officials were promoting unrest among the Cherokee and Catawba Indians. Consequently, when news got out about an expected cargo of gunpowder due to arrive on board the merchantman *Philippa*, South Carolinians teamed up with a band of Georgia rebels to intercept it. See Kenneth Kellow, "Capture of the *Philippa*: 10 July 1775," American War of Independence at Sea, http://www.awiatsea.com/incidents/10%20July%201775%20Capture%20of%20the%20Philippa.html, accessed January 17, 2013.

Chapter 21 — Three Generals and a Lady

1. Edward Barrington de Fonblanque, *Political and Military Episodes in the Latter Half of the Eighteenth Century, Derived from the Life and Correspondence of the*

Right Hon. John Burgoyne, General, Statesman, Dramatist (London: Macmillan, 1876), 119.

2. Allen French, *The First Year of the American Revolution* (Boston: Houghton Mifflin, 1934), 196.

3. French, *First Year*, 199.

4. Debate in House of Commons, May 20, 1774, *AA4*, 1:164.

5. French, *First Year*, 200–201. Major General Frederick Haldimand was also momentarily there as Gage's second in command.

6. French, *First Year*, 201.

7. French, *First Year*, 202.

8. French, *First Year*, 202.

9. Burgoyne to North, July 14, 1775, de Fonblanque, *Political and Military Episodes*, 138–39.

10. Gage proclamation, June 12, 1775, *AA4*, 2:968–69.

11. Gage proclamation, June 12, 1775, *AA4*, 2:969–70.

12. French, *First Year*, 205.

13. Germain to Suffolk, June 16 or 17, 1775, Henry Steele Commager and Richard B. Morris, eds., *The Spirit of 'Seventy-Six: The Story of the American Revolution as Told by Participants* (New York: Harper & Row, 1958), 119–20.

14. de Fonblanque, *Political and Military Episodes*, 116n4.

15. Elbridge Henry Goss, *The Life of Colonel Paul Revere* (Boston: Howard W. Spurr, 1906), 235.

16. Charles Ferris Gettemy, *The True Story of Paul Revere* (Boston: Little, Brown, 1905), 83; see entire discussion at pp. 81–91.

17. David Hackett Fischer, *Paul Revere's Ride* (New York: Oxford University Press, 1994), 387n13.

18. Peter Orlando Hutchinson, ed., *The Diary and Letters of His Excellency Thomas Hutchinson, Esq* (London: Sampson Low, Marston, Searle & Rivington, 1883), 476, entry dated June 24, 1775.

19. Fischer, *Paul Revere's Ride*, 290.

20. Darryl Lundy, "General Hon. Thomas Gage," The Peerage, http://the peerage.com/p2617.htm#i26163, accessed October 15, 2012; *Charming Nancy* crossing time, French, *First Year*, 323–24.

21. *Town and Country Magazine* 13 (1781), 233–36. An example of the magazine's usual editorial content is "Comparative View of Wives and Mistresses," on p. 29 of the same volume.

22. John Richard Alden, *General Gage in America: Being Principally a History of His Role in the American Revolution* (Baton Rouge: Louisiana State University Press, 1948), 293–94.

23. One of the strongest defenses of Margaret Gage is in John Alden's biography of her husband, *General Gage in America*, 248–50, although Alden repeats the gossip of *Town and Country Magazine*, 287–88. For J. L. Bell's usual rigor in these matters, see his posts in *Boston 1775* at http://boston1775.blogspot.com/search/label/Margaret%20Gage.

Chapter 22 — What Course Now, Gentlemen?

1. J. Adams to A. Adams, June 17, 1775, L. H. Butterfield et al., eds., *Adams Family Correspondence*, vol. 1, *December 1761–May 1776* (Cambridge, Mass.: Belknap Press of Harvard University Press, 1963), 216.

2. *JCC*, June 12, 1775, 2:87–88.

3. *JCC*, June 13–14, 1775, 2:89–90; "the most accurate Marksmen," J. Adams to A. Adams, June 17, 1775, *Adams Family Correspondence*, 215.

4. *JCC*, June 15, 1775, 2:91.

5. L. H. Butterfield, ed., *Diary & Autobiography of John Adams* (New York: Atheneum, 1964), 3:321–22.

6. Butterfield, *Diary & Autobiography*, 3:322.

7. Butterfield, *Diary & Autobiography*, 3:323. This account was written a quarter of a century after these events, after Washington's modesty had become a staple of American history.

8. Butterfield, *Diary & Autobiography*, 3:323.

9. *JCC*, June 15, 1775, 2:91.

10. Dyer to Trumbull, June 17, 1775, Edward C. Burnett, ed., *Letters of Members of the Continental Congress*, vol. 1, *August 29, 1774, to July 4, 1776* (Washington, D.C.: The Carnegie Institution of Washington, 1921), 127–28.

11. Hancock to Warren, June 18, 1775, *Letters of Members of the Continental Congress*, 134.

12. *JCC*, June 16, 1775, 2:92.

13. For the latter, see Walter R. Borneman, "Which Road to Fort Duquesne? Colonel Washington Proves 'Obstinate,'" *Western Pennsylvania History* 90 (summer 2007), 36–43.

14. *JCC*, June 16, 1775, 2:92.

15. Washington's commission, *JCC*, June 17, 1775, 2:96; G. Washington to M. Washington, June 18, 1775, The Papers of George Washington, "Documents," http://gwpapers.virginia.edu/documents/revolution/martha.html, accessed November 7, 2012.

16. *JCC*, June 16, 1775, 2:93–94; J. Adams to Gerry, June 18, 1775, *Letters of Delegates to the Continental Congress*, 135; Samuel H. Williamson, "Seven Ways to Compute the Relative Value of a U.S. Dollar Amount—1774 to

Present," MeasuringWorth.com, http://www.measuringworth.com/
uscompare/result.php?year_source=1775&amount=2000000&year
_result=2010, accessed November 14, 2012.

17. *JCC*, June 20, 1775, 2:100.

18. *Pennsylvania Gazette*, June 21, 1775.

19. Gary B. Nash, *The Unknown American Revolution: The Unruly Birth of Democracy and the Struggle to Create America* (New York: Viking, 2005), 121.

20. Records of the committee of safety, *The Journals of Each Provincial Congress of Massachusetts in 1774 and 1775, and of the Committee of Safety, with an Appendix* (Boston: Dutton and Wentworth, 1838), 553, entry dated May 20, 1775.

21. Nash, *Unknown American Revolution*, 156–57.

22. Nash, *Unknown American Revolution*, 157.

23. A. Adams to J. Adams, March 31, 1776, *Adams Family Correspondence*, 369–70.

24. J. Adams to A. Adams, April 14, 1776, *Adams Family Correspondence*, 382.

25. Adams to Sullivan, May 26, 1776, Robert J. Taylor, et al., eds., *Papers of John Adams*, vol. 4 of *The Adams Papers* (Cambridge, Mass.: Belknap Press of Harvard University Press, 1977), 211–12.

26. Thomas B. Allen, *Tories: Fighting for the King in America's First Civil War* (New York: Harper, 2010), 114.

27. Allen, *Tories*, 115.

28. James H. Stark, *The Loyalists of Massachusetts and the Other Side of the American Revolution* (Boston: W. B. Clarke, 1910), 458. The Robies were among those loyalists who returned to America after the Revolution, but Marblehead remembered Mary Robie's taunt, and she and her husband were forced to depart from their ship in Salem under the cover of darkness.

29. Howe to Harvey, June 12, 1775, Allen French, *The First Year of the American Revolution* (Boston: Houghton Mifflin, 1934), 207.

30. French, *First Year*, 20.

31. French, *First Year*, 19–21.

32. French, *First Year*, 30–31.

33. William Farrand Livingston, *Israel Putnam, Pioneer, Ranger, and Major-General, 1718–1790* (New York: G. P. Putnam's Sons, 1901), 200.

34. "Amos Farnsworth's Diary," *Proceedings of the Massachusetts Historical Society* 12 (1899), 79, entry dated May 11, 1775.

35. Barker diary, May 13, 1775, Elizabeth Ellery Dana, ed., *The British in Boston: Being the Diary of Lieutenant John Barker of the King's Own Regiment from November 15, 1774 to May 31, 1776; with Notes* (Cambridge, Mass.: Harvard University Press, 1924), 46–47.

36. J. Warren to M. Warren, May 18, 1775, H. C. Lodge, et al., eds., *Warren-Adams Letters, Being Chiefly a Correspondence among John Adams, Samuel Adams, and James Warren* (Boston: Massachusetts Historical Society, 1917), 50.

37. "Why a situation," C[harles]. Stedman, *The History of the Origin, Progress, and Termination of the American War* (London, 1794), 125; "my two colleagues," Burgoyne to Stanley, June 25, 1775, *AA4*, 2:1094.

38. W. Howe to R. Howe, June 12, 1775, French, *First Year*, 208.

39. New Hampshire committee of safety to Massachusetts Provincial Congress, June 13, 1775, *AA4*, 2:979.

40. Massachusetts committee of safety, June 13, 1775, *AA4*, 2:1352.

41. Gilman to New Hampshire committee of safety, June 16, 1775, *AA4*, 2:1013.

42. Willard Sterne Randall, *Ethan Allen: His Life and Times* (New York: Norton, 2011), 333.

43. Report of Joint Committee, May 12, 1775, *AA4*, 2:755. Dr. Benjamin Church signed for the committee of safety.

44. Richard Frothingham, *The Life and Times of Joseph Warren* (Boston: Little, Brown, 1865), 505; Richard Frothingham, *History of the Siege of Boston, and of the Battles of Lexington, Concord, and Bunker Hill* (Boston: Charles C. Little and James Brown, 1849), 116.

45. *Journals of Each Provincial Congress*, June 15, 1775, 334; Massachusetts Committee of Safety, June 15, 1775, *AA4*, 2:1354.

46. Charles Martyn, *The Life of Artemas Ward: The First Commander-in-Chief of the American Revolution* (New York: Artemas Ward, 1921), 120; French, *First Year*, 214, doubts Ward's personal visit.

47. Martyn, *Ward*, 122–23.

48. P. Brown to S. Brown, June 25, 1775, Massachusetts Historical Society, "The Coming of the American Revolution," https://www.masshist.org/revolution/image-viewer.php?item_id=725&img_step=1&tpc=&pid=2&mode=transcript&tpc=&pid=2#page1, accessed October 26, 2012.

Chapter 23—"The White of Their Gaiters"

1. Richard Frothingham, *History of the Siege of Boston, and of the Battles of Lexington, Concord, and Bunker Hill* (Boston: Charles C. Little and James Brown, 1849), 119–20.

2. Allen French, *The First Year of the American Revolution* (Boston: Houghton Mifflin, 1934), 215.

3. French, *First Year*, 215–16.

4. French, *First Year*, 209–10.

5. Howe to [? Adjutant-General], June 22 and 24, 1775, Sir John Fortescue, ed., *The Correspondence of King George the Third, from 1760 to December 1783*, vol. 3, *July 1773 to December 1777* (London: Frank Cass, 1967), 221.

6. "Journal of His Majesty's Ship Lively, Captain Thomas Bishop, Commanding," *NDAR*, 1:700.

7. French, *First Year*, 220.

8. French, *First Year*, 217.

9. P. Brown to S. Brown, June 25, 1775, Massachusetts Historical Society, "The Coming of the American Revolution," https://www.masshist.org/revolution/image-viewer.php?item_id=725&mode=transcript&img_step=2&tpc=#page2, accessed October 26, 2012.

10. P. Brown to S. Brown, p. 2.

11. French, *First Year*, 217–18.

12. Burgoyne to Stanley, June 25, 1775, *AA4*, 2:1094–95.

13. Paul Lockhart, *The Whites of Their Eyes: Bunker Hill, the First American Army, and the Emergence of George Washington* (New York: Harper, 2011), 211–13.

14. French, *First Year*, 221; Lockhart, *Whites of Their Eyes*, 212, maintains Clinton's plan was from the Mystic side.

15. W. Howe to R. Howe, June 22, 1775, Great Britain Historical Manuscripts Commission, *Report on the Manuscripts of Mrs. Stopford-Sackville, of Drayton House, Northhamptonshire*, vol. 2 (Boston: Gregg Press, 1972), 4, http://books.google.com/books?id=X9JRQTECDuYC&pg=PP6&lpg=PP6&dq=stopford-sackville+papers+report+2&source=bl&ots=zDOp1M8LQZ&sig=EZkE7ASTv3DfVi2I1MooQB7WfAk&hl=en&sa=X&ei=28KrUK2wAcOzywGooIDgCA&ved=0CC4Q6AewAA.

16. French, *First Year*, 222. Howe's infantry might well have splashed ashore and gotten their gaiters wet at less than high tide, but the high tide was essential to landing Howe's few pieces of artillery.

17. "General Morning Orders, Saturday, June 17th 1775," French, *First Year*, 740.

18. Lorenzo Sabine, *The American Loyalists, or Biographical Sketches of Adherents to the British Crown in the War of the Revolution* (Boston: Charles C. Little and James Brown, 1847), 706.

19. *The Journals of Each Provincial Congress of Massachusetts in 1774 and 1775, and of the Committee of Safety, with an Appendix* (Boston: Dutton and Wentworth, 1838), 333, entry dated June 14, 1775.

20. Warren to S. Adams, May 26, 1775, Richard Frothingham, *The Life and Times of Joseph Warren* (Boston: Little, Brown, 1865), 495.

21. There are a number of sources for these events—some conflicting—but this summary is generally from Frothingham, *Life of Warren*, 509–15.

22. Percy to Northumberland, June 19, 1775, Charles Knowles Bolton, ed., *Letters of Hugh Earl Percy from Boston and New York 1774–1776* (Boston: Charles E. Goodspeed, 1902), 57; John Richard Alden, *General Gage in America: Being Principally a History of His Role in the American Revolution* (Baton Rouge: Louisiana State University Press, 1948), 267–68.

23. French, *First Year*, 223–24.

24. W. Howe to R. Howe, June 22, 1775, *Stopford-Sackville Manuscripts*, 2:4.

25. W. Howe to R. Howe, June 22, 1775, *Stopford-Sackville Manuscripts*, 2:4.

26. "An Account of the Battle of Bunker's Hill, by Major General Henry Dearborn," in Charles Coffin, ed., *History of the Battle of Breed's Hill* (Saco, Maine: William J. Condon, 1831), 18.

27. "Dearborn Memoir," Coffin, *History of the Battle of Bunker's Hill*, 18–19.

28. French, *First Year*, 227.

29. French, *First Year*, 230.

30. "Narrative of Vice Admiral Samuel Graves," June 17, 1775, *NDAR*, 1:704; see also French, *First Year*, 742–43.

31. W. Howe to R. Howe, June 22, 1775, *Stopford-Sackville Manuscripts*, 2:4.

32. W. Howe to R. Howe, June 22, 1775, *Stopford-Sackville Manuscripts*, 2:4.

33. P. Brown to S. Brown, 2–3.

34. Massachusetts Provincial Congress Minutes, June 23, 1775, *AA4*, 2:1438.

35. French, *First Year*, 235n8.

36. W. Howe to R. Howe, June 22, 1775, *Stopford-Sackville Manuscripts*, 2:4.

37. French, *First Year*, 234.

38. Massachusetts Provincial Congress, Committee of Safety Report, July 25, 1775, *AA4*, 2:1374.

39. Burgoyne to Stanley, June 25, 1775, *AA4*, 2:1095.

40. Coffin, *History of the Battle of Breed's Hill*, 12; Lloyd A. Brown and Howard H. Peckham, eds., *Revolutionary War Journals of Henry Dearborn, 1775–1783* (Chicago: Caxton Club, 1939), 5–6.

Chapter 24 — "A Dear Bought Victory"

1. Burgoyne to Stanley, June 25, 1775, *AA4*, 2:1095.

2. Allen French, *The First Year of the American Revolution* (Boston: Houghton Mifflin, 1934), 233.

3. French, *First Year*, 237.

4. *Rivington's New-York Gazetteer*, August 3, 1775.

5. Howe to [? Adjutant-General], June 22 and 24, 1775, Sir John Fortescue, ed., *The Correspondence of King George the Third, from 1760 to December 1783*, vol. 3, *July 1773 to December 1777* (London: Frank Cass, 1967), 222.

6. French, *First Year*, 238–39.

7. French, *First Year*, 242n.

8. French, *First Year*, 243.

9. French, *First Year*, 246.

10. In Ward's defense, see Charles Martyn's highly pro-Ward biography, particularly p. 131, as to dispatching troops, as well as French, *First Year*, 246.

11. Chester to Fish, July 22, 1775, Richard Frothingham, *History of the Siege of Boston, and of the Battles of Lexington, Concord, and Bunker Hill* (Boston: Charles C. Little and James Brown, 1849), 391.

12. Isaac J. Greenwood, ed., *The Revolutionary Services of John Greenwood of Boston and New York, 1775–1783* (New York: De Vinne Press, 1922), 12–13.

13. French, *First Year*, 242.

14. Prescott to Adams, August 25, 1775, Massachusetts Historical Society, "'The Decisive Day Is Come': The Battle of Bunker Hill," http://www.masshist.org/bh/prescott.html.

15. Waller to friend, June 21, 1775, Massachusetts Historical Society, http://www.masshist.org/bh/wallerp2text.html; for one account of Peter Salem, see J. H. Temple, *History of Framingham, Massachusetts* (Framingham, Mass.: Town of Framingham, 1887), 324–25.

16. French, *First Year*, 250.

17. French, *First Year*, 247.

18. Waller to friend, June 21, 1775.

19. C[harles]. Stedman, *The History of the Origin, Progress, and Termination of the American War* (London, 1794), 127.

20. W. Howe to R. Howe, June 22, 1775, Great Britain Historical Manuscripts Commission, *Report on the Manuscripts of Mrs. Stopford-Sackville, of Drayton House, Northhamptonshire*, vol. 2 (Boston: Gregg Press, 1972), 5, http://books.google.com/books?id=X9JRQTECDuYC&pg=PP6&lpg=PP6&dq=stopford-sackville+papers+report+2&source=bl&ots=zDOp1M8LQZ&sig=EZkE7ASTv3DfVi2I1MooQB7WfAk&hl=en&sa=X&ei=28KrUK2wAcOzywGooIDgCA&ved=0CC4Q6AewAA.

21. P. Brown to S. Brown, June 25, 1775, Massachusetts Historical Society, "The Coming of the American Revolution," https://www.masshist.org/revolution/image-viewer.php?item_id=725&mode=transcript&img_step=3&tpc=#page3, accessed October 26, 2012, pp. 3–4.

22. Chester to Fish, July 22, 1775, Frothingham, *Siege of Boston*, 291; Webb to Webb, June 19, 1775, Worthington Chauncey Ford, ed., *Correspondence and Journals of Samuel Blachley Webb*, vol. 1, *1772–1777* (Lancaster, Pa.: Wickersham Press, 1893), 64.

23. French, *First Year*, 251–52.

24. French, *First Year*, 253.

25. French, *First Year*, 253.

26. Letter from Boston to Scotland, June 25, 1775, *AA4*, 2:1094.

27. "Dearborn Memoir," Charles Coffin, ed., *History of the Battle of Breed's Hill* (Saco, Maine: William J. Condon, 1831), 22.

28. French, *First Year*, 255.

29. French, *First Year*, 254.

30. For a British historian's perspective on British mistakes, see Stedman, *Origin, Progress, and Termination of the American War*, 128–29.

31. French, *First Year*, 256–57. That Howe was stunned by these losses and never recovered emotionally as a military leader is a theory that grew after he abandoned Boston and after his hesitant performances at the battles of Long Island and White Plains. Nonetheless, Howe managed to best George Washington at Brandywine and Germantown and capture Philadelphia before resigning his command. For different recent interpretations of the influence of the Battle of Bunker Hill on Howe's subsequent career, see James L. Nelson, *With Fire and Sword: The Battle of Bunker Hill and the Beginning of the American Revolution* (New York: St. Martin's, 2011), and Paul Lockhart, *The Whites of Their Eyes: Bunker Hill, the First American Army, and the Emergence of George Washington* (New York: Harper, 2011).

32. Ann Hulton, June 20, 1775, Henry Steele Commager and Richard B. Morris, eds., *The Spirit of 'Seventy-Six: The Story of the American Revolution as Told by Participants* (New York: Harper & Row, 1958), 137.

33. Jeremy Lister, *Concord Fight, Being So Much of the Narrative of Ensign Jeremy Lister of the 10th Regiment of Foot as Pertains to His Services on the 19th of April, 1775, and to His Experiences in Boston during the Early Months of the Siege* (Cambridge, Mass.: Harvard University Press, 1931), 43.

34. Richard M. Ketchum, *Decisive Day: The Battle for Bunker Hill* (Garden City, New York: Doubleday, 1962), 193.

35. N. Greene to J. Greene, June 28, 1775, *AA4*, 2:1126.

36. Ketchum, *Decisive Day*, 199.

37. J. Warren to M. Warren, June 18, 1775, H. C. Lodge, et al., eds., *Warren-Adams Letters, Being Chiefly a Correspondence among John Adams, Samuel Adams, and James Warren* (Boston: Massachusetts Historical Society, 1917), 59–60.

38. G[ideon]. D[elaplaine]. Scull, ed., *Memoir and Letters of Captain W. Glanville Evelyn, of the 4th Regiment, ("King's Own,"), from North America, 1774–1776* (Oxford: James Parker, 1879), 71.

39. W. Howe to R. Howe, June 22, 1775, *Stopford-Sackville Manuscripts*, 2:5.

40. Burgoyne to Germain, August 20, 1775, *Stopford-Sackville Manuscripts*, 2:6–7.

41. Gage to Dartmouth (no. 33), June 25, 1775, Clarence Edwin Carter, ed., *The Correspondence of General Thomas Gage with the Secretaries of State, and with the War Office and the Treasury, 1763–1775* (Hamden, Conn.: Archon Books, 1969), 1:406.

42. Gage to Dartmouth (private), June 25, 1775, *Correspondence of Gage*, 1:406–7.

43. Gage to Barrington, June 26, 1775, *Correspondence of Gage*, 2:686–87.

44. John Richard Alden, *General Gage in America: Being Principally a History of His Role in the American Revolution* (Baton Rouge: Louisiana State University Press, 1948), 283.

Epilogue — Monday, July 3, 1775

1. *JCC*, June 27, 1775, 2:109–10.

2. George III to Sandwich, July 1, 1775, G. R. Barnes and J. H. Owen, eds., *The Private Papers of John, Earl of Sandwich, First Lord of the Admiralty, 1771–1782* (London: Naval Records Society, 1932),1:63.

3. Bradford to Madison, July 18, 1775, J. C. A. Stagg, ed., *The Papers of James Madison Digital Edition* (subscription only), Charlottesville: University of Virginia Press, Rotunda, 2010, congressional ser., 1, 157, http://rotunda .upress.virginia.edu/founders/JSMN-01-01-02-0049, accessed December 18, 2012.

4. Mercy [Otis] Warren, *History of the Rise, Progress and Termination of the American Revolution* (Boston: E. Larkin, 1805), 3:392.

5. S. Ward to H. Ward, October 11, 1775, Henry Steele Commager and Richard B. Morris, eds., *The Spirit of 'Seventy-Six: The Story of the American Revolution as Told by Participants* (New York: Harper & Row, 1958), 736.

6. *The Journals of Each Provincial Congress of Massachusetts in 1774 and 1775, and of the Committee of Safety, with an Appendix* (Boston: Dutton and Wentworth, 1838), 439, entry dated July 1, 1775.

7. Reports of Washington's arrival in Cambridge and assuming command the next day are sketchy and frequently coated with the hyperbole of hindsight. This description is based on analysis in Charles Martyn, *The Life of Artemas Ward: The First Commander-in-Chief of the American Revolution* (New York: Artemas Ward, 1921), 150–51, and Paul Lockhart, *The Whites of Their Eyes: Bunker Hill, the First American Army, and the Emergence of George Washington* (New York: Harper, 2011), 331–32.

BIBLIOGRAPHY

~

Abbreviations

AA4—*American Archives, fourth series.* Edited and compiled by Peter Force (1790–1868), the *American Archives*, comprising six series, were originally published under an act of Congress in 1833. The fourth series, itself consisting of four volumes, is subtitled *Containing a Documentary History of the English Colonies in North America, from the King's Message to Parliament, of March 7, 1774, to the Declaration of Independence by the United States.* Accessed online at http://dig.lib.niu.edu/amarch/contents.php.

Franklin Papers—The papers of Benjamin Franklin as collected and edited by scholars at Yale University and digitized by the Packard Humanities Institute, accessed at http://www.franklinpapers.org.

JCC—*Journals of the Continental Congress,* accessed online at http://memory.loc.gov/ammem/amlaw/lwjclink.html#vol.

NDAR—*Naval Documents of the American Revolution,* originally published by the United States Government Printing Office in 1964 and electronically published by the American Naval Records Society of Bolton Landing, New York, in 2012. Accessed online at www.navalrecords.org.

Works of John Adams—John Adams, *The Works of John Adams, Second President of the United States: with a Life of the Author, Notes and Illustrations, by His Grandson Charles Francis Adams* (Boston: Little, Brown and Co., 1856). 10 volumes. Accessed from http://oll.libertyfund.org/title/2098 and not to be confused with *The Papers of John Adams.*

Diaries, Correspondence, and Personal Papers and Reminiscences

Adams, Charles Francis. *Letters of Mrs. Adams, the Wife of John Adams* (Boston: Wilkins, Carter, 1848).

Adams, Josiah. *Letter to Lemuel Shattuck, Esq. of Boston* (Boston: Damrell & Moore, 1850).

Allen, Ethan. *A Narrative of Colonel Ethan Allen's Captivity* (Burlington, Vt.: H. Johnson, 1838).

Bailyn, Bernard, ed. *Pamphlets of the American Revolution, 1750–1776*. Vol. 1, *1750–1765* (Cambridge, Mass.: Belknap Press of Harvard University Press, 1965).

Barnes, G. R., and J. H. Owen, eds. *The Private Papers of John, Earl of Sandwich, First Lord of the Admiralty, 1771–1782* (London: Naval Records Society, 1932).

Bernard, Francis. *Select Letters on the Trade and Government of America* (London: Bowyer and Nichols, 1774).

Bolton, Charles Knowles, ed. *Letters of Hugh Earl Percy from Boston and New York, 1774–1776* (Boston: Charles E. Goodspeed, 1902).

Brown, Lloyd A., and Howard H. Peckham, eds. *Revolutionary War Journals of Henry Dearborn, 1775–1783* (Chicago: Caxton Club, 1939).

Butterfield, L. H., et al., eds. *Adams Family Correspondence*. Vol. 1, *December 1761–May 1776* (Cambridge, Mass.: Belknap Press of Harvard University Press, 1963).

Butterfield, L. H., ed. *Diary & Autobiography of John Adams*, 4 vols. (New York: Atheneum, 1964).

Carter, Clarence Edwin, ed. *The Correspondence of General Thomas Gage with the Secretaries of State, and with the War Office and the Treasury, 1763–1775*, 2 vols. (Hamden, Conn.: Archon Books, 1969).

Clarke, Jonas. *Opening of the War of the Revolution, 19th of April 1775, A Brief Narrative of the Principal Transactions of That Day* (Lexington, Mass.: Lexington Historical Society, 1901).

Clinton, Henry. *Observations on Mr. Stedman's History of the American War* (London: J. Debrett, 1794).

Cushing, Harry Alonzo, ed. *The Writings of Samuel Adams* (New York: G. P. Putnam's Sons, 1907).

Dana, Elizabeth Ellery, ed. *The British in Boston: Being the Diary of Lieutenant John Barker of the King's Own Regiment from November 15, 1774 to May 31, 1776; with Notes* (Cambridge, Mass.: Harvard University Press, 1924).

de Fonblanque, Edward Barrington. *Political and Military Episodes in the Latter Half of the Eighteenth Century, Derived from the Life and Correspondence of the Right Hon. John Burgoyne, General, Statesman, Dramatist* (London: Macmillan, 1876).

Documents and Records Relating to the Province of New-Hampshire from 1764 to 1776 (Nashua, N.H.: Green C. Moore, State Printer, 1873).

Donne, W. Bodham, ed. *The Correspondence of King George the Third with Lord North, 1768 to 1783* (London: John Murray, 1867).

Elofson, W. M., and John A. Woods, eds. *The Writings and Speeches of Edmund Burke*. Vol. 3, *Party, Parliament, and the American War, 1774–1780* (Oxford: Clarendon Press, 1996).

Emerson, Amelia Forbes, ed. *Diaries and Letters of William Emerson, 1743–1776* (Boston: Thomas Todd, 1972).

Farmer, A. W. [Samuel Seabury]. *The Congress Canvassed: Or, an Examination into the Conduct of the Delegates, at the Grand Convention Held in Philadelphia, Sept. 1, 1774* (London: Richardson and Urquhart, 1775).

Ford, Worthington Chauncey, ed. *Correspondence and Journals of Samuel Blachley Webb*. Vol. 1, *1772–1777* (Lancaster, Pa: Wickersham Press, 1893).

Fortescue, Sir John, ed. *The Correspondence of King George the Third, from 1760 to December 1783*. Vol. 3, *July 1773 to December 1777* (London: Frank Cass, 1967).

[Gray, Harrison]. *A Few Remarks upon Some of the Votes and Resolutions of the Continental Congress and the Provincial Congress Held at Cambridge in November 1774* (Boston, 1775).

Guttridge, George H., ed. *The Correspondence of Edmund Burke*, Vol. 3 (Cambridge: Cambridge University Press, 1961).

Hall, Charles S. *Life and Letters of Samuel Holden Parsons* (Binghamton, N.Y.: Otseningo, 1905).

Heath, William. *Memoirs of Major-General William Heath* (New York: William Abbatt, 1901).

Hosmer, Jerome Carter, ed. *The Narrative of General Gage's Spies* (Boston: Bostonian Society, 1912).

Hutchinson, Peter Orlando, ed. *The Diary and Letters of His Excellency Thomas Hutchinson, Esq* (London: Sampson Low, Marston, Searle & Rivington, 1883).

Jackson, Donald, and Dorothy Twohig, eds. *The Diaries of George Washington*. Vol. 3, *1771–75, 1780–81* (Charlottesville: University Press of Virginia, 1978).

Jensen, Merrill, ed. *English Historical Documents: American Colonial Documents to 1776*, vol. 9 (London: Eyre & Spottiswoode, 1955).

Kennedy, John Pendleton, ed. *Journals of the House of Burgesses of Virginia, 1773–1776* (Richmond, Va., 1905).

Lister, Jeremy. *Concord Fight, Being So Much of the Narrative of Ensign Jeremy Lister of the 10th Regiment of Foot as Pertains to His Services on the 19th of April, 1775, and to His Experiences in Boston during the Early Months of the Siege* (Cambridge, Mass.: Harvard University Press, 1931).

Lodge, H. C., et al., eds. *Warren-Adams Letters, Being Chiefly a Correspondence among John Adams, Samuel Adams, and James Warren* (Boston: Massachusetts Historical Society, 1917).

Mackenzie, Frederick. *Diary of Frederick Mackenzie* (Cambridge, Mass.: Harvard University Press, 1930).

Mason, Bernard, ed. *The American Colonial Crisis: The Daniel Leonard–John Adams Letters to the Press, 1774–1775* (New York: Harper & Row, 1972).

Massachusetts Provincial Congress. *The Journals of Each Provincial Congress of Massachusetts in 1774 and 1775, and of the Committee of Safety, with an Appendix* (Boston: Dutton and Wentworth, 1838).

New-York Historical Society. "The Kemble Papers" in *Collections of the New-York Historical Society for the Year 1883* (New York: New-York Historical Society, 1884).

Niles, H[ezekiah]., ed. *Principles and Acts of the Revolution in America* (Baltimore: W. O. Niles, 1822).

Parliament of Great Britain. *The Parliamentary History of England*, Vols. 17 and 18, *from the Earliest Period to the Year 1803* (London: T. C. Hansard, 1813).

Phinney, Elias. *History of the Battle at Lexington, on the Morning of the 19th April, 1775* (Boston: Phelps and Farnham, 1825).

Quincy, Josiah. *Memoir of the Life of Josiah Quincy Jun.* (Boston: Cummings, Hilliard, 1825).

Ricord, Frederick W., and William Nelson, eds. *Documents Relating to the Colonial History of the State of New Jersey*. Vol. 10, *Administration of Governor William Franklin, 1767–1776* (Newark, N.J.: Daily Advertiser Printing House, 1886).

Ripley, Ezra. *A History of the Fight at Concord, 19th of April, 1775* (Concord, Mass.: Allen & Atwell, 1827).

Scribner, Robert L., ed. *Revolutionary Virginia: The Road to Independence*. Vol. 3, *The Breaking Storm and the Third Convention, 1775: A Documentary Record* (Charlottesville: University Press of Virginia, 1977).

Scull, G[ideon]. D[elaplaine]., ed. *Memoir and Letters of Captain W. Glanville Evelyn, of the 4th Regiment, ("King's Own,"), from North America, 1774–1776* (Oxford: James Parker, 1879).

Sparks, Jared, ed. *The Writings of George Washington* (Boston: Charles Tappan, 1846).

Sutherland, William, and Richard Pope. *Late News of the Excursion and Ravages of the King's Troops on the Nineteenth of April, 1775* (Cambridge, Mass.: Harvard College, 1927).

Taylor, Robert J., et al., eds. *Papers of John Adams*. Vol. 4 of *The Adams Papers* (Cambridge, Mass.: Belknap Press of Harvard University Press, 1977).

True, Henry. *Journal and Letters of Rev. Henry True, of Hampstead, New Hampshire: Also an Account of the Battle of Concord by Captain Amos Barrett, a Minute Man and Participant* (Marion, Ohio, 1900).

Viator [pseud.]. *The Thoughts of a Traveller upon our American Disputes* (London: J. Ridley, 1774).

Willard, Margaret Wheeler, ed. *Letters on the American Revolution, 1774–1776* (Boston: Houghton Mifflin, 1925).

Willcox, William B., ed. *The American Revolution: Sir Henry Clinton's Narrative of His Campaigns, 1775–1782* (New Haven, Conn.: Yale University Press, 1954).

Willcox, William B., et al., eds. *The Papers of Benjamin Franklin.* Vol. 21, *January 1, 1774, through March 22, 1775* (New Haven, Conn.: Yale University Press, 1978).

Secondary Sources

Alden, John Richard. *General Gage in America: Being Principally a History of His Role in the American Revolution* (Baton Rouge: Louisiana State University Press, 1948).

Allen, Thomas B. *Tories: Fighting for the King in America's First Civil War* (New York: Harper, 2010).

Ayer, Mary Farwell. *Check-List of Boston Newspapers, 1704–1780.* Vol. 9 of *Publications of the Colonial Society of Massachusetts* (Boston, 1907).

Baxter, W. T. *The House of Hancock: Business in Boston, 1724–1775* (Cambridge, Mass.: Harvard University Press, 1945).

Borneman, Walter R. *The French and Indian War: Deciding the Fate of North America* (New York: HarperCollins, 2006).

Boudinot, Elias. *Journal of Events in the Revolution* (Trenton, N.J.: Traver, 1899).

Bouvé, Thomas Tracy, et al. *History of the Town of Hingham, Massachusetts,* Vol. 1 (Cambridge: Cambridge University Press, 1893).

Bradley, Patricia. *Slavery, Propaganda, and the American Revolution* (Jackson: University Press of Mississippi, 1998).

Breen, T. H. *American Insurgents, American Patriots: The Revolution of the People* (New York: Hill and Wang, 2010).

Burns, Eric. *Infamous Scribblers: The Founding Fathers and the Rowdy Beginnings of American Journalism* (New York: Public Affairs, 2006).

Calloway, Colin G. *The American Revolution in Indian Country: Crisis and Diversity in Native American Communities* (Cambridge: Cambridge University Press, 1995).

Chamberlain, Mellen, et al. *A Documentary History of Chelsea Including the Boston Precincts of Winnisimmet, Rumney Marsh, and Pullen Point, 1624–1824* (Boston: Massachusetts Historical Society, 1908).

Chase, Ellen. *The Beginnings of the American Revolution,* Vol. 3 (New York: Baker and Taylor, 1910).

Coburn, Frank Warren. *The Battle of April 19, 1775 in Lexington, Concord, Lincoln, Arlington, Cambridge, Somerville and Charlestown Massachusetts* (Lexington, Mass.: Lexington Historical Society, 1922).

Coffin, Charles, ed. *History of the Battle of Breed's Hill* (Saco, Maine: William J. Condon, 1831).

Cohen, Eliot A. *Conquered into Liberty: Two Centuries of Battles along the Great Warpath That Made the American Way of War* (New York: Free Press, 2011).

Commager, Henry Steele, and Richard B. Morris, eds. *The Spirit of 'Seventy-Six: The Story of the American Revolution as Told by Participants* (New York: Harper & Row, 1958).

Davies, Kate. *Catharine Macaulay and Mercy Otis Warren: The Revolutionary Atlantic and the Politics of Gender* (London: Oxford University Press, 2005).

The Detail and Conduct of the American War under Generals Gage, Howe, Burgoyne, and Vice Admiral Lord Howe (London: Richardson and Urquhart, 1780).

Eaton, Arthur Wentworth Hamilton. *The Famous Mather Byles* (Boston: W. A. Butterfield, 1914).

Ellet, Elizabeth F. *The Women of the American Revolution* (New York: Baker & Scribner, 1849).

Ferling, John. *A Leap in the Dark: The Struggle to Create the American Republic* (New York: Oxford University Press, 2003).

Fischer, David Hackett. *Paul Revere's Ride* (New York: Oxford University Press, 1994).

Fleming, Thomas. *The First Stroke: Lexington, Concord, and the Beginning of the American Revolution* (Washington, D.C.: National Park Service, 1978).

————. *Liberty! The American Revolution* (New York: Viking, 1997).

Forman, Samuel A. *Dr. Joseph Warren: The Boston Tea Party, Bunker Hill, and the Birth of American Liberty* (Gretna, La.: Pelican Publishing, 2011).

Fowler, William M., Jr. *The Baron of Beacon Hill: A Biography of John Hancock* (Boston: Houghton Mifflin, 1980).

————. *Samuel Adams: Radical Puritan* (New York: Longman, 1997).

French, Allen. *The Day of Concord and Lexington: The Nineteenth of April, 1775* (Boston: Little, Brown, 1925).

————. *The First Year of the American Revolution* (Boston: Houghton Mifflin, 1934).

————. *General Gage's Informers: New Material upon Lexington & Concord* (Ann Arbor: University of Michigan Press, 1932).

————. *Historic Concord & the Lexington Fight* (Ipswich, Conn.: Gambit, 1978).

Frey, Sylvia R. *Water from the Rock: Black Resistance in a Revolutionary Age* (Princeton, N.J.: Princeton University Press, 1991).

Frothingham, Richard. *History of the Siege of Boston, and of the Battles of Lexington, Concord, and Bunker Hill* (Boston: Charles C. Little and James Brown, 1849).

————. *Life and Times of Joseph Warren* (Boston: Little, Brown, 1865).

Galvin, John R. *The Minute Men: The First Fight: Myths and Realities of the American Revolution* (Washington, D.C.: Brassey's, 1996).

Garraty, John A. *The American Nation* (New York: Harper & Row, 1966).

Gettemy, Charles Ferris. *The True Story of Paul Revere* (Boston: Little, Brown, 1905).

Gilbert, Alan. *Black Patriots and Loyalists: Fighting for Emancipation in the War for Independence* (Chicago: University of Chicago Press, 2012).

Gordon, John W. *South Carolina and the American Revolution: A Battlefield History* (Columbia: University of South Carolina Press, 2003).

Gordon, William. *The History of the Rise, Progress, and Establishment, of the Independence of the United States of America: Including an Account of the Late War; and of the Thirteen Colonies, from Their Origin to That Period* (London, 1788).

Goss, Elbridge Henry. *The Life of Colonel Paul Revere* (Boston: Howard W. Spurr, 1906).

Greenwood, Isaac J., ed. *The Revolutionary Services of John Greenwood of Boston and New York, 1775–1783* (New York: De Vinne Press, 1922).

Hamilton, Edward P. *Fort Ticonderoga: Key to a Continent* (Boston: Little, Brown, 1964).

Harris, J. William. *The Hanging of Thomas Jeremiah: A Free Black Man's Encounter with Liberty* (New Haven, Conn.: Yale University Press, 2009).

Hinkle, Alice M. *Prince Estabrook: Slave and Soldier* (Lexington, Mass.: Pleasant Mountain Press, 2001).

Howe, Archibald M. *Colonel John Brown, of Pittsfield, Massachusetts, The Brave Accuser of Benedict Arnold* (Boston: W. B. Clarke, 1908).

Isaacson, Walter. *Benjamin Franklin: An American Life* (New York: Simon & Schuster, 2003).

Jasanoff, Maya. *Liberty's Exiles: American Loyalists in the Revolutionary World* (New York: Random House, 2011).

Jones, Thomas. *History of New York During the Revolutionary War* (New York: New-York Historical Society, 1879).

Kerber, Linda K. *Toward an Intellectual History of Women* (Chapel Hill: University of North Carolina Press, 1997).

Ketchum, Richard M. *Decisive Day: The Battle for Bunker Hill* (Garden City, New York: Doubleday, 1962).

Livingston, William Farrand. *Israel Putnam, Pioneer, Ranger, and Major-General, 1718–1790* (New York: G. P. Putnam's Sons, 1901).

Lockhart, Paul. *The Whites of Their Eyes: Bunker Hill, the First American Army, and the Emergence of George Washington* (New York: Harper, 2011).

Maier, Pauline. *From Resistance to Revolution: Colonial Radicals and the Development of American Opposition to Britain, 1765–1776* (New York: Vintage, 1974).

Martyn, Charles. *The Life of Artemas Ward: The First Commander-in-Chief of the American Revolution* (New York: Artemas Ward, 1921).

Mayer, Henry. *A Son of Thunder: Patrick Henry and the American Republic* (New York: Grove, 1991).

Middlekauff, Robert. *The Glorious Cause: The American Revolution, 1763–1789* (New York: Oxford University Press, 1982).

Miller, John C. *Origins of the American Revolution* (Boston: Little, Brown, 1943).

Morgan, Edward Sears, and Helen M. Morgan. *The Stamp Act Crisis: Prologue to Revolution* (Chapel Hill: University of North Carolina Press, 1995).

Nash, Gary B. *The Unknown American Revolution: The Unruly Birth of Democracy and the Struggle to Create America* (New York: Viking, 2005).

Nelson, James L. *With Fire and Sword: The Battle of Bunker Hill and the Beginning of the American Revolution* (New York: St. Martin's, 2011).

Phillips, Kevin. *1775: A Good Year for Revolution* (New York: Viking, 2012).

Pickering, Octavius, and Charles W. Upham. *The Life of Timothy Pickering*, Vol. 1 (Boston: Little, Brown, 1867).

Quintal, George, Jr. *Patriots of Color—"A Peculiar Beauty and Merit": African Americans and Native Americans at Battle Road & Bunker Hill* (Division of Cultural Resources, Boston National Historical Park, 2004).

Randall, Willard Sterne. *Benedict Arnold: Patriot and Traitor* (New York: William Morrow, 1990).

———. *Ethan Allen: His Life and Times* (New York: Norton, 2011).

Ryan, William R. *The World of Thomas Jeremiah: Charles Town on the Eve of the American Revolution* (Oxford: Oxford University Press, 2010).

Sabin, Douglas P. *April 19, 1775: A Historiographical Study* (n.p.: Sinclair Street Publishing, 2011).

Sabine, Lorenzo. *The American Loyalists, or Biographical Sketches of Adherents to the British Crown in the War of the Revolution* (Boston: Charles C. Little and James Brown, 1847).

Shattuck, Lemuel. *A History of the Town of Concord* (Boston: Russell, Ordiorne and Company, 1935).

Sheets, Robert Newman. *Robert Newman: The Life and Times of the Sexton Who April 18, 1775 Held Two Lanterns Aloft in Christ Church Steeple, Boston* (Denver, Colo., 1975).

Smith, Page. *A New Age Now Begins: A People's History of the American Revolution*, vol. 1 of *A People's History of the United States* (New York: McGraw-Hill, 1976).

Spring, Matthew H. *With Zeal and with Bayonets Only* (Norman: University of Oklahoma Press, 2010).

Stark, James H. *The Loyalists of Massachusetts and the Other Side of the American Revolution* (Boston: W. B. Clarke, 1910).

Stedman, C[harles]. *The History of the Origin, Progress, and Termination of the American War.* 2 vols. (London, 1794).

Stoll, Ira. *Samuel Adams: A Life* (New York: Free Press, 2008).

Stuart, Nancy Rubin. *The Muse of the Revolution: The Secret Pen of Mercy Otis Warren and the Founding of a Nation* (Boston: Beacon Press, 2008).

Temple, J. H. *History of Framingham, Massachusetts* (Framingham, Mass.: Town of Framingham, 1887).

Tourtellot, Arthur B. *Lexington and Concord: The Beginning of the War of the American Revolution* (New York: Norton, 1959).

Trevelyan, George Otto. *The American Revolution, Part I, 1766–1776* (New York: Longmans, Green, 1899).

Trumbull, John. *M'Fingal: An Epic Poem* (New York: American Book Exchange, 1881).

Unger, Harlow Giles. *John Hancock: Merchant King and American Patriot* (New York: John Wiley, 2000).

Warren, Mercy [Otis]. *History of the Rise, Progress and Termination of the American Revolution* (Boston: E. Larkin, 1805).

Weston, Thomas. *History of the Town of Middleboro, Massachusetts* (Boston: Houghton Mifflin, 1906).

Wheildon, William W. *History of Paul Revere's Signal Lanterns, April 18, 1775, in the Steeple of the North Church* (Concord, Mass., 1878).

Articles

Andrews, John. "Letters of John Andrews, Esq. of Boston, 1772–1776," *Massachusetts Historical Society Proceedings* 8 (1864–65), 392.

Baxter, Beverly. "Grace Growden Galloway: Survival of a Loyalist, 1778–79," *Frontiers: A Journal of Women Studies* 3, no. 1 (spring 1978), 62–67.

Belknap, Jeremy. "Journal of My Tour to the Camp and the Observations I Made There," entry dated October 25, 1775, *Proceedings of the Massachusetts Historical Society* 4 (1858–60), 84–86.

Borneman, Walter R. "Which Road to Fort Duquesne? Colonel Washington Proves 'Obstinate,'" *Western Pennsylvania History* 90 (summer 2007), 36–43.

Chamberlain, Mellen. "Why Capt. Levi Preston Fought," *The Historical Collections of the Danvers Historical Society* 8 (1920), 69–70.

De Berniere, Henry. "Narrative of Occurrences, 1775," *Collections of the Massachusetts Historical Society*, 2nd ser., 4 (1816), 216.

Deming, Sarah Winslow. "Journal of Sarah Winslow Deming," *American Monthly Magazine* 4 (January–July 1894), 45–49.

Farmar, Eliza. "Letters of Eliza Farmar to Her Nephew," *Pennsylvania Magazine of History and Biography* 40, no. 2 (1916), 199–207.

Maier, Pauline. "Coming to Terms with Samuel Adams," *American Historical Review* 81, no. 1 (February 1976), 12–37.

Parker, Elizabeth S. "Captain John Parker," *Proceedings of Lexington Historical Society and Papers Relating to the History of the Town* 1 (1890).

Proceedings of the Essex Institute 1, "Mr. William Gavett's Account," 1848–1856 (1856).

Rantoul, Robert S. "The Cruise of the *Quero*," *Essex Institute Historical Collections* 36 (1900).

Town and Country Magazine 13, "Histories of the Tête-à-Tête" (1781), 233–36.

Sumner, W[illia]m. H. "Reminiscences by Gen. Wm. H. Sumner," *New England Historical and Genealogical Record* 8 (1854), 187–88.

Vance, Clarence H., ed. "Letters of a Westchester Farmer (1774–1775)," *Publications of the Westchester County Historical Society* 8 (1930), 43–62.

Online Resources

Baigent, Elizabeth. "Pitcairn, John," *Oxford Dictionary of National Biography*, May 2008, www.oxforddnb.com/view/printable/53715.

Bell, J. L. "Comparing Bissell and Revere," *Boston 1775* (blog), May 3, 2010, http://boston1775.blogspot.com/2010/05/comparing-bissell-and-revere.html.

———. "The Legend of Israel Bissell," *Boston 1775* (blog), May 2, 2010, http://boston1775.blogspot.com/2010/05/legend-of-israel-bissell.html.

———. "'To Alarm the Country Quite to Connecticut,'" *Boston 1775* (blog), May 1, 2010, http://boston1775.blogspot.com/2010/05/to-alarm-country-quite-to-connecticut.html.

———. "The True Story of Isaac Bissell," *Boston 1775* (blog), May 4, 2010, http://boston1775.blogspot.com/2010/05/true-story-of-isaac-bissell.html.

Berkin, Carol. "Leonard, Daniel," *American National Biography Online* (subscription only), February 2000, http://www.anb.org/articles/0101-00513.html.

Berthelson, Robert L. "An Alarm from Lexington," the Connecticut Society of the Sons of the American Revolution, accessed August 14, 2012, http://www.connecticutsar.org/articles/lexington_alarm.htm.

Blood, Thaddeus. "Statement on Battle of April 19," National Park Service website, accessed June 27, 2012, www.nps.gov/mima/forteachers/upload/Thaddeus%20Blood.pdf.

Brown, John. Letter to John Adams and the Massachusetts committee of correspondence, March 29, 1775, Fort Ticonderoga website, accessed June 7, 2012, http://www.fortticonderoga.org/learn/re-enactors/1775-capture/re-enactor/brown.

Brown, Peter. Letter to Sarah Brown, June 25, 1775, Massachusetts Historical Society, "The Coming of the American Revolution," accessed October 26, 2012, https://www.masshist.org/revolution/image-viewer.php?item_id=725&img_step=1&tpc=&pid=2&mode=transcript&tpc=&pid=2#page1.

"Events of April 18, 1775," The Old North Church: Christ Church in the City of Boston, accessed March 25, 2012, http://www.oldnorth.com/history/april18.htm.

Fuhrer, Mary, Judith Broggi, et al. "Using Primary Sources to Reconstruct the Past," *Learning at the Scottish Rite Masonic Museum and Library (National Heritage Museum)* (blog; contains information about Prince Estabrook), accessed August 22, 2012, http://nationalheritagemuseum.typepad.com/learning/.

Harrison, Jemima Condict. North American Women's Letters and Diaries: Colonial to 1950 (subscription only), accessed January 3, 2012, http://solomon.nwld.alexanderstreet.com/cgi-bin/asp/philo/nwld/getdoc.pl!S34-Do25.

Historical Manuscripts Commission, Great Britain. *Report on the Manuscripts of Mrs. Stopford-Sackville, of Drayton House, Northhamptonshire,* vol. 2 (Boston: Gregg Press, 1972), http://books.google.com/books?id=X9JRQTECDuYC&pg=PP6&lpg=PP6&dq=stopford-sackville+papers+report+2&source=bl&ots=zDOp1M8LQZ&sig=EZkE7ASTv3DfVi2I1MooQB7WfAk&hl=en&sa=X&ei=28KrUK2wAcOzywGooIDgCA&ved=0CC4Q6AewAA.

Kellow, Kenneth. "Recapture of the *Falcon*'s Prizes: The First Naval Encounter of the War, 14 May 1775," American War of Independence at Sea, http://www.awiatsea.com/incidents/14%20May%201775%20Recapture%20of%20Falcon's%20Prizes.html#B000048T.

Klein, Christopher. "A Forgotten Battle," PatriotLedger.com, May 17, 2008, http://www.patriotledger.com/opinions/x1880506383/A-FORGOTTEN-BATTLE#ixzz26wxvoZjc.

Lundy, Darryl. "General Hon. Thomas Gage," The Peerage, last edited April 9, 2011, http://thepeerage.com/p2617.htm#i26163.

Miles, Lion G. "The True Story of Bissell's Ride in 1775," iBerkshires.com, July 21, 2004, http://www.iberkshires.com/printerFriendly.php?story_id=15001.

Oberg, Barbara B., and J. Jefferson Looney, eds. *The Papers of Thomas Jefferson Digital Edition* (subscription only), Charlottesville: University of Virginia

Press, Rotunda, 2008, main ser., 1 (accessed December 16, 2012), 105, http://rotunda.upress.virginia.edu/founders/TSJN-01-01-02-0082.

Pitcairn, John. "Major John Pitcairn's Report to General Gage, April 26, 1775," Digital History, "Explorations of the Revolutionary War," accessed January 9, 2013, http://www.digitalhistory.uh.edu/learning_history/revolution/account3-lexington.cfm.

Prescott, William. Letter to John Adams, August 25, 1775, Massachusetts Historical Society, "'The Decisive Day Is Come': The Battle of Bunker Hill," http://www.masshist.org/bh/prescott.html.

Revere, Paul. Deposition, fair copy, circa 1775, Massachusetts Historical Society, accessed March 12, 2012, www.masshist.org/database/img-viewer .php?item_id=98&img_step=1&tpc=&pid=&mode=transcript&tpc=&pid=#page1.

———. Letter to Jeremy Belknap, circa 1798, Massachusetts Historical Society, accessed March 14, 2012, http://www.masshist.org/database/img -viewer.php?item_id=99&mode=small&img_step=2&tpc=&pid=#page2.

Ryan, D. Michael. "White Cockade: A Jacobite Air at the North Bridge?" https://www2.bc.edu/~hafner/lmm/music-articles/white_cockade _ryan.html.

Stagg, J. C. A., ed. *The Papers of James Madison Digital Edition* (subscription only), Charlottesville: University of Virginia Press, Rotunda, 2010, congressional ser., 1 (accessed December 16, 2012), 144–45, http://rotunda.upress.vir ginia.edu/founders/JSMN-01-01-02-0044.

Stark, James H. "Samuel Quincy, Solicitor General," 8n, *The Loyalists of Massachusetts* (1910), http://www.robertsewell.ca/loyalmass.htm#_ftn8.

Waller, John. Letter to a friend, June 21, 1775, Massachusetts Historical Society, http://www.masshist.org/bh/wallerp2text.html.

Washington, George. Letter to Martha Washington, June 18, 1775, The Papers of George Washington, "Documents," accessed November 7, 2012, http:// gwpapers.virginia.edu/documents/revolution/martha.html.

Williamson, Samuel H. "Seven Ways to Compute the Relative Value of a U.S. Dollar Amount — 1774 to Present," MeasuringWorth.com, accessed November 14, 2012, http://www.measuringworth.com/uscompare/ result.php?year_source=1775&amount=2000000&year_result=2010.

Newspapers

Boston Evening-Post
Boston Gazette and Country Journal
Boston News-Letter

Boston Post-Boy
Connecticut Courant
Essex Gazette
Essex Journal and Merimack Packet
Massachusetts Gazette and the Boston Post-Boy and Advertiser
Massachusetts Spy
New-Hampshire Gazette
New-York Gazette and the Weekly Mercury
Rivington's New-York Gazetteer
Pennsylvania Gazette
Pennsylvania Packet
South-Carolina and American General Gazette

INDEX

~

ABOUT THE AUTHOR

~

WALTER R. BORNEMAN is the author of eight works of nonfiction, including *The Admirals, 1812, The French and Indian War,* and *Polk.* He lives in Colorado.

Also by WALTER R. BORNEMAN

The Admirals

Nimitz, Halsey, Leahy, and King—The Five-Star Admirals Who Won the War at Sea

"In his superbly reported new book, historian Walter R. Borneman tackles the essential question of military leadership: What makes some men, but not others, able to motivate a fighting force into battle?" —Tony Perry, *Los Angeles Times*

"The first book to deal with the four admirals together, focusing on their intertwined lives, friendships, and rivalries.... A very well-crafted book." —John Lehman, *Washington Post*

"Engagingly written and deeply researched." —Andrew Roberts, *Wall Street Journal*

"A brilliant, intriguing, and important book.... In *The Admirals* Borneman not only presents balanced mini-biographies of his four principal subjects but also gives an overview of the evolution of the navy from the late-nineteenth to mid-twentieth centuries and provides fascinating details about the naval, political, and diplomatic aspects of World War II." —Timothy J. Lockhart, *Virginian-Pilot*

Back Bay Books
Available wherever books are sold

Also by WALTER R. BORNEMAN

Iron Horses

America's Race to Bring the Railroads West

"A riveting history of the frenetic race to construct a railroad across the great American Southwest following the Civil War. Borneman is masterful at writing seamless narrative. Every page sings with fine writing." —Douglas Brinkley, professor of history at Rice University and author of *The Wilderness Warrior: Theodore Roosevelt and the Crusade for America*

"Brisk, colorful, and exciting." —Jay Freeman, *Booklist*

"Borneman's telling of this story is admirable foremost because of its detail and historical accuracy; his extensive research is put to good use. But he also is a gifted storyteller, and he introduces his readers to an array of characters who are part of this transcontinental treasure hunt. . . . An enjoyable read for railroad buffs, Old West aficionados, serious-minded historians, and anyone who finds romance in the sound of a train whistle in the night." —*BookPage*

Back Bay Books
Available wherever books are sold